Traces In The Dust

Carbondale's Black Heritage
1852-1964

Melvin LeRoy Green Macklin

Edited by
Dr. Elizabeth I. Mosley-Lewin

Illustrated by
Chan Oi Lin
"Cat"

Cover Design by
Leslie Wallace

Ingenuity Press
Magnolia, Texas

Traces In The Dust: Carbondale's Black Heritage, 1852-1964. Copyright © 2001 by Melvin LeRoy Green Macklin. No part of the materials appearing in this publication may be duplicated or reproduced without the permission of the author or Ingenuity Press.

ISBN: 978-1-68162-215-6

Library of Congress Cataloging-in-Publication Data

Macklin, Melvin L. G.

Traces In The Dust: Carbondale's Black Heritage, 1852-1964. A history of the African American residents of Jackson County and Carbondale, Illinois from the founding of the city (1852) through the year 1964.

Includes:

> General Index
> Bibliographical references

1. African Americans in Jackson County, Illinois--History (1807--1900).

   > Slavery in Jackson County, the 1800s--Slave owners.
   > Registers--African American births, marriages, and deaths in Jackson County--Genealogy.
   > Demography--Jackson County--Population growth and expansion.

2. African American Settlement of Carbondale, Illinois (1852--1964)

   > Demography--Expansion--History.
   > Early black families and residents--Genealogy--Heads of families and households.
   > Registers--African American births, marriages, and deaths in Carbondale--Civic and Community Leaders

Ingenuity Press
Magnolia, Texas

For nine courageous African American women of Carbondale whose lives and teachings helped anchor my past and steady me for the future--

    Ernell Marie France Glasby
    Allean Brown Gordon
    Martha Green
    Estelle Chappell
    Misanna Ikard
    Bertha Mitchell
    Luella Davis
    Wanda Perkins Haynes
    Julia Mae Thompson

Dedication

This book is dedicated, with love, to Ernell Marie France Green Glasby, a mother who was always there--a mother filled with warmth, understanding, compassion, and forgiveness.

In Memorial

To the memory of "Momean" and all the others of Carbondale who have gone before, leaving behind the marvelous treasures of their memories, wisdom, and inspiration.

To the memory of "Cousin Jenny," who would heal the sick and us "young'uns" suffering from the flu, colds, and other maladies with her many strange, but then quite common, home remedies and concoctions. Her potent medicines of cow manure and hog hoof teas; health rubs, and tablespoon size doses created from mutton and goose grease; and dish water washes were "guaranteed to do the trick.." "But, just in case," as she used to say, left in ready reserve were coal oil and sugar mixes; camphor salves and various poultices; leaf filled asphyxia bags which hung about the neck; and "special" balms she would mix herself. All these she made with herbs and different roots and grasses from places in the back woods known only to her and a few other of the highly respected healing women.

In Appreciation

To Johnetta Jones, whose treatise on the Negro settlement of Jackson County added much to my limited knowledge, and P. Michael Jones for his lifetime devotion to keeping alive the history of Southern Illinois and shedding much light on the Black experience in Murphysboro and the surrounding area.

Acknowledgements

Rarely is a literary work solely the result of the efforts of one person, especially a text which purports to be historical in nature. Over the past six years, many persons have unselfishly shared with me their time, effort, and knowledge in the creation of this book. It is their collective strengths, grounded in the grace and goodness of our Almighty Father, which have proven to be my greatest source of inspiration.

To my mother, Ernell Marie France Glasby, who taught me to trust God for the things I desired from life--and who provided every conceivable type of assistance including putting in much of the "leg work" in the Carbondale community--I give my love and thanks. Without her moral and financial support and laborious endeavors, this work truly would not have come to fruition.

I wish to thank my sister, Sherlene; my "Aunt Dean," Gloria Aiken; my cousin, Arthur Chappell; and my dad, Leonard Glasby, for doing all they could to help me reach the end of an arduous journey. I am also grateful to my cousin Patricia "Pat" Chappell for her vision in helping me to solidify the aims and objectives of the book; my niece, Ulisa Bowles, for her diligent review of the text; and William Irvin Smith and Barbara Tender for aiding in the gathering of resources. Special thanks is extended to my former Attucks classmate Gwendolyn Cavitt Gails, who has been a behind-the-scenes "dynamo" taking on every responsibility from the day *Traces In The Dust* was first conceptualized, and to Margaret Jean Nesbitt, Everlene Chambers, and my uncle, William Chappell, for their honest appraisals and additional contributions.

I remain indebted to historian Kenneth E. Cochran for reviewing the manuscript and author P. Michael Jones for his observations and comments. Likewise, I am grateful to my long time friends and "comrades in the cause," Hardin Allen Davis and Tommie Bell, whose advice and suggestions resulted in the culmination of a broader and more cogent text; and to Marilyn Tipton Brown for her kindhearted efforts and knack for getting things done. Most of all I am grateful to all those special persons who took the effort to provide contributions of oral histories, photos, articles, and biographies on the northeast community and its subsequent Black development and expansion in Carbondale.

Bob Thornton, Nettie Hayes, Louberta Cavitt, Louvenia McKinley, Virginia Clark, Stella Ivy, and my Aunt Mary, the wife of the late James Arthur France, allowed me unrestricted use of their rare and treasured collections of documents and photos. Verna Roseman, Hortense Edward, Gloria Aiken, and Mrs. Helen Greene-Jennings brought additional materials and information to the manuscript. Many other residents of the former "New Addition," where I grew up, gave wonderful stories and accounts of the people who lived among us and the events that took place in our part of town--much of which I had long since forgotten.

Thanks is extended to the wonderful people at the Jackson County Historical Society who went far "beyond the call" in navigating me through the foundation's myriad of files and records. In addition to that of Ken Cochran, the enthusiasm and camaraderie of Phoebe Cox, Clifton Swafford, and Robert Morefield added many moments of fun and spontaneity to the otherwise laborious job of research.

Appreciation is extended to Dr. Elizabeth I. Mosley-Lewin for consenting to edit *Traces*; and to Yolonda Johnson Gregory; my cousin, Hazel Chappell Law ("Little Ludy"); Ernell Glasby; and Gwendolyn Gails for undertaking the tedious tasks of technical proofing. Again, thanks is extended to Mike Jones for sharing with me so much of his experiences and vast knowledge on the era of the Negro slaves in Southern Illinois; and to Johnetta Jones for allowing me to tap into her pioneer research and discoveries on local black lore and history.

I wish to express my deep bond of affection and appreciation to my lifelong friend, Cozette Bell Spinner, who, after finding such joy and delight in reading one of my previous writings, *1393-K*, helped inspire me to make the final commitment to write *Traces*.

I can not end without adding a word of appreciation to my former graduate professors at Prairie View A&M University of Texas: Drs. Edward Mason, Joan Clark, and Ollie J. Davis, for showing me how to develop and further enhance my skills; Professor Darlington I. Ndubuike, for helping me to fully appreciate the beauty and significance of our African ancestry; and Professor Clarissa Gamble Booker, for opening my eyes to one of the greatest of gifts: the insight to understand the tremendous power of books and the unlimited rewards of reading.

If *Traces In The Dust* stirs our imagination and recalls for us days of laughter and fond memories, I will be delighted; if it encourages us to remain forever vigilant against the tyranny of prejudice and societal neglect wrought by man and the dust of time, I will be grateful. However, if it teaches us to cherish the proud past given to us by our forefathers and to appreciate the present, which has been bought and paid for by the sweat of their black brows, I will be thankful--for only then will this work have truly accomplished its purpose.

Significant contributions to this work came from several persons who, sadly, are no longer with us. I am very grateful that our lives touched here on this earth:

Beulah Mae Brown; Clubs and Organizations
Kathleen Thornton; Early Life and Public Welfare
Reverend Loyd C. Sumner; Religion and The African American Church
Mary "Priss" Bell; Expansion of Development .theast Community
Albert "Flat top" Mason; Early Residents and Families
Della Matthews; Early Carbondale and Families
Michael Wayne France; Early History of Southern Illinois: The Development of "Little Egypt"
Cardella Scott; Social Institutions, Organizations, and Public Welfare
Cora Gibbs; Early Carbondale-Expansion and Development
Dorothy Marie Mackey McAttee, St. Louis, Mo.; Families and Residents

Special thanks to:

Kenny Swafford, President, Jackson County Historical Society: Murphysboro, Illinois
Dr. Elizabeth Mosely-Lewin, Superintendent; Carbondale Elementary School District 95
Judy Travelstead, Librarian, Southern Illinoisan Newspaper; Carbondale, Illinois
Katharine A. Salzmann, Archivist, Southern Illinois University at Carbondale
The James France family; Philadelphia, Pennsylvania
The City of Carbondale, Development Services
Morris Library, Southern Illinois University at Carbondale
Dr. Robbie Lieberman, Professor of History, Southern Illinois University at Carbondale
Fred Wills, President, The Spirit of Attucks Organization; Carbondale, Illinois
Delores Albritton; Director, Eurma Hayes Center; Carbondale, Illinois
Julia Ann Thomas Brown, Elgin, Illinois
Carbondale Main Street; Carbondale, Illinois.
David Ahlfield, Photo Center Manager, Wal-Mart Photo Center; Carbondale, Illinois
Angela Hunziker, Photo Specialist, Wal-Mart Photo Center; Carbondale, Illinois
Phyllis Halekakis; Conroe, Texas
Elaine A. Wilkins West, The Woodlands, Texas
Erin Kathleen West, The Woodlands, Texas
Steven R. Sabens, Superintendent; Carbondale Community High School District 165
The Southern Illinois University Alumni Association; Carbondale, Illinois
Fred Montgomery, Curator of The Alex Hailey Museum and Mayor of Henning, Tennessee
Gail Anders, Department of Journalism, Magnolia High School; Magnolia, Texas
The students of the Community Service Program of Magnolia High School
Elizabeth Blake and the students of the History Club of Magnolia High School: Emily Martinez, Jaime Fuentes, Melissa Flores, Andrea Morehead, Kelly Skinner, and Cecilia Blake.

Some photos have been reproduced by special permission of Mr. Arthur Newbern; Olan Mills Studios; Morris Library, Southern Illinois University at Carbondale; the Southern Illinoisan Newspaper; and the Jackson County Historical Society, Murphysboro, Illinois.

Front Cover Photo: "Papa Lilly." Charles Lilly, known mostly by "Papa Lilly," was one of the earliest black settlers of the northeast Carbondale community of the 1900s. "Papa Lilly was the late husband of Hattie Bell Clark Davis Lilly and was the father of numerous children (and step children) including four fun loving sons: Willie Dee, Charles, Harry, and Buster Lilly. "Papa Lilly" always had time to sit down and tell me a story--a story which always made one think. And from somewhere in his overalls, he could always manage to dig out a piece of candy or a nickel or dime for us "young'uns."

Rear Cover Photo: Early U. S. Army Honorable Discharge of Grant Barnett; exited with "Excellent Character" from the 9th Cavalry, Troop B; January 18, 1911. Courtesy of Odell Robison.

Contributors

The Early Negro Settlement: Jackson County and Carbondale

Annie Mae Dunlap Wakefield
Kenneth E. Cochran
P. Michael Jones
Johnetta Jones
Clifton Swafford
Phoebe Cox
Bob Morefield

The Northeast Community

Nettie Hayes
Gloria Dean Brown Aiken
Margaret Nesbitt
Louvenia McKinley
Louberta Cavitt
Darnecea "Nish" Smith Moultree

Bob Thornton
Irene Hayden (Mamarene)
William Chappell
Mildred Harrington Jordan
Frances Armour
Hortense Edward

Oral History

Julia Mae Thompson
Annie Mae Wakefield
Dorothy Sykes
Helen Green
Della Lambus
Stella Ivy

Biography and Photo Credits

Gloria Dean Aiken, Carbondale, Ill.; Delores Albritton, Carbondale, Ill.; Delmar Algee, Jr., Cairo, Ill.; Jacqueline Armstrong, Chicago, Ill.; Flossie Bell, Carbondale, Ill.; Jasper Boykin, Carbondale, Ill.; the late Beulah Mae Brown, Carbondale, Ill.; Julia Ann Thomas Brown, Elgin, Ill.; Arthur Chappell, Carbondale, Ill.; Patricia Chappell, Dolton, Illinois; William Chappell, Carbondale, Ill.; Celestine Cavitt, Carbondale, Ill.; Louberta Cavitt, Carbondale, Ill; Everlene Chambers, Carbondale, Ill.; Dorcus Cunningham Davis, Chicago, Ill.; Hardin Allen Davis, Carbondale, Ill.; Brenda Devers, Chicago, Ill.; Charlie Dixon; Hortense Edward, Carbondale, Ill.; Robert Lee McCall Foster, Murphysboro, Ill.; George France, Columbia, Md; Mary France, Philadelphia, Penn.; Gwendolyn Cavitt Gails, Carbondale, Ill.; Anita Mason Gibbs, Carbondale, Ill.; Ernell France Green Glasby, Salem, Va.; Helen Green-Jennings, Carbondale, Illinois; Gladys and Warren Grigsby, Carbondale, Ill.; Nettie Hayes, Carbondale, Ill.; Melvin "Pepper" Holder; Carbondale, Ill.; Beatrice Hudson, Carbondale, Ill.; Janice Bell Humphrey; Detroit, Mich.; Stella Ivy, Carbondale, Ill.; Katie Mae Kelly, Carbondale, Ill.; Dr. Elizabeth Mosley Lewin, Carbondale, Ill.; Willie B. Mackey, Jr., Carbondale, Ill.; Edna Brooks Mason, Carbondale, Ill.; Kenneth Mason, Carbondale, Ill.; Marie Mason, Carbondale, Ill.; Vickie Mason, Carbondale, Ill.; Cleveland Matthews, Carbondale, Ill.; Louvenia McKinley, Carbondale, Ill.; Evelyn Merideth, East Saint Louis, Ill.; Lee Merideth, Cahokia, Ill.; Dorothy Miller, Carbondale, Ill.; Henry Morgan, Carbondale, Ill.; Darnecea Moultrie, Carbondale, Ill.; Margaret Jean Nesbitt, Carbondale, Ill; Etta and Arthur E. Newbern; Carbondale, Ill.; Booker O'Neal, Jr., Carbondale, Ill; Emily Palmer, Carbondale, Ill.; Veronica Powridge, Ripley, Tenn.; Calvin Scott, Carbondale, Illinois; Cozette Bell Spinner, Detroit, Mich.; Doris and the late Walter Steele, Carbondale, Ill.; Bertha Mitchell, Carbondale, Ill; Earl Mitchell, Carbondale, Ill.; Odell Robison, Carbondale, Ill.; Verna Roseman, Carbondale, Ill; Julia Rowe, Carbondale, Illinois; Barbara Scott, Carbondale, Ill.; the late Cardella Scott, Carbondale, Ill.; Jewell Slaughter, Carbondale, Ill.; William Irvin and Irvin Smith, Carbondale, Ill.; Julia Mae Thompson, Carbondale, Ill.; Bob Thornton, Carbondale, Ill.; Marilyn Brown Tipton, Carbondale, Ill.; Naomi Shird Tucker, Peoria, Ill.; Darnella Wakefield-Morrison, Carbondale, Ill.; Joseph L. Washington, Inglewood, Ca.; Vivian France West; St. Louis, Mo.; David Dean Williams, Carbondale, Ill.; Fred Wills, Carbondale, Ill.; Brad Woods, Carbondale, Ill.; Barbara Wooley; Carbondale, Ill.

CONTENTS

Dedication		iv
Acknowledgements		v
Contributors		vii
Biography and Photo Credits		vii
Preface		xi
Introduction		xii
Prologue: The Wonder Years		xv
Part I.	The African American Settlement of Jackson County and Carbondale: An Overview	1
	Slavery in Jackson County	2
Part II.	African Americans in Jackson County	8
	Negro Slaves in Jackson County	9
	Negro Slaves in Jackson County, 1820	10
	African American Residents in Jackson County, 1870	11
	African Americans in Jackson County, 1900	20
	African American Deaths in Jackson County	25
	African American Deaths in Jackson County, 1877 to 1940	27
	African American Marriages in Jackson County, 1800-1900	38
	African American Marriages in Jackson County, 1859-1890	39
Part III.	African Americans in Carbondale, 1852-1900	47
	Black Growth and Expansion in Carbondale, 1860	49
	The First African American Births in Carbondale and the First Families	51
	Early African American Settlers of Carbondale, 1865	52
	Negro Personal and Realty Holdings in Carbondale in 1870	53
	Early Black Residents of Carbondale	54
	Black Families in Carbondale in 1880	57

Part IV.	African American Residents in Carbondale, 1900-1964	62
	African American Households in Carbondale in 1905	64
Part V.	Around The Town	149
Part VI.	African American Families, 1900-1964	177
Part VII.	In Service To Their People: Labors and Achievements	308
Epilogue:	Voices Past and Present	334
	Photography Notes	353
	Bibliography	354
	Index	356

Each and every one of us, no matter who we are, no matter where we come from--man woman, or child-- leaves an indelible mark and a path which others may eventually follow. And no matter how dark the way or how obscure that path may be, if those who come afterward look closely enough and sift through the ashes of time, they will uncover the unique remnants of a wondrous past and a glorious heritage left by those who have gone before. They need only to discover the traces in the dust.

Melvin LeRoy Green Macklin

Preface

Traces in the Dust focuses upon the African American families and residents of Carbondale since the founding of the Carbondale Township (1852). It is meant to provide a glimpse of the growth, progress, and development of the Black American community in the city through the exploration of recorded data and oral history. The book begins with the Black settlement of Jackson County and tracts the expansion of the Negro family in Carbondale through the year 1964. Individuals seeking a broader understanding of the local African American experience should read Johnetta Jones's detailed historical masters thesis, *Negroes In Jackson County, 1850-1910* (1968). More information on African Americans in Carbondale can also be found in Dr. Madlyn Stalls's, PhD Dissertation, *A History Of African Americans At Southern Illinois University At Carbondale 1915-1987* (1990) and in the work, *In Unity There Is Strength* (1999), produced by the Little Egypt Chapter of the Afro-American Historical and Genealogical Society.

Like the works mentioned above, *Traces In The Dust* attempts to hold up to light the contributions Blacks have made to their culture and society during their roughly 200 year history in the area. Although close examination has been given to historical documents and details have been recorded with great care and scrutiny, this book is by no means to be viewed as a definitive treatise on the complete history of the African American in Carbondale over the past one hundred and fifty years. Such an undertaking would require several volumes to complete. Rather, the ultimate goal of this work is simply to enable the reader to understand life in Carbondale from the black perspective and from the viewpoint of one growing up in the city in the early 1950's. Enabling the reader to know something of who the early black families and residents were and the parts they played in the city's development is the one primary concern. Caution should also be given here to those looking for a vehicle for carrying out extensive family research. While it is possible to conduct a certain amount of genealogical investigation using this book, the information provided on individuals and families is purposely limited. This book is not (nor was it ever) meant to be a pure work of Black genealogy; therefore, no extended family bloodlines are traced; no family trees appear.

Traces--through the reporting of factual data--seeks first to draw attention to those life styles, institutions, and economic and social factors which have held great significance and impact on the lives of ensuing generations of blacks since the arrival of the first families from the South. Secondly, it endeavors throughout its pages to shed light on the black battle for survival and recognition by highlighting those individuals who were the backbone and the "glue" of the predominantly Black northeast community of Carbondale. To this end, many months have been spent in research, and countless hours and seemingly endless days have been expended in the pursuits of interviewing, documenting, and the verifying of facts.

In the final analysis, it is hoped that this work prevails as a memorial to the undying spirit and the indomitable will of a remarkable people during turbulent times of struggle and scarcity. It is offered as a tribute to our black heritage: a present and future paved for us by those persons and institutions we knew and loved so well.

Some of the vocabulary contained herein may be deemed offensive by some individuals. Such terms as "nappy headed," "black ass," and "nigger"--descriptions liberally used by my grandmother and other old timed personages of my childhood in that part of town known as "The Hoodlums"--are in no way intended as a slight against anyone or any group of people. However, to omit these expressions from this book would, in essence, amount to an attempt to deny or gloss over this particular aspect inherent within the framework of the black historical experience in the United States of America. Idioms are as much an essential part of history as are locations and events. The reader is asked to consider these references in this light.

Introduction

It is often said that luck is a fickle lady. One's understanding of history, like luck, is equally as fickle. One signed document buried away for decades in a trunk in the attic can change long standing theories in less than a day's time; a souvenir, an old relic, or an outdated family heirloom can create an entirely new and different picture from that which was originally thought to be--and can do so overnight. One letter or notarized statement, socked away among old personal belongings for centuries, can drastically alter previously held conceptions of one's family's history which had stood unchallenged for generations. History, as Dr. Madlyn Stalls confirms, is the reproduction of what has been previously recorded, preserved, and stowed away. And like "Lady Luck" anything previously recorded and accepted as true can change with a "trump card" of a single new piece of evidence. As long as man can inquire into the past, concepts of history are never constant although events themselves, once taken place, can never be undone. It is with these assumptions in mind that this book has been written.

In the Spring of 1995, when I first began gathering data for *Traces In The Dust,* a major problem immediately emerged: the lack of available data on many black residents and families who occupied Jackson County and Carbondale, especially in the middle 1800s and between the years 1900 and 1930. Such mysteries as the disappearance of three huge volumes of early Jackson County birth records and other records for Blacks born in Jackson County unexplainably ending up in the annals of other counties help account for the gaps in the historical time line.

In documenting families and residents of early Carbondale, several reasons directly account for the lack of information on many individuals. The deaths of family heads and high mobility through the years contribute significantly to the loss of vital files. In a good deal of cases, the heads of families and their children had all moved away (or passed away) and could not be found. Even when distant relatives and surviving descendants were located, many had grown very elderly themselves and were unable to clearly distinguish details of the past. Ironically, other descendants were much too young to remember their deceased relatives.

A second explanation for the absence of biographical information on some early residents is the aforementioned lack of official documents. The earliest residents were delivered by midwives or family members who did not keep birth records, and relatively few of those individuals moving into the area from other states brought birth records or other documents with them. For those who did, these records were not required to be filed with any official agency and a majority of them were lost over time. Because it could not be determined where these residents originally came from, they were not able to be traced. Even when death occurred, the death records--which were little more than crude notes by today's standards--contained only data relative to the deceased at that immediate moment, and very little, if anything at all, could be learned about the person's origins. Thus, we see various vital statistics reports today with a minimal of details.

The destruction of official records at the former Jackson County Seat at Brownsville also contributes to the gap in Jackson County history. The Brownsville Courthouse was burned to the ground on January 10, 1843 and Murphysboro was chosen as the new county seat. The impact of the number of records lost in the Brownsville disaster is greatly felt by present day researchers studying Jackson County's past. Every record helps to produce the whole picture of a culture's past; each piece of evidence lost ultimately means a history which is fragmented and incomplete.

A third explanation why many persons are not included in this book--especially those residents of fairly recent Carbondale history (1950 to 1964)--is due to the failure of family members to submit the requested data. Moreover, in a number of cases, the persons contacted opted not to have themselves or their families included in this work. It should also be noted that many birth dates and other facts have been omitted upon request of the residents themselves.

Finally, the restriction of public access to birth documents after 1916 and other records on file at the Jackson County Court House proved a major hindrance. For example, the restrictions made it virtually impossible to get information on the hundreds of African American residents and families living in Carbondale from 1930 through the 1960s. In many instances no other records were available, leaving the county files as the only known sources of facts on the residents of this time period. Not being able to examine these records significantly contributes to the large gap noted in the listing of Blacks for the final twenty-five years which *Traces* explores. Within the last five years, many historical documents and Jackson County books, each containing hundreds of residents and families, have been painstakingly examined to produce this work. In addition to these, a substantial quantity of materials donated by individual residents and private institutions were scrutinized. Still, the combination of the above factors (and others) should lead the reader to understand that despite all efforts to produce an accurate picture of

Blacks in Carbondale during its first one hundred year history, only a relatively small percentage of African Americans in the city spanning that era are represented in this work.

In addition to the problems involved with documentation, a second concern constantly nagged at me. This was the issue of avoiding fiction, hearsay, and controversy. The answer to the first problem of the lack of historical data became self evident: do as thorough a job of research and fact finding as humanly possible and, in the cases where residents were omitted, take solace in knowing that every available avenue to find, retrieve, and enter information related to them was explored.

As to the second dilemma, the solution was not so simple. It was not until after many months of research and hours spent conversing with family and friends--and with advisors and experts in the discipline of history--that a plausible solution surfaced. It became apparent that first of all, no matter what preventive measures were taken, all controversy could never be totally eliminated due to the fact that controversy is inherently a part of history itself and constitutes an integral part of everyone's lives. At best, any controversy could only be minimized. With this in mind--and in order to meet the goals of the book--only one option remained: limitations which would restrict or eliminate unwanted speculation and unproductive individual bias would have to be imposed, and data would have to be scrutinized to guard against the introduction of irrelevant and detracting material. Also, I realized that I would have to remain alert to my own preconceptions and not let these interfere with the truthful recording and preservation of facts. Thus, I have, at all times, vigorously endeavored to present factual data in the hope that this book remains a true and historical account of a group of people and not a sensationalized work on the lives of individuals.

In keeping with the task of insuring historical integrity, authenticity, and accuracy, I have sought to substantiate all information through historical investigation. Consequently, the materials presented in these pages are supported by in-office records and other accessible reports. Likewise, various methods have been taken to insure the authentication of photographs and the identification of individuals. Dates of weddings, births, residency, deaths, and burials are ascertained from census reports, marriage certificates, and death notices found in area libraries and the annals of the Jackson County Historical Society. However, since Illinois law prohibits public access to birth records after 1916 and impose similar restrictions to other important files--and because of county and state "red tape" which hampers effective research--a large amount of the information found in this book comes from individual contributors and privately owned documents and family papers.

A final point concerning this work needs to be brought out here. Some may find data which appears to be in contradiction with traditional lore. While *Traces* is certainly not a deliberate attack on any long standing traditions or tenets concerning Blacks in Carbondale, it will, no doubt, impact a few current ideas and beliefs long held by some. Indeed, even some of my own views have been greatly augmented over the past five years of researching the materials for this book. This "new" insight manifests itself in the underlying philosophy of *Traces* which, in turn, is reflected in the wording and writing style of the book.

An example of this is found in the approach to the recording of subject matter. I have, for instance, opted not to overly concentrate on the issue of "firsts." It is a well known fact that many historians place great importance on discovering who the first person was to be associated with a certain event, and understandably so. This defines for them their meaning of history, and any other approach to the study of history is unacceptable. But because history is so dependent on records and verifiable pieces of information, and because the very documents which we use to determine history are themselves many times suspect or lacking in some respect--if not missing altogether--I have purposefully shied away from using absolute terms such as "the first Black person . . ." or "the only Black . . ." Past experience has taught me that, in many cases, years of concentrated effort are required to provide proof of such claims, checking record against record for confirmation. Many early birth records and other later documents examined for this work were themselves fraught with errors and inconsistencies of every conceivable type; consequently, throughout this book, readers are continuously cautioned to compare and cross-reference files before forming final conclusions. The greatest lesson learned from writing this book is that the researcher must always keep an open mind. Therefore, fixed and resolute pronouncements only appear in this book when indisputable proof warrants their use. In lieu of these rigid terms, the reader encounters such descriptions and phrases as the "first known African American"; the "earliest known Black to date"; and the "first black, according to . . ."; etc. The worth of *Traces* lies in its attempt to extol the virtue of a cultural group as a whole, not in the aim to glorify individualism.

The Text

The different topic areas of the book are divided into seven parts. Part I, The Black Settlement of Carbondale: An Overview, briefly addresses the history behind the Black movement into the Southern Illinois area of Jackson County and its subsequent expansion into Carbondale. Part II, African-Americans in Jackson County, describes the populations of Blacks in Jackson County and their movements within the county from 1807 to 1900. This time period encompasses two major events impacting the black family: the demise of slavery in Jackson County (c. 1830) and African Americans in the Civil War (1861). Part III, African Americans in Carbondale, 1852-1900, and Part IV, African American Residents in Carbondale, 1900-1964, highlight individual African American residents during the early development of the city. These sections also chronicle the black families who settled in Carbondale after its founding through the mid 1960s. It is 1964 when the impact of integration and the closing of Attucks, the Negro educational institution in Carbondale, spells an abrupt end to the close-knit, community structure Blacks had known for generations. The advent of desegregation in Carbondale (1963-64) for which Blacks had fought, ultimately proved to be a two edged sword. While it ushered in a supposedly "new age of progress and opportunity for African Americans," it also launched the Black community in Carbondale on a journey never witnessed before--one which was to forever detract from the Black way of life.

Part V, Around the Town; and Part VI, African American Families continue the themes of Parts III and IV, showing scenes of events, places, and people of Carbondale from the 1800s to the mid-1960s. These sections pictorially depict the first generations of the city's early black families and highlight their contributions to Carbondale's social and cultural history. *Traces* ends with Part VII, In Service to Their People: Labors and Achievements. This section highlights several of early Carbondale's black community leaders who waged the campaign for the benefit of blacks and the betterment of the human condition within the northeast neighborhood. Arrangement of Listings of Persons

Of necessity, family histories are largely limited to brief, biographical sketches of the heads of families. In the majority of cases, names of persons are arranged according to the date individuals were born or when they first settled in Carbondale (or by the earliest known date that links the person to the city). In cases when the exact dates are unknown, individuals can be located by other chronological data or by alphabetical listing. It is hoped that such arrangement will enable the reader to perceive the deep significance of a continuing African American historical experience. A general index is given to expedite locating families, individual residents, and other information.

Prologue

The Wonder Years

The absolute, most wonderful years of my life have to be those spent growing up in Carbondale and my junior and senior years at Attucks High School. They were years of unfulfilled promises and dreams and of hopes yet to come. As a young child and as a teenager, life for me was full of wonder, and the world I knew was made of expectations and limitless possibilities.

It was a world of people loving and caring about people--neighbors were truly neighborly. Everyone made it their business to look out for everyone else. Teachers were more than teachers--they were friends and confidants; they were mothers and fathers. At Attucks, Mrs. Ikard spoke to each of us in her quiet, soft-tone manner as though she were talking to her son or daughter; Mrs. Luella Davis, taking us under her wings, cautioned us to always "think it through" before acting on a thing; and Mr. John Q. Clark, loving to play with big words, seemed to always feel the immediate need to regale us with one of his lofty speeches on how important it was for us students to have "perspicacity." The fact that none of us knew what perspicacity was or where to get it really didn't matter. To Professor Clark, it seemed sufficient that we were made aware of that precious quality.

It was a time of boys and girls together and wondering what the next day would bring. We worried little about the future then; we were more concerned about who would take whom to the next big movie at the Rogers theater or the Varsity. We laughed; we smiled, and we cried, but not from worry about ourselves. When we cried, we cried for each other.

It was days full of love and kindness. It was days of friendships, girlfriends and boyfriends--days of buddies, and pals. It was dancing the new dances at Jones cafe, and showing off at the "Rec." It was days of attending Sunday School as a young child and, later, as a young adult, attending the youth meetings and singing in the church choir as we traveled to other churches as near as the next few blocks or as far away as Wisconsin and Alabama. Our group, The Inspirational Singers, performed at the Walter Hawkins's Workshop in Champaign, Illinois, and at the James Cleveland Workshop in St. Louis, Missouri. We sang at Grambling Louisiana State College, and we won 1st place in the Kappa Talent Show at SIU.

It was a time when we visited and enjoyed our friends' houses as much as we did our own. In a real sense, our friends' houses were, in fact, our houses. Their mothers were our mothers--their fathers, our fathers. It was a time I shall never, ever forget. A time now long since passed that is talked about only when the residents of that era return home to visit old acquaintances and family.

And even before the era of my high school days, I remember those times of first attending class and being on the playground at the old Attucks Grade School. The grade school was comprised of the first through the sixth grades; Junior High School was the seventh and eighth grades; and the high school in the newer, separate building housed grades nine through twelve. However, in those days and in the preceding generations of our mothers and grandmothers, not much attention was given to technicalities--everything was just plain Attucks!

Attucks meant more than just learning--it meant days of swinging and playing in the sun. The merry-go-rounds--which really weren't the types of merry-go-rounds like the carousels one could see at the carnivals which came to town each year--were a series of green boards connected to one another which went around and around. Merry-go-rounds which went as slow or as fast as the slowest or fastest pusher could power them. The see-saws went up and down, up and down--the most fun part of course was when we "bucked" them, trying to see if you could unseat your playmate on the opposite end.

Attucks meant days of Mrs. Jones waiting at the door of the grade school house at the back of the main building for us to line up and come in--and getting her "bolo" bat on your back side if you messed up in the classroom. The "bolo" bat was a toy mostly girls would play with. But some of the teachers used the paddle for instilling values and reinforcing their points. And there was no mistaking it when some one messed up, it seemed you could hear the "whacks" all over the school grounds. Attucks meant days of trying to please your favorite teacher and not ever being able to fully do so because of the fact that all of them were so very special. Mrs. Versa White would always have a piece of candy for us; Mrs. Jenny Jones always had a smile and a big hug; and Mrs. Perkins, Mrs. Grace Kelly, and Mrs. Florence Crim were always the most beautiful and gracious ladies I had ever seen.

Attucks meant days of us young children whooping and hollering on the playground on what could only have been the tallest sliding board in the world, and the giant swing that seemingly reached clear to the top of the little white school house itself. Attucks meant days of wonder and days of vigor and vibrant youth that could never be denied!

It was in this marvelous atmosphere that we played our parts, living out our energetic and never ending lives of wonder and amazement. How could one ever put into words the lives we knew, the experiences we had, the wonders God brought to our lives day after day after day. Clearly, what Attucks would come to mean to the black citizens of Carbondale in future years would be, as Harold McCroy described, nothing less than a legacy.

I suppose there is (or at one time was) an Attucks in most every small town throughout America--a special place with a special meaning for its people, young and old. For truly, throughout rural America there always has been that little area across the tracks, that small, nondescript neighborhood occupied by the town's black population and separated from the white section. Those ever present train tracks always ran dead center through "up town." And in every such town, there surely must always have been those special teachers at that one special black school exerting a special impact on the lives of its progeny generation after generation. How magnificent is God that in His omnipotence and wisdom, He gave to each succeeding group of people the opportunity to experience the greatest gift of all--the love of a people one generation to the next.

This was a love that was shown by Mrs. Willie Norman who taught us about Jesus in Sunday School and about whom "Momean" and "Aunt Marie" and all the others sang each Sunday at Olivet Freewill Baptist Church. It was a life reflected by Mama Cecil and Mama Irene--who was better known as "Mamarene"--when they admonished us kids for our misdeeds, the boys for misbehaving and the girls for acting "fass," which, of course, meant "fast." This, by the way, was a curious expression which was to say that the girls were wise beyond their years and too grown-up like for their own good. It was curious because the word itself, as noted Blacks writers have observed, invariably came out aloud as [fass], no matter who pronounced it. It was never pronounced [fast].

It was a time when my grandmother, Allean Gordon, whom we all called "Momean," would cook supper as though she was preparing for a small military squad. Early Saturday and every Sunday morning before daylight broke, you would hear the sounds of pots and pans rattling and banging about in the kitchen. You knew the cooking had begun. Beans that were soaked all night; chicken and meats that were unthawed and cleaned; greens that were picked over and washed four or five times--all of this was so diligently and swiftly done in those wee morning hours. By seven o'clock, there would be so many sweet smelling aromas in the kitchen, a body could hardly stand it. Of course, much of the gathering of foods had been done by us "chu'luns" (as the older women called us) one or two days before.

There was always the garden in back from which came most all of our beans, okra, and tomatoes. Other food stuffs came from Dillinger's Feed Store up town. The fruits of the garden vines were the biggest and ripest that I would ever see. And the taste was absolutely astounding, compared to what one gets from the stores today. But for me--when I reflect on this aspect of living and growing up on Allman Street--I think the best time of all when it came to foods, was cutting into the large, delicious watermelons my grandfather Doe-Doe would bring home in the hot summer months.

Doe-Doe was the nickname given to Arthur Brown, husband to Allean Brown and father of Hattie Gloria Dean Brown, and I remember it was he and Mr. Albert Franklin, along with the other men out in the "Hoodlums" who served up those gigantic mouthwatering slices of the coldest, sweetest, juiciest, black seeded melons with such great pride and joy. It was at these times that all us kids (or chu'luns) would have an absolute ball! Especially on the Fourth of July when Charles Brown, "Uncle Albert," "Aunt Tank," and all the other women and deacons at our church would organize the big, annual picnic out to Crab Orchard Lake. The families would gather seemingly by the hundreds and the foods and drinks would appear as if by magic. And like my grandmother, who always cooked for anyone who wanted or needed "som'um-t'eat,"--the local, black vernacular for "something to eat," which was pronounced [sump'um-teet] with the voiceless "p" forming a sort of hard, abrupt stop which died out in the throat--anyone was just as apt to cook and serve anyone else. It didn't matter if the person was a family member or not. In those days, when food was cooked at my grandmother's house, anyone passing by could drop in for a meal. The door was open and literally unlocked at all times. We slept on pallets on the front porch or out in the yard. There was no need for locked doors on Allman Street. No one broke in his neighbor's house or destroyed his property.

Another time everyone gathered together was during the slaughterings. My grandfather Doe-Doe and Mr. Mitchell led and directed these festivities. Mr. Mitchell, whom everyone called "Mitch" or "Big Mitch," lived on the next street which was Barnes Street. He was a very outgoing person who was well liked by all and was the father of my classmates Bernadine and Geraldine Greer--and their brothers, David Dean, Michael and John Wayne. Mitch would teach us young boys about hunting, fishing, and skinning hogs. He and "Aunt Duck," who was Willie Mae Lilly, the wife of "Uncle Dee," would always lend me fishing worms or a long cane fishing pole if I didn't have them on a particular fishing trip. But the more spectacular event, without a doubt, was hog killing time, and at that Big Mitch was a master!

At Play

Children on the Merry-Go-Round at the Attucks playground.

    I remember how my eyes almost popped out the first time Mr. Mitchell pulled out his tremendously long skinning knife. I had never seen anything like it in my life! It was the biggest, shiniest, most fierce looking thing I had every seen. Not even my grandpa had anything to match it! Even today, I can still see that magnificent and awesome blade and Big Mitch as he and the other men expertly went about their work--all the while shooing us boys away who were, of course, always under foot.
    The men worked like surgeons, deftly splitting open the strung up dead hog, and before you knew it, the old number ten washtub would be filling up with steaming, stinking, reeking hog guts--the blood from that old boar or sow just a spewing and gushing out like water over Niagra Falls. And all the while, the hog just hanging there with what I thought was the most stupid grin on its face. I never understood why the hog could have such a dumb look of happiness on its countenance, after all it had just been gutted with a foot long blade. But each time I studied the dead hog's snout, sure enough there would be all those teeth showing in that silly, frozen grin spread across its jowls from end to end. It was a most fantastic and curious phenomenon.

The sows were lucky mostly; they were left around to have more little piglets. But if they got too mean or too old or too ornery, "Blam!" a dead-aim shot right between the eyes put a decisive end to its temperament once and for all. I was always excited at the time of the hog slaughtering because it meant a big plate, piled up with a heaping helping of chittlings and hog maws the next day. However, hog slaughtering also had a down side: it meant the feared lye soap, which my grandmother, Momean, taught my sister, Sherlene, and me to make from rendering the lard from the dead hog. We were not at all fond of that lye soap. True enough, it could whiten up faded white sheets and dingy clothes like nothing you had ever seen; dirty dish rags, pillow cases, long Johns and baby diapers came out as white as the driven snow. Unfortunately, the main ingredient for making the soap--the "Red Devil" lye--was true to its name. It had a nasty little side effect of nearly burning the hide right off your hands and fingers if you messed with it for too long. But in all, it too was a time I yet cherish, and one I shall never forget--a time long since passed which is talked about now only when residents of that age return home to visit old acquaintances. Those were the times I remember in my youth as a small child growing up in the northeast part of Carbondale. It was indeed a time of wonder, a time of running with friends and cousins.

The wonder years meant days of swimming out back in Mrs. Isalee's back yard with my best friends, Kent Mason and James Morgan, whom we all called "Stank." On the days the heavy rains would come, Stank's back yard would flood, and the water would rise three or four feet. That was our "swimming hole." I suppose because we were so young, we didn't focus on the snakes Mrs. Isalee was always so worried about. To us boys--so filled with robust energy and dare-devil attitudes--our only concern was seeing who could get up on the back porch and dive off the fastest.

Sometimes we surfaced with baseball size knots and cuts from landing head first into a rock or a broken bottle laying at the bottom of the muddy water. That was a great honor! The person with the biggest and deepest gashes naturally became the envy of all the other divers; that is, if he didn't start bawling like a girl. Crying brought instant dishonor and scorn for all time. The gash was one's symbol of manhood--even though we were only ten and eleven. That didn't matter because only the manliest of all could sustain such self-inflicted wounds and live to brag about it. My, how we strutted around with those abrasions like peacocks displaying during courting season. And like the medal of honor awarded for bravery in the face of the enemy, we wore our "red badges of courage" with pride and dignity. Sometimes, however, that pride and dignity earned us an extra beating from our mothers when we got home. They would say things like, "Get in here. Didn't I tell you to stop jumping off into that water like some crazy fool! Go get me a switch!" But my grandmother--the most feared disciplinarian in the neighborhood--didn't mince or refine her words at all. She would say stuff like, "Boy! You little nappy headed fool! I told you to keep yo' black behind out of that water! I ain't goin' to be paying no hospital bill! Brang yo' buck eyed, knotty head over here, right now! I'm gon'na beat all the black off'en yo' ass!" And she always said "brang" when she got mad, never the word "bring." However, we boys cared naught for the whipping we got. The beating was only another confirmation and mark of our manliness.

Sometimes someone would crack under the pain that came along with the bodily damage suffered in the swim--that poor, unfortunate fellow was just about exiled from the neighborhood. Everyone knew, of course, that "real" men didn't cry, therefore "sissies" and "mama's boys" were simply not tolerated. And if the fellow cried too loudly and showed too much weakness, he was subject to have more bodily harm rained down upon him right there on the spot by the rest of his intolerant companions. Our playing was much more than mere play; indeed, it was a sort of rite of passage, much akin to the rites of the college and university frat houses. Great was the one who took his aches and bruises like a man! All the lowly, less fortunate divers crowded about, patting him on the back and congratulating him for his bravery (and injuries), and that guy became like a god and was the talk of our gang--Hail the conquering Caesar! And so reigned the mighty king--well at least until the next rains came, and new hero was declared.

Sometimes at Stank's, we made use of the planks which fashioned a bridge connecting the back porch of Mrs. Isalee's main house to the doorway of her wash house. To walk those narrow boards without falling off into the water was also a test of one's courage and the greatest source of pride. We prided ourselves on determining who was the one true Tarzan or Jungle Jim.

The wonder years were times of climbing the box cars that sat idly on the Illinois Central Railway tracks just up the hill from Stank's house on the way to the "junk yard," or the city dump. Those box cars became irresistible to curious, vivacious young boys, and we would scale them like climbers scampering up Mount Everest, being ever so watchful for the railroad yard man who was always on the prowl making his rounds. During these times, we contemplated the merits of diving off into the creosote pools which our fathers and grandfathers said were used to soak the railroad ties and make them fit to hold the great spikes that would be driven into them--spikes which, in turn, would hold down the train tracks of the Illinois Central rail line. However, even the most gallant of us boys never went so far as to actually dive off into the depths of the creosote pools, not even Bud Miller. Bud Miller was even more daring than I, and my uncle Mike always told me I was one notorious little fellow. That was my uncle's word for me: notorious. I never knew what he was talking about until I got up some size and understood the meaning of the word. But if I was notorious, then my friend Bud Miller had to have been down right crazy because that boy would do anything anyone dared him not to do. However, as I said, not even Bud would go jumping off into a creosote pool. Those black, thickened, lakes of oil contained tar and acids, we were told--acids that could eat a body's flesh clean down to the bone. And having suffered through many tortuous experiences with my grandmother's home made lye soap, I knew enough to make it a point to avoid anything that contained even the slightest amounts of acid. Certainly, I wasn't about to leap into the greasy, foul smelling stuff lining the surfaces of the creosote pools.

Those extraordinary times meant days of walking in the sun and the rain in the summer, and trodding through mud and ice in winter. We walked not so much out of wanting to, but rather out of necessity. Truthfully, none of us ever gave much thought about getting around any other way for the mere fact that few of the black families of our neighborhood in the early fifties had cars; so, the issue was a moot point anyway. I suppose "simple" is the word to describe it--we merely did whatever it was that had to be done. It was a simple life lived in a simple manner. Today, as I think back, I feel because we went about our lives without wrangling about it, it was this very simplicity to which we now owe our inherent joy and happiness.

The rains heralded the best of times because, in addition to swimming, those were also the times the craw dads came out. Then it was a race to see who could come up with the biggest and best craw dads of all. Like ducks after a piece of bread, boys and girls ran jumping and plopping into the rushing, gushing ditches with their raging torrents. We hollered and screamed--falling into the muddy water--laughing and yelling while grabbing at the fleeting craw dads as they squirted backwards into the culverts and drain pipes. It was somewhat of a mystery to me that some of the girls seemed to be better at catching craw dads than a lot of us boys. After all, it was common knowledge that girls were a nuisance and really couldn't do any "real, manly thing" very well.

The favorite ditch was the one that ran just next to "Aunt Ferne's." Aunt Ferne was Ferne Gray, who was a daughter of Mama Cecil. At the first sign of the swelling of the water, the whole pack of neighborhood kids from Fisher, Barnes, Burke, and Allman Streets would be out in that ditch that ran down to her house from the back of "Mama Steele's" store which was called "Steele's Place." All of the Browns, the Mason kids, and my cousins and I--as well as a whole pack of unseemly characters from other blocks--would be in on the great craw dad hunt. Since I and my group of friends were in our adolescent years and older than the Brown children, it figured that we would be the ones to control the contest and dominate over the younger ones. Not so! The little ones would out best us bigger boys just about all the time.

Little Jeffrey Gray and my cousin, "Ronie Bell," were the champion craw dad catchers of all time. Jeffrey was a little fellow as fast as lightning. He could snatch them up when nobody else could. How he did it I was never able to figure out. The water in the ditches could be waist high or only ankle deep, it didn't matter to Jeffrey. His long arms would shoot down in a flash, and when he brought them up, sure enough, there emerged a nasty, ugly looking beast, just a pinching and a squirming every which way it could twist its long, agile body. It was indeed hard to acknowledge such a little guy as Jeffrey as being the master over us bigger guys.

Larone, whom everybody called "Ronie Bell," except for my Aunt Dean, was just as good. My aunt Dean always would call her son "Larone" or "Brother"--mostly it was "Brother." Sometimes we would call him other things; that was mostly when "Ronie Bell," stationed unseen somewhere off in the distance like some secret assassin, would sail a rock through the air and plant it straight upside someone's head. And true to the assassin's code, you never knew it was coming. You only heard the "zing" of the missile as it sliced through the air. By then it was too late! The piercing weapon had found its mark. "Ronie Bell," it seemed, always found his target. And it didn't matter if you were standing still or dodging about. In fact, he seemed to be even a better thrower while on the run--he simply never missed!

As for the craw dads, I always thought "Ronie Bell" was so good at catching the critters because his arms were short and he was so low to the water. Being on the short side, he never had far to stoop to snatch up the lightning fast, escaping crayfish--or as we called them, "craw dads." (Other people called them "crawfish.") At least that was my considered opinion of my cousin. Like Jeffery, Ronie Bell seemed to possess some type of crawfish "ESP."

Next to Jeffrey and Ronie Bell was Cheryl Brown. For a girl, she could always come up with a big craw dad. And if someone came up and tried to grab it from her, he was as likely as not to get his head knocked off! Cheryl could duke it out with the toughest boy. Everybody knew not to fool with her. "Aunt Ferne" would sometimes holler out at us, warning us that if we kept messing with Cheryl, we were liable to have some serious hurt inflicted upon our person. "All right," she would say, "if Cheryl smacks you in the mouth, don't come telling me nothing because I done told ya'll fools to leave that girl alone! Ya'll know good and well Cheryl'll slap the tar out of you!" And she was right; Cheryl was left alone.

I always enjoyed getting after little Mayola with the craw dads. Mayola was the cutest little girl in our neighborhood. She had the bright skin color of the Louisiana Creole and the longest, thickest black hair to complement those features. And on top of all this, she had the most amazing, biggest and brightest pair of eyes anyone had ever seen. However, she had one trait the other girls did not have, and that was what made her my favorite target: Mayola could scream the loudest!

Whenever we boys came near her with one of those craw dad monsters--its claws snapping, trying to get hold of any human fingers that ventured too close its pinchers--little Mayola would cut loose with a piercing scream that could make your teeth rattle and just about deafen you for life. Then she'd take off down the road like a rocket going to tell "Aunt Ferne." But by the time she got to her house, we boys had all split. Nobody waited around for "Aunt Ferne" to appear; that was too much like committing suicide!

Now, there were also times in our community when it seemed no one could get along with anyone else. Most often this occurred on the days of the event to end all events--the great baseball game! This was serious business, and two prerequisites were crucial. First, and of utmost importance, one had to choose the team's players with the greatest of care. The one chosen as captain became an instant drill sergeant, scrutinizing everyone else to make sure he or she was fit to play: no broken bones; no blindness or otherwise poor eye sight; no rotten teeth that was subject to ache and cause one to lose concentration on the all-important game; etc. All the known players with anything remotely associated with the slightest semblance of skill or athletic ability were naturally picked first--the ball droppers, the blind, the lame and crippled runners, the clumsy and otherwise undesirables came in dead last. The last group--the downright idiotic--didn't have a prayer! They were confined to the benches in hopes of getting in the next week's game.

The second most important aspect of the game concerned the playing field. One had to choose the ball arena carefully because if you weren't careful, or if you were in a heated argument and not paying attention to oncoming missiles, you were apt to end up a casualty of a fast moving, non-breaking T-Model Ford whose road we kids had confiscated. Since we lived in the "Hoodlums" and the Attucks playground was "up town," over in "Puppy Tail," we had to use the dusty roads of Allman and Burke Streets and empty yards for our ball "stadiums." "Puppy Tail" was so named because Green Street once curved around into Oak Street, forming a sort of puppy tail shape. According to local historian Hardin A. Davis, the greater part of the land in "Puppy Tail," on which the Attucks Playground stood, had been farm land owned by Dan and Grace Powers. We boys, at that time, never knew the history of the playground; we simply always dreamed of playing our games at the big diamond field there. However, in the 1950s our parents didn't let us kids wander all over town and so, playing in the immediate vicinity of our homes was the only option. We didn't dare think of sneaking off. After all, we wanted to live to see adulthood!

Saturdays were especially hazardous times for baseball playing because this meant it was the weekend, and to some of the young men who were old enough to get a license--and to some of the older adults as well--weekends meant "laying" or "kicking back" with a glass or two of "home brew;" or even worse, a half pint Mason canning jar of home made "mule kick." And when a good mouthful or two of that concoction got into you, all hell was subject to break loose! Sometimes the cars would fly down Barnes Street half backwards, turning corners in a hail of dust clouds, flying gravel, and deafening, ear splitting squeals of rubber! When detected in time, us kids went scattering like a flock of sheep--across the ditches and scurrying out of the way up onto the nearest front porch or up into the nearest tree like a cat with a bulldog on his tail.

One could easily tell when that home made corn liquor had gotten the best of somebody. Years before when I was about seven, I had come across a clear jar full of the stuff in my grand daddy Doe Doe's coal shed. How it got there or whose it was, I never knew. I could only remember feeling like dying after I had gulped down a good quantity of the stuff. I also remember feeling like being on fire-- engulfed by a fierce heat--and thinking that actual death wouldn't be so bad compared to the pain and nauseating misery I was suffering. When Doe Doe got home, he diagnosed the case and immediately gave me some buttermilk which made me wretch like a witch. I stood gagging and violently vomiting up what I felt to be my entire system of bodily organs. Needless to say, I have shied away from corn whiskey in any shape, form, or fashion to this very day.

As for the street games, they always took place under the watchful eyes of our parents. And to protect life and limb from those "crazy, no count, damn fools," (as Cousin Jenny and Mrs. Partlow called them), we young'uns (young children up to the teen years) and the "crumb snatchers" usually ended up playing in Mr. John Brown's and Mama Cecil's big drive way, which, in turn, ended in an even larger front yard in front of their home known as the "Big House." Actually, the "crumb snatchers" were too little to play ball; they were mostly kept out of the way by the mothers or by the bigger kids who weren't actually playing in the game. These little ones were mostly of toddler age and were always crawling or ambling about looking for candy, sweets, scraps of food, and other crumbs that happen to fall from the table; thus, the term "crumb snatchers."

The baseball game was an even greater affair than the craw dad hunting, and at the very mention of the momentous occasion, every kid in our neck of the woods--and half the grown ups--turned out. The kids came to play; the adults came to make sure the kids came home in one piece. Next to Sunday Service and a funeral, the baseball game was the most serious and sacred event of which one could partake. One wrong call by the umpire or one widely thrown pitch and it was "fist city!" One slip of the tongue when calling somebody's name--unintentionally or not--and it was a "sho nuff" just cause for war! Even a stolen base could be taken as a signal to try and rearrange somebody's teeth!

And wild calls were a dime a dozen! Most of the time, nobody really knew when a home run had been hit because no one was ever truly certain of just where the bases were. Many a pair of players had come to blows because the batter ran to get on base at the fence, while the pitcher threw him out at the base which he and all his team mates had declared to be the light pole. But usually after all the fussing and fighting and kicking and yelling, everybody would somehow emerge unscathed, and each player would march off to his home content and bragging that he had put on a great show--and absolutely convinced--at least in his or her own mind--that he or she was the greatest ball player the Carbondale northeast neighborhood had every seen.

The wonder years also meant evenings of watching the free movies out in the big clearings at the outskirts of the neighborhood called "The Fields" or at Huckiebuck's when Mr. "Jelly" Gibbs showed the films at Mrs. Fletcher's. The movies always came served up with big, mouthwatering pickles and endless bags of fresh hot popcorn. As we entered our teen years, the movies seemed to become less and less interesting. There wasn't anything wrong with the films; it was just that members of the opposite sex were becoming more appealing. Girls suddenly were becoming rather pleasing; whereas before, they were merely pests. Now, more and more when the movies began, boys and girls could be observed pairing up and sitting a bit closer together than before. Now, when the watchful eyes of parents were averted, boys and girls could be seen trying to steal a quick kiss behind a tree--and dashing back to the crowds before their presence could be detected.

The wonder years were lifetimes of endless days having to sit getting your hair cut at Bear's--the uptown barber shop of Charles Arnett--and sitting on the hard flat board that stretched across the arms of his big barber chair. The very first haircut was the most terrifying because, as a small child sitting so high up, you were terrified to look down to the floor which seemed so far down. The wonder years were days of getting the best ice-cream cones at Jacob's store, the best bowls of chili at "Mrs. Carter's," and the absolute best hamburgers at Jones's Cafe. And, again, they were days of picking peas and the many others vegetables from my grandmother's garden, and taking baskets filled with large quantities of produce to the neighbors and members of our church.

Then there were the black neighborhood stores such as "Mr. Fletcher's," with its coal burning, pot bellied stove; and Hinchey's store, which was really a makeshift room in one part of his house set up to serve and dispense sandwiches, snacks, candies, and other assorted items. Everybody, it seemed, had a store on just about every corner. Besides Fletcher's and Hinchey's Stores, there was Campbell's Store, Hillsman's Store, Russell's Store, and Fisher Store--and there was Steele's Place on Allman Street in the "New Addition," also known as "Renfro Addition." There was Isom's Store, owned by Mrs. Fannie Isom, and, of course, Jacob's Store to which everybody would flock for the most delicious ice cream in the world! There was also Johnson's Store, and there was one operated by the Banks. Also, the Westley's at one time had a store. It was in such revered establishments as these where pieces of candy went two-for-a-penny and where the largest, most luscious, juiciest pickles went for a nickel each. In short, it was a kid's paradise. If you had a quarter, it was like dying and going to heaven!

There were two women of our neighborhood who held a particular fascination for me: "Mama Cecil" and "Cousin Jenny." "Mama Cecil," who was Mr. John Brown's wife, was a kind, old soul with a pleasant disposition and an easy going manner. She always would get on to us kids if she noticed us doing anything wrong. She always had her cane or a stick with her she'd use to chase off the dogs, and when she caught one of us young'uns 'up to mischief or no good," she would point that stick at us and say, "You all stop that or I'm going to tell Allean." Well, Allean was my grandmother, and the last thing we wanted was for anyone to mention our bad behavior to Momean. That was like signing your own death warrant.

Mama Cecil, like all the women of the time, could work wonders in the kitchen, and if you were lucky enough to be at the "big house" in the early morning, you'd be treated to a mouth-watering breakfast of fresh buttered biscuits and thick slabs of fat-back served up with a nice helping of molasses. I made it a point on several occasions to be at Papa John's early in the day before he'd strike out for the day in his wagon. And even if you missed Papa John, you could always say you wanted to catch Billy before he got away. However, everyone was well aware that a small boy showing up at Mama Cecil's door so early in the dawn meant only one thing: he was on a treasure hunt, and Mama Cecil's biscuits was the target.

It was always a revelation when "Cousin Jenny" came ambling down the street because she always had a story to tell or a lesson to teach. "Cousin Jenny's" real name was Jenny Beard, and she always thought the destruction of the nation was due to the "Jay-Panos." According to her, anything that was wrong with the United States of America was due to the insidious takeover by the Japanese government, which was violent and sneaky in all its doings. Consequently, she was always down on the "Jay-Panos." It was hilarious to stand and listen to her; she could go on and on for hours about the no good, low down Jay-Panos and how the President ought to bomb them all to hell! She couldn't understand for the life of her how a God fearing nation like the United States could allow such "riff-raff" to set foot on its sacred soil. I came to the conclusion that it all had to do with the early 1940s and World War II. Since I was born at the end of the great war of infamy, I just could never figure it all out. Eventually, I stop trying and would simply nod my head in agreement with whatever Cousin Jenny had to say about the "low down foreigners." It was dangerous to get her started because you were liable to be held a captive audience well into the evening.

Nobody seemed to know exactly how old Cousin Jenny was either. She herself was apt to tell you she was eighty something one day, and then a few days later, she would be ninety-three. It was only when I grew up that I realized that "Mama Cecil" was older than any of the women on our street and that she had been born in the 1800s. However, I was to later learn that it was cousin Jenny who lived the longest. I wondered at how something so significant could have gone so unnoticed. All this time I had been residing less than half a block away from living history itself and never knew it. Not once could I recall having ever been told our history or any of the history surrounding Mama Cecil or Cousin Jenny.

Within recent years, I learned that Cousin Jenny lived to be one hundred and six years old. She was the oldest African American ever in post-1900 Carbondale history. Only one other African American from Carbondale was ever documented to live to age 106, and she died in the 1800s.

When I was about six years old, my mother built the house at 811 North Washington Street. Now there were new pals to romp around with and new experiences to encounter. Leonard, Earl, and "Peachum" were "Blue" Mitchell and Bertha Mitchell's sons. We all called her "Aunt Bertha"; it just didn't sound right any other way. Well, when we boys got together--Earl, Leonard, my Uncle Michael France, and I--the trouble we didn't get into! Catching tadpoles in the "swamp" under the oil tanks across the street was always fun, but jumping off the old garage shed in back of the Mitchell's was our most favorite past time of all. Aunt Bertha would yell at us to "get down off that roof before you break your dog gone necks." Well, we would get down, but as soon as she went back inside, we'd be back up on that roof quicker than a bat in a church tower. Mothers somehow couldn't understand that it was just a natural inclination for young boys to jump off things.

Also, over at Lincoln Junior High School, which at that time was attended by whites, was a fire escape attached to the back of the school. It wasn't a series of stairs as are modern fire escapes, but it was a closed in structure sort of like a water shoot ride at a water park. You had to climb into this structure and slide down all the way down from the top of Lincoln school to the ground. Well, that fire escape became one of our favorite "rides." The entrance door to the thing was never locked and we boys would climb up to the top of the two story roof and jump into the chute, and away we would zip. I was always the first to lead the way. That was when my uncle Mike first started calling me notorious. The inside of the chute was pitch black; you couldn't see a thing--only a light that became visible after the chute made a series of turns and ended near the ground level. The chute was a spiral and it went around and around as one descended toward the ground. Well, since it was pitch black inside the thing, everyone was always scared to go first except me. I would go up to the roof and jump right in--feet first with absolutely no hesitation at all. Everyone else, after waiting to see what would happen, would naturally follow.

To sum it all up, my life as a child in Carbondale was simply the best. Running and jumping up onto Mr. John Brown's horse and wagon and riding from the east side of Carbondale to the rural roads north, south, and west of the city was truly an adventure--the likes of which I have never experienced since. Sometimes, Mr. John Brown would even turn over the reigns to one of us little fellows, and we would be the "big boss" for the moment, driving the horse crazy as it tried to figure out which way we were directing it to go. How delighted it was to coax the horse into the alley way in back of Dillinger's to load up the wagon with bags of feed and flour and rice.

Such moments were virtually the best of times--the friends, the picnics, the shared days and nights with our families were times I fear we shall never see again. It surely must have been such times as these the writer was recalling to mind when he coined the phrase "you can't go home again." How sad, but true. True because time is ever changing; and so, as the times change, the people change likewise.

Part I

The African American Settlement of Jackson County and Carbondale

An Overview

The African American Settlement of Jackson County and Carbondale: An Overview

Of Slaves and Freed Men

The Black settlement of the Carbondale area begins with a look at the migration of the Afro-Americans who came predominantly from the south. Most came seeking better lives in the north; others came because they had no choice. The earliest records at the Jackson County Court House and the Jackson County Historical Society in Murphysboro depicting the movement of blacks into the area date back to the early 1800's. These include census reports, birth registrations, and death certificates showing the blacks who had arrived in Illinois and settled in Jackson County.

Information from these annals and other works reveal that the first Blacks were in Jackson County as early as 1807 (P. Michael Jones, 1994). Examination of the various historical documents reveals that the majority of these residents arrived from Tennessee and Kentucky. Others made their way into Illinois mostly from the southern states of Louisiana, Missouri, Georgia, Mississippi, Alabama, Virginia, the Carolinas, Alabama, and Maryland. Then there were blacks traveling north from as far as Florida and those arriving from the northern states and from Canada.

The earliest slaves came in and out of Southern Illinois and Jackson County largely by means of the underground railroads. Two of these ran from Chester to Sparta toward the north and from Cairo northward using the Illinois Central Railroad (Jon Musgrave, 1997). According to authors Hodges and Levene, the starting points of three of the best known routes were Chester, Alton, and Quincy, all towns along the Mississippi River (Illinois History Makers, 1964). By 1830, protests to abolish slavery in Illinois had already begun. The underground railroads were great threats to the slave owners. Each time a slave successfully made his way to freedom, a slave owner could lose an investment from $700.00 to $2,000.00 (Hodges and Levene, p. 11). Slavery clearly was not far away from its demise. By 1860, the growing rumors of Lincoln's inclination toward emancipation and the looming Civil War had spawned the faith and belief that freedom was not far away. The African Americans who came to Southern Illinois after the abolishment of slavery shared the same dreams and hopes of those who arrived before slavery's end. No matter where their journey began, Blacks every where sought to reach a place where they could have the means to prosper and grow.

Just how many of our Black forefathers in the area realized their dreams is not clear. It would seem to be a very low number, since these same records reveal that the majority of Blacks--upon reaching their northern destinations--lived in impoverished conditions, suffered extremely bad health, and began to die fairly early of various diseases and the harsh Illinois winters. Verna Cooley notes, "Slaves entering Illinois from the South and Southeast found a hostile territory and were obliged to depend on their own resources" (Jon Musgrave, 1997). Additionally, in his work, The Underground Railroad ran both ways in Southern Illinois, Musgrave points out a major hazard of the slaves' travels:

> In antebellum Southern Illinois the Underground Railroad ran both ways. Both ran contrary to the law of the land, but while one was a righteous crusade, the other was for criminal profit. The legitimate one ran north, helping Blacks escape slavery for freedom. The other one ran in reverse, enslaving free Blacks back into bondage.

Slavery in Jackson County

One of the earliest works written exclusively on the black slaves in Jackson County is *Forgotten Soldiers* by P. Michael Jones (1994). As previously mentioned, Jones notes that slaves began entry into the area beginning in the early 1800s--with the first documented cases seen in 1807. In 1818, the year Jackson County is established, Jones cites the number of slaves at 53. The Jackson County Census of 1820 shows that in the ensuing two year period the number of slaves had decreased to 39.

As previously stated, several factors collectively indicate that the number of slaves in Jackson County could easily have been higher than reported. First, there were some positions which were commonly held by slaves especially trained for these duties. Many references are made to the young women and teenage girls as being "house girls" or "house servants." Other positions such as "Dray man," (a coach driver); "Teamster," (a mule or horse team driver in the fields); Blacksmith, "field boy;" and "house boy" also indicate slave positions held by men. Of course, any of these jobs could have been worked by freed blacks, and undoubtedly were. But such positions as "house maids" and "chamber maids" had traditionally been held by black slaves and indentured servants who had been schooled for these duties. It was ironic that such lowly positions called for the highest quality of "refinement" and "mannerisms" and only the most genteel of servants would do.

Secondly, the nationalities of most of the early Afro-Americans are given as "Black," "Colored," or "Negro." Black women are also referred to by the term "Negress." Yet, in many instances, the descriptions "African" appears on the individual's report--particularly so in the death records. Obviously, this distinction could have been merely a designation for Blacks who had come to the States either directly or indirectly from Africa, with no implication that the person was a slave. The term could also have been a way of identifying local persons from new arrivals. On the other hand, in the time that slavery did endure, it could very well have been a means some whites could use to specifically identify slaves, or ex-slaves. (Alex Hailey's notes make it clear that in the novel *Roots*, "The African" was a term specifically used for his grandfather, a plantation slave brought from Africa to Tennessee.) Was this situation unique only to this one individual out of hundreds of thousands of slaves? This would seem unlikely. If the term "African" did, in fact, signify a slave, even if only in a small amount of cases, then greater numbers of slaves would have been around than were being reported.

The issue of whether or not the term "African" was synonymous with "slave" is as interesting as it is questionable. Words have different meanings for different people--meanings which change with time and usage. Until more research on this issue is undertaken, any possible answers to the question will remain essentially invalidated.

A more plausible explanation effecting the accuracy of slave data is the fact that early census reports were often not conducted in a consistent manner among census takers and, thus, were highly unsophisticated by modern standards. In 1820 two census takers were responsible for providing data in Illinois. One took the state count for Jackson County; the second took the federal census count. There is an obvious discrepancy between the two reports, and inconsistencies and miscounts are seen even within the individual report for Jackson County prepared by Matthew Duncan.

It is quite evident that different recorders used different codes and abbreviations that others were unfamiliar with. This created confusion in trying to put together the final copy of a report. Handwriting was often illegible and, in certain cases, completely unreadable; no one knows who for sure who provided the information; spelling and recording was fraught with misspellings and incorrect personal data. Most importantly, early census takers only counted residents by the surnames of the persons residing in each household and did not count each and every individual. Thus, many blacks (and whites as well) were obviously overlooked (or otherwise unaccounted for) in the tally of numbers in the census reports. Johnetta Jones relates that in May of 1855, Jackson County authorities granted a certificate of freedom to "Bijab, a man of color, twenty-two or twenty-three years old, son of Hannah, a free woman of color" (Jones, p. 11). In a time frame when slavery was supposedly non-existent in the county, such facts argue strongly to the contrary, and it is no small wonder that later documents describe the numbers of slaves cited in the early 1800s reports as "estimates."

However, the most compelling argument for the lack of larger number of slaves being reported has to be the historical time period of slavery itself. Since slavery as institution wasn't officially declared ended until 1863, history shows that prior to this event, all blacks (except those who carried proof of their freedom) were legally considered "property" and not human individuals. As such, even in areas where official slave numbers were relatively low, the actual number of slaves could have been significantly higher--including the state of Illinois--which was ostensibly a "free" state after 1834.

Other factors were also at work which could have lowered the slave counts. The fact that slaves who were being set free could purchase the freedom of other slaves helped to reduced the number of slaves being reported. Slaves could also be married off or sold to other farms or to other locations. However, the one of the main causes of inaccurate slave counts was the result of the direct action of the slave owners themselves. This stems from the one hard fact that slaves were property, and because they were property, they could be taxed. Consequently, many white slave owners--much like tax dodgers today-- often took deliberate, planned illegal measures to assure their individual slave counts were lower than they actually were. Any owner wishing to lessen his tax burden, could either change the status of a slave to indentured servant, or, if conditions permitted, he could simply move the slave into his home and list him on paper as a family member (census reports show that Blacks routinely resided in white households in Jackson County in the mid-1860s). It should be made clear that the intent here is not to dispute any existing slave documents; after all, such records are the means by which we gauge and interpret history.

Traces In The Dust

The purpose here is only to draw attention to the fact that because of human error--intentional or not--many areas of history remain open to speculation and conjecture, and the need for further investigation always persists.

Obviously, the question of the number of slaves in the area is a matter not easily sorted out. After 1830, the practice of listing specific slave numbers seemed to have stopped. By 1840, for instance, no other census report for Jackson County listed slaves, even though evidence suggest some slaves still lived in the county. Various reasons could account for this demise of slave counts. One, the migration north and the constant movement of blacks from one area to another would certainly make it difficult to keep accurate records. Two, at times it may simply have been too arduous a task trying to determine the black slaves from indentured servants and free blacks. This would have been particularly so during the mid-1800s when the different anti-slavery movements and uprisings, and the various activities of the abolitionist leaders were under full steam. Hodges and Levene (1964) and (O'Neill, 1973), enable us to understand how anti-slavery sentiment and the constant black rebellions--along with the efforts of the Black leaders of the resistance movement in the North--coupled with the establishment of the Maroon Camps and the underground railroads of the South, were all factors which could have limited or prevented altogether the accurate listing of slaves every where in the country the practice thrived. Finally, the size of plantations themselves and the amount of land area they encompassed could have added to the problem. Plantations varied greatly throughout the South. Kennell Jackson, in his work, America Is Me, notes that in 1860 some plantations had as little as twenty slaves while a great number of establishments had well over one hundred.

Another factor that directly decreased the number of slaves--and perhaps in doing so, detracted from the logic of keeping slave records--was the ability of the black slaves and indentured servants to "self-purchase" their freedom (Franklin and Moss, Jr., 1994) In addition to these forces at work, there were still bigger shadows hanging over the heads of slave owners which reeked constant concern: the civil war and the ever pending approach of the Emancipation Proclamation. Many slaves joined the war effort, as it was ultimately seen as the most expedient means to freedom, and the approach of Lincoln's official act of freeing the slaves had long since caused sleepless nights for slave advocates. In addition to these factors, slave violence and acts of resistance, too, had always been cause for whites across the nation to question the effort and personal cost of keeping slaves (O'Neill, 1973).

One could argue logically, of course, that slaves were less in number in Jackson County simply because there never had been that much slave activity. Using this line of thought, the number of slaves in Jackson County would well have been lower than the average number of slaves per county in the South, for example. Since slavery had, for all intents and purposes, ended by 1934 (about 30 years before the signing of the Emancipation Proclamation) due largely to the legal steps taken by the slave, Juliet Gaston in 1930 (P. Michael Jones, 1994), there obviously wouldn't be any more slaves to account for after this time.

The scarcity of slaves in Jackson County seems apparently due to the territory of Illinois's early status as a quasi-free state; however, it was more likely because of a combination of factors--coupled with the rapidly approaching (and inevitable) end of slavery as a whole. And although historical documentation suggests slavery in Jackson County's early history existed on a relatively small scale, the nagging suspicion of the possibility of a larger and more robust slave activity in the area is not easily ignored.

The Color of Identity--Then and Now

In the majority of cases, the earliest African Americans in the area were described as "Colored," "Negroid," "Negro," "African," or "Ethiopian." They were also referred to by descriptives of color such as "Dark," "Tan," and "Brown." Other labels found among historical documents employed such dubious combinations as "Black Negro," "African Negro," "Yellow African," "Brown African," and "Black African." A certain Charles Elvoy of Mount Carbon, Illinois was deemed a "Yellow Negro," who on December 22, 1882 married Celia E. Sperman of Mount Carbon, also a "Yellow Negro." And in several marriages and deaths in the 1870s, the negative term "Darkie" appears. Still, other descriptions used were such terms as "Mixed," "Yellow," "Mulatto," "Light American," and just plain "Light." The description "Copper" was generally thought to refer to those individuals who were of Negro and

American Indian descent. This is distinguishable from "Mulatto" which referred primarily to those of mixed Caucasian and Negro ancestry. Mulattos were typically characterized by various shades of fair complexion skin tones--from smooth olive brown to light tan.

Strangely enough, due to the large variety of colors of non-whites in the 1800s, it was not always known exactly what some individuals should be called. The term appearing most often in official archives of early Jackson County is "Black." Next on the scale is the term Negro followed by "Colored" and "African" which appear just about evenly. However, these universal categories would not adequately suffice, again because of individuals of various colors and, too, due to the existence of other races. It is said that necessity is the mother of invention, and of necessity, the new invented phrase for the non-typical blacks and persons of other races in Jackson County became "Fair Americans." The term was born in the late 1800s and worked excellently as a way to save the time and trouble of properly identifying one's race. To identify a person correctly required tracking one's roots, and most blacks had no papers or certificates of birth. "Fair Americans" could accommodate anyone who wasn't readily distinguishable as to his proper race. There was no mistaking the term to mean White people. In all Jackson County documents, Whites were clearly distinguishable by the terms "White" or "Caucasian," or "White American." "Fair Americans," as well as "Light" and "Light Americans," referred strictly to individuals bright in color and of European descent. Through tracing and comparison of the various available documents, several of these "Fair" and "Light Americans," oddly enough, were proven to be really creole or mulatto. In a word, they were black.

Also in use at the time was the term "Dark American." As previously stated, the word "Dark" denoted Blacks. "Dark American," on the other hand, referred to other races of color. Whereas "Light Americans" referred predominantly the light colored Europeans, "Dark American," referred largely to Europeans of darker shades of skin tones such as the Italians and Greeks. It also was applicable to Mexicans and Native American Indians. In documents containing over three thousand marriage notices along, only three instances were noted where "dark Americans" were found to be of Negro descent. It is clear, then, that when the term "Dark American" was used, the word "American" did not carry the same connotation it did when applied to the white race. When referring to the dark races, the word "American" was strictly a label employed solely as a means to racially classify the individual; it was not used in the sense of the person belonging to or being a part of the nation. In a sense, it was a brand-- much like a rancher would brand his cattle. Non-whites were invariably grouped and referred to by the shade and color of their skin or by ethnic origin. The somewhat redundant terms "Black Ethiopian" (said of Henry Robinson, 1878) and "Dark African" (said of Jordan Anderson, 1883) discovered among marriage documents are only two of a myriad illustrations of this.

Creole and "Negro Creole" were also terms which had several connotations. Creole commonly referred to a descendant of the French who settle in Louisiana and spread to a few other parts of the South. However, "Negro Creole" was used by southern whites to distinguish the Negro born in the Western Hemisphere and who used a Creole dialect from the Negro who came from Africa. Creole also was applied to a person of Spanish or Portuguese descent, as well as to a person of European descent born in the West Indies. The term "Indian Negro" was used in the North to denote a person of Negro and Indian ancestry (See Twombly, Robert C. *Black Resistance to Slavery in Massachusetts* in *Insights And Parallels,* 1973).

Some of the terms used to describe blacks were more than mere terms of identity; they held greater significance because of what they implied. Two such terms which survived to modern times are "yellow" and "high yellow." "Yellow" was synonymous with "Light American" and denoted a very pretty, light tone with just a hint of color. To be "yellow" was considered to be very beautiful at times. On other occasions, however, it could be considered a curse. It all depended upon the circumstances.

"High yellow" had reference to an extremely light complexion. A "high yellow gal," for instance, was a Negro female whose skin was so light and whose facial appearances were so Caucasian-like, she could easily be mistaken as a white person. Yet, like the term "yellow," "high yellow" also carried a negative connotation and was often used in a derogatory sense; it too was a put down. Because of their extremely light colored skin, "high yellow" Blacks often felt somehow superior to darker colored Blacks; consequently, the darker toned Afro-Americans used the term as an expression of scorn and derision. In the black northeast community of Carbondale, to about the mid-1960s, was often heard the expression, "yellow wench." For one black female to be called such by another black female was an aspersion cast upon her honor. To be called a "high yellow wench," or a "high yellow heffa" was the ultimate insult--"heffa" meaning "heifer," or a cow. How often would I hear the women of our neighborhood say, "Just because she's high yellow, she ain't no better than me." Even today, it is not uncommon to hear such expressions in the vernacular of the older generations of African-Americans.

The most offensive term ascribed to Blacks is the vulgarism "Nigger." Evidence suggests the term came into the American dialect originally from the from the French term [*Negre*] which referred to dark skinned people. The early English dialect had in use the terms Neger and Neeger. In 1619, the term "Negar" referred to the first Black slaves and other non-whites who came into the colonies (Jackson, 1966). It was more a term of identification as opposed to one of scorn or derision. The ethnic term "Negro" stems from the Spanish [*Negro*] which denoted the first blacks arriving from Africa and landing in the Caribbean islands and South and Central America. According to Jackson, slaves were not routinely brought directly from Africa into English North American until the late 1700s (*America Is Me*, p. 59).

In early Jackson County, the word "Negro" ranked second in official use following the term "Black." The expression "Nigger" understandably does not appear in any official Jackson County documents examined either before or after the demise of slavery. It would not be used in any official capacity because of the obvious derogatory and offensive nature of the word. According to Jackson, "nigger" was used interchangeably with "slave" or "negro" beginning with the seventeenth century. This can be construed to mean that the word, in such cases, was used as a means of identification. It is quite obvious, however, that it wasn't too long before the word acquired a separate and distinctly infamous usage: to express utter contempt and derision for the black race. From the multitude of written works on the slave era, it seems most likely that this usage of the word (i.e, to show hatred) derived directly from the Early English [Neeger] and that it most likely originated sometime during the middle 1700s and the early 1800s. In the later 1700s before Blacks began to build their own churches, for example, "Nigger pews" referred to the balcony and other segregated areas of the White buildings where Blacks were forced to sit (Jackson, 1996). By the middle 1800s, "Nigger" was used extensively to compare Blacks to cutthroats, pagans, animals, and immoral beings; it was also used to denote personal and exchangeable possessions known as "chattel." This is evidenced by Mattie's speech in 1866, "The niggers are on the warpath again" from *The Story of Mattie J. Jackson* (Thompson, 1866), and by some white slave owners' claims as "my own neegers" (Jackson, 1996). The concept that Blacks were "property" and not people was carried over into the twentieth century by Mark Twain's use of "Nigger" in mainstream American literature (The Adventures of Huckleberry Finn, 1884). Today, the term "Nigger," or "Nigga," as used by bigots and racists extends indiscriminately to all Blacks and Africans in the United States.

Another reference to Blacks in both slavery and post-slavery America was the word "mammy," and it, too, had multiple usages and connotations. Depending upon who was using it and how it was used, it could be harmless or as equally as bad as the other derogatory terms--or worse! In the South during slavery, the word "mammy" originated simply as a derivation of "mama," both of which meant nothing more than "mother." And it was used by both blacks and whites. However, at some point, probably around the middle to late 1800s, it began to take on more negative tones, eventually evolving into the early 1900s slur of the word "mother."

The more intense one's dislike for the female grew, the worse the connotations of "mammy" became. Its most vicious use obviously was as a direct attack on one's mother, and the degree of viciousness implied was in direct proportion to the vindictiveness with which the word was uttered. It could also be used as a roundabout way to insult one's relatives. By belittling the mother, one belittled the entire family. From accounts of oral history, it seems evident that by the early 1900s in Carbondale, one black person could no longer refer to another black person's mother using the word "mammy." By this time, "Mammy" had evolved to denote a female was of flawed character or that she was literally a bad mother when it came to her family. Still in use, although to a much lesser extent (and mostly by the older generations of Blacks), the term--in addition to its original meanings--now includes a more specific, modernized connotation: a mother who abandons or neglects her children; especially a mother who puts "her man" before her children. Today, the term "mammy" is clearly an expression of one's disgust (or disrespect) for a female individual. Even if used in jest, the person to whom the term is uttered would most likely be highly offended.

As previously mentioned, none of the available historical documents indicate any person was enslaved in Jackson County due to their race after 1830. Death certificates show the majority of the men in the middle 1800s to be common laborers and field hands who lived, worked, and died on farms or tracks of land they either owned or share cropped. Some of the men had acquired specialized skills ranging from horse trainers, and shoe makers to coal miners and blacksmiths. The position of "Teamster" is listed in many instances. The majority of the females did cooking, cleaning, or washing. Others are listed simply as "housewives." Even though the blacks occupying Jackson County after 1830 continued to work in slave positions and occupations, it seems clear that the institution of slavery in Jackson County had ended by this time and that one's color had more to do with ethnic identification than with slavery.

Today, along with the term "Black," American society has produced a new term in vogue at the moment: "African or Afro- American." I say "at the moment" because history has proven that language is perpetually in a constant state of change, and all labels born of politically correct interests are destined to fall into disuse. Blacks have been the only group in American history to suffer a major crisis of identity. As a group of people, they have gone full circle from being Black or African to Negroes; from being Negroes to Colored; from being Colored to "Bro," "Sister," and "People of Color"; from being "People of Color" to Afro-American and back to Black again. The tragedy is underscored by the fact that within the black social structure, each of these terms is equally offensive to someone of the culture. "Black" is highly offensive to many older people of the Negro race who prefer the term "Colored." Conversely "Colored" is disagreeable to those who call themselves "Black;" notwithstanding the fact that during the fifties, "Black" was the worst of insults, and a "fighting" word. The person calling another individual black was immediately beset upon.

The word "Negro" has all but fallen into total oblivion; it is dismissed by most everyone today who is of the black race. One person who followed the Muslim religion told me in the fall of 1999 that the words "Negro" and "African American" were old and new contrivances of the white people and had no meaning. It was a ploy by them (whites) to further distance the black race from their heritage. "Colored people, by virtue of their African heritage were Black and should always be addressed as 'Blacks,'" he stated. Well, I didn't know quite what to say to that since I had once called a man from Nigeria "black" and what a horrible experience that turned out to be!

It was at Southern Illinois University in Carbondale in 1963. I was talking with an individual from Nigeria about his native costume he was wearing, and I, in my blissful ignorance, referred to him as "Black." I was promptly informed (and in no uncertain terms) that he was not a "Black" man (that is to say, an American black) and that if I wanted to address him at all, I should properly refer to him as "African." "You Blacks are a lost people," he informed me, "and I have a culture and a home!" "I am African!" To this very day, I have never forgotten that harsh lesson taught to me so vehemently and unceremoniously. That was one of the few times in my life I felt lower than dirt. With the exception, of course, of the time I attempted to converse with a Mexican national using the Spanish language. Again, I was promptly assailed for belittling and putting the man down. "I speak English," he immediately told me with an angry scowl. "I am American. You speak English to me." It was at this moment I finally understood why it is so hard to get Mexican children to use their native language at school.

About six years ago, I was approached by a fellow colleague at a South Texas junior college where I taught English to Mexican nationals. My friend, who was white, was truly perplexed by the use of today's nomenclature and was perturbed at not knowing what term to use when addressing Blacks. "I just don't know what to call you all," she said. "Do I say black people or colored or what?" "Well," I replied somewhat diplomatically, "the safest approach is to find out the preference of the person to whom you are talking." Seeing that this answer didn't do much to allay her fears, I assured her that any of the terms she chose would be fine with me, but then I was only one Black individual. Since my friend was about my age, I knew she had been around in the sixties; so, I reminded her that since we were of the era of James Brown's "Say it Loud, I'm Black and Proud!" I would certainly not be offended by being called "Black." Indeed, I personally preferred that word to some of the other alternatives. I also informed her that there was certainly nothing wrong with the simple term "American."

It should be clear that in this work, as in the works of most black authors, the term "Black" is used exclusively to identify a nation and a people, and, at the same time, it signifies a proud history of a cultural group. Certainly, no offense should be taken to its use. The term "African-American" or "Afro-American" (a contrivance or not) did not exist in the early days of black history in Jackson County; as such, it is used in this work not so much for its historical merit, but mostly because someone coined the phrase and it is, as previously mentioned, the acceptable expression of current use. Also as previously mentioned, like all other politically motivated, popular expressions, it too is destined to be replaced over time. One certainty remains, however: as long as society insists upon ethnic labeling and refuses to accept all groups of people as Americans equal in every respect, the crisis of identity for Blacks will continue.

Part II

African Americans In Jackson County

African Americans In Jackson County

In her work, *Negroes In Jackson County, 1850-1910*, Johnetta Jones reiterates that the presence of black Americans in Jackson County is traceable to the early 1800s. She notes that by 1820 the black population stood at 39, a decrease in the number of the Negro slave population which previously stood at 53 in 1818, as noted by P. Michael Jones (1994, p. 15). The count continues with increases (and some decreases) from then on. In 1840, there were 43 Blacks in Jackson County, but only 29 in 1860. By 1910, the year which concludes Jones's research, the Black population in Jackson County stood at 2,696.

Negro Slaves in Jackson County

According to Illinois Census Returns (Norton, 1969), the 1820 state census was taken by Matthew Duncan sometime between August 1 and December 1. Two hundred and eighty-one families are listed. There were two hundred and fifty-three families given for the federal census of that year. The discrepancies came about most likely because both census reports were taken by different individuals and at different times. Also, many of the residents were single men and presumably on the move looking for a permanent location. The total population of Jackson county in 1820 was 1572. Of that total, 40 residents (by Norton's count) were African Americans. Of these 40 black individuals, who were scattered throughout the county, only one is listed as a "free colored." The remaining 39 individuals were all Negro slaves.

The state census of 1820 does not list the thirty-nine slaves and the one free black resident by name. Only the heads of the households--presumably the slave owners--and the number of slaves owned are given. Neither is the exact age of the slave given; all of the slaves were listed according to age groupings. The one free black resident is counted with the household of Charles Garner, a white family of seven persons.

Negro Slaves in Jackson County in 1820

Source: Illinois Census Returns, 1820; edited by Margaret Cross Norton

Free White Males: 867
Free White Females: 665
Free persons of color 1
Servants or slaves <u>39</u>

Total Population 1572

Heads of households having slaves   **No. of slaves in household and age group**

James S. Dorris   1 male (14-26)
James Hall, Senior   2 females; 1 under fourteen; 1 (26-45)
James Hall, Jr.   1 male under fourteen
Robert Henderson   1 male under fourteen
Francis Thornbury   1 male under fourteen
Samuel Smith   1 male under fourteen
Thomas Burns   4 Total. 1 male under fourteen; 1 male (26-45)
                                1 female under fourteen; 1 female (14-26)
Samuel Cochran   4 Total. 1 male under ten; 1 male (16-26)
                                1 female under ten; 1 female (10 and Upwards)
James Gill   1 male (16-26)
Benjamin Henson   1 male (26-46)
William Boon   4 Total. 2 males under fourteen and 1 male (26-45)
                                1 female (26-45)
T. French   4 Total. Sex and ages not given
William Linn   3 Total. 1 male under twenty-one; 1 male over twenty-one;
                                1 female under twenty-one
Matthew Duncan   5 Total. 2 males under twenty-one; 1 male over twenty-one;
                                2 females over fourteen
Jo. Duncan   1 female over 14
C. Davis   <u>5</u> Total. 3 males under twenty-one; 2 males over twenty-one

Total number of slaves: 39

"There is but one free person of color in this county a male over 21 years of age."
--Matthew Duncan, Censor of Jackson County, 1820

Traces In The Dust

African American Residents in Jackson County, 1870

(Census of 1870)

Source: 1870 U. S. Census of Jackson County. All information given as shown on original document. Census conducted by the surname of the head of household (including the first person listed of each different surname in the same household); residents not counted individually.

(*)denotes Mulatto; (---------) denotes unknown information; (?) denotes unclear spelling, origin, or meaning; information difficult to decipher.

Surname	Age	Place of Birth	Occupation	Township
Abernathy, Mary	25	Kentucky	Domestic	Makanda
Adams, Sandy	50	Tennessee	Laborer	Grand Tower
Aikens, James	40	Kentucky	Day Laborer	Carbondale
Alexander, Manirva	40	Tennessee	Housekeeping	Carbondale
Alford, Hack	37	Georgia	Drayman	Grand Tower
Allen, John	50	Kentucky	Day Laborer	Carbondale
Allen, Peter	20	Alabama	-----------	Carbondale
Alpha, Murray	35	Mississippi	Farm hand	Carbondale
Anderson, Jordon	35	Virginia	Farming	Carbondale
Anting, Ann	26	Missouri	-----------	Grand Tower
Armstead, Sam	30	Alabama	Day Laborer	Carbondale
Armstead, Shelton	35	Tennessee	Farmer	Murphysboro
Arnell, Ellie	18	Mississippi	Boarding	Carbondale
Aslin, George Wm.	30	Virginia	Teamster	Murphysboro
Austin, Alax	26	Virginia	Laborer	Grand Tower
Austin, Isaac	25	Tennessee	Farm hand	Ridge
Austin, Sandy	26	Kentucky	Drayman	Grand Tower
Bandymore, An't	29	Illinois	Barber	De Soto
Barfield, Dole	45	Tennessee	-----------	Makanda
Barfield, Sam	9	Tennessee	-----------	Makanda
Barfield, Sherman	3	Tennessee	-----------	Makanda
Barfield, Squire	25	Kentucky	Farm Laborer	Makanda
Barnes, John	47	Tennessee	Day Laborer	Carbondale
Barnes, Joseph	22	From the South	Laborer	Grand Tower
Barnes, William	25	Tennessee	Day Laborer	Carbondale
Barton, Thomas	26	Alabama	Black Smith	Carbondale
Bass, John	56	North Carolina	Farm hand	Makanda
Bastic, Catharine	24	Tennessee	-----------	Murphysboro
Bastic, Hardin	29	Tennessee	Farmer	Murphysboro
Bastic, Stephen	26	Tennessee	Farmer	Murphysboro
Bastic, William	27	Tennessee	Farmer	Murphysboro
Bates, Henry	28	Tennessee	Farm hand	Murphysboro
Bates, Mat	21	Alabama	Laborer	Grand Tower

African Americans In Jackson County

Bates, Sarah	13	Alabama	----------	Carbondale
Beadley, Madison	40	Pennsylvania	Cook	Grand Tower
Beanter, Allen	56	Mississippi	Farm hand	Murphysboro
Beaver, Alexander	41	Tennessee	Farm work	De Soto
Belcher, Anderson	22	Kentucky	Farm work	Makanda
Belcher, Sarah	21	Kentucky	----------	Makanda
Belle, Anna	24	Virginia	Keeping house	Grand Tower
Belle, Hiram	30	Tennessee	Farm hand	Ridge
Berry, Caroline	23	Kentucky	----------	Makanda
Berry, Charles	26	Kentucky	Farmer	Makanda
Berry, Ellen	6	Kentucky	----------	Makanda
Berry, George William	33	Virginia	Farm hand	Kincaid
Berry, George	50	Mississippi	Teamster	Murphysboro
Berry, George	3	Kentucky	----------	Makanda
Berry, (?) (female)	1	Tennessee	----------	Makanda
Birdsong, Hiram	39	Kentucky	Farmer	Elk Prairie
Birum, Fannie	40	Virginia	----------	Grand Tower
Blize, James	1	Arkansas	----------	Makanda
Blize, Betsy	3	Arkansas	----------	Makanda
Blize, Isaac	33	Arkansas	Farm Laborer	Makanda
Blize, Johanna	24	Arkansas	----------	Makanda
Blize, Rose	5	Arkansas	----------	Makanda
Bodro, John*	29	Missouri	Laborer	Grand Tower
Boon, Paul	34	Louisiana	Butler	Grand Tower
Booth, William	50	Georgia	Farm hand	Carbondale
Bostic, Dudley	25	Tennessee	Farmer	Murphysboro
Boyd, George	28	Virginia	Farm hand	Murphysboro
Boyd, John	25	Kentucky	Farm hand	Kincaid
Boyd, John	42	Arkansas	Brick moulder	Carbondale
Branch, Amanda (m)	49	Virginia	Farm hand	Carbondale
Brown, Andrew	40	Tennessee	Farm hand	Carbondale
Brown, Sarah	41	Kentucky	Housekeeper	Elk Prairie
Brown, William	40	District of Columbia	Works in stable	Carbondale
Bruam, Phillip	20	Tennessee	Farm hand	Elk Prairie
Buck, Robert	19	Virginia	----------	Grand Tower
Buckner, Jackson	30	Kentucky	Farm hand	De Soto
Burkhalter, Jerry	49	Georgia	Farmer	Elk Prairie
Buss, Hattie	45	Kentucky	----------	Makanda
Buss, John	56	North Carolina	Farm hand	Makanda
Buttler, Charles	28	Tennessee	Day laborer	Carbondale
Caldwell, George	45	Illinois	Farmer	Elk Prairie
Cale, Henry	25	Kentucky	----------	Grand Tower
Calson, John	16	Kentucky	Farm hand	Makanda
Carter, Edwin	26	Tennessee	Laborer	Grand Tower
Cary, George	36	District of Columbia	Barber	Carbondale
Caslin, John	30	Missouri	Barber	Murphysboro
Chaberlong, Iona	28	Missouri	Chamber maid	Grand Tower
Chambers, Andy	19	Mississippi	----------	Murphysboro
Chambers, George	10	Kentucky	----------	Carbondale
Chappell, Jeff	26	Kentucky	Farm hand	Makanda
Chappell, Martha	21	Kentucky	----------	Makanda

Traces In The Dust

Chapman, Blue	68	Kentucky	Farmer	De Soto
Cheaver, Wesley	20	Tennessee	Laborer	Murphysboro
Clements, Isaac	50	Louisiana	Day laborer	Carbondale
Clivetan, William	24	Illinois	----------	Murphysboro
Coal, Simon	45	Virginia	Day laborer	Carbondale
Crawford, Hyrum	28	Tennessee	Day laborer	Carbondale
Cummins, James	43	Arkansas	Farmer	Elk Prairie
Curd, C.	21	Kentucky	----------	Makanda
Curd, Easter	18	Kentucky	----------	Makanda
Curd, Gideon	45	Kentucky	Farm hand	Makanda
Curd, Rachel	40	Kentucky	----------	Makanda
Curtis, Henry	27	Louisiana	Laborer	Grand Tower
Dalton, Sam	27	Virginia	Day laborer	Carbondale
Davis, Christopher	16	Kentucky	Servant boy	Carbondale
Davis, Robert	30	Maryland	Laborer	Grand Tower
Davison, Teller	50	Illinois	Farm hand	Carbondale
Dayly, Martha	47	Kentucky	Housekeeping	Grand Tower
Deam, Henry	33	Tennessee	Farmer	De Soto
Desna, Ellen*	35	Missouri	Seamstress	Grand Tower
Desna, Nancy*	60	Tennessee	Cook	Grand Tower
Douglas, Ellen	15	Mississippi	----------	Carbondale
Dudley, Phillip	40	Virginia	Farmer	Murphysboro
Eason, Jack	35	Illinois	Farmer	Elk Prairie
Elcun, William	16	Tennessee	----------	Grand Tower
Emerson, Mattie	22	Missouri	----------	Grand Tower
Evans, Frederick	21	Illinois	Domestic	Murphysboro
Everheart, Isaac	59	Illinois	Farmer	Carbondale
Felix, Alex	24	Alabama	----------	Carbondale
Flinn, Margaret	11	Missouri	----------	Grand Tower
Floyd, Jack	38	North Carolina	----------	Carbondale
Fowler, Jordon	56	Virginia	Laborer	Grand Tower
Franklin, Ben	38	Virginia	Making Tiers	Carbondale
Furgerson, Isaac	25	Virginia	Farm hand	Carbondale
Gadss (?), Hamilton	15	Kentucky	Laborer	Murphysboro
Gaines, Maria	40	Kentucky	Washing	Carbondale
Gaines, Osnus (?)	30	Kentucky	Day laborer	Carbondale
Glaces, Harris	23	Tennessee	Laborer	Grand Tower
Glenn, Hilliard*	30	Tennessee	Farm hand	Murphysboro
Glover, John	30	Kentucky	Laborer	Grand Tower
Goe, Jim	35	Tennessee	Day laborer	Carbondale
Good, Maria	18	Alabama	----------	Carbondale
Goodson, George	14	Louisiana	----------	Carbondale
Grayson, Barry	52	Kentucky	Shoe and Boot Maker	Carbondale
Gray, Robert	10	Tennessee	----------	Grand Tower
Green, Harris	70	Kentucky	Farm hand	Carbondale
Green, Simpson	24	Alabama	Laborer	Murphysboro
Green, William	20	Virginia (?)	Barber	Carbondale
Greenwood, William	34	Maryland	Barber	Carbondale
Greer, Peter	35	Georgia	Farmer	Elk Prairie
Guy, Fleming	45	Virginia	Farmer	Elk Prairie
Guy, Henry	43	Alabama	Farmer	Elk Prairie

African Americans In Jackson County

Hailstock, John	18	Illinois	----------	Grand Tower
Hall, Malissa	30	Kentucky	Domestic Servant	De Soto
Hall, Minerva	28	Alabama	Domestic	Carbondale
Hamilton, John	4 mo.	Illinois	----------	Carbondale
Hamilton, William	18	Maryland	Brick moulder	Murphysboro
Hanes, Church	55	North Carolina	Farm hand	Carbondale
Harrison, Gabriel	30	From the South	Day laborer	Grand Tower
Harris, George	35	Tennessee	Day laborer	Carbondale
Harris, John	26	Alabama	Laborer	Grand Tower
Harris, Levi	45	Mississippi	Laborer	Grand Tower
Harris, Richard	35	Illinois	Farmer	Elk Prairie
Harris, William	25	Tennessee	Laborer	Grand Tower
Hauldook, Amanda	22	Alabama	----------	Makanda
Hauldook, John	24	Louisiana	----------	Makanda
Hauldook, Lincoln	2	Illinois	----------	Makanda
Hauldook, Selden	7	Illinois	----------	Makanda
Hay, David	51	North Carolina	Farmer	Murphysboro
Hays, Dick	19	Tennessee	----------	Murphysboro
Henderson, Joseph	54	Louisiana	Day laborer	Carbondale
Herd, Thomas	24	Tennessee	Laborer	Grand Tower
Hester, Rachel	106	North Carolina	Boarder	Makanda
Hestor, Elizabeth	50	Kentucky	----------	Makanda
Hestor, Jessie	20	Tennessee	----------	Makanda
Hestor, Martha	52	North Carolina	Farmer	Makanda
Hestor, Nancy	16	Tennessee	----------	Makanda
Hestor, Thomas	10	North Carolina	----------	Makanda
Hestor, William	18	Kentucky	----------	Makanda
Hickam, Lucinda	26	Mississippi	House keeping	Carbondale
Hill, George	30	Mississippi	Laborer	Levan
Hill, Jefferson	23	Mississippi	Laborer	Murphysboro
Hockins, Charles	50	Virginia	Farm hand	Carbondale
Hodge, Nathan	38	Missouri	Farm hand	Murphysboro
Hollama, Jim	29	Tennessee	----------	Carbondale
Holland, Dick	22	Louisiana	Farm hand	Carbondale
Holland, Louisa	33	Missouri	House keeping	Grand Tower
Hon (?), Beckey	90	Virginia	The old woman of ale	Carbondale
Hopkins, Barney	27	Kentucky	----------	Murphysboro
Hopkins, Barry	25	Maryland	Laborer	Murphysboro
Hunter, Eli	22	Louisiana	Day laborer	Carbondale
Icum, Taylor	35	Kentucky	Drayman	Grand Tower
Isom, Charles	45	Tennessee	Laborer	Levan
Jackson, David	28	Alabama	Farmer	Elk Prairie
Jackson, Ellen	45	Tennessee	Domestic	Grand Tower
Jackson, Henry	56	Kentucky	Farmer	Makanda
Jackson, James	30	Alabama	Farmer	Elk Prairie
Jackson, John	50	Virginia	Farm day laborer	Carbondale
Jackson, John	53	Alabama	Farmer	Elk Prairie
Jackson, Peter	27	Tennessee	----------	Carbondale
Jackson, Sam	50	District of Columbia	Farmer	Carbondale
Jackson, Samuel	49	Kentucky	Day laborer	Ridge
Jackson, Stonewall	25	Tennessee	Laborer	Grand Tower

Traces In The Dust

James, Alex	35	North Carolina	Laborer	Levan
Johnson, Arthur	37	Kentucky	Farmer	Elk Prairie
Johnson, Ella	05	Illinois	----------	Carbondale
Johnson, Sophia	12	Kentucky	----------	Kincaid
Johnson, Sophia	17	Kentucky	----------	Murphysboro
Johnson, William	26	Louisiana	Day laborer	Carbondale
Joines (?), Edmond	05	Tennessee	----------	Carbondale
Jona (?), Jordon	40	Mississippi	Laborer	Grand Tower
Jones, Aaron	25	South Carolina	Farm hand	Carbondale
Jones, Cittria	18	Missouri	Domestic	Grand Tower
Jones, George	27	North Carolina	Laborer	Grand Tower
Julius (?), Smith	18	Tennessee	----------	Grand Tower
Kane, Andrew	48	Tennessee	Laborer	Grand Tower
King, Amanda (m)	57	Kentucky	Farmer	Elk Prairie
Laberely, Peter	26	Missouri	Butcher	Grand Tower
Lee, Josephine	22	Louisiana	Domestic Servant	Carbondale
Lee, Martha	06	Illinois	----------	Carbondale
Lee, Nathan	55	Virginia	Farmer	Carbondale
Lee, Sarah	50	Virginia	----------	Carbondale
Lewis, John	18	Maryland	----------	Grand Tower
Lewis, Paul	26	Louisiana	Day laborer	Carbondale
Lewis, Seymore	50	Tennessee	Farm hand	Carbondale
Lipsey, Jordan	34	Tennessee	Farmer	Elk Prairie
Lockridge, William	70	Kentucky	Retired	Carbondale
Long, Alfred	30	Virginia	Laborer	Grand Tower
Long, Willis	28	Kentucky	Farmer	Elk Prairie
Lucas, William	40	Mississippi	Laborer	Grand Tower
Lytle, Henry	35	Tennessee	Farmer	Murphysboro
McCay (?), Samuel	28	Tennessee	Farm hand	Makanda
McClernon, Wyatt	40	Alabama	Show hand	Carbondale
McClure, Rufus	24	Tennessee	Farm laborer	Makanda
McClure, Susan	33	Virginia	----------	Makanda
McCormick, Isaac	30	Tennessee	House keeping	Grand Tower
McCoy, Caroline 1	8	Tennessee	----------	Makanda
McCoy, Jacob	36	North Carolina	Farmer	Makanda
McCoy, Samuel	23	Tennessee	Farm hand	Makanda
McDavis, Sina	28	Tennessee	Laborer	Grand Tower
McFagion, Porter	32	Virginia	Laborer	Grand Tower
McLane, Adolph	26	Missouri	Laborer	Degonia
Macan, Matilda*	30	Virginia	Keeping house	Grand Tower
Maderly, Mary	23	Alabama	Laborer	Grand Tower
Malone, Brutus	17	Kentucky	----------	Makanda
Malone, Easter	9	Kentucky	----------	Makanda
Malone, Frank	2	Kentucky	----------	Makanda
Malone, Grant	7	Kentucky	Illinois	Makanda
Malone, George	10	Kentucky	----------	Makanda
Malone, Gideon	7	Kentucky	----------	Makanda
Malone, Lucy	13	Kentucky	----------	Makanda
Malone, Mary	38	Kentucky	----------	Makanda
Malone, Mary	4	Kentucky	----------	Makanda
Malone, Samuel	15	Kentucky	----------	Makanda

African Americans In Jackson County

Malone, Sanford	36	Kentucky	Farm hand	Makanda
Manley, John	39	Illinois	Laborer	Levan
Margrave, Isaac	36	Virginia	Farm Hand	Murphysboro
Mason, Carrie	4	Illinois	----------	Makanda
Mason, John	16	Kentucky	----------	Makanda
Mason, Lizzie	2	Illinois	----------	Makanda
Mason, Lori	22	Kentucky	Keeping house	Makanda
Mathews, George	56	Mississippi	Day laborer	Carbondale
Merideth, James	38	Kentucky	----------	Makanda
Meridieth, James	06	Kentucky	----------	Makanda
Meridieth, M.	65	Kentucky	Farm work	De Soto
Meridieth, Van	30	Kentucky	Farmer	De Soto
Meriweather, Edward	30	Tennessee	Day laborer	Carbondale
Miles (?), Henry	50	Maryland	Day laborer	Carbondale
Miller, George	47	Illinois	Farmer	Makanda
Miller, Amanda	27	Kentucky	----------	Makanda
Miller, Isaac	30	Virginia (?)	Day laborer	Carbondale
Miller, Lucida	5	Kentucky	----------	Makanda
Miller, Rachel	35	Missouri	Domestic	Grand Tower
Miller, Thomas	12	Kentucky	----------	Makanda
Minor, John	43	District of Columbia	Farm hand	Carbondale
Montgomery, Lewis	53	Kentucky	Farmer	Murphysboro
Moon, Freid	55	Tennessee	Teacher	Carbondale
Moon, Hary	19	Alabama	----------	Carbondale
Moor, Robert	23	Kentucky	Laborer	Grand Tower
Morgan, John	25	Kentucky	Laborer	Grand Tower
Moseley, Henry	22	Illinois	Laborer	Grand Tower
Mosley, Lizzie	15	Illinois	----------	Grand Tower
Moss, Arther	23	Mississippi	----------	Carbondale
Murray, Wilson	22	Arkansas	----------	De Soto
Murty, Alex	40	Kentucky	Day laborer	Carbondale
Myers, Mary	35	North Carolina	Keeping house	De Soto
Myers, Spencer	25	Virginia	Day laborer	Carbondale
Nash, James	25	Massachusetts	Laborer	Grand Tower
Negro, Margaret	14	Louisiana	----------	Carbondale
Nelson, Henry	23	Kentucky	Farm hand	Makanda
Nelson, Jacob	35	Maryland	Laborer	Grand Tower
Nelson, Willis	35	Mississippi	Day laborer	Carbondale
Nowles, John	25	Kentucky	Farm laborer	Makanda
Paschal, George	29	Illinois	Barber	Carbondale
Parrot, Emily	18	Arkansas	----------	Makanda
Parrot, William	25	Kentucky	Farm laborer	Makanda
Perkins, Mary	19	Alabama	----------	Carbondale
Phillips, Henry	56	Virginia	Farm worker	Carbondale
Pierce, Malinda	---	Virginia	----------	Makanda
Pierce, Randale	53	Virginia	Farm Laborer	Makanda
Pierce, Susan	54	Virginia	----------	Makanda
Pope, Clark	21	Illinois	Porter	Grand Tower
Powell, Isham	23	Tennessee	Farm worker	De Soto
Prim, James	25	Tennessee	Laborer	Grand Tower
Primm, Henry	45	Mississippi	Farm hand	Carbondale

Traces In The Dust

Purson, Samuel	28	Tennessee	Laborer	Murphysboro
Redman, Arther	26	Maryland	Drayman	Grand Tower
Reese, Henry	05	Illinois	----------	Carbondale
Reese, Richard	52	Tennessee	Drayman	Carbondale
Ridge, Wayne	39	Kentucky	Laborer	Grand Tower
Ringo, Lewis	52	Kentucky	Farm hand	Carbondale
Robinson, Perry	55	Kentucky	Black smith	Carbondale
Rogers, George	50	Tennessee	Farm hand	Carbondale
Rush (?), Ann	20	Kentucky	Keeping house	Grand Tower
Sanders, James	38	Kentucky	Farm hand	Murphysboro
Sanders, Joseph	27	North Carolina	Laborer	Grand Tower
Sanford, Albert	10	Kentucky	----------	Makanda
Sanford, Henry	5	Kentucky	----------	Makanda
Sanford, Joseph	60	Kentucky	Farmer	Makanda
Sanford, Phyllis	25	Virginia	----------	Makanda
Sanford, Willis	13	Kentucky	----------	Makanda
Scott, Dan	24	Virginia	----------	Grand Tower
Scott, Emaline	18	Kentucky	----------	Makanda
Scott, John	24	Tennessee	Servant	Grand Tower
Scroggs, Dan	30	Alabama	Gardener	Carbondale
Settlors, Alex	30	Mississippi	Farm hand	Carbondale
Shaw, Charles	27	Tennessee	Laborer	Grand Tower
Shaw, John	40	Tennessee	Day laborer	Carbondale
Shelles, Abner	10	Missouri	----------	Degonia
Sherod, Isaac	21	Alabama	----------	Grand Tower
Simons, James	20	Georgia	Laborer	Grand Tower
Sims, Henry	50	Virginia	Farmer	Carbondale
Smith, Henry	23	Kentucky	Farm hand	Carbondale
Smith, William	50	Alabama	Farmer	Carbondale
Smith, William	25	Kentucky	Laborer	Grand Tower
Smith, William	26	Mississippi	Day laborer	Carbondale
Smith, William	25	Tennessee	Worker at Depot	Carbondale
Smith (?), Julius	18	Tennessee	----------	Grand Tower
Snider, Miles J.	33	Illinois	Farmer	Carbondale
Snow, Beverly	40	Virginia	Laborer	Grand Tower
Spencer, Susan	26	Tennessee	Keeping house	Carbondale
Starks, Boyd	30	Kentucky	Farm hand	Makanda
Starks, Easter	55	Virginia	----------	Makanda
Starks, Elisa	73	Kentucky	----------	Makanda
Starks, Emilie	8	Kentucky	----------	Makanda
Starks, George W.	55	Kentucky	Farmer	Makanda
Starks, Judy	30	Kentucky	----------	Makanda
Starks, Lewis	---	Tennessee	----------	Makanda
Starks, William	3	Illinois	----------	Makanda
Starks, Woodson	40	Kentucky	----------	Makanda
Stepenson, Watley	60	Kentucky	Farm hand	Carbondale
Stephens, George	49	Alabama	Day laborer	Carbondale
Stephens, John	20	Tennessee	Day laborer	Carbondale
Stewart, Dennis	52	Louisiana	Farm hand	Carbondale
Stobaugh, James	22	Tennessee	Day laborer	Carbondale
Stoner, Wash	19	Kentucky	----------	Carbondale

African Americans In Jackson County

Strickland, Ella	1	Illinois	----------	Makanda
Strickland, Maria	37	Tennessee	----------	Makanda
Strickland, Rosa	---	Illinois	----------	Makanda
Strickland, Ruby	---	Tennessee	----------	Makanda
Strickland, Squire	36	Georgia	Farmer	Makanda
Summers, James	39	Illinois	Cook	Grand Tower
Sykes, William	35	Tennessee	Farm hand	Carbondale
Taylor, Ann	50	Virginia	Keeping house	Carbondale
Taylor, Ed	18	Tennessee	Laborer	Grand Tower
Taylor, John	26	Kentucky	Farm hand	Carbondale
Taylor, Richard	19	Florida	Day laborer	Carbondale
Taylor, Samuel	48	Maryland	Laborer	Degonia
Thomas, Dalna (?) (m)	40	Kentucky	----------	Carbondale
Thomas, David	26	Kentucky	Servant	Carbondale
Thomas, Eliz	25	Mississippi	Day laborer	Carbondale
Thomas, Jane	40	Tennessee	Domestic	Levan
Thomas, Kate	42	Louisiana	Keeping house	Carbondale
Thomas, William	27	Tennessee	Day laborer	Carbondale
Thompson, Henry	14	Alabama	----------	Elk Prairie
Thompson, Lib	25	North Carolina	----------	Makanda
Tillman, Peter	50	Indiana	Livery stable worker	Carbondale
Tisda, Caroline	50	Kentucky	Keeping house	Makanda
Tisslon, Caroline	50	Kentucky	----------	Makanda
Vincent, Frank	18	Kentucky	----------	Ridge
Walker, John	30	Tennessee	Laborer	Grand Tower
Walker, Lawrence	47	North Carolina	Farmer	Murphysboro
Wallace, Reid	20	Tennessee	----------	Grand Tower
Ward, Emma	22	Missouri	Keeping house	Grand Tower
Ware, Wills	30	Kentucky	laborer	Grand Tower
Washington, Charles	48	Mississippi	Day laborer	Carbondale
Washington, Lara	35	Tennessee	----------	Elk Prairie
Watson, Harold	17	Mississippi	----------	Carbondale
Watson, William	47	Tennessee	Laborer	Grand Tower
Wells, Alfred	25	Mississippi	Laborer	Grand Tower
Wells, Diana	23	Alabama	----------	Makanda
Wells, Henry	28	Mississippi	Farm laborer	Makanda
Wheeler, John	50	Tennessee	Laborer	Grand Tower
White, Samuel	28	Tennessee	Farm hand	Murphysboro
Wilkins, Daniel	19	Kentucky	----------	Makanda
Wilkins, Easter	13	Kentucky	----------	Makanda
Wilkins, Elisa	15	Kentucky	----------	Makanda
Wilkins, Lucy	46	Kentucky	----------	Makanda
Wilkins, M.	17	Kentucky	----------	Makanda
Wilkins, Robert	60	Kentucky	Farmer	Makanda
William, John	50	Georgia	Farmer	Elk Prairie
Williams, Gaston	27	North Carolina	Teamster	Murphysboro
Williams, George	22	Maryland	Servant	Carbondale
Williams, George	48	Pennsylvania	Barber	Grand Tower
Williams, Green	50	Tennessee	Day laborer	Carbondale
Williams, John	23	Mississippi	Laborer	Grand Tower
Williams, John	27	South Carolina	Day laborer	Carbondale

Traces In The Dust

Williams, John	50	Tennessee	Farm hand	Carbondale
Williams, Louisa*	09	Kentucky	----------	Makanda
Williams, Mary	25	Tennessee	----------	Murphysboro
Williams, Mat	50	Georgia	Farmer	De Soto
Williams, Spencer	45	Missouri	Day laborer	Carbondale
Williams, William	25	Louisiana	Hotel Cook	Carbondale
Williamson, Robert	50	North Carolina	Laborer	Grand Tower
Wilson, William	08	Kentucky	----------	Carbondale
Winn, Caroline	20	From the South	Servant	Carbondale
Woodrick, Mary	14	From the South	----------	Degonia
Woods, David	28	From the South	----------	Carbondale
Woods, Levi	25	Tennessee	Laborer	Grand Tower
Woodward, Mary	40	Virginia	Washing	Carbondale
Wright, Isabela	04	Mississippi	----------	Carbondale
Wright, Jessie	30	Tennessee	Farmer	Carbondale
Wright, Lucinda	02	Illinois	----------	Carbondale
Wright, Mack	60	Mississippi	Day laborer	Carbondale
Wright, Sim	50	North Carolina	Day laborer	Carbondale
Yarber, Jerry	40	Georgia	Farm hand	Carbondale

Unidentified African Americans, 1870

Female from Kentucky. Age 9. Residence: Makanda. Last name begins "Mc."
Female from Kentucky. Age 3. Residence: Makanda. First name unknown. Last name given as Miller.

African Americans in Jackson County, 1900
(Carbondale Excluded)

Murphysboro, Wards 1-2

Name	Age	Birth	Place of Birth	Occupation
Abernathy, Alex	33	March 1867	Mo	Day laborer
Anderson, Emily	69	December 1830	Tenn	----------
Armstrong, Gabe	45	January 1855	Ky	Upholsterer
Armstrong, Alla	45	July 1854	Ky	----------
Armstrong, Fanny	20	December 1879	Tenn	----------
Armstrong, Anna	17	June 1882	Ky	In school
Armstrong, Gabe	15	March 1885	Ky	In school
Armstrong, Maggie	12	January 1878	Ky	In school
Armstrong, Willard	3	July 1896	Ky	In school
Band, Mary	55	February 1845	Ala	Wash woman
Band, Myrtle	14	December 1885	Ill	In school
Banks, Harwell	33	March 1867	Ark	Laborer
Banks, Eliza	43	March 1857	Tenn	----------
Biggs, Everett	20	December 1879	Ill	----------
Bostick, Addie	28	May 1872	Ill	Cook
Bowden, Charley	42	October 1857	Ky	Saloon porter
Brewster, Silas	50	January 1850	Va	Coal miner
Brown, Albert	4	March 1896	Ill	----------
Brown, Anderson	45	January 1855	Tenn	Railroad laborer
Brown, Charley	50	November 1849	Ark	Day laborer
Brown, Ethel	7	November 1892	Ill	In school
Brown, Emma	49	January 1851	Ill	----------
Brown, Howard	6	December 1893	Ill	In school
Brown, Frank	45	August 1854	Va	Coal miner
Brown, McDowel	16	December 1883	Ill	----------
Brown, Oscar	11	November 1888	Ill	In school
Brown, Susan	39	July 1860	Mo	----------
Brown, Tille (f)	49	June 1850	Ky	----------
Buford, Amos	22	October 1877	Ill	Barbershop porter
Buford, David	19	April 1881	Ill	----------
Buford, Manning	11	October 1888	Ill	In school
Burford(?), Martha J.	16	September 1883	Mo	Servant
Burns, Charlotte	29	December 1870	Ill	----------
Burns, William H.	30	January 1870	Ill	Hotel porter
Dodson, Andrew	27	May 1873	Ill	Postroad keeper
Dodson, Fanny	47	December 1852	SC	----------
Dodson, Isreal	6	June 1893	Ill	In school
Dodson, James	50	October 1849	Va	Day laborer
Dodson, Loue	18	March 1882	Ill	----------
Duzzie, Wesley	11	April 1889	Ill	Servant
English, Liza	20	September 1879	Ill	----------
Evans, John	35	April 1865	Tenn	Railroad laborer
Evans, Mary	27	January 1873	Mo	----------
Everhart, Walter	10	January 1890	Ill	In school

Traces In The Dust

Name	Age	Date	State	Occupation
Frod, William	30	January 1870	Miss	Coal miner
Forester, Jarrett	21	June 1878	Ill	----------
Foseay, Edward	30	September 1869	Ill	Hotel porter
Galaway, Georgia	25	October 1874	Ill	----------
Galaway, Sam	27	March 1873	Ill	Railroad laborer
Gard, James	25	October 1874	Ill	----------
Givens, William	80	April 1820	NC	----------
Gray, Prunie	18	April 1882	Ky	----------
Gray, William	26	July 1873	Tenn	Day laborer
Green, James	31	April 1869	Tenn	Hotel cook
Griffy, Henry	8	September 1891	Ill	In school
Griffy, Nancy	27	June 1872	Ill	Servant
Guy, Hanah	67	January 1833	NC	----------
Guy, Henry	73	September 1826	Al	Minister
Hamilton, Sally	53	August 1846	Ky	Wash woman
Hamilton, Sally	14	June 1885	Ill	In school
Harris, Julia	29	December 1870	Mo	Servant
Harris, Lucy	29	August 1870	Ky	Wash woman
Hill, Maggie	21	January 1879	Ill	Servant
Humpfry, Alice	10	January 1890	Ill	In school
Humpfry, Eva	30	May 1870	Ill	----------
Jackson, George	30	March 1870	Tenn	Railroad laborer
Jackson, James	31	October 1868	Tenn	Railroad laborer
James, Fanny	86	April 1814	NC	----------
Johnson, Louie	6	June 1893	Ill	In school
Johnson, William	23	January 1877	Ky	Coal miner
Lane, Nancy	19	July 1880	Ill	----------
Lee Rosa	10	January 1890	Ill	In school
Lee, Robert	14	January 1886	Ark	----------
Lichman, Ben	26	July 1873	Tenn	Cook
Logan Bessie	13	September 1886	Mo	In school
Logan, Homer	3	April 1897	Mo	----------
Logan, James	1	August 1884	Mo	In school
Logan, Missouri	39	September 1860	Mo	----------
McKenny, Edgar	6	November 1893	Ill	In school
McKinley, Pink	28	August 1871	Miss	Day laborer
McKinley, Sarah	43	July 1856	Va	----------
Manley, Frank	54	January 1856	Tenn	Day laborer
Manley, Mattie	50	January 1850	Tenn	----------
Martin, Selth	13	January 1887	Ill	----------
Mays, Nancy	59	February 1841	Mo	----------
Murry, Bennie	18	January 1882	Ill	----------
Murry, Hary	13	April 1887	Ill	----------
Murry, Nellie	48	February 1852	Tenn	----------
Murry, Wilson	50	January 1850	NC	----------
Pelly, Herbert	12	May 1888	Ill	In school
Porter, Ada	29	January 1871	Ill	Wash woman
Porter, Fred	4	June 1895	Ill	----------
Porter, John H. T.	20	January 1880	Ill	Coachman
Porter, William	3	June 1896	Ill	----------
Powell, Owen	22	August 1877	Ill	Saloon porter

Powell, Ivory	19	September 1880	Ill	----------
Randells, Blanche	28	March 1872	Ill	----------
Randells, William	26	May 1874	Mo	Coal miner
Riley, Edith	4	March 1896	Ill	----------
Riley, Frank	24	July 1875	Ill	----------
Riley, Goldie	1	February 1899	Ill	----------
Riley, Nancy	21	November 1878	Ill	----------
Robinson, June	52	November 1847	Tenn	----------
Rush, Jane	68	September 1831	NC	Servant
Sims, Samuel A.	58	August 1841	Tenn	Day laborer
Smith, Harry	59	January 1841	Tenn	----------
Simmons, Hattie	34	October 1865	Ill	Hotel keeper
Simmons, Plese	12	July 1887	Ill	In school
Simmons, Ruth	6	February 1894	Ill	In school
Thomas, John	31	March 1869	Ala	----------
Thompson, Jeff	20	September 1879	Ill	Barbershop porter
Turner, Mattie	23	October 1876	Ill	Laundress
Tyler, Mary M.	61	April 1839	Va	Wash woman
Ware, Jasper	48	January 1852	Miss	Day Laborer
Williams, Arthur	46	April 1854	Tenn	Coal miner
Williams, Henry	30	February 1870	Ill	Saloon Porter
Williams, Julia	13	July 1886	Ill	In school
Williams, Mary	46	April 1854	Ill	----------
Woods, Anna	31	October 1868	Tenn	----------
Woods John	33	June 1866	Ark	Fireman
Young, Annie	5	May 1895	Tenn	In school
Young, Lizzie	30	March 1870	Tenn	----------
Young, William	25	March 1875	Tenn	Railroad laborer

De Soto Township

Birdsong, Alice	21	1875	Ill	----------
Birdsong, Hiram	70	October 1829	Al	----------
Birdsong, Hiram	1	March 1899	Ill	----------
Birdsong, Peter	24	December 1875	Ill	Miner
Birdsong, Sarah	70	1829	Al	----------
Dean, Edith	32	July 1867	Ill	----------
Dean, Osborn	32	December 1867	Ill	Farm laborer
Dean, Perry	11	November 1889	Ill	----------
Hayes, Amos	26	August 1873	Ill	Farm laborer
McCord, Anna	68	May 1836	OH	----------
Smith, Addie	19	September 1880	Ill	----------
Smith, Emmie	17	February 1883	Ill	----------
Smith, Frances	5	April 1895	Ill	----------
Smith Meray	44	March 1856	Ga	----------
Smith, Nora	9	December 1890	Ill	----------
Smith, Paul	11	August 1888	Ill	----------
Smith, Payton	46	October 1853	Tenn	Farmer
Smith, Ruth	14	September 1885	Ill	----------
Williams, Charles	23	July 1876	Ill	----------
Williams Colenmter(?)	22	February 1878	Ill	----------
Williams, Ellen	14	September 1886	Ill	----------

Traces In The Dust

Williams, Bessie	11	November 1888	Ill	----------
Williams, John	16	February 1888(?)	Ill	----------
Williams Lillie	48	April 1852	Ga	----------
Williams, Mary	20	November 1879	Ill	----------
Williams, Maud	7	August 1882	Ill	----------
Williams, Nathan	52	August 1847	Ga	----------
Williams, Ollie	18	April 1882	Ill	----------

Makanda Township

Allen, Albert	41	September 1858	Tenn	----------
Bass, Mitilla	28	September 1871	Ill	----------
Bell, George E.	27	December 1872	Ill	Restaurant owner
Bell, George S.	4	June 1895	Ill	----------
Bell, Helen	1	December 1898	Ill	----------
Bell, Lou	28	June 1871	Ill	----------
Bell, Lucinda	51	May 1849	Miss	----------
Brooks, Thomas	20	July 1879	Ill	----------
Edmons, Adam	30	December 1864	Ill	----------
Edwards, Frank	23	January 1876	Ill	----------
Gibson, Fronnie	10	November	Ark	----------
Hesbbin(?) William	22	June 1877	Ill	----------
Jenson (?) Shehamer	22	February 1888	Tx	----------
Jones, Grace	12	November 1887	Ill	----------
Jones, Sam	39	February 1858	Ky	----------
Lawrence, David	9	July 1890	Ark	----------
Lawrence, Henry	6	April 1894	Ark	----------
Lawrence, Ida	32	December 1867	Ark	----------
Lawrence, Lulu	12	December 1887	Ark	----------
Lawrence, Millie	16	May 1884	Ark	----------
Lawrence, Wade	14	March 1886	Ark	----------
Liles, Grace L.	18	August 1881	Ill	----------
Liles, Lovie C. D.	17	April 1883	Ill	----------
Liles, Parlee	40	October 1859	Ill	----------
Liles, Pery J.	40	October 1859	Ky	Railroad laborer
Liles, Stelli M.	15	February 1885	Ill	----------
Lipe, Richard	24	August 1875	Ill	----------
Malone, Geva L.	4	July 1895	Ill	----------
Malone, Gideon	39	March 1861	Ky	Railroad laborer
Malone, Harry	16	December 1883	Ill	Railroad laborer
Malone, Mary	39	April 1861	Ill	----------
Malone, Oscar D.	8	January 1892	Ill	In school
Malone, William D.	12	May 12878	Ill	In school
McKire, Person	30	October 1864	Ill	----------
Parrott, Emley	47	October 1852	Ark	----------
Parrott, Girtyie M.	21	October 1878	Ill	----------
Parrott, Henry W.	28	November 1871	Ill	Railroad laborer
Parrott, Lillian B.	19	August 1890	Ill	In school
Parrott, Maud	13	December 1886	Ill	In school
Parrott, William	60	May 1839	Va	Railroad laborer
Peacher, Robert	28	October 1871	Ill	----------
Pierce, Randall	88	December 1811	Va	----------

Name	Age	Date	State	Occupation
Rice, Harriet	18	April 1882	Ark	----------
Pierce, Susan	71	September 1828	Va	----------
Rice, George	15	December 1884	Ark	Farm laborer
Rice, James	23	December 1876	Ark	Farm laborer
Rice, Mary	20	October 1879	Ark	----------
Rice, Nellie	60	January 1840	Miss	----------
Rice, Wesley	57	March 1843	SC	Farmer
Ritley, Wesley	36	October 1869	Tenn	----------
Rosell, Robert	19	December 1882	Ky	----------
Russell, Charles	22	June 1877	Tenn	----------
Sander, William	22	March 1877	Ala	----------
Shaffer, Muerroe	26	November 1883	Ky	----------
Semples, Porter	21	February 1878	Ky	----------
Simpson, Isabell	24	December 1875	Ill	Restaurant cook
Smith, Harry	23	May 1877	Ill	----------
Starks, Elbert L.	16	October 1883	Ill	----------
Starks, Ida O.	37	January 1862	WI	----------
Starks, Lewis	40	July 1854	Ky	Railroad laborer
Starks, Waller	14	May 1886	Ill	----------
Waldon, Johana	20	March 1880	Tenn	----------
Waldon, Morgan	24	April 1875	Miss	Railroad laborer
Wingo, Achabal	14	February 1886	Ill	In school
Wingo, John	68	May 1832	Tenn	Farm laborer
Wingo, Leroy	3	February 1900	Ill	
Wingo, Nora	49	April 1851	Ala	----------

Traces In The Dust

African American Deaths in Jackson County

Jackson County death record indexes show 2,850 deaths occurring in Jackson County from the early 1800s to 1906. For several reasons, this number must be regarded as an approximate count of all the deaths occurring in the county during this time span. Primarily, because early death records were haphazardly maintained, there was no consistency to their collection. Many of the earliest deaths were recorded in family Bibles and not reported by official representatives; others were recorded in cemetery reports. Secondly, the first death records were hand written and often illegible, making accurate recording virtually impossible. Finally, because Illinois death reports were not legally required by law until 1916, many deaths were not recorded at all. (For statistics and more complete information on death inquests, see "Index to Death Records 1844-1906, Jackson County, Illinois compiled by Valerie P. Gildehaus.)

The earliest death report for a Black resident in Jackson County was traced to the year 1877 with the death of Rachel Garner. Rachel was a 50 year old farmer's wife who died December 18, 1877 in Jackson County of Malaria. She was buried in Murphysboro. Although it is not known when she first arrived in Jackson County, it is known that she had lived in Illinois for at least twelve years. No earlier death record for a Black resident of Jackson County was found.

The earliest death record for a black resident of Carbondale was traced to the year 1878 with the death of Sora Bird. Sora was listed as an African child who died of pneumonia. Her death notice states she was 3 years old when she died on January 30, 1878. It also states she was born in Carbondale and places her birth in the year 1875. However, 1875 was not the earliest date indicated for a black birth in Carbondale (See Early Black Families of Carbondale).

Between 1878 and 1880, the years showing the greatest amount of deaths among Blacks, most of the young men who died were listed as "single." Still, there were couples listed as "married" even though there were no specific references as to the dates of these marriages. Also, the reports make no mention of the numbers of children of these couples.

African Americans in the 1800s apparently lived a relatively short life span, an average of 40 to 45 years. It is interesting to note that during the late 1800s, the majority of Black citizens who died in the Carbondale-Makanda area had died of Pneumonia, Typhoid Fever, Lung Disease, or Consumption and had expired after several days or weeks of suffering from these illnesses. This, no doubt, attests to the extreme harsh and unhealthy living conditions the early settlers had to endure.

The remainder of the Blacks died from various other illnesses, or fatalities, and a few suffered accidental deaths. The records indicate that the majority of African Americans in Jackson County were buried in Makanda, Carbondale, and Grand Tower, but the vagueness of these files and the scarcity of details still allow for a great deal of speculation about the locations of specific graves or living areas. Until around 1910, those reporting deaths did not do so in any consistent or conscientious manner; what information was recorded was simply left to the whim of the one filling out the report. In 1916, when the filing of Death certificates became mandatory, the reports began to be filled out in a more detailed and prescribed form.

Historical documents reveal that in Jackson County roughly between 1850 and 1865--there were only a handful of Black residents. The actual number is less than thirty. The Reed family of Kincaid, two Black residents of Carbondale (1860) and a few others sprinkled throughout area made up this group. The first Black residents and families in Jackson County arrived around 1833. The first Black birth for the town of Carbondale was Boston Williams, who was born in 1867.

What accounts for the low numbers of Blacks in Jackson County during these early periods? Did the "Black Laws" (legislation prohibiting the entry of Blacks into Illinois) succeed in keeping all other Blacks out of Jackson County during the periods in question, or did the Black citizens simply desire to reside in other locations in Southern Illinois? Were there suddenly better opportunities or more tolerable conditions in other townships along the Illinois Central Rail Road between 1850 and 1867? These are only a few of the many questions that demand further investigation in order to piece together the complete history of Blacks in Illinois. (For information on the Black Laws of 1853, see *"African Americans in Jackson County"* in *Forgotten Soldiers* by P. M. Jones.)

A final point needs to be footnoted here because certain data are missing, data, which, were it available, could alter the story of Blacks in Jackson County and the city of Carbondale in the 1800s. These refer to the number of unidentifiable deaths and unknown black graves. At first glance, such information might seem insignificant, yet it is highly relevant from a historical point of view.

In these cases, the burial cites, dates, and names of the deceased are listed simply as unknown, and it is unlikely that the identities of these unidentified blacks buried throughout the county will ever be known. Documents on hand show five such unidentified black graves for Jackson County, which is a relatively low number for a period of time spanning over a hundred and twenty years. Moreover, the impact these five deaths may exert on local history may be of little consequence because of the simple fact that their lifespans were cut much too short--far shorter than any of the other blacks in Carbondale at that time. However, if a relatively larger number of unmarked or unknown black graves existed (and if those individuals had longer life spans), then these pages conceivably would have to be rewritten.

The history of our Negro forefathers in Jackson County is vital to us today. It not only provides a record of our past, it enables us to more deeply appreciate our circumstances and those of our predecessors in Carbondale and throughout the Southern Illinois region. It lets us understand much about how our culture, our traditions, and our very way of life came to be and why present conditions exist as they do. It is so important that the present and future generations continue to track the links and find those small, little traces that are forever present. By doing so, we can never lose grasp of who we are.

Traces In The Dust

African American Deaths In Jackson County
1877-1940

Sources: (A) Index to Death Records, 1844-1906; Jackson County, Illinois. Compiled by Valerie Phillips Gildehaus. (B) Register of Deaths, Jackson County, Illinois; Sept 18, 1877 to May 16, 1901. (C) Deaths for Carbondale, Illinois, 1877-1952. Compiled by Louise Morehouse, Carbondale, Illinois. (D) Family Death Records to 1964.

* indicates death occurring in Carbondale

Abernathy, Jack. Male. Black. 88 years old. Widow. Born in Perry Co., Missouri. Died April 17, 1917. Buried at Jackson County Farm Cemetery.

*Adams, Barbra. Female. Black. Married. Born October 1854 in Mississippi. Died December 13, 1918 in Carbondale. Buried in Cobden Cemetery at Cobden, Ill.

Adams, Frank B. Male. 6 months old. Born in Grand Tower. Died in Grand Tower of Colitis, July 5, 1902. Burial data not given.

*Alexander, Alfred. Male. African. 9 months old. Born in Carbondale. Died Feb. 11, 1878 in Carbondale, Ill. Cause: Broncho Pneumonia. Buried in Carbondale. Undertaker: R. Roming. Doctor returning death certificate: E. B. Chafin.

*Alexander, Mathew George. Male. 9 years old. Born in Carbondale 1872. Died in Carbondale Nov 15, 1881 of a throat condition. Buried in New Cemetery in Carbondale. Date unavailable.

*Allen, Ira. Black. 34 years old. Died June 4, 1921 in Carbondale. Buried in Oakland Cemetery, Carbondale.

Anderson, George. Male. 2 years old. Born in Carbondale. Died in Murphysboro May 4, 1882. Cause: Suffering 10 days of Pneumonia. Buried on May 5, 1882 at Carbondale, Cemetery.

*Ashburry, Louisa. Female. Widow. Mulatto. 50 years old. Born in Kentucky. Lived 10 years in Illinois. Occupation: Wash woman. Died in Carbondale Sept. 14, 1879. Cause: Typhoid Fever. Buried in New Cemetery at Carbondale, Sept. 15, 1879.

Armor, Harry Jr. Black male. Born in Mississippi. Died 25 of June 1916 in De Soto. 21 years old.

*Arnold, Bertram C. Black male. Died April 2, 1930 in Carbondale. Buried in Oakland Cemetery, Carbondale.

*Atkins, Anthony. Black male. Married. Born Jan. 2, 1856 in Tennessee. Died July 8, 1929 in Carbondale. Buried in Carbondale.

*Atkins, Dorothy F. Black female. Born 26 Jan. 1925 in Carbondale. Single. Died 13 June 1925. Buried in Oakland Cemetery.

Austin, Cornelius. Black. Died March 20, 1880. Two years old. Born in Grand Tower. Died in Grand Tower following 28 days of suffering from Meningitis. Buried in Grand Tower.

Austin, J. Van.
Died in July of 1880. 9 years old.

Bailey, Albert. Male. 3 months old. Born in Murphysboro. Died in Murphysboro, May 28, 1902 of Capillary Bronchitis. Buried in Oddfellows Cemetery. Burial date not recorded.

Baldridge, Gertrude. Female. 1 month old. Born in Grand Tower. Died Feb. 5, 1902 in Grand Tower. Cause: Bronchial Pneumonia. Burial Date and Place: Unknown.

*Band, Edda. Single. Black Male. Born in Carbondale in 1871. 10 years old.

*Barrow, Baby. Infant Male. Born in Illinois.
Died 23 Nov. 1910 in Carbondale. Buried in Oakland Cemetery.

Bass, John. Male. 67 years old. Laborer. Born in North Carolina. Laborer. Lived 15 years in Illinois.
Died June 7, 1880 near the city of Grand Tower after 12 days of Dysentery. Buried at Grand Tower Cemetery, June 8, 1880. Dr. Ebenezer Day, Physician.

*Bass, Mary E. Black Female. Married. Born in Missouri. Died 5 Dec. 1917 in Carbondale. Buried in Oakland Cemetery. Age 50.

Bates, Bessie. Female. Black. 8 years old. Single. Born in Grand Tower.Died August 12, 1883. Buried in Grand Tower Cemetery August 13, 1883.

Bates, Junius. Died February of 1880. ll mos. old.

*Belew, Erna. Black. Male. Single. Born May 9, 1921 in Tennessee. Died 8 August 1924 in Carbondale. Buried in Oakland Cemetery.

Bird, Dolla. Single. Black Female. 6 mos. old. Born in Jackson Co., Ill. Died: May 7, 1881 of Chronic Hydrocephalus. Buried: New Cemetery in Carbondale on May 8, 1881 by Jerry Bird. Doctor returning death certificate: John F. McAnally.

*Bird, Sora. African female. 3 years old. Born in Carbondale. Died Jan. 30, 1878 in Carbondale. Cause: Pneumonia and neglect on part of mother. Buried in Carbondale on the 31st of January, 1878. Doctor returning death certificate: E. B. Chafin of Carbondale.

Blanch, Julius. Died May of 1880. 5 years old.

*Bogan, Fannie. Black. Female. Single. Born in Tennessee. Died October 23, 1919 in Carbondale. Buried in Oakland Cemetery in Carbondale.

*Bogans, Anna. Black. Female. Widow. Born in South Carolina. Died Nov. 10, 1918 in Carbondale. Buried in Oakland Cemetery in Carbondale.

Bostic, Ella Gorden. Female. Married. 20 years old. Died August 7, 1886. Born in Tennessee. Died in Jackson County, Illinois. Burial data unavailable.

Bostic, Robert. Male. Age 53. Born in Tennessee. Lived in Illinois for 35 years. Occupation: Farmer. Died Feb 17, 1902 in Grand Tower. Buried at Walker Hill Cemetery in Grand Tower on Feb. 18, 1902.

*Boston, Ezekiel. Colored. Male. Married. Born in Mississippi in 1888. Died Oct. 29, 1928 in Carbondale. Buried in Oakland Cemetery. Cause: Tuberculosis. Buried in Carbondale in Oakland Cemetery Oct. 31, 1928. Doctor returning death certificate: Dr. Etherton. Undertaker: W. S. Brown.

Bradshaw, Benjamin.
Died February, 1880. 5 years old.

Brooks, Jacob. Black male. 30 year old married laborer. Died Sept. 18, 1885 in Makanda of Dropsy.
Buried in Makanda, Illinois Sept. 19, 1885.

Brown, Carroll. Black male. Born in Tennessee. 1 year old. Died Aug. 14, 1902. Buried in Oakland Cemetery Aug. 15, 1902.

Brown, Stella Katy. Lived 2 months and 2 days.
Died March 5, 1882. Died in Grand Tower of Acute Bronchitis. Buried March 6, 1882 in Grand Tower Cemetery.

*Brown, William. Male. Black. Married. Born in Virginia. 52 years old. Worked as a teamster.
Died 19 Feb. 1878 in Carbondale. Buried in Carbondale. Cause: Suffered 8 days of Pneumonia. Doctor returning death certificate: Dr. J. B. Bricker.

Bruce, Robert. 40 years old. Born in Kentucky. Occupation: Laborer. Died Aug 12, 1902 in Grand Tower. Cause: Accident. Buried at Tower Grove Cemetery. Burial date unavailable.

Burkhalter, May M. Black female. 21 years old. Single. Housekeeper. Born in Georgia. Resided 14 years in Ill. Died March 3, 1882 in Elk Township.
Cause: Bleeding of the Lungs. Buried at Rees Cemetery, date unknown.

*Campbell, Cora. Single. African. Female. 3 years, 6 mos. old. Born in Carbondale. Died: July 28, 1881 in Carbondale of Congestion of the Brain. Buried: July 29, 1881. Doctor returning death certificate: Dr. John O'Hara of Carbondale.

Carter, Albert. 14 years old. Born in Grand Tower. Died May 26, 1902 at Grand Tower.

*Cherry, Cornelia. Black. Female. 13 years old. House girl. Born in Hardin Co., Tennessee. Lived twelve years

Traces In The Dust

in Illinois. Died in Carbondale. Oct. 26, 1881 after suffering ten days of Acute Bronchitis. Buried: New Cemetery. Date unknown. Undertaker: R. Roming. Doctor returning death certificate: J. F. McAnally.

Cherry, Henry. 1 year old. Black. Male. Born in Carbondale. Died: Oct 24, 1881. Cause: Cholera. Buried in New Cemetery in Carbondale. Undertaker: Roming Doctor returning death certificate: J. F. McAnally.

*Clay, Richard. Black. Male. Married. Born Carroll Co., Tennessee. Died May 6, 1918 in Carbondale. Buried in Oakland Cemetery, Carbondale.

Clements, Elizabeth. 3 years old. Born in Illinois 1877. Died Nov. 23, 1880 in Grand Tower on Market Street from severe burns as a result of clothes catching afire. Buried in Carbondale Nov. 24, 1880.

Clements, Martin. Married black male. 26 years old. Laborer from Louisiana. Died in Grand Tower of Small Pox, 1:00 am, July 31, 1882. Buried in Grand Tower July 31, 1882.

*Clinton, Jennie. Black Female. Born in Tennessee. 50 years old. Died 20 Dec. 1916 in Carbondale. Buried in Oakland Cemetery in Carbondale.

Coleman, Nancy. 12 years old. Born in Jackson, Tennessee. Died in Murphysboro at 1915 Logan St., on August 2, 1902. Cause: Entero Colitis. Burial data not listed.

Coushionbery, Ellen B. Died in March of 1880. 3 days old.

Crawford, Vera. Black. Female. Lived 19 days. Born in Grand Tower. Died July 3, 1902 in Grand Tower. Cause: Entero Colitis. Buried at Walker Hill. Date unavailable.

Crawford, William. Died May 1880. 18 years old.

Crook, Viney. Female. Widow. 64 years old. Died in Murphysboro Feb 18, 1882. Cause: Malaria. Buried in Murphysboro by George Kennedy, Jr.

Cross, Henderson. Male Black. Died April 11, 1901 in Greenville. Buried in Oakland Cemetery, Carbondale.

*Cross, William. Black Male. Married. Born in Tennessee. Died 17 Oct. 1923 in Carbondale. Buried in Oakland, Cemetery in Carbondale.

Curd, Rachel. Black. Female. 89 years old. Lived in Illinois for 33 years. Occupation: Housewife. Died April 1, 1902 at Hallidayboro of Paralysis. Burial data unavailable.

*Daniels, Olly. Single. Male. 7 months old. Born in Carbondale. Died: Feb 25, 1884 in Carbondale. Cause: Typhoid and Pneumonia Hydrocephalus.
Buried: New Cemetery. Feb 26, 1884. Doctor returning death certificate: J. F. McAnally.

Davis, Julia. Black female. Widow. Died June 23, 1887 in Makanda of Pneumonia. Buried June 26, 1887.

*Deidley, Martha. Female. From Tennessee. 26 years old. Married. Died April 21, 1879 in Carbondale. Cause: Four weeks of suffering of a malignant sore at the throat. Buried in New Cemetery in Carbondale. Burial date unavailable.

Delassus, Isaac. Died February, 1880 at age 54.

Denton, Noah. Colored. 59 years old. Born in Tenn. Occupation: Farmer. Died March 20, 1902 in Makanda after 5 months of Gangrene. Buried at Sheppard Cemetery on March 21, 1902.

*Dill, Luela. Black. Born in Appleton, Missouri. Died 1 May 1902 in Carbondale. Buried in Oakland Cemetery. Age 14 yrs. and 7 mos.

Dudley, Warner. Died July, 1879. 7 mos. old.

Duncan, Ana. Single. Female. Colored Laborer. 31 years old. Died in Elk Township April 18, 1878. Place and date of birth unavailable. Cause: Suspected pneumonia. Buried at Elk. No burial date.

*Dunlap, Nettie. Single Black. Female. Age 7 yrs. and 6 mos. Born in Tennessee. Died July 14, 1916 in Carbondale. Buried in Tennessee.

Emry, Walter. Male. 25 years old. Laborer. Died Jan 16, 1902 in Grand Tower. Cause: Pneumonia. Buried in Grand on Jan 17, 1902.

Gains, William. Male. 41 years old. Laborer. Am. Married. Born in Louisville, Ky. Died March 5, 1880.

29

Cause: Pneumonia. Buried in Carbondale March 6, 1880. Doctor returning death certificate: Dr. R. P. Lightfoot.

*Gaiters, Carl. Black. Male. Married. Born in Illinois in 1888. 29 years old. Died 28 January 1917 in Carbondale. Buried in Oakland Cemetery.

Garner, Rachel. 50 years old. Lived 12 years in Illinois. Died in Jackson Co. Occupation: Farmer's Wife. Died December 18, 1877 in Jackson County. Cause: Malaria. Buried in Murphysboro.

*Gibson, Percy. Black. Male. Born 25 September 1921 in Carbondale. Died 6 November. 1921 in Carbondale Township. Buried in Oakland Cemetery in Carbondale.

*Goodlaw, Adalade. Single. Female. 10 years old. Died in Carbondale on March 21, 1884 after an illness of ten days with inflammation of the Brain. Buried in New Cemetery on March 22, 1884.

Gray, Ardella. Mulatto. Died September 1879.

Gray, Virginia May. Black. Female. Born May 16, 1926 in Ward. Died June 21, 1926 in De Soto Township. Buried in Hallidayboro. Daughter of Robert and Naomi Ross Gray of Ward.

Grear, Amanda. 58 years old. Lived 37 years in Illinois. Born in Georgia. Died Oct. 25, 1902 in Elk Township. Cause: Dropsy and head disease. Buried Oct. 26, 1902 in Grear Cemetery by family.

*Green, Harrison. Black. Male. Married. Born 25 May 1846 in Missouri. Died January 1, 1929 in Carbondale. Buried in Oakland Cemetery.

Greer, Magnolia. Black Female. Born in Centralia. Died August 27, 1928 in Carbondale. Buried in Centralia. Age 23.

*Hall, Luella. Female. Black. 14 years old. Born in Missouri. Died in Carbondale on May 1, 1902. Cause: Tuberculosis. Buried in Oakland Cemetery on May 2, 1902.

Hall, William R. Male. Laborer. 26 years old. Married. Born in Cape Girardeau, Missouri. Died of Plithisis in the Negro quarters in Grand Tower March 3, 1878. Buried in the Grand Tower Cemetery March 4, 1878.

Hampton, King. Male. Colored. 13 years old. Born in Illinois. Life resident in the state. Died at Muyphysboro of Accidental Drowning of June 21, 1888. Buried in Murphysboro.

Harley, Mannie. Female. 28 years old. Occupation: Housewife. Born in Jackson, Tennessee. Died April 1, 1902 at Murphysboro. Cause: Acute Tuberculosis. Buried in Jackson, Tennessee April 4, 1902.

Harris. Ben. Died January 1880. 7 years old.

*Harris, Ben. Male. Black. 8 years old. Lifetime resident of Illinois. Died September 23, 1878 in Carbondale, Ill. after suffering 2 days of Spinal Meningitis. Buried in Oak Grove Cemetery. Doctor returning death certificate.: Dr. John O'Hara.

*Harris, Carrie. Black. Female. Married. Born in Georgia. Died 30 June 1931 in Carbondale. Buried at Jackson County Farm Cemetery.

Harris, Narcissa. Died August 1880. 12 years old.

Harrison, George. Negro Male. 9 years old. Born in Carbondale in 1871. Died: Nov. 11, 1880 ten days after contracting Typhoid Fever. Buried at New Cemetery in Carbondale on Nov. 12, 1880. Doctor returning death certificate: Heber Robarts.

*Harrison, Martha. 25 years old. From Kentucky. Lived in Illinois for three years. Married. Died in Carbondale April 7, 1879, eight days after contracting pleuro-pneumonia. Buried on April 9, 1879 in New Cemetery in Carbondale. Doctor returning death certificate: Dr. J. Bricker of Carbondale.

Hawkins, Jane. Female. Black. Widow. Died 29 Jan. 1906 in Jackson Co. Buried at Jackson County Farm Cemetery. Age 78.

Hawkins, Lizzie. Black female. Single. 19 years old. Born in Tennessee. Lived 6 years in Illinois. Died July 10, 1881 in Murphysboro after suffering 6 months of Consumption. Buried July 11, 1881 in Carbondale.

*Hawkins, Margaret. Female. African. 45 years old. Occupation: Housewife. Born in Tennessee. Lived 45 years in Illinois. Died at 6:00 a.m. Nov. 17, 1878 on West Street in Carbondale after six months of consumption. Buried in New Cemetery, Carbondale, Ill. Dr. returning death certificate: Dr. James Roberts.

*Hayes, Jesse. Black Married. Born 19 March 1885 in Carbondale. Died 21 Dec. 1944 in Carbondale. Buried in Oakland Cemetery.

*Hays, David. African. Male. Widower. Born in Kentucky. Occupation: Farmer. 56 years old. Lived 8 years in Ill. Died in Carbondale after 16 days of pneumonia on April 16, 1878. Buried at Union Hill April 17, 1878.

*Hays, Mary. Black Female. Age 19. Married. From Tennessee. Lived 12 years in Illinois. Died Jan. 22, 1880 in Carbondale after 1 month of Consumption. Burial date and place unavailable. Doctor returning death certificate: Dr. J. Bricker.

*Hays, William Henry. Male. 7 years old. Born in Carbondale, Illinois 1877. Died: Aug. 8, 1884 in Carbondale after 15 days of suffering with Typhoid Fever. Buried in New Cemetery in Carbondale. Undertaker: Roming. Doctor returning death certificate: Dr. John F. McAnally. Death was recorded September 4, 1884.

Hern, Charlie Hester. Mulatto. Died March 1880. 2 years old.

*Hester, Thomas. African. Male. 23 years old. Laborer. From Mayfield, Ky. Died Aug. 15, 1884 in Carbondale after suffering from plithisis for 18 months. Buried in New Cemetery on August 16, 1884.

*Hillsman, Pearlie. Black. Female. Married. Born May 6, 1884 in Murray, TN. Died 9 Feb. 1928 in Carbondale. Buried at Trezevant, Tennessee.

Hinton, Mary Alice. 5 years old. Black female. Born in Cairo, Illinois. Died of fever in Ward 2 in Grand Tower, Illinois August 17, 1878. Buried in Grand Tower at Walker Hill Cemetery. Date unknown.

Hollands, William. Male. 16 years old. Laborer. Born in Jackson County. Life time resident of Illinois. Died Jan. 26, 1902 in Grand Tower of Nervous Exhaustion and Paralysis. Burial Date and Place: Unknown.

*Hunter, George. Colored. Male. Single. 80 years old. Occupation: Wood Sawer. Died: Nov. 25, 1886 in Carbondale. Cause: Old age and Heart Disease. Burial site and date: Unknown. Death certificate returned by John Dillinger, Coroner.

Jacobs, Moses. Male. Laborer. Age unknown. Died March 29, 1888 in Murphysboro. Cause: Plithisis Pulmonalis. Burial date and place unknown.

*Jenkins, Julias Brance. Negro. Male. Single. 5 years old. Born in Carbondale 1875. Died in Carbondale on May 16, 1880, about 26 hours after scalding by boiling soap. Buried in New Cemetery in Carbondale. Undertaker: Jake Swaar. Physician returning death certificate: Heber Robarts

*Jennings, Dan. Black. Male. Single. Born in Mississippi. Date unknown. Died 13 April 1931 in Carbondale. Buried in Mississippi.

*Johnson, L. D. Black. Widower. Died 17 April 1904 in Carbondale. Buried in Oakland Cemetery in Carbondale.

*Jones, Bernice. Black. Female. Infant. Born in Harrisburg. Died 5 Sept. 1916 in Carbondale. Buried in Oakland Cemetery in Carbondale.

*Jones, Frances Bell. Also Fannie Bell. African. Female. Single. 19 years old. Worked as a House girl. Native of Tennessee. Lived eleven years in the state of Illinois. Died April 27, 1882 in Carbondale. Cause: Plithisis Pulmonalis. Buried in County Line Cemetery. Doctor returning death certificate: J. P. McAnally

Jones, Franklin. 1 year, 18 days old. Born in Carbondale. Died March 23, 1880 after suffering 3 weeks of Bronchial Pneumonia. Buried March 24, 1880 in Carbondale. Undertaker: Jacob Swaur. Doctor returning death certificate: Dr. R.P. Lightfoot.

*Jones, Isom. Black. Single Born 1860 in Tennessee. Died 6 Feb. 1920 in Carbondale and buried in Oakland Cemetery. Age 60.

Jones, Josephine. Female. 49 years old. Lifetime resident of Illinois. Wife of a laborer. Died Feb. 10, 1902 in Grand Tower of Heart Failure. Buried at Walker Hill Cemetery, Feb. 11, 1902.

Jordan, David. Died July 1879. 8 years old.

*Joy, Jonnie. Black Male. Single. Born in Tennessee. Died March 1, 1918 in Carbondale. Buried in Oakland Cemetery.

*Joy, Richard. Black Male. Single. Born 2 May 1883

in Bolivar, Tennessee. Died 18 August 1917 in Carbondale. Buried in Oakland Cemetery in Carbondale.

Kelly, William. Black. Divorced. Died November 26, 1922 in Jackson Co. Buried at Jackson County Farm Cemetery. Age 76.

Kinner, James. Male. 10 years old. Born in Carbondale. Died: August 28, 1880 of an injury. Buried: Aug. 30, 1880 in Carbondale. Doctor returning death certificate: Heber Robarts.

Lain, James. Black male. Married. 22 years old. Farmer. Born in Alabama. Died June 16, 1881 in Murphysboro of Consumption. Buried in Murphysboro June 22, 1881.

Lane, David. Died May 1880. 25 years old.

Lee, Laura. Died March 27, 1890.

*Lee, Thomas. Black. Born 29 Jan 1846, Stewart Co., Tennessee. Died 20 Sept. 1929 in Carbondale. Buried, Oakland Cemetery., Carbondale.

Lindsey, Tillman Jr. Died February 1880. Age 10.

Loving, Charles. Black male. 7 years old. Born in Columbus, Kentucky. Died February 25, 1880 in "Red Town" in Grand Tower after suffering 7 days from Pneumonia. Buried in Grand Tower Cemetery February 26, 1880.

*Lowrey, George Wesley. Male. Married. Born 3 Feb. 1887 in Tennessee. Died 1 February 1916 in Carbondale. Buried in Oakland Cemetery.

*McKernan, Wyatt. Yellow male. Married. Died December 1879. 49 years old. Shoemaker from Alabama. Lived in Illinois 15 years. Died in Carbondale of inflammation of the bladder and rectum. Death occurred December 18, 1879. Buried in Carbondale December 20, 1879.

*McCourtney, Mose. Male. Black. Married. .Died 16 October 1922 in Carbondale. Buried in St. Louis, Mo.
*McCracken, Elizabeth. Black. Widower. Born 21 Oct. 1857 in Kentucky. Died March 13, 1929 in Carbondale. Buried, Oakland Cemetery, Carbondale.

*McCracken, Leonard J. Black. Died. 18 April 1928, in Carbondale. Buried, Oakland Cemetery, Carbondale.

*McDonnell, William. Negro Male. Single. 29 years old. Laborer. Born in Kentucky. Died: March 26, 1882 in Carbondale, Illinois at 8:00 a.m. Cause: Congestion of the Lungs and Typhoid Fever. Buried in New Cemetery in Carbondale. Undertaker: Jacob Swaar.

*Mack, Louise. Born in Carbondale. Died 13 Feb. 1911 in Carbondale. Buried, Oakland Cemetery, Carbondale.

*Mailing, Edith. Black. Female. Single. Born in Kentucky. Died 9 August 1916 in Carbondale. Buried, Oakland Cemetery, Carbondale.

*Marshall, John. Male. 69 years old. Widower. Laborer from Georgia. Died April 10, 1880 in Carbondale. Cause: Congestion of Lungs. Buried April 11, 1880 in Carbondale. Doctor returning death certificate.: R.P. Lightfoot of Carbondale

*Mason, Sam. Died 13 February 1922 in Carbondale. Buried at Elkville.

Mathews, Eliza Ann. Mulatto. Died May 1890. 31 years old.

Mathews, William Franklin. Mulatto. Died September 1879. 6 years old.

Matthews, F. Died February 1880. 35 years old.

Matthews, Josephus. Mulatto. Died February 1880. 42 years old.

Mays, Nancy. Black. Female. 53 Years old. Born in Missouri. Occupation: Housekeeper. Died July 28, 1902 at Murphysboro. Cause: Breast Cancer. Buried at Murphysboro. Date and location not given.

Merideth, Irene. 1 year old. Born in Jackson County. Died of Whooping Cough in Elk Prairie October 10, 1878. Buried in District Cemetery October 11, 1878.

*Miles, Catharine. Female. Occupation: Cook. 63 years old. Born, NC. Died in Carbondale on Jan 28, 1881 of a malignancy. Buried at New Cemetery Jan 30. 1881.

Miner, Louisa. Female. Copper. 56 years old. Lived in Illinois 12 years. Housewife. Married. Born in

Traces In The Dust

Kentucky.
Died of Malaria Jan. 25, 1881. Buried in City Cemetery, town unknown. January 26, 1881. Doctor reporting death: D. H. Baysinger of Grand Tower.

Mitchell, Cinderella. Female. Black. Single. Born in Jackson County, Illinois. Died in Murphysboro, Illinois of Meningitis Sept. 24, 1883. Burial date unavailable.

Mitchell, Hattie. Female. 23 years old. Born in Randolph Co., Ill. Died Jan. 26, 1902 in Degonia Township. Cause: Heart Failure. Buried on a farm in Randolph Co.

Morgan, John. Mulatto. Died July 1879. 10 mos old.

*Mousehart, Rena. Female. Mixed: African/English. Housekeeper. Married. Birthplace unknown. 35 years old. Died In Carbondale on Nov. 16, 1887. Cause: Pneumonia with complications of Typhoid Fever. Buried in Thedford Cemetery, Nov. 18, 1887.

*Muse, John H. 58 years old. Lived in Illinois 25 years. Born in Tennessee. Occupation: Horse Trainer. Died in Carbondale on July 13, 1902. Cause: Heart Disease. Buried in Oakland Cemetery July 14, 1902.

*Neusome, Reuben. Age 56. Lived in Illinois 30 years. Born in Alabama. Died in Carbondale May 9, 1902. Cause: Unknown. Buried in Oakland Cemetery.

Parker, Martha. Female. Widow. Born 17 March 1844 in New Madrid, Mo. Died. 13 Sept. 1939 in Dewmaine. Buried in Oakland Cemetery in Carbondale.

Penick, Andrew Walter Nelson. 14 years old. Black male. Single. Born in Henry County, Tennessee. Died October 16, 1884 in Makanda. Cause: Typhoid Fever. Buried in Makanda Cemetery.

Perkins, Francis E. Black. Female. 2 years, 8 mos old. Born in Villa Ridge. Died July 28, 1880 at 3:30 p.m. in Carbondale. Cause: Some type of unknown malignancy. Buried in New Cemetery. Undertaker: J. Roming.
Doctor returning death certificate: Heber Robarts.

Perkins, Paul Lafayette. Died August, 1879. 7 mos old. Burial date unavailable.

*Perrin, James. Male. Black. Born in Tennessee. Died 13 May 1905 in Carbondale. Buried, Oakland Cemetery in Carbondale.

Phillips, Shadrock. Black male. 12 years old. Single. Born in Du Quoin, Illinois. Died in Grand Tower of Small Pox June 15, 1882. Buried in Grand Tower; place and date unknown.

*Pollod, Andrew. Male. Negro. Single. 39 years old. Occupation: Farmer. Died March 16, 1882 in Carbondale Township. Cause: Pneumonia. Buried in New Cemetery in Carbondale on March 17, 1882. Doctor returning death certificate: H. Roberts.

Primm, Amy. Female. Occupation: Housewife. 30 years old. Born in Tennessee. Lived 8 years in Illinois. Died in Grand Tower of Bronchitis June 5, 1878. Buried in Grand Tower Cemetery June 6, 1878.

*Redden, Isaac Frank. Black male born in Tennessee. Son of Bos. Redden of North Carolina. Age 57. Died 12 September 1918 in Carbondale. Buried in Oakland Cemetery.

Reid, Harry. 3 year old black male. Born in Hickman, Kentucky. Died in Mt. Carbon Flats of Cholera July 20, 1882. Burial date and place unknown.

Rein, John A. Single black male born in Ohio. Died at age 63 in Jackson County on March 23, 1924. Buried at Jackson County Farm Cemetery.

Ritter, Annie B. Died July, 1879. 18 years old.

*Quigley, Franklin. Male. Widower. Laborer. 26 years old. Born in Ballard Co., Kentucky. Died October 18, 1883 in Carbondale. Buried in New Cemetery in Carbondale Township on October 19, 1883. Undertaker: R. Roming.

Doctor returning death certificate: Dr. John F. McAnally.

Randle, Ida. Black female infant. 9 months old. Born in Murphysboro. Died in Murphysboro July 23, 1880 of Spinal Meningitis.
Buried July 24, 1880 in Murphysboro, Illinois.

*Redden, Isaac F. Male. Black. Born in Tennessee. Died Sept. 12, 1918 in Carbondale. Buried at Oakland Cemetery in Carbondale.

Rein, John A. Black Single. Born in Ohio. Age 63. Died 23 March 1924 in Jackson Co. Buried at Jackson

County Farm Cemetery.

*Rice, Millie. Widow. Born in Mississippi. Died May 20, 1916 in Carbondale. Buried, Oakland Cemetery in Carbondale.

Riley, James. Male. Black. 49 years old. Married. Born in Mobile, Alabama. Died Feb. 12, 1886 in Murphysboro. Buried in Murphysboro.

*Ringo, Sarah K. Female. Single. 17 years old. House girl. Died in Carbondale of Typhoid Fever on July 14, 1883 at 12:30 p.m. Expired after suffering fourteen days of inflammation of the brain. Buried in New Cemetery, Carbondale July 15, 1883. Undertaker: R.Roming.

Roach, Oscar Thomas. Male. Black. 5 months old. Born in Carbondale. Died in Carbondale January 17, 1887 after 5 months and 2 days of suspected pneumonia. Buried in Oak Cemetery on January 18, 1887. Undertaker: Roming. Doctor returning death certificate: J. F. McAnally.

Robertson, Stephen. 49 years old. Lived 16 years in Illinois. Occupation: Farmer. Married. Born in Va. Died in Jackson County at Rickles Place on April 13, 1879. Cause: Pneumonia. Buried at Bradshaw School House. Date unavailable. Doctor returning death certificate: E. Teague.

*Robinson, John. Married. Born in Mississippi. Died 3 Sept. 1917 in Carbondale. Buried in West Point, Mississippi.

*Robinson, Rachael. Black. Female. Single. 19 years old. Born in Jackson Co., Illinois. Lifetime resident of the state of Illinois. Housekeeper. Died March 26, 1902 in Carbondale at 11:45 p.m. Cause of death: Consumption. Buried in Oakland Cemetery March 28, 1902.

*Rogers, Jerry. Black. Widower. Born in Tennessee. Died 10 March 1907 in Carbondale. Buried, Oakland Cemetery in Carbondale.

*Rose, Zella Reed. Widow. Born January 1, 1897 in Pulaski Co. Died 31 Aug. 1917 in Carbondale.

*Sanford, Joseph. 62 years old. Black male. Farmer. Married. From Kentucky. Died March 17, 1880 at 11:00 p.m. in Carbondale. Buried by the County on March 18, 1880. Doctor returning death certificate: Herber Robarts

Shaw, Lewis. Black. 84 years old. Died 7 March 1915, Jackson Co. Buried Jackson County Farm Cemetery.

Shearror, Anna. African Female. Married. Laborer. 36 years old. Born in Lexington, Kentucky. Lived 11 years in Illinois. Died in the third ward of Grand Tower of intestinal disease on May 14, 1878. Buried in Grand Tower.

*Shepherd, Anna Lucille. Born August 1, 1909 in Jackson Co. Daughter of Joe Shepherd of Cape Co., Mo. and Lula Barnes Shepherd of Perry Co., Missouri. Died December 18, 1911 in Carbondale. Buried in Carbondale, Oakland Cemetery.

*Shird, James. Black male invalid. 23 years old. Born in Carbondale. Died Sept. 5, 1902. Unknown cause of death.

Sims, James. Male. Dark. Occupation: Laborer. Born in Missouri. Died of Pneumonia. April 17, 1902 in Murphysboro. Buried at Tower Grove Cemetery, April 18, 1902.

Sisca, Roy. Male. 9 months old. Born in Grand Tower. Died February 17, 1902 of Bronchial Pneumonia. Buried in Grand Tower Feb. 18, 1902

Smith, Henry. Mulatto male. 2 years old. Born in Jackson County. Died March 3, 1882 of Meningitis in Somerset Township. Burial date and place unknown.

*Smith, Henry. 24 years old. Lived 1 year in Illinois. Born in Carbondale. Occupation: Laborer. Died March 28, 1902 at 3 p.m. in an alley in the city of Carbondale. Unknown cause of death. Buried in Oakland Cemetery March 28, 1902.

Smith, J. Van. 9 years old. Born in Carbondale. Lifetime resident of Illinois. Died of Plithisis Pulmonalis in Grand Tower July 25, 1879. Buried in Grand Tower. Date unknown.

*Smith, Melinda. Female. Black. 51 years old. Lived in Illinois 6 years. Born in North Carolina. House Worker. Died in Carbondale, Ill. on Jan. 13, 1902 of Pneumonia. Buried January 15, 1902 in Oakland Cemetery. Death certificate signed by J. P. McAnally on Jan 14, 1902. Recorded by County Clerk D. Bower, Dec.

Traces In The Dust

20, 1902.

*Smith, Robert G. Single. Born in Tennessee. Son of Alfred and Nell Brush Smith of Tennessee. Died 18 Feb. 1928 in Carbondale. Buried in Oakland Cemetery in Carbondale.

*Smoots, Willie. Female. Black. Married. Born February 1, 1889 in Tennessee. Daughter of Edmond McCrary of Denver, Tenn. and Jane Wiley McCrary of Jonhsonville, Tennessee. Died 16 June 1935 in Carbondale. Buried, Oakland Cemetery in Carbondale.

*South, Ella. Black female. 49 years old. Lived 46 years in Illinois. Born in Tennessee. Housewife. Died in Carbondale on July 7, 1902 at 4:00 p.m. Cause: Dropsy. Buried in Oakland Cemetery.

Spaulding, Charles. African. Infant. Lived for one and one half days. Born in Grand Tower, Illinois. Died in Grand Tower. Cause: Astherria. Buried at Walker Hill Cemetery on August 12, 1878.

*Steptoe, Charles. Single. Born 10 February 1887 in Missouri. Son of C. Steptoe of Missouri and Clara Steptoe of Louisiana. Buried in St. Louis, Missouri.

Strickland, Mattie. 30 years old. House worker. Died June 28, 1902 in St. Louis, Mo. Cause: Plithisis. Buried in Carbondale. Date not given.

*Swafford, Elizabeth. 30 year old, female from Tenn. Married. Occupation: Wash woman. Lived 8 years in Illinois. Died in Carbondale Oct. 7, 1879 at 8:00 a.m due to premature labor. Buried in Carbondale. Date and place of burial unknown. Doctor returning death certificate: James Roberts, Carbondale.

Talford, Luke. 1 month old black male born in Grand Tower. Died of fever March 29, 1881, one mile south of Grand Tower. Buried March 30, 1881 in Grand Tower.

*Thomas, Hester. 23 year old male laborer. Born in Mayfield, Kentucky. Died August 15, 1884 in Carbondale of Plithisis. Buried in New Cemetery in Carbondale on August 16, 1884.

Thompson, Alfred. 77 years old. Lived in Illinois 7 years. Born in Alabama. Occupation: Farmer. Died June 27, 1902 at 4 p.m. Cause: Cysto-Prostitis. Buried in Elkville at Grear Cemetery. Date not given.

Thompson, Melissa. Female. 39 years old. Born in Tennessee. Occupation: Housekeeper. Died June 20, 1902 in Elkville of Apoplexy. Buried in Elkville at Grear Cemetery. Date of burial is unknown.

*Thompson, Oliver Benjamin. Black. Male. Married to Emma Mae Thompson. Born 10 Sept. 1873 in New Orleans, Louisiana. Son of Oliver Thompson of Louisiana. Died 15 Feb. 1927 in Carbondale. Buried, Oakland Cemetery in Carbondale.

*Vaughn, Rosa. Born in Louisiana. About 56 years old. Died December, 28 1910 in Carbondale. Buried, Oakland Cemetery in Carbondale.

Walbridge, Anthony. Male. 23 years old. Single. Born in Virginia. Lived 6 months in Illinois. Occupation: Coal Miner. Died in the poor house in Jackson County on June 20, 1878. Cause: Consumption.
Buried at the poor farm on June 21, 1878.

Wars, Jasper. Died 7 Sept. 1904 in Jackson Co. Buried Jackson Co. Farm Cemetery. 45 years old.

Washington, Fanny. Female widow. 70 years old. Born in Tennessee. Lived 10 years in Illinois.
Died October 19, 1878 in Murphysboro. Occupation: Washing. Cause: Typhoid Fever.
Buried at Murphysboro October 20, 1878.

Washington, Mariah E. Black female. 18 years old. Single. Lived in Illinois four years.
Died May 28, 1880 of perontinitis caused by filth and neglect of midwife.
Buried in Grand Tower. Burial data unavailable.

*Waufford, Daughn. 13 year old single male. Born in Fulton County, Kentucky. Died July 16, 1881 in Carbondale of Dropsy and of having no medical attention. Buried in New Cemetery in Carbondale on July 17, 1881 by W.H. Waufford.

Wells, Hannah. Born in Alabama. Daughter of Richard and Hannah Woods. Died 23 November 1910 in Carbondale Township. Buried in Oakland Cemetery at age 74.

Whitington, Myrtle. 4 years old. Born in Jackson, Tennessee. Died May 29, 1902 in Murphysboro of Bronchitis. Buried in Jackson, Tenn., June 1, 1902.

Williams, Carolina. Died in May of 1880.

*Williams, Desdaina. Black. Married Female. Born November 29, 1901 in Carbondale. Daughter of John and Lillian Russell Woods of Tennessee. Died 3 February 1923 in Carbondale. Buried in Carbondale, Oakland Cemetery. Burial date unrecorded.

Williams, Frank. Single black male. 18 years old. Laborer. Born in Illinois. Died May 4, 1882 in Jackson County of Consumption. Buried May 5, 1882. Burial site unknown.

Williams, John. Black. Male. Widower. 75 years old. Died February 28, 1909 in Jackson Co. Buried at Jackson County Farm Cemetery.

Williams, Sim. Black male. Miner. Died November 16, 1886 in the mines at Sommerset. Burial site and location unknown.

*Williams, Spencer. Male. Yellow. 50 years old. From Missouri. Resided 12 years in Illinois. Laborer. Died in Carbondale December 17, 1879. Cause of death: Pneumonia. Buried in New Cemetery at Carbondale December 19, 1879.

Williams, Wilburn. Black male. 17 year old farmer. Single. Born in Georgia. Died April 16, 1884 in Elk Township of Pneumonia. Buried April 7, 1884.

*Wilson, Mary. Black. Widow. Born Carroll, Co., Tennessee. Daughter of Fannie Harris of Tennessee. Died September 27, 1922 in Carbondale. Buried in Carbondale, Oakland Cemetery. About 60 years old.

Wingo, Danny. Black. Male. 80 years old. Lived 20 years in Illinois. From Tennessee. Occupation: Laborer. Died April 8, 1902 at Makanda. Cause: Old Age. Buried in Goodwin Cemetery. Date not given.

Wood, William. Black. Male. Married. Born in Mound City. Son of Lancey Metcalf Wood. 31 years old.
Died 28 Feb. 1922 in Carbondale. Buried in Du Quoin.
Woods, Hattie. Female Black. 18 years old. Lifetime resident of Illinois. Born in the city of Carbondale, Ill. 1884. Died in Grand Tower on Nov. 10, 1902. Cause: Consumption. Buried Nov. 11, 1902 at Walker Hill Cemetery in Grand Tower.

Woods, Otto. 3 years old. Born in Jackson Co. Died July 20, 1902. Cause: Meningitis. Buried at Oakland Cemetery on July 21, 1902.

*Wright, James R. Son of Sim Wright. Died 12 August 1925 in Carbondale. Buried in Carbondale, Oakland Cemetery. Age 57.

*Wright, Juda. Black female. 56 years old. Lived 35 years in Illinois. Occupation: Housekeeper. Died in Carbondale Sept. 6, 1902 at 9 p.m. Cause: Unknown. Buried in Oakland Cemetery on Sept. 7, 1902.

*Yearkins, Alice. Black Female. Born in Carbondale. 7 years old. Life-time resident of Illinois. Died in Carbondale Feb. 23, 1878 Cause: Mumps. Buried in Greenwoods Cemetery on Feb. 25, 1878.
Doctor returning death certificate: Dr. J. B. Bricker.

Unidentified Deaths

Died May 1880. Baby boy. Known only by last name of Glover. Stillborn.

*Died July 8, 1881 in Carbondale. A 1 month old baby boy. Black. Cause: Suspected case of Thrush. Buried: July 9, 1881 in New Cemetery at Carbondale.
Doctor returning death Certificate: J. F. McAnally of Carbondale.

Died October 22, 1881. A male infant with the surname of Starks. Lived less than 1 month. Born and died in Makanda. Buried October 24, 1881 in Toppingtown in Union County.

Died August 1, 1885 in Makanda, Illinois. Black male. Cause of death: Dysentery.
Buried in Makanda August 1, 1885.

Died May 20, 1894. Listed only as "Black man."
Died September 5, 1898. Colored man.

Died December 8, 1898. Listed only as "colored."

*Died in Carbondale April 7, 1900. Baby girl by the name of Shannon. Buried in Oakland Cemetery.
*Died May 1, 1900 in Carbondale. Infant female by the name of White. Listed as daughter of Hy White.

Died May 3, 1901. Unknown Negro.

May 9, 1901. Unknown Negro.

Died May 20, 1901. Unknown Negro.

Traces In The Dust

Died May 21, 1901. Unknown Negro.

Died June 1, 1901. Unknown Negro.

Died June 8, 1901. Unknown Negro.

June 17, 1901. Unknown Negro.

*Died March 12, 1902. Baby girl. Known only as S. James. Stillborn in Carbondale, Ill. Buried March, 13, 1902.

*Died April 18, 1902. Baby girl. Known only as a stillborn infant of Mary Rach. Born and died in Carbondale. Buried at Oakland Cemetery.

Died May 27, 1902 in Murphysboro. Baby girl. Entered as "Baby Guy." Lived 30 days. Born at Murphysboro. Buried in Oddfellows Cemetery.

Died Oct. 28, 1902 Baby boy. First name: Johnny. Middle name: Wesley. Last name unidentifiable due to irresponsible record keeping and illegible writing. 1 year, 5 months old. Born in Elk. Died at 6:00 p.m. in Elk. Cause: Burns from clothing being caught on fire. Burial data not given.

Died. April 23, 1903. Unknown Negro.

Died June 8, 1905. Unknown Negro.
Died December 19, 1905. Unknown Negro.

Died. Two Black males. Dates of birth and death also unknown.

African American Marriages in Jackson County
1800-1900

The earliest document found for an African American marriage in Jackson County dates back to 1859. The bride and groom, John and Elizabeth Brandymore, were identified simply as "colored people." Black marriages are identified up to the year 1875.

The original register of marriages for the years 1880 to 1900 was unavailable and presumably lost in the courthouse fire of 1843. However, reproduced records for some years between 1878 and 1900 were available. By cross-referencing these documents, further identification of other African American marriages to the year 1890 was possible. Files reproduced after 1890 lacked the data necessary to complete cross-referencing. Consequently, no African American marriages are shown for the period 1890 to 1900.

Available registers of marriages prior to 1859 do not specify race, and reproduced documents for this period do not provide adequate data to identify Blacks through document comparison. Additionally, very few of the marriage documents of the 1800s give the individual townships (within Jackson County) where the marriages occurred. Some errors and inconsistencies found in reproduced indexes have been corrected in the following register. Also, marriages that were omitted from previously reproduced indexes have been added.

Traces In The Dust

African American Marriages in Jackson County
1859-1890

Sources: (A) Marriage Registers, 1800-1900; Jackson County Historical Society. (B) Marriages Recorded From 1843 to 1875, Jackson County, Illinois. Compiled≥ . by Roberta McDaniel Ellis and Helen Falkenheim Williams. (C) Marriage in Jackson County, 1878-1890. Compiled by P. Michael Jones.
(D) Marriage filed at Jackson County Courthouse, 1860-1890.
(*) indicates marriages occured in Carbondale or one or both parties were residents of the city.

April 16, 1859	John W. Smothers to Elizabeth Brandymore
January 4, 1866	William Steel to Sealia Starks
June 5, 1866	Joseph Sanders to Catherine Wilson
July 7, 1866	George Henderson to Francis (?) Surname omitted.
August 11, 1866	Daniel Scruggs to Caroline Casey
October 27, 1866	Benjamin Clay to Louisa Christopher
December 1, 1866	Thomas H. Williams to Winney Glass
December 31, 1866	David Woods to Winnie Skyes
January 6, 1867	Woodson Starks to Julia Ahl
January 10, 1867	Dudley Boston to Winney Boston
January 20, 1867	Edward Morgan to Anna Jones
February 26, 1867	Thomas Scott to Adline Smith
May 18, 1867	James Philips to Harriet Bass
May 28, 1867	Henry Miles to Catherine Williams
June 8, 1967	John Noles to Maggie Crason
July 17, 1867	John Cropper to Easter Loveless
July 19, 1867	Frank Manley to Martha Hill
July 21, 1867	Squire Strickland to Maria Hoods
July 18, 1867	Van Meredy to Ann Blue
September 23, 1867	George Berry to Charlotte Mayo
October 19, 1867	Hiram Crawford to Eliza Woods
April 14, 1868	John Humphreys to Fanny Ose
April 25, 1868	Ballad Burns to Rebecca Ross
June 28, 1868	John Manly to Margaret Patterson
September 10, 1868	James Hays to Nancy Smith
January 21, 1869	Stephen Bostick to Jeaney Wood
February 13, 1869	Gideon Curd to Rachel Curd
March 6, 1869	Samuel Edward to Nancy Arington
March 21, 1869	William Hamilton to Margaret Rees
June 26, 1869	Alfred Murray to Matilda Norton
September 19, 1869	John Harris to Milly Slaughter
September 21, 1869	James Ward to Emeline Stephenson
November 13, 1869	Alexander Arnold to Ellen Hudson
November 25, 1869	Isaac Sherrod to Annie Evans
December 1, 1869	William M. Phillips to Nancy Manson

December 2, 1869	Aaron Jones to Eliza Jane Allen
December 4, 1869	Isaac Austin to Darcus Vincent
December 6, 1869	Isaac Ferguson to Emeline Hale
December 9, 1869	William Smith to Charlotte Smith
December 13, 1869	George Washington to Martha White
December 21, 1869	Silas Ward to Mary Washington
January 11, 1870	Esom Taylor to Ellen Thomas
February 10, 1870	Gideon Curd to Rachel Curd
February 11, 1870	Donald Jordan to Margaret Jones
February 14, 1870	Henry Jackson to Joyce Jackson
March 19, 1870	Edmond Carter to Lon Lapson
March 24, 1870	Samuel H. Dolton to Mary A. Stanton
April 2, 1870	Calvin Williams to Mary A. Umpkins
July 12, 1870	Alexander Gray to Polley Harris
July 22, 1870	Isaac Bledge to Johanna Leney
October 1, 1870	Alexander Woods to Franky Eglson
December 21, 1870	Peter Greer to Amanda Williams
December 26, 1870	Washington Alexander to Ellin Bostick
December 26, 1870	Richard Hayes to Clemma Bostty(?)
December 31, 1870	George Roberts to Jennie Jones
December 31, 1870	Thomas Lee to Laura Morris
February 22, 1871	William Bostick to Emma Fletcher
March 25, 1871	Andrew Price to Elsa Brown
July 22, 1871	Lib Thompson to Mary J. Miles
August 4, 1871	Robert Wilkins to Mary Douglas
September 15, 1871	William Hamilton to Jane McAlister
January 20, 1872	John James to Carrie Jones
January 28, 1872	Charles Calwell and Lucy Thomas
March 2, 1872	Charles Hampton to Mary Crumble(?)
April 8, 1872	Hack Alford to Rosa Boyd
April 8, 1872	Hiram Bell to Sarah Simpson
May 29, 1872	George Butler to Rebecca Graves
July 30, 1872	James Sanders to Sarah E. Fethesson(?)
August 10, 1872	Horace Glapgow to Lucretia Cooper
October 14, 1872	David Hay and Manda Love
December 30, 1872	Nelson Hale to Mary Roore(?)
April 23, 1873	Lawrence Walker to Nancy Walker
April 28, 1873	George Mathews to Adelia Mathews
April 28, 1873	Hiram Birdsong to Sarah Brown
April 9, 1873	Wade Hampton to Annie Jackson
May 2, 1873	Dabner Thomas to Clarrisa Smith
May 27, 1873	John Lee to Jennie Nelson
June 28, 1873	John Roberts to Matilda Philips
September 4, 1873	Peter Allen to Catherine Jones
September 20, 1873	Lewis Hicks to Emily Reed
September 22, 1873	John Veneable to Sarah McKerney
December 19, 1873	Oscar Wilkins to Martha Kent
December 23, 1873	Henry Simms to Rhoda Kent
December 24, 1873	John Glover to Maggie Simons
December 24, 1873	Ferdinand Bostwick to Mary Glenn
December 27, 1873	Starling Boston to Ellen Dunn

Traces In The Dust

December 30, 1873	Alfred Campbell to Mattie Asbell
January 10, 1874	Robert Wright to Ella Shaw
January 15, 1874	Daniel Hamilton to Ella Hall
February 19, 1874	John Titworth to Catharine Bates
February 24, 1874	Thomas Irvin to Martha S. Powers
February 24, 1874	Horace Augusta to Sarah Branch
March 3, 1874	Stonewall Jackson to Kate Sanders
March 5, 1874	Joseph M. Reed to Nancy Skipworth
March 18, 1874	William Goldbow to Caroline McCoy
March 23, 1874	George Dye to Cary Ann Taylor
March 24, 1874	Silas Brewster to Easter Cropper
March 24, 1874	Alex Meekins to Rebecca Henderson
March 25, 1874	Jacob Newby to Mary Walker
May 30, 1874	John Davis to Fanny Cook
June 19, 1874	Jonas Mosley to Caroline Valentine
June 23, 1874	Nash Bryan to Nancy Harris
August 1, 1874	Jasper Goode to Hannah Griffin
September 12, 1874	Charles Holland to Caroline Barton
September 30, 1874	Clem Martin to Mary Malone
October 5, 1874	Joseph Jones to Hester Ferby
October 17, 1874	William Givens to Emily Howell
October 24, 1874	John Jackson to Margaret Hogans
November 11, 1874	George W. Randall to Susan Simmons
December 9, 1874	Albert Jones to Susan Jackson
December 22, 1874	James Johnson to Adeline Butoler
December 23, 1874	Martin Bartee to mary Bostick
December 24, 1874	David Jones to Antonett Jackson
December 25, 1874	William Bird to Willie Smith
December 25, 1874	Shelton Armstead to Emma Greene
December 30, 1874	Isaac Clemons to Nancy Yearkins
February 17, 1875	John Hunter to Ellen Harris
March 2, 1875	Henry A. Brown to Rutha Brown
March 5, 1875	William Sykes to Susan Williams
March 19, 1875	Daniel Smith to Elenore Shaw
March 23, 1875	John Gillmore to Caroline Mathew
April 5, 1875	George Paschal to Laura Johnson
April 22, 1875	Jordon Geder to Adaline Felleson
May 6, 1875	John Bass to Martha Reed
Mary 19, 1875	Solomon Cox to Mattie Wallace
June 5, 1875	Robert Bass to Synthia O'Neal
July 10, 1875	Isaac Essick to Sarah Cole
July 16, 1875	Thomas Lee to Laura Jones
August 6, 1875	John Sherard to Sophia Lewis
August 26, 1875	Charles Carter to Rachel Hughes
September 6, 1875	Abe Glass to Harriet Adams
September 25, 1875	George Rogers to Catherine Jones
November 2, 1875	George Washington to Matilda Simmons
November 18, 1875	James Thompson to Edy Campbell
November 19, 1875	Joseph Mitchell to Amelia Mathews
December 2, 1875	Richard Lovey to Eliza Starks
January 11, 1876	James Holmes to Fannie Young

January 11, 1876	Edward Fredrickson to Delpha Jackson
January 21, 1876	Samuel Thompson to Emily Hicks
February 24, 1876	Cyrus Shird to Caroline Perkins
Mrch 16, 1876	Charles Jones to Henrietta Taylor
April 17, 1876	James Jones to Jane Stanholt
May 27, 1876	Berry Irvin to Maggie Lee
June 2, 1876	Jacob Dudley to Emma Cook
June 2, 1876	James Ham to Elizabeth Williams
June 3, 1876	Rufus Hester to Eliza Wilkins
June 12, 1876	Van Buren Johnson to Sarah Cooper
June 20, 1876	Charles M. Lovey to Sarah F. Neely
July 29, 1876	Janson R. Marshall to Sarah E. Black
August 3, 1876	Edward Williams to Sophia Jackson
August 3, 1876	Henry Gossberry to Amanda Jones
August 3, 1876	Robert Wilkins to Fannie Umphrey
October 26, 1876	Thomas Ganes to Sarah Robinson
January 19, 1877	Arthur Williams to Mary Ann Washington
January 31, 1877	Henry Smith to Artimes Morgan
February 3, 1877	J. R. Frely (?) to Anna Lewis
February 24, 1877	Green Williams to Caroline Montgomery
February 26, 1877	James W. Wheeler to Laura Wilcox
April 17, 1877	Moses Larrey to Alsie Jackson
April 25, 1877	Scott Plesant to Ella Douglass
June 6, 1877	John Roberts to Minnie Reynolds
September 29, 1877	Hiram A. Hayes to Mary J. Rees
October 29, 1877	Anderson Green to Mary Sykes
October 31, 1877	Augustus Scott to Rosa Perkins
November 12, 1877	Frank Malone to Anna Morgan
November 19, 1877	Frank Brown to Jania Ray
December 26, 1877	Jessie Lefleir to Emma Shelton
April 4, 1878 (Date filed)	Augustus Woods to Lucinda Partee
April 28, 1878	Charles Henry Dejoie to Carrie Hall
May 30, 1878	William Swafford to Elizabeth Kinner
June 29, 1878	Tony Jenkins to Anna Branch
*July 5, 1878	Henry Robinson to Elizabeth Brown Baker
August 11, 1878	George W. Snider to Jane Lang
August 17, 1878	Jackson Buckner to Fanny Glenn
August 20, 1878	Alfred Cushionberry (*also* Cushenberry) to Mattie Burkhalter
*September 30, 1878	Henry Lee to Ellen Pelly
October 12, 1878	William Botts to Tennessee Bowyers
*October 12, 1878	George Vaughn to Rose Thomas
November 15, 1878	Dick Smith to Rosetta Harris
December 4, 1878	Stephen Richarson to Lida Anderson
December 30, 1878	Henry Kelley to Francis Ann Roberson
January 6, 1879	Edward Letcher to Rutha Woods
*January 12, 1879	Jesse Wright to Mary Brown
January 18, 1879	Levi Farer to Lan Philips
January 29, 1879	Jacob Garner to Bell Rodney
February 2, 1879	Richard Holland to Mary McClain
March 2, 1879	John Burkhalter to Emily Birdsong
April 18, 1879	Newton Stewart to Merener Roulett Elliott

Traces In The Dust

*May 4, 1879	Richard Green to Celia Bird
May 9, 1879	Alfred Robinson to Catherine Miles
June 15, 1879	Newton McClean to Elizabeth Williams
July 8, 1879	Daniel W. Davis to Lucinda Davis
*August 19, 1879	Spencer Miles to Hariet Anderson
August 28, 1879	Isaac Coffee to Charlotte Wiggins
September 23, 1879	Payton Smith to Marietta E. Williams
September 28, 1879	Henry Blackwell to Anna Dodd
October 8, 1879	Wilson Guy to Mariah Reed
*October 9, 1879	Arch Vorace to Benanna O'Brinct(?)
October 28, 1879 (date filed)	Luther Allen to Martha Bass
October 28, 1879 (date filed)	Joseph Robinson to Louisa Adams
*October 28. 1879	Frank Malone to Drucilla O'Brien
*December 5, 1879	James Riley to Caroline Harris
January 14, 1880	William Hamilton to Tempy Overton
*February 29, 1880	William Boyd to Annie Fry
April 13, 1880	Nathan Loden to Satty Beeler
April 23, 1880	Oliver F. C. Hinton to Iris Macon
*May 18, 1880	Joseph Allen to Easter B. Starks
*May 20, 1880	Smith Johnson to Georgia A. Smith Stout
*June 11, 1880	Thomas Jones to Frona Sheppherd
June 18, 1880	Albert R. Green to Rachael A. Wilkins
June 27, 1880	John H. Jones to Hannah Thomas Scott
July 6, 1880	George W. Stoner to Josephine Buler(?)
August 6, 1880	Richard Goodlow to Isabelle Miller
*August 16, 1880	William Johnson to Anna Taylor Mitchell
August 21, 1880	Ed McCloud to Francis Coffield
August 23, 1880	Lee Creghead to Alice Ridgeway
August 29, 1880	Mason Smith to Nasan Morgan
October 26, 1880	George Malone to Julia Mitchell
*November 26, 1880	James Black to Mary Williams Hamilton
*December 5, 1880	Daniel Cragwell to Jane Hustion Allin
December 20, 1880	George Barten to Emma Little
*December 29, 1880	Sam Asbell to Hattie Grayson
*September 1, 1880	H. C. Rodney to Mary Starks
November 12, 1880	Dick Towns to Anna Scott
February 15, 1881	James Williams to Mary A. Jackson
January 16, 1881	William Afford to Mahala Ann McKurnie
January 28, 1881 (date filed)	Thomas Spearman to Madartha Glenn
*February 23, 1881	Alexander Lane to Cornelia Crawford
*April 7, 1881	David Clay to Laura Lee Wheeler
May 1, 1881	Albert Robinson to Jane Glenn
*May 20, 1881	Robert Wright to Mariah Stephenson
May 28, 1881	James Simons to Fannie Walter
*June 16, 1881	Tolbert Roach to Mariah J. Harrison
*June 27, 1881	Albert Henson to Penlia Hunter
July 10, 1881	Albert Huse(?) to Priscilla Stettsberry
July 27, 1881	James McCampbell to Melvina Hays
August 10, 1881	William C. Robinson to Jennie Westbrook
August 10, 1881	Harvey Roberts to Sarah Guy
August 11, 1881	Fred Evans to Susan Ballard

African Americans In Jackson County

September 8, 1881	Lawrence Logan to Missouri Hall
October 8, 1881	David Pickett to Kaziah Dukes
October 9, 1881	George W. Merida to Louisa Reed
*November 17, 1881	Charles Stevenson to Lou Mason
*December 9, 1881	James Gentry to Mary Hancock Bineman
January 7, 1882	William Bonds to Leanna Walker
January 24, 1882	John Taylor to Mariah Wade
March 22, 1882	Joseph Vessels to Eliza Prussells(?)
*March 20, 1882	Henry Woodward to Eliza Wilkins
*March 29, 1882	Thomas H. Lee (Tenn.) to Mollie Lee (Tenn.)
*May 23, 1882	Thomas Fisher to Kate Etherton
June 4, 1882	J. Benjamin Muray to Nancy Caroline Doty
April 23, 1882	Henry Philips to Malinda Ozburu
June 8, 1882	John Walker to Mary Cuningham
July 3, 1882	Henry Guy to Frankie Wilkins
July 12, 1882	James Price to Martha Wright
August 12, 1882	Frank Dunbar to Clory(?) James
*August 29, 1882	Richard C. Lawson to Josephine Sheffey
August 29, 1882	Isaac Morgan to Ellen Ballard
December 18, 1882	Adam Hays to Allice Halstall
December 22, 1882	Charles Elvoy to Celia E. Spearman
January 18, 1883	Grundy J. Bostwick to Susan Woods
February 25, 1883	Charles Dejoie to Lizzie Cunningham
*March 22, 1883	William H. Fleming to Florence Hays
*April 22, 1883	David Thomas to Talitha E. Coffey
April 25, 1883	John Francisco to Isabelle Miller
*May 5, 1883	Jordon Anderson to Phoebe Thompson
May 19, 1883	John Glenn to Martha A. Foster
July 2, 1883	Lucien Minor (African) to Matilda Mackey (White American)
*July 7, 1883	William Robinson to Amanda Lewis
July 21, 1883	Henry Franklin to Lucy Reynolds
August 3, 1883	David Smith to Mary Perkins
*August 12, 1883	Alexander Lane to Isabell Holland
Sept 20, 1883	William Redferd to Caroline Bree
*September 23, 1883	Henry Sykes to Elizia Clement
*October 1, 1883	Louis A. Meeks to Mariah Cherry
October 16, 1883	Charles Crutchfield to Rachel Pelly
October 13, 1883	Philip Hinton to Josephine Rodney
October 25, 1883	W. R. Jerret to Julia Ann Duks(?)
October 29, 1883	Adison King to Laura Scott
December 22, 1883	Johnny Stovell to Mary M. Lee
*December 24, 1883	Henderson Stratton to Sophia Murphy
December 24, 1883	Savire(?) Spearman to Sarah Primm
December 25, 1883	George Pelley to Annie Guy
*March 20, 1884	Henry Johnson to Fannie Smith
April 20, 1884	Sam Edward to Annie Merryday
April 10, 1884	Richard Thompson to Fanny Simms
*April 12, 1884	Benjamin Moore to Jennie McFarlan
*May 20, 1884	James D. Lewis to Laura McKernan
May 20, 1884	Charles Hines to Ann Crumwell
*June 23, 1884	James R. Dodge to Mary Breekenridge

Traces In The Dust

*June 13, 1884	Reuben H. Terrill to Molley Willanham
*July 17, 1884	James T. Daniels to Lula Haynes
July 20, 1884	Philip White to Bettie Lockridge
*August 10, 1884	Leroy Thompson to Lizzie Mathews
*August 22, 1884	William Branch to Ellen Beck
August 28, 1884	Other Matington to Amelia Goodlow
September 1, 1884	Charles Brown to Elizabeth Bordeau
November 9, 1884	Henry Givens to Hester Jones
*October 28, 1884	Robert Woodward to Laura Wright
*October 31, 1884	Henry Woodward to Sarah Brown
*November 27, 1884	Collins Wilson to Ovia Goodlow
December 22, 1884	Charles Wiggins to Alice Adams
*January 14, 1885	Humphrey Ealey to Annie Wheeler
March 10, 1885	Henry Morgan to Surena Hines
March 19, 1885	John Williams to Emma Thompson
April 13, 1885	Isaac Campbell to Lucinda Porter
April 19, 1885 (Date filed)	Shadrach Dowell to Elizabeth Totten(?)
April 30, 1885	Benjamin Henderson to Amy Colley
*May 20, 1885	Charley Powell to Minnie Reese
May 23, 1885	Calvin Gardner to Belle Davis
May 23, 1885	David McLane to Lydia Ann Brown
*June 18, 1885	Daniel Wilcox to Cherry Williams
July 20, 1885	Larken Jackson to Fany Buckner
July 26, 1885	Daniel Scott to Nanie Walker
August 3, 1885	John Snider to Mollie(?) Morgan
August 14, 1885	Jackson Powers to Adaline Townsen
August 15, 1885	Edward Latchin to Dosha Scott
*October 7, 1885	T. J. Roach to America Martin
October 14, 1885	John Wilson to Fanny Fisher
October 21, 1885	John Hunter to Martha McCampbell
*December 5, 1885	Robert Black to Anna Bradley
December 24, 1885	Thomas Rankins to Amanda Jane Cully
January 3, 1886	Pursley White to Mary Stewart
*January 17, 1886	Reed Wallace to Ida Stanton
February 28, 1886	Scott Hinton to Belle Flemmings
March 30, 1886	Samuel Taylor to Margaret Jones
March 31, 1886	Silas Brewster to Mattie Jones
May 6, 1886	R. B. Bostick to Louella C. Woods
*May 26, 1886	William H. Woods to Louisa Goodlow
June 3, 1886	Starland Bostick to Ella Gardner
June 4, 1886	Louis Campbell to Mattie Dukes
*July 29, 1886	Albert Everhardt to Eliza Jackson
August 11, 1886	John Winter to Hattie Bovee
August 21, 1886	Lee McCaslin to Winnie Luella Pelly
*October 28, 1886	Solomon Goodlow (Ala.) to Martha Beany Goodlow (Mo.)
November 25, 1886	James Madison to Jane Tait
*November 27, 1886	William Brown to Laura Gaines
December 1, 1886	Peter Williams to Martha Birdsong
December 17, 1886	James Brown to Sarah Essick
December 19, 1886	Lark Barker to Alice Williams
December 13, 1886	El Paty to Mary Lee

*January 27, 1887	Thomas Lee to Laura E. Buttler
March 24, 1887	Jerry G. Tilman to Abigail D. Ward Tilman
*June 21, 1887	Thomas Wilson to Lizzie Harris
June 4, 1887	William Spearman to Rose Worthington
June 12, 1887	Irvin Thompson to Flora Burkhalter
*June 15, 1887	Walter D. Holland to Mattie J. Allen
*July 27, 1887	John Venerable to Susan Davidson
August 22, 1887	Robert Crockett to Sallie Allen
September 16, 1887	Charley Jones to Elizabeth Mathias
September 18, 1887	Charles Smith to Daisy Glen
October 22, 1887	James Baldridge to Susian Bufford
*November 2, 1887	Albert Hicks to Artimissa Cross
November 24, 1887	R. E. Wisely to Iona A. Wight(?)
December 24, 1887	John Jackson (Va.) to Malinda J. Martin Jackson (Ky.)
January 22, 1888	Levi Robinson (Ala.) to Rena Robinson (Elkville, Ill.)
March 8, 1888	Samuel Wingo to Jennie Blize
April 18, 1888	J. D. Lewis to Laura Jones Jordon
May 31, 1888	James E. Oates to Laura Lewis
June 22, 1888	Charles Brown to Emily Jacobs
*December 4, 1889	William Cross to Sallie Hall
December 27, 1888	Henry Cornelius to Sallie Mathus
January 6, 1889	Isaac Wheeler to Susan Davis
February 3, 1889	John L. Taborn to Catharine Coffee
March 11, 1889	Henry Morgan to Lizzie Wilson
*March 11, 1889	Jordon Anderson to Parlee Hayes
March 16, 1889	Edwin Freeman to Nora Hunt
*April 16, 1889	James Goodloe to Emma Muse
April 16, 1889	Nelson Sisson to Rosa D. Cobb
May 26, 1889	Edward Mattingly to Mary Hamilton
*June 26, 1889	Leroy Vaughn to Annie Walker
July 24, 1889	Daniel Washington to Martha Jennie Reed Jones
July 31, 1889	Henry Vaughn to Malinda Bradley
August 14, 1889	Peter W. Tate to Nettie Russell
August 15, 1889	Charles Simpson to America Brown
September 2, 1889 (Date Filed)	Jefferson Murray to Lucy Reed
*September 3, 1889	Willie Bates to Elenora Johnson Bates
*September 12, 1889	John Clemans (Ill.) to Hannah Donning Clemans (Ala.)
*August 29, 1889	Boston Williams to Josey M. Williams
*October 6, 1889	James F. Blackwell to Mary A. Knowles
*November 7, 1889	Frank Silver to Sarah Silver
December 23, 1889	Joseph H. Schrader to Nora Will
December 26, 1889	James Wilson to Mary Hickman Johnson
February 12, 1890	Charles L. Anderson to Mary Friarson

Part III

African Americans in Carbondale

1852-1900

African Americans In Carbondale, 1852-1900

P. Michael Jones, who has conducted extensive research on Jackson County and has made historical excavations related to his research on the history of Murphysboro, distinguishes three separate populations of Blacks who settled in Jackson County and demonstrates a pattern in the settlement of Murphysboro and surrounding areas. The first population of Blacks largely consisted of two groups: the slaves and indentured servants brought into the area by their white owners. This took place beginning around 1820 and lasted to about 1830. The second population of Blacks consisted of the freed men and ex-slaves declared to be free by the Emancipation Proclamation of 1863, and the immediate descendants of slaves. The Blacks who became soldiers and veterans of the Civil War belonged to this group (See *African Americans in the Civil War*, P. Michael Jones). The third population were those blacks who moved into the area beginning around 1900 who came in search of jobs with the railroad companies and those who came to join family and neighbors who had previously left the South.

The black establishment of Carbondale closely parallels this pattern. Like the earlier settlement of Murphysboro (founded in 1843, nearly 10 years earlier than Carbondale), the settling of Carbondale also can be divided into phases or stages. However, it would be extremely difficult, if not ludicrous, to try to site specific dates and times to show precisely when one phase ends and another begins. Suffice it to say that each phase overlaps the other. Whenever one examines periods of development in black history or the separation of black groups, he must remember to consider the fact that free blacks (and rich free blacks) have always lived throughout the period of slavery. It is now known, for example, that the first twenty blacks to come over from Africa were not slaves at all, but indentured Blacks who were to be trained in the English language and used as interpreters. From this perspective, one could argue that Black American history has always been one continuum with each phase interwoven one with the other.

Distinguishing such periods of development, particularly as it relates to the early social history of African Americans, is more than merely a matter of quoting dates; it relies greatly upon the scrutiny and examination of observable phenomena. It also depends to a large extent upon arbitrary division. The African American settlement of Carbondale, for example, can be divided into four phases. And even though these share a certain degree of commonality, each is uniquely characterized by its own dynamics and differences.

The first stage, or phase, logically commences with the arrival of Blacks in Jackson County in the early 1800s--the age of the slaves and indentured servants. The second stage spans from approximately 1834 to 1852, the year Carbondale is founded. It begins with the new era of the ex-slaves and their descendants and continues to the era of the new incoming black residents of the 1860s.

The the third stage begins with the first black families at the turn of the century (1900) and runs to the middle 1940s. It is during this period that more blacks settle into the area attracted by the railroad. By 1940, 7.7 percent of the total population of Jackson County is African American, (Southern Illinois, p. 32). This third phase of growth is also a period when the war effort of the 1940s called on the services of the black men--taking them away from their homes and drastically impacting the black family in Carbondale. The final stage begins with Carbondale's "Modern Age" for blacks (1945 to 1964). During this era, change becomes inevitable and by the early sixties, the unstoppable, external forces of time and "progress" begin to alter the make-up and "soul" of the predominantly Black northeast community forever.

Demography

The incorporation of Carbondale marks the mid-way point of the second phase of its development as it relates to the Black settlement. It is during this period that the black population experiences comparatively rapid growth with an influx of new black settlers arriving mostly from the South. Among this group were the ex-slaves and the sons and daughters of slaves and ex-slaves. Also, coming into Carbondale at this time were members of families who had previously resided in the surrounding towns of Jackson County. Two such residents, who resided in Carbondale for a time, were slaves who had previously served in the Civil War: Samuel Dalton was born a slave in 1839; the other was William Lewis Sykes, a field slave (P. Michael Jones, p. 1994).

Black Growth and Expansion in Carbondale, 1860

Records on Black populations are themselves a puzzlement. According to Wright's History of Early Carbondale (1977), Carbondale was founded by Daniel Harmon Brush in 1852, and fours years later in March of 1856 it was formally incorporated by action of the Illinois legislature (Wright, p. 18). However, the date of incorporation inscribed on the present day city hall building and at the Brush gravesite in Carbondale is 1873.

The first documented African American residents in Carbondale in the archives for Jackson County appear in 1860. It is more likely, however, that Blacks had been in the city much earlier. As Mike Jones has noted, a few Blacks were always in the township area. The 1850 Census, for example, shows that the total population for Jackson County was 5,862; there were 33 "free colored" individuals reported. Johnetta Jones records that by 1860, this number had dropped to twenty-nine. "This small group of Negroes," Jones writes, "was spread fairly evenly over the southern and central sections of the county." The problem in determining Black populations at any specific time, again, stems from the fact that few of the early census reporters bothered to take pains to seek Blacks out and file detailed reports. The Eight Census of the United States (1860), for example, shows two Black individuals in Carbondale in that year. These were Baker Ward, a fifteen year old male servant from Kentucky and Fannie Ward, a fourteen year old female servant, also from Kentucky. Those are only two registered African American individuals out of one or two Black families who, according to John Wright, might have been residing in the town. The population counters did not provide the total number for all the members of the black families.

Johnetta Jones cites two reasons for the low numbers of African Americans in Jackson County between 1850 and 1860: the anti-Negro migration bill of 1853 and "the general anti-Negro attitude" of the area. The total population of Jackson County by 1860 had risen to 9,589, according to the 1860 census. Twenty-nine Blacks, a very low number by comparison, are accounted for as "free colored."

By 1865, the number of Blacks in Carbondale had risen to ninety-six out of a total Carbondale population of 1,127. As previously mentioned, the early census takers counted the population by listing family surnames, and did not name each and every individual within the home. Many times, a single dwelling would house persons with two or more different last names. It is due to this practice that thirty-one of the ninety-six African Americans in Carbondale in 1865 were not identified by name, but were included in the count for the white households in which they were working (or residing) at the time the census was being conducted. The remaining sixty-five blacks lived in fourteen separate black households. They were identified only by the fourteen different family surnames (and any other surnames) used by the individuals of those dwellings.

By 1870 when the total population had reached roughly 1,500, the number of Blacks in Carbondale had increased to about 150. Wright points out that the exact number could not be determined since there was a separate population count for citizens living in the city and another count for those residents who lived in the township area (subdivisions outside of the city limits). "In the whole township," Wright notes, "there were more than 300 Blacks in 1870." By the year 1880, when the total population for Carbondale had risen to approximately 2,100, the Black population had risen to 422.

The Separation of Blacks and Whites in The Township

It is quite evident that in the very beginning in Carbondale (as well as in many other towns of the nation), most Blacks and Whites lived in the same general areas in close proximity with each other. This would account for those Black families living to the south and on the west side of town later in the early 1900s, and would likewise explain the relatively large amounts of land owned by blacks in virtually every part of Carbondale. It is almost impossible to say exactly when a split within a community occurs because it is an ongoing, developing process which does not take place as a tangible, observable event. It only becomes evident after its full manifestation. Studies of records indicate that the "parting" of races in the Carbondale Township begins to occur on a noticeable scale during the period roughly between 1900 and 1915, and that two factors played a large part in this phenomena.

Many Blacks arriving later in the city came to join relatives already settled in the city, and there was the natural tendency to settle close to kin. However, another and more sinister force was also at work; it was the group which would become infamously known as the KKK. The deliberate and organized separation of Blacks from Whites coincides remarkably with the rise of Klu Klux Klan activity. This

Traces In The Dust

theory, as espoused by Jones, is highly plausible because it can be supported by Klan ideology and activity. Reorganizing in 1915 in Georgia as the Knights of the Ku Klux Klan, this group continued the aims of the old secret society organized after the Civil War. One of its principal tenets has always been the segregation of the white and non-white ethnic groups, especially the black race. Branching out from the South through vigorous campaigns of terror and intimidation, the Klan spreaded it views, virtually infiltrating nearly every major city and rural area of the North. By 1928, the pattern of separation and the concept of the "black community" is already well defined in Carbondale as evidenced by the heavy concentration of Blacks "across the tracks" in the northeast sector of town.

A final point must be taken into consideration when determining the reliability of early population counts. It is the previously mentioned fact that most early census recorders seemed to devote most of their energy to the easily accessible populated areas. There were no set, standardized laws governing the early census takers, and they were, after all, only human. Inclement weather and unpredictable conditions, washed out paths and roads, and distances often dictated how far one could or would go into a region or area. There is sufficient evidence that in areas of very sparse population, only "educated" guesses or the word of other neighboring individuals were used to establish "official" counts.

In 1852, Samuel Brush--and the other elected or appointed city officials--filed the Carbondale land plat at the Jackson County Courthouse. It showed that the Carbondale Township lay between Oak Street and Walnut Street to the north and south, and between Marion Street and Missouri Street, to the east and west. In 1853, the Carbondale Township covered more than 360 acres, but the early census reports themselves again indicate not much attention was given to those households located outside the "central limits." Thus, the question of the number of individuals (both black and white) who may have been excluded from those early, official population rolls will always remain.

Most population counts of the early 1900s seem to have been conducted almost as haphazardly as those of the 1800s. The practices of counting populations by the heads of households and concentrating on citizens of the central town area seems to have been the universal rule among virtually all early statisticians, and not just by census takers. During the late 1890s, the overall population of Carbondale stood at about 4,000 citizens. Still, a relatively few years later, in 1905, when Hoffman compiled that year's City Directory, we continue to see a major fault in the counting of residents. By 1905 the population of the city stood in excess of 4,700. Yet, by Hoffman's own admission, there were approximately 1,600 persons living in the rural areas of Carbondale who were not listed by name in his directory for that year. He also did not indicate how many of these were Blacks.

Black population growth remains fairly consistent throughout the history of Carbondale; however, declines and "spurts" are noted from time to time. The population continued to increase, spurred on by the abundance of jobs working with the railroad and the coal mines. Blacks from the southern states who already had relatives in the city came to join them, and more blacks from nearby towns in Jackson County steadily poured into Carbondale as more opportunities opened up.

The time period from 1920 to 1940 saw the largest growth in the black families in Carbondale. Even though the depression had begun, individually owned Black enterprises had began to crop up in the northeast community; black families had become landowners; the all black school of Attucks had been built; and more black individuals were being employed with the railroad--although under conditions far less agreeable than those of the white employees. Also, by the mid-forties, blacks were finding work at the Southern Illinois Normal University in Carbondale. Even though the times seemed to indicate more advantages for African Americans, the fact remains that the majority of Blacks still were engaged in employment as laborers, house workers, field hands, and custodians. Those Blacks who did manage to find employment in plants or at professional establishments outside of the northeast community, were usually confined to positions of menial labor. By 1940, the Carbondale Township had a total population of 10,247. The city population was 8,550. The black population consisted of 846 males and 855 females in the Township--a total of 1,701 African Americans. In 1950 there was a drop in the non-white popuation which now stood at 1,688. However, by 1960, when the total population for the city had reached 14,670 and the Carbondale Township population had reached 19,579, the Black population totaled 1,984 for the city and 2,085 for the Carbondale Township, figures which illustrate the continuing trend of steady Negro migration into the city.

African Americans In Carbondale, 1852-1900

The First African American Births in Carbondale and the First Families

Johnetta Jones documented that the first free Black to be born in Carbondale was Boston Williams who was born in 1867. A marriage document found in the Jackson County archives gives Williams's age at the time of his marriage and the name of his bride. Williams's birth was followed by that of James Kinner (born in 1870); Edda Band (a Negro male born in May of 1871); and George Alexander (born in 1872).

The first black recorded females births in Carbondale are those of Alice Yearkins (born in February 1871); Lullu Parran (1877); Cora Campbell (1878); and Hattie Woods (1884). These are followed by the births of "Mama Cecil" (Cecil Brown, June of 1894) and Araminta McCracken (October of 1894).

Among the first female births of the 1900s are those of Beulah May Jones (1904), Mrs. Ida Edgar (1905), and Cleo Belle Williams (1906). The earliest birth record found for a Negro boy born in Carbondale in the 1900s is that of Leonard Woods (August 11, 1909). Following are the births of "Baby" Haron, a son born to Mattie Green Haron, (August, 1909) and the birth of James C. Pitts (August 27, 1909).

Today, the oldest African American families of Carbondale are the Armsteads, the Browns, the Parrans, the Woods, and the Alexanders with the Armsteads probably being the oldest. Primary historical sources show that Sam Armstead, a 30 year old day laborer from Alabama and the first known Armstead to settled in Carbondale, arrived in the year 1870. Shelton Armstead (believed to be a cousin) was the second Armstead to arrive in Jackson County. Shelton was a 35 year old farmer who also arrived from Tennessee in 1870. He settled in the Murphysboro Township.

Rapid Development and Growth

With the arrival of the 1900s, the Black expansion of Carbondale began in earnest--the population ever increasing year after year. The "Golden Age" of Blacks in Carbondale (1900-1945) was born. It was during this period that the northeast community realizes its fastest growth in building and development and the greatest rises in population. By the era of World War II, the first black churches have been long since been established; the Attucks school system has come into its own; and, as more Blacks come into the city, the need for goods and services increase. Previous employment for the black men had largely meant rail road or common labor work; by the mid-1920s however, more African Americans were beginning to think "business." Now, small black enterprises (stores, shops, and cafes) are begun and by 1930, a new network of black, family owned operations are firmly established. Also during the 1930s, new plants are operating in the city and Southern Illinois Normal University add additional job opportunities to the market place--although for Blacks, these "opportunities" were yet in the lower paying, menial positions and provided very little, if any real opportunity at all. For African Americans in Carbondale, such a period of rapid growth and development would not be seen again until the 1960s, when broad and sweeping change would come to the northeast community--change blown in by the wings of desegregation.

Traces In The Dust

Early African American Settlers of Carbondale
1865
Population: 96

Note: The African American population of Carbondale in the year 1865 was listed at 96. Thirty-one of these persons were not identified, as they were counted as part of the white households for whom they worked. The remaining 65 residents resided in 14 separate households. In the accompanying list, the head of the household is identified followed by the total number of blacks in that family.

Source: Wright, John W. D. *A History of Early Carbondale, Illinois: 1852-1905*, 1977.

Unidentified Residents	31
F. Ailver	3
I. Clemens	5
S. Jordan	10
N. Lee	4
A. Losson (Lawson?)	5
T. Madison	2
I. Miller	2
P. Overton	6
Reuben (no last name given)	2
J. Simpson	5
W. Sykes	9
Tom and Charlotte (listed as couple)	2
A. Williams	6
G. Williams	4
No. of black residents	96

African Americans in Carbondale, 1852-1900

Negro Personal and Realty Holdings in Carbondale in 1870
Source: *Negroes In jackson County, 1850-1910.* Johnetta L. Jones, 1968.

Name	Occupation	Real Estate	Personal
Gerome Daivs	Garderer	$ 200.00	$-----
John Collins	Day laborer	500.00	-----
William Smith	Farmer	2000.00	100.00
Chas. Washington	Day laborer	300.00	-----
Peter Tillman	Livery Stable worker	750.00	-----
John Shaw	Day laborer	200.00	-----
Wm. Smith	Day laborer	200.00	-----
L. Hickenson	Housekeeping	200.00	-----
John Durnes	Day laborer	200.00	-----
___(?)___ Williamson	Day laborer	200.00	-----
E. Eveskin	Brick mason	100.00	-----
Travis Gabirn	Day laborer	200.00	-----
P. Robinson	Blacksmith	500.00	-----
W. Brown	Stable worker	400.00	-----
S. Meyers	Day laborer	400.00	-----
I. Clements	Day laborer	400.00	-----
H. Willis	Day laborer	200.00	-----
Mary ___(?)___	Wash woman	200.00	-----
R. Reese	Drayman	300.00	-----
I. Miller	Day laborer	500.00	-----
J. Anderson	Farmer	1000.00	100.00
___(?)___ Livingston	Barber	700.00	-----
G. Lievry	Barber	3000.00	-----
B. Grason	Shoe maker	600.00	-----
S. Jackson	Farmer	-----	300.00
S. Lewis	Farm hand	-----	250.00
L. Rogers	Farmer	-----	100.00
V. Stephenson	Farmer	1000.00	130.00
N. Lee	Retired	150.00	150.00
W. Sachrigl	Day laborer	-----	100.00
S. Wright	Day laborer	500.00	100.00
S. Cosil	Farm hand	-----	200.00
M. Alexander	Farm hand	-----	200.00
H. Simons	Farm hand	-----	100.00
H. Green	Farm hand	-----	200.00
L. Ringo	Farm hand	-----	200.00
M. Alfwher	Farm hand	-----	200.00

Early Black Residents of Carbondale
(From the Founding of the City in 1852 to 1900)

Boston Williams

Boston Williams was born in Carbondale in 1867. He was the son of John and Jennie Williams. On August 29, 1889 when he was twenty-two years old, Boston married twenty year old Josey M. Withis Williams of Illinois, the daughter of Ed M. Withis. Available documents confirm that Boston Williams was the first known black resident born in Carbondale.

James Kinner

James Kinner was born in August of 1870 in the township of Carbondale. Little else is known of him. Records show he was ten years old when he died and that his birth occurred in Carbondale. James died August 28, 1880. He was buried August 30, 1880 in Carbondale.

Alice Yearkins

Alice Yearkins was a seven year old female born in Carbondale. The report of her death filed by Dr. J. B. Bricker puts her birth date at February of 1871. This officially makes her the first black female born in the Carbondale Township. Heretofore, no earlier records of a black female birth in Carbondale have been found. Alice died in Carbondale February 23, 1878 of Mumps. She was buried in Greenwoods Cemetery on Feb. 25, 1878.

Edda Band

Edda Band born in Carbondale in May of 1871. Edda was 10 years old when he died of diabetes in Carbondale on May 12, 1881. He was buried on May 13, 1881 at New Cemetery in Carbondale.

William Brown

William Brown was born in Virginia in 1826. The circumstances of his arrival in Carbondale are unknown. He lived in Illinois 14 years and died in Carbondale on February 19, 1878 after suffering 8 days with pneumonia. At the time of his death, he was married and was 52 years old. He was buried in Carbondale.

Margaret Hawkins

Margaret Hawkins, an African female and housewife, was born in Tennessee in 1833. The circumstances of Margaret's arrival in Carbondale are unknown; however, it is known that she lived 45 years in Illinois.

Margaret passed away Nov. 17, 1878 on West Street in Carbondale after suffering six months of consumption. She was buried in New Cemetery, Carbondale, Ill.

Elizabeth Swafford

Elizabeth Swafford, from Tennessee was born in 1849. She was 30 years old and married when she died. The question of how and when she arrived in Carbondale is unknown. It is only known that she worked as a wash woman and had lived in Illinois for eight years. Mrs. Swafford died in Carbondale Oct. 7, 1879 due to premature labor. She was buried in Carbondale.

Martha Harrison

Martha Harrison came from Kentucky. She was born in 1854. She was 25 years old and had resided in Illinois for three years. Her death report reveals little else other than she was married when she died.

Martha passed away in Carbondale April 7, 1879, eight days after contracting pleuro-pneumonia. She was buried on April 9, 1879 in New Cemetery in Carbondale.

Martha Deidley

Martha Deidley was born in 1853. She was from Tennessee. Little is known of her except that she was 26 years old and married at the time of her death. She died April 21, 1879 of a malignancy at the throat. She was buried in New Cementary in Carbondale.

Mary Hays

Mary Hays is described as a black female who came from Tennessee. She was born in 1861. She lived to be 19 years old. It is not known when she came to Carbondale. It is known that at the time of her death on January 22, 1880 she was married. She died in Carbondale of Consumption. Her attending physician was Dr. J. Bricker.

William Gains

William Gains, a laborer, was from Louisville, Kentucky, was born in 1839. He was married when he passed away. It is not known when he came to Carbondale. William died March 5, 1880 at age 41 of what was described as Pluro Pneumonia. He was buried in Carbondale on March 6, 1880.

Catharine Miles

Catharine Miles was a black female from North Carolina. She was born in 1818. She worked as a cook. When she came to Carbondale is not known.

Mrs. Miles died in Carbondale on Jan 28, 1881 of a malignancy and was buried at New Cemetery, Jan 30, 1881.

Daughn Waufford

Daughn Waufford was born in 1868. He was from Fulton Co. Kentucky. He died at age 13 on July 16, 1881 of Dropsy and the lack of medical attention. Daughn was buried in New Cemetery in Carbondale on July 17, 1881 by W.H. Wofford.

Cornelia Cherry

Cornelia Churry, a 13 year old house girl from Hardin Co., Tennesse was born in 1868. She lived twelve years in Illinois. Cornelia died Oct. 26, 1881 in Carbondale after suffering ten days of acute Bronchitis. She was buried in New Cemetery by undertaker R. Roming.

Andrew Pollard

Andrew Pollard was a Negro farmer. He was born in 1843. It is not known where he came from or when he came to Carbondale. He was single at the time of his death. Mr. Pollard died March 16, 1882 at age 39 in the Carbondale Township. The cause of death was pneumonia. He was buried in Carbondale March 16, 1882.

Sarah Ringo

Sarah Ringo was born in 1866. Her birthplace and parentage remain unknown. It is known that she worked as a house girl and was 17 years old when she died. She died in Carbondale of Typhoid Fever on July 14, 1883 after suffering from inflammation of the brain. Sarah was buried in New Cemetery in Carbondale July 15, 1883.

Kate Simpson

Born, 1867; died, 1959.

Ben Harris

Ben Harris was born in 1870. When he died, he was 8 years old and a lifetime resident of Illinois. His exact birthplace is unknown, nor it is not known how long he or his family had lived in Carbondale. It is only known that Ben died in Carbondale on September 23, 1878 after suffering 2 days of Spinal Meningitis. He was buried in Oak Grove Cemetery.

George Harrison

George was a Negro male, 9 years of age. He was born in Carbondale around November of 1871 and died Nov. 11, 1880. According to his death report, George died ten days after contracting Typhoid Fever. He was buried at New Cemetery in Carbondale on Nov. 12, 1880.

George Alexander

George Alexander was a 9 year old boy born in Carbondale in November of 1872. He died November 15, 1881 of a throat condition. The date and location of his burial is unknown.

William Henry Hays

William Henry Hays was a seven year old child born in Carbondale in August of 1877. He died August 8, 1884 in Carbondale after suffering with Typhoid Fever. William was buried in New Cemetery. His death was not filed until September 4, 1884 and no burial date is given.

Lullu Bertha Parran

Lullu Bertha Parran, a lifetime resident, was born in Carbondale March 7, 1877. She was the mother of Jerrold Parran. She was a member of Rock Hill Baptist Church.

Mrs. Parran died in 1967 at the home of her daughter, Mrs. Geneva Betty Curtis of East St. Louis. She was 90 years old. Funeral services were held at 2 o'clock at the Rock Hill Baptist Church June 7, 1967--the Reverend Lenus Turley officiating. Mrs. Parran's survivors included her son, three grandchildren and two great grandchildren. She was buried in Oakland Cemetery. Jackson Funeral Home was in charge of the arrangements.

Sora Bird

Sora Bird, described simply as an African child, was born around January of 1875. Her birthplace is unknown. She was three years old when she died of pneumonia on January 30, 1878 in Carbondale. She was buried in Carbondale on Jan 31, 1878.

Alfred Alexander

Alfred Alexander was a 9 month old African male. The exact date and place of his birth is unknown; records only indicate that he was born sometime during the year 1877.

Alice Isbell
1878-1967

Mary Edna Hamilton
Born, 1878; died, 1970.

Cora Campbell

Cora Campbell, described as an "African female," was born in Carbondale in January of 1878. She was 3 years, 6 months old at the time of her death. Cora died July 28, 1881 in Carbondale of Congestion of the Brain. She was buried July 29, 1881. Her attending physician was Dr. John O'Hara of Carbondale.

Franklin Jones

Franklin Jones was an infant born in Carbondale in March 5, 1879 who lived to be 1 year and 18 days old. He died March 23, 1880 and was buried March 24, 1880.

Charley Fisher

Charley Fisher was born in 1879. His place of birth is unknown. It is known that he was married. Charley died July 11, 1962.

Joseph Sanford

Joseph Sanford was a 62 year old farmer from Kentucky. He was married at the time of his death on March 17, 1880. He died in Carbondale and was buried by the county on March 18, 1880.

John Marshall

John Marshall was 69 years old. He was from Georgia. He died April 10, 1880 in Carbondale of lung congestion. He was buried April 11, 1880 in Carbondale.

Julias B. Jenkins

Julias Brance(?) Jenkins was a Negro male born in Carbondale. The date of his birth and his age at the time of his death are unknown. He was single when passed away in Carbondale on May 16, 1880 following a scalding accident. Julias was buried in New Cemetery in Carbondale.

George Anderson

George Anderson was born in Carbondale in the spring of 1880. He died at age two in Murphysboro, Illinois on May 4, 1882 of pneumonia. He was buried on May 5, 1882 at Carbondale Cemetery.

Frances E. Perkins

Frances E. Perkins was a black female child who was born in Villa Ridge. Her arrival date in Carbondale is unknown. The only information known is that Frances died in Carbondale July 28, 1880 of a malignancy. She was 2 years, 8 months old and was buried in New Cemetery by Undertaker J. Roming.

Henry Cherry

Henry Cherry was a one year old infant boy born in Carbondale in October of 1880. He died October 24, 1881 of Cholera. He was buried in New Cemetery in Carbondale.

Dolla Bird

Dolla Bird was a 6 months old female born in Jackson Co., Ill. in 1880. She died on May 7, 1881 of Chronic Hydrocephalus and was buried in New Cemetery at Carbondale on May 8, 1881. No other information is known about her.

Arthur Jones
Born, 1880; died 1974.

African Americans in Carbondale, 1852-1900

Black Families in Carbondale in 1880

Source: Wright, John W. D. *A History of Early Carbondale, Illinois: 1852-1905*, 1977.

According to Wright's findings by 1880, the number of black residents in Carbondale had risen to 422. In this year, blacks were listed in a separate section from others in the township. Wright gives the following list which details the number of family members in a household for the census year 1880. The name of the head of household is given first followed by his or her age and occupation, and the total number of individuals in the household. The number preceding the name is the census number. The list is shown as it appears in the original work; spellings and data should be compared to that found in other documents when questions arise.

10	Beverly Grayson, 63, Shoemaker-3	239	Susan Hopkins, 67, Wash woman-2
19	Hayes, 15, Servant-1	240	P. G. Loving, 82, Physician-3
30	Jemima Johnson, 33, Wash woman; 3		Richard Reese, 62, Laborer-5
46	Adam Hall, 37, Farmer-6	241	Harry Gooseberry, 47, Laborer-8
70	John Knowles, 41, Laborer-6	242	Caleb Toney, 45, Works in Barber Shop-6
104	James Holland, 40, Laborer-6		
107	Tradon Gaters, 32, Laborer-6	243	Jane Allen, 32-2
109	Johnson, 35, Laborer-6	244	Benj. Irving, 40, Teamster-2
111	Harry Perkins, 35, Laborer-3		Jordan Anderson, 51, Laborer-4
114	Issac Clemence, 60, Laborer-1	245	Mason Clark, 35, Laborer-8
124	Dabney Thomas, 50, Laborer-4	246	Richard Richardson, 50, Laborer-4
125	John Cherry, 30, Laborer-7	247	Horace Augusta, 51, Laborer-6
139	Nathan Bates, 55, Laborer-4	264	Joseph Allen, 22, Mill Worker-1
145	Caroline Marbley, 55-3		Martha Alexander, 18, Servant-1
147	John Williams, 38, Drayman-5	275	Green Williams, 56, Drayman-5
148	Isaac Miller, 40, Laborer-7	285	Wesley Stevenson, 69, Laborer-8
174	Mary Price, 20, Servant-1	286	George Vaughan, 29, Laborer-4
180	George Paschal, 39, Barber-4	288	John Shaw, 45, Laborer-3
181	William R. Curtis, 40, Barber -5	289	Daniel Smith, 32, Laborer-3
186	George Liggins, 13, Servant-1	300	Eli Hunter, 30, Mill Worker-6
189	A. Campbell, 30, Laborer	301	Mark Bradshaw, 36, Laborer-6
	Asberry, 21, Works in Barber Shop-7	305	Rebecca Vaughn, 55-9
	Monroe Asberry, 19, Laborer	306	Samuel Omstead, 39, Laborer-5
198	Martha Wright, 30, Servant-1	307	Daniel Scruggs, 34, Laborer-3
203	Frank Ailver, 49, Farmer-9	309	Charles Butler, 48, Laborer-3
204	Lewis Ringo, 55, Farmer-6	310	John Shurd, 35, Laborer-11
205	David Woods, 35, Farmer-10	311	Jesse Jones, 52, Laborer-4
206	Anderson Green, 23, Farmer-6	323	Spencer Miles, 45, Mill Worker-3
212	Godfrey Bates, 35, Laborer-8	324	Charles Carter, 27, Laborer-4
213	Reed Wallace, 35, Farmer-1		Henry Lawson, 45, Laborer-4
222	Murphy, 56, Laborer-5	325	Thomas Gains, 23, Laborer-4
226	William Hayes, Drayman-5	326	Joseph Henderson, 50, Laborer-3
	Hiram Hayes, 22, Laborer-1	327	William Boots, 49, Laborer-7
227	Salina Kinner, 24, Boarding house-8	328	Peter Harris, 54, Laborer-2
228	John Guinn, 32, Carpenter-3	329	Alfred Parker, 39, Farmer-7
231	John Bonns, 50, Laborer-5		William Bird, 33, Laborer-3
232	Joyce Jackson (m), 55, Laborer-2	330	George Harris, 39, Laborer-4

Traces In The Dust

331	Lucy Williams, 36-7
	-------(?)-------, Everheart, 75-3
	Jerry Bird, 32, Laborer-3
345	Mary Binum, 30-3
346	Isaac Essick, 50, Laborer-3
347	Ann Mitchell, 59-5
348	Geo. Rogers, 50, Express Wagon Driver-4
349	Alex Washington, 30, Mill Worker-7
350	John Burrell, 37, Laborer-3
351	Philip Dudley, 50, Laborer-6
360	James Thompson, 49, Janitor-6
361	Polly Woodward, 70-3
362	Adeline Bond, 35-3
363	Ed Merriweather, 38, Laborer-4
364	Adeline Bond, 35-3
374	A. W. Suttler, 40-4
397	Stuart Price, 55, Farm Worker-4
402	Mack Wright, 50, Laborer-4
403	Andrew Brown, 47, Laborer-4
406	Mary Wright, 45-3
<u>424</u>	Toney Jenkins, 60, Farm Worker-7
422	**Total blacks in Carbondale in 1880**

William McDonnell

William McDonnell was a single Negro male who was born in Kentucky. He worked as a laborer. William died March 26, 1882 at age 29 in Carbondale of lung congestion and Typhoid Fever. He was buried in New Cemetery.

Frances Bell Jones

Frances Bell Jones was described as a single, African female. She was also known as Fannie Bell Jones. She was born in 1863 and came from Tennessee. She was a house girl who had resided eleven years in Illinois.

Frances died at the age of 19 on April 27, 1882 in Carbondale of Plithisis Pulmonalis. She was buried at County Line Cemetery.

Thomas Hester

Thomas Hester, born in 1861, was described as an African male twenty-three years old. He came from Mayfield, Kentucky and worked as a laborer. Thomas died Aug. 15, 1884 in Carbondale after suffering from plithisis, a common disease among blacks in Jackson County in the 1800s. He was buried in New Cemetery on August 16, 1884.

Olly Daniels

Olly Daniels was a 7 month old male infant born in Carbondale in July of 1883. He died February 25, 1884 of Typhoid Fever complicated by Pneumonia Hydrocephalus. He was buried in New Cemetery Feb. 26, 1884.

Franklin Quigley

Franklin Quigley born in Ballard Co. Kentucky in 1857. He was 26 years of age and worked as a laborer. He died a widower on October 18, 1883. He was buried October 19, 1883 in New Cemetery in the Carbondale Township. Dr. J. P. McAnally was the attending physician.

James "Bud" Cawthon
Born, 1883; died, 1974.

Adalade Goodlaw

Adalade Goodlaw's death certificate indicates she was born in March of 1874. Her birthplace and the date she arrived in Carbondale are unknown. It is known that she lived to be ten years old and that she died in Carbondale on March 21, 1884 after ten days of suffering with inflammation of the brain. Adalade was buried in New Cemetery on March 22, 1884.

Hattie Woods

Hattie Woods was an 18 year old black female whose death records show she was born in the city of Carbondale in November of 1884. She was also known to have lived her entire life in Illinois. Hattie died in Grand Tower on Nov. 10, 1902 of consumption. She was buried Nov. 11, 1902 at Walker Hill Cemetery in Grand Tower.

Nathaniel Mason
Born, 1884; died, 1967.

George Hunter

George Hunter was born in 1806. He was known to have been a wood cutter. He was described simply as a "colored" male. Little is known of him except that he was one of the oldest residents to live in Carbondale during the 1800s and that he was single when he died.

It is not known when George came to Carbondale. He died November 25, 1886 in Carbondale at age 80. The cause of death was determined to be heart trouble and old age. The Hunter burial site and date are unknown. His death certificate was filed by John Dillinger who was a Coroner at that time.

Oscar T. Roach

Oscar Thomas Roach was a five month old infant boy born in Carbondale in 1886. He died in Carbondale January 17, 1887 at the age of 5 months of what was suspected as pneumonia. Oscar was buried in Oak Cemetery on January 18, 1887. Doctor J. F. McAnally, attending physician.

Daniel Green

Daniel Green was born in 1886 and died in 1967. His funeral was held at Rock Hill Baptist Church in Carbondale January 7, 1967.

Percell Carter
Born, 1886; died, 1970.

Rena Mousehart

Rena Mousehart was a female of mixed African and English descent. She was born in November of 1852. Her birthplace is unknown. Rena was a 35 year old housekeeper and was married. She died of pneumonia complicated by Typhoid Fever in Carbondale on Nov. 16, 1887. She was buried in Thedford Cemetery on Nov. 18, 1887.

Traces In The Dust

Andrew Wilson

Andrew Wilson was born in Carbondale in August of 1889. His father was an African from Kentucky.

March Mayfield
Born, 1889; died, 1967.

Lonnie Mayfield
Born, 1890; died, 1973.

Anna Wilson
Born, 1890; died, 1970.

Mittie Virginia London

Mittie Virginia London was born in 1892. The date of her arrival in Carbondale is unknown. She died in 1978. Funeral services held at Rock Hill Baptist church March 13, 1978.

Willie Hudson
1892-1957

Joseph Martin
Born, 1893; died, 1965

Maude Couthon
Born, 1893; died, 1967

Cecil Branch Woods Brown
"Mama Cecil"

Mrs. Cecil Brown, was born June 21, 1894 in Carbondale. She was the daughter of Hattie Johnson Branch and Alfred Branch. Mrs. Brown was the matriarch of one of Carbondale's earliest black families following the turn of the century.

The rise and growth of the Brown family began with Cecil's first marriage to Val Woods in Carbondale and the birth of her first two children, Frances and Evelyn.

Available records indicate that Mama Cecil was one of the very few African Americans born in Carbondale in the 1880s to survived to the turn of the century (1900). Stories are often recalled of her being ridiculed by whites as "that little black girl," or worse, whenever she had to walk the dusty streets of uptown Carbondale.

Mama Cecil was later married to John Brown in Carbondale. To this union, nine children were born, Mayola, Willard, Ferne, Charles, Billy, Harold, Betty Lou, Johnnie, and Ronald.

Mama Cecil and her family belonged to Olivet Freewill Baptist Church where she served and worshipped throughout her long life of one hundred and one years. This gave her the distinction of being one of five African Americans in the history of Carbondale to live to the age of 100 or longer.

Mrs. Cecil Brown died in Carbondale May 12, 1995. Mrs. Brown had a total of thirteen children, twenty-nine grandchildren; thirty-seven great grandchildren, and twelve great-great grandchildren. Several of her children preceded her in death.

Araminta McCracken Ford

Araminta McCracken Ford, formerly of 317 Pecan St., was born in Carbondale at 317 W. Pecan Street on October 18, 1894. She was the tenth child of Elizabeth Murray McCracken of Eddyville, Kentucky. Her father, John Henry McCracken, was a forty-one year old carpenter from Grand River, Kentucky. Her birth was reported years later to County Clerk Boyd Thorp by her brother George S. McCracken of Detroit, Michigan. The midwife attending the birth had long since died.

Mrs. Ford spent her entire life in the field of education (See The Legacy of Attucks). She was a former member of Bethel A.M.E. Church and later was affiliated with St. Andrew's Episcopal Church of Carbondale. She was a charter member of the former Music and Book Lover's Club. She also participated in the Carbondale Community Club, the Hospital Volunteer Service Auxiliary, and the Mariam Chapter No. 17 Order of the Eastern Star.

In addition to her parents, Mrs. Ford lost three of her sisters, five brothers, and one niece prior to her death. She was survived by a sister, Mable McCracken; two nieces, Mary Cason and Evelyn Howard; and one nephew, James Wiley. Mrs. Ford was a foster sister to Mabel Dellum Davis.

Mrs. Ford passed away at the Jackson County Nursing Home in Murphysboro, Illinois on March 15,

1984 at the age of 89.

Sarah Scott
Born, 1897; died, 1974.

Caurdie Clayton
Born (?); died, 1977.

Deaths in Carbondale
(Dates of death unknown)

David Hays

David Hays was a 56 year old farmer who resided in Illinois for eight years. The township where he lived is unknown. Also unknown are the circumstances surrounding his birth and his death. Mr. Hayes was buried at Union Hill Cemetery.

Louise Ashberry

Louise Ashburry was a 50 year old mulatto negro. It is known that Louise had lived in Illinois for 10 years. How much of that time she resided in Carbondale is not known. At the time of her death she was a wash woman. Louise died of Typhoid Fever and was buried at New Cemetery in Carbondale.

Spencer Williams

Spencer Williams is described as a yellow male who was fifty years old. He resided 12 years in Illinois working as a laborer. Spencer died in Carbondale of pneumonia and was buried in New Cemetery at Carbondale. Nothing is known of his birth or where he lived prior to coming to Illinois.

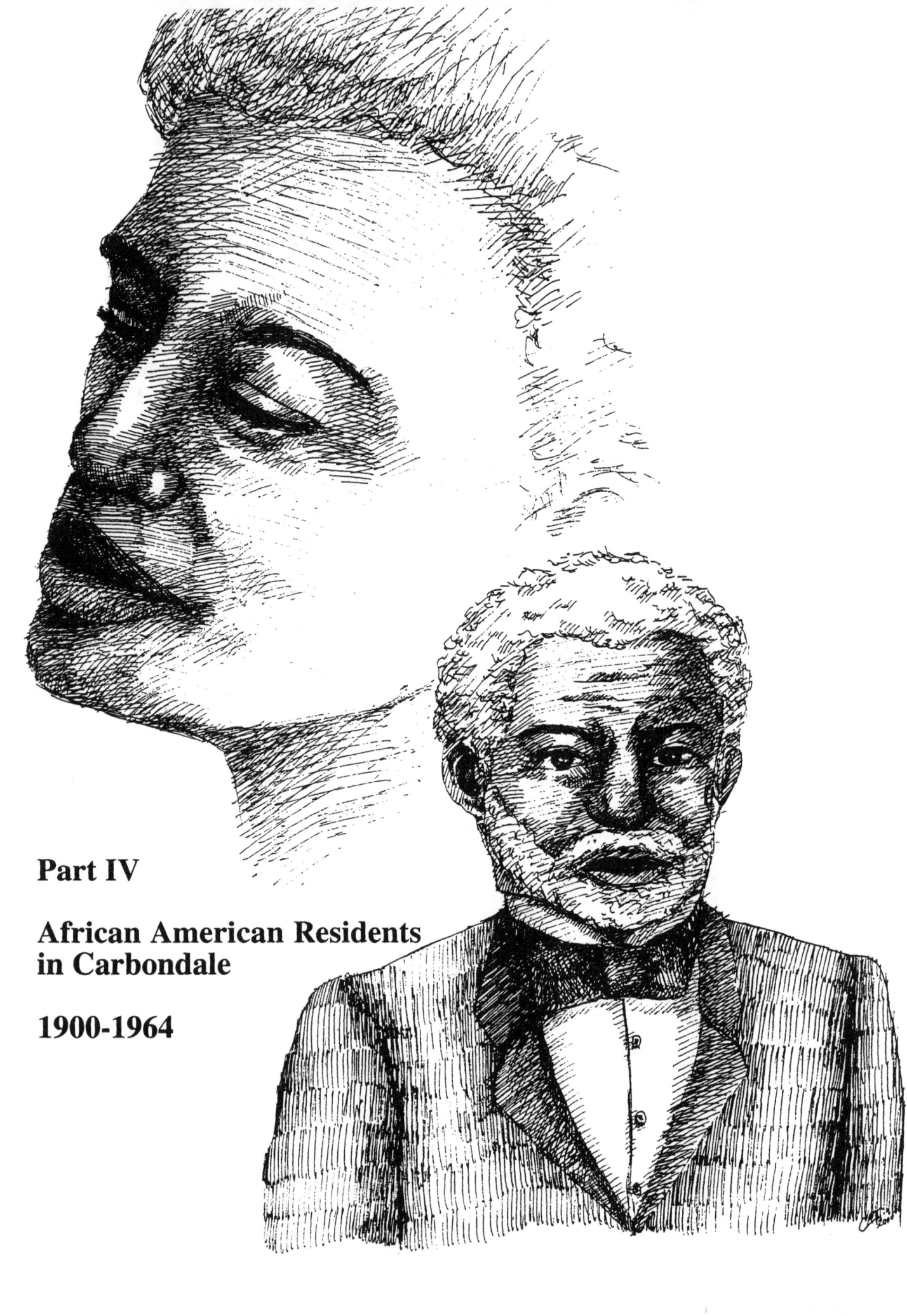

Part IV

African American Residents in Carbondale

1900-1964

George Wesley Crim
Born, 1902; died, 1977.

Mary Elizabeth Morrow
Born, 1903; died, 1976.

Beulah May Jones

Beulah May Jones, born February 12, 1904 was born to Ina Franklin Jones, a twenty-one year old native of Illinois. Her father, Samuel Jones, was a thirty-one year old laborer from Tennessee.

Lillian E. Ellis
Born, 1904; died, 1983

Ella J. Watson

Ella J. Watson, a native of Render, Kentucky, was born November 30, 1900. She was the daughter of James and Cora Strather Jarnigan. She was married to John W. Watson in Alton, Illinois on April 18, 1921. He died on december 22, 1963.

Mrs. Watson was a member of Hopewell Baptist Church. She died at her residence on South Marion Street April 25, 1984. She was survived by a niece, Mariilyn Clark, and a nephew, Eugene Jarnigan.

Ida Marie Harris Edgar

Ida Edgar, the daughter of Levi Harris and Mattie Denwiddie Harris, was born June 21, 1905 in Carbondale on North Street. In 1927 she was united in marriage to Mr. Charles Edgar. She was Sunday School teacher for a number of years at Hopewell Baptist Church, and she was a member of the Triple 4 Club.

Mrs. Edgar passed away January 9, 1990. Mrs. Edgar was the mother of a son, Charles Harris, and a daughter, Imogene Washington. She had four grandchildren, Samuel Washington, Gena Harris, Tena Jeremiah, and Joseph Washington; four great-grandchildren, Gena Lockett, and Rashid, Samuel Ali, and Laila Washington; and one great great-grandson, Gary Williams. She was an aunt of Helen Stone and Mattie Clinton and was the stepmother of Charlie Ann Bell and Theotrice Price.

Traces In The Dust

African American Households in Carbondale in 1905
Source: *Hoffman's Carbondale City Directory, 1905.* (Jno=Junior)

Abbot, Thomas	Laborer	Dudley Alley
Acron, Jno	Laborer	206 Birch
Adams, Jos. and Sarah	Laborer	420 N. West
Adkins, Adolph	Porter	Edwards House
Aker, Bud and Juda	Laborer	310 E. Green
Alexander, Charles	Laborer	304 W. Oak
Alexander, Louis and Julia	Carpenter	411 S. Marion
Algee, James	Laborer	418 E. North
Anderson, Charles	Barber	437 N. West
Anderson, Jno	Laborer	406 E. Green
Atkins, Anthony and Susan	Laborer	217 N. Wall
Atkins, Marcus	Laborer	217 N. Wall
Baird, Jno	Laborer	202 E. Oak
Baker, James and Anna	Laborer	707 N. East
Bartee, Martin and Mary,	Laborer	Dudley Alley
Barnett, Ella	----------	505 Green
Barnett, Grant	Laborer	505 Green
Barnett, Ida	----------	505 Green
Barnett, Joe and Mary	Laborer	505 Green
Barnett, Susan	----------	505 Green
Barnett, William	Miner	505 Green
Bass, George and Mary	Laborer	321 N. West
Bass, James	Laborer	307 N. West
Bass, Tilda	----------	320 Pecan
Bates, Narcise	Widow	436 N. West
Beetworth, Britta	Cook	209 W. Elm
Beck, Dave	----------	427 E. North
Beck, Jno and Roenia	Laborer	427 E. North
Bell, Eugene	Laborer	504 N. East
Benberry, Andrew and Sadie	----------	418 N. West
Benberry, George	Laborer	418 N. West
Berry, Thomas and Mora	Laborer	419 E. North
Billips, Jno and Amoma(?)	Laborer	409 N. West
Billips, Jack and Lucy	Laborer	409 N. West
Bird, Jerry and Easter	Laborer	517 N. Marion
Bishop, LeRoy and Annie	Laborer	428 N. West
Blandfield, Jennie	----------	406 E. Green
Bogen, Annie	----------	429 N. West
Bogen, Fannie	----------	429 N. West
Bond, Henry and Ella	Laborer	325 E. Oak
Bowers, Andrew J. and Iibbe	Laborer	415 S. West
Bowers, Frank and Priscilla	Laborer	422 S. Marion
Bounds, Roena	Widow	Dudley Alley
Boyd, Clifford and Mattie	Laborer	502 N. Marion
Boyd, Rhoda	Widow	318 E. North
Branch, Hattie	----------	421 E. North
Branch, William and Ellen	Laborer	516 E. Main

African American Residents In Carbondale, 1900-1964

Bridgeman, Henry and Ella	Laborer	216 E. Walnut
Broady, Grace	Widow	200 W. Oak
Brooks, Henry and T. W.	Laborer	409 S. Marion
Brown, Abe	----------	415 S. Marion
Brown, Jos. and Mattie	Carpenter	415 S. Marion
Burse, Colman	Laborer	418 E. Main
Butler, Charles and Lulu	Laborer	415 E. Oak
Butler, George	Laborer	415 E. Oak
Butler, Margaret	----------	505 Green
Campbell, B. and Mellissa	Laborer	500 N. East
Carr, Annie	----------	417 N. West
Carson, Lulu	----------	417 N. West
Carter, Alexander	Laborer	437 N. West
Carter, Garrett and Lena	Laborer	517 E. Oak
Carter, Jno	Laborer	504 N. East
Casey, Thomas and Lena	Cook	508 W. Main
Cauthon, Bud and Carrie	Laborer	414 N. Marion
Cauthon, Carrie	----------	414 N. Marion
Churcher, Harriet	----------	408 S. Marion
Clarke, Mattie	Cook	416 W. Main
Clarkson, Arthur and Willis	Bartender	330 N. West
Clay, Richard and Sarah	Teamster	418 E. North
Collier, Andy and Mallie	Laborer	405 S. Marion
Collins, Isaac	Upholsterer	207 S. West
Conner, B. F. and Mollie	Laborer	304 E. College
Cross, Agnes	----------	508 S. Marion
Cross, Charles and Matilda	Laborer	411 N. Marion
Cross, James	Laborer	313 Pecan
Cross, William and Sallie	Laborer	213 E. Elm
Crutcher, David and Eva	Laborer	309 E. Walnut
Crutcher, Lucy A.	Widow	440 N. West
Cupper, Alex	Laborer	316 N. West
Darnel, Bost and Bettie	Laborer	416 S. Marion
Daniel, E. F. Rev. and Mary	Minister	438 N. West
Davis, Jos. and Lizzie	Laborer	421 N. West
Davis, Otto	Laborer	310 E. Green
Deamond, Frank and Clarissa	Laborer	321 E. Walnut
Denton, Milberry	----------	413 North Oakland
Devan, Mohala	----------	423 N. West
Dodge, James and Mary	Laborer	316 Pecan
Dudley, Lucrecia	Domestic	208 E. Oak
Ealey, W. H. and Eliza	Laborer	313 Pecan
Eckerson, Carrie	Laborer	320 Pecan
Eckerson, Edgar	Laborer	320 Pecan
Eckersoll, Elvis and Lorie	Laborer	320 Pecan
Elder, Charles	Laborer	Dudley Alley
Ellis, Wiley	Laborer	437 N. West
Ellison, Ben and Anna	Laborer	320 E. North
Ellsworth, Charles and Josephine	Laborer	421 N. West
English, Alonzo	Laborer	413 N. Marion
English, Ed and Mary	Laborer	413 N. Marion

Traces In The Dust

English, Charles	Laborer	413 N. Marion
English, Walter	Laborer	413 N. Marion
English, William and Carrie	Laborer	511 Green
Evans, Mary	----------	307 N. West
Everhart, Alfred and Eva	Laborer	422 E. Main
Ewingburg, Bertha	Teacher	412 S. West
Exum, Rueber and Drucella	Laborer	324 E. North
Foster, J. W.	Bartender	202 E. Oak
Fox, Ella	----------	437 N. West
Franklin, John and Bessie	Laborer	304 S. Marion
Franklin, Phillip and Selina	Laborer	Dudley Alley
Frazer, Jno and Lucinda	Laborer	410 N. West
Fry, Jno and Rosa	----------	423 N. Marion
Fuget, Lewis	Laborer	411 N. West
Gaines, Sarah	Widow	431 E. North
Gaines, Charles	Laborer	431 E. North
Gaines, Mirah	Widow	213 E. Walnut
Gambil, Charles	Laborer	437 N. West
Gaters, James	Laborer	418 S. Marion
Gaters, Travis and Elizabeth	Laborer	418 S. Marion
Gilbert, Ann	----------	415 S. Marion
Gilbert, Green	Laborer	415 S. Marion
Gordon, Sam and Vina	Laborer	410 S. Marion
Green, Anderson and Mary	Laborer	410 S. West
Green, David and Joannah	Teamster	410 S. West
Green, Julia	----------	419 N. West
Green, Richmond and Celia	Laborer	402 S. Marion
Green, William	Laborer	410 S. West
Green, William and Anna	Laborer	207 Willow
Griffin, Samuel and Caroline	Teamster	330 N. West
Grissom, James	Porter	Edwards House
Grundy, Anna	Widow	413 E. North
Grundy, Henry	Laborer	413 E. North
Grundy, Nora	----------	413 E. North
Grundy, Victoria	----------	413 E. North
Hagler, R. H. and Sallie	Laborer	414 S. Marion
Hagler, W. and T. W.	Laborer	405 S. Marion
Hampton, D. W.	Laborer	219 E. Green
Hampton, Jessie	----------	219 E. Green
Hannah, Gussie	----------	321 Pecan
Hardin, Ben and Inezzie(?)	Laborer	325 E. Oak
Harris, George and Sarah	Laborer	415 N. Marion
Harris, Ida Marie	Infant	424 E. North
Harris, Lew and Julia	Laborer	207 Willow
Harris, Levy and Mattie	Laborer	424 E. North
Harris, Nance	Widow	325 E. Oak
Harroll, William and Mary	Laborer	417 E. North
Harrison, Robert	Laborer	437 N. West
Hawkins, Bob	Laborer	412 S. Marion
Hayes, Mary	----------	Dudley Alley
Hayes, Abe	Laborer	Dudley Alley
Hayes, Richard and Clementine	Laborer	Dudley Alley

African American Residents In Carbondale, 1900-1964

Hayes, William	Teamster	420 N. West
Hayes, William	Laborer	413 S. Marion
Herron, Robert and Mattie	Laborer	422 E. Main
Hicks, Albert and Artie	Laborer	408 S. Marion
Hill, Charles and Mary	Laborer	216 E. Walnut
Hill, Gus and Elsie	Laborer	423 Willow
Hinchey, Wayman	Laborer	304 E. College
Holland, James	Laborer	420 E. North
Holland, Mattie	School teacher	302 Pecan
Holman, S.	----------	413 E. Oak
Homes, Sarah	----------	419 N. West
Hopkins, Rufus and Rhoda	Laborer	407 N. Marion
Howard, Charles and Vinnie	Laborer	412 S. Marion
Howelton, Nannie	----------	208 E. Elm
Hudson, Henry	Laborer	416 S. Marion
Hudson, John and Ella	Laborer	403 S. Marion
Hudson, Mary Bell	----------	411 N. West
Hughes, Ona	----------	414 N. Marion
Hull, Jno	----------	217 E. Green
Hundley, William	----------	Dudley Alley
Hyde, Mose	Laborer	Dudley Alley
Jackson, A. and Florence	Laborer	707 S. West
Jackson, Charles and Mattie	Laborer	401 S. Marion
Jackson, Frank	Laborer	306 S. Marion
Jackson, Hainey	Laborer	437 N. West
Jackson, Henry and Addie	Laborer	437 N. West
Jackson, William	Laborer	409 N. West
Jeffrey, Florence	----------	428 N. West
Jenkins, Walter and Garry	----------	Dudley Alley
Johnson, Dan and Nannie	Porter	213 E. South
Johnson, Easter	----------	410 E. Main
Johnson, Manel	Laborer	410 E. Main
Johnson, Moses	Laborer	411 E. Oak
Johnson, Richard and Bettie	Laborer	429 N. West
Johnson, Walter	Laborer	206 Birch
Johnson, Wiley and Lizzie	Laborer	420 E. Main
Jones, Charles and Cora	Laborer	411 S. Marion
Jones, I. J.	Fireman	1009 Thompson
Jones, James	Laborer	413 N. West
Jones, Lewis	Laborer	418 E. Main
Jones, Noah and Fanny	Laborer	305 E. Oak
Jones, Olmstead and Mattie	Laborer	314 E. Green
Jones, Sam and Iva	Laborer	311 Pecan
Jowels, William and Harriet	Laborer	407 S. Marion
Joy, Charles and Mary	Laborer	419 N. Marion
Kelly, Stella	----------	200 W. Oak
Kelly, J. H. and Anna M.	Operator	200 W. Oak
Kennybrne(?), Charles	Laborer	408 S. Marion
King, Filmore and Rosa	Laborer	412 N. West
Knox, Sophia	Widow	309 E. Oak
Lawler, Squire and Pearl	Laborer	210 E. Walnut

Traces In The Dust

Lawson, Amanda	----------	219 E. Green
Lee, Laura	Widow	212 E. South
Lee, Thomas and Susan	Laborer	519 W. Main
Lewis, Charles and Mary	Laborer	504 E. Main
Lewis, Emma	----------	119 N. Wall
Lewis, Jno	Laborer	119 N. Wall
Lewis, J. P. and Maggie	Laborer	119 N. Wall
Lewis, Narcise	Widow	408 N. Normal
Lewis, Nettie	----------	119 N. Wall
Logan, Jno	Laborer	504 N. East
Long, Adam	Laborer	411 E. Oak
Long, William	Laborer	411 E. Oak
Love, James and Lucy	Laborer	426 N. West
Malone, Rogers and Mary	Laborer	307 E. Walnut
Mardy, Judge and Celia	Laborer	318 E. North
Marshall, Ella	----------	413 S. Marion
Marshall, Samuel and Henrietta	----------	442 N. West
Mathews, Frank and Maggie	Laborer	700 Barnes
Mathews, Marcella	----------	700 Barnes
Means, Ada	Domestic	405 W. Walnut
Miller, Ed and Laura	Laborer	519 E. Oak
Miller, Simon and Carrie	Miner	301 S. Marion
Milligan, Horace and Toma	----------	211 N. Marion
Mitchell, Kate	----------	413 E. Oak
Mitchell, William and Ella	----------	417 N. West
Moody, Sarah	----------	208 E. Oak
Moore, W. A.	Minister	221 E. Green
Montgomery, James and Fanny	Laborer	Dudley Alley
Morgan, Calvin	Laborer	408 S. Marion
Morgan, Melvin	Laborer	408 S. Marion
Morton, Rosie	Widow	436 N. West, in rear
Morris, Arthur and Lucy	Laborer	429 E. North
Mosley, Idella	Laborer	213 E. Walnut
Mosley, Jake and Ida	Laborer	213 E. Walnut
Murphy, Eliza	----------	437 N. West
Murray, R. and Lena	Miner	411 S. West
Murry, Jeff	Laborer	406 S. Marion
Muse, Ernest and Alice	Laborer	415 N. East
Muse, Jno Mrs.	----------	415 N. East
Muse, Marie	----------	415 N. East
McClure, Verda	----------	306 S. Marion
McCracken, Eva	----------	317 Pecan
McCracken, George	Laborer	317 Pecan
McCracken, Gilbert	Laborer	317 Pecan
McCracken, Kate	----------	317 Pecan
McCracken, Lewis	Laborer	317 Pecan
McKernen, Laura	----------	306 S. Marion
Nance, Ella	----------	310 E. North
Nance, Emma	----------	310 E. North
Nance, Jno and Isabella	Saloon keeper	501 Chestnut
Nauman, Walter and Connie	Laborer	439 N. West
Nealy, Mattie	----------	400 E. Green

African American Residents In Carbondale, 1900-1964

Nicholas, Flagg	Barber	214 N. East
Nichols, Thomas	Laborer	414 S. Marion
Offutt, M.	----------	306 S. Marion
Owen, Cornelius	Laborer	423 N. Marion
Owen, Robert	Laborer	423 N. Marion
Ozburn, Lou	----------	524 W. Sycamore
Palmer, Era	----------	217 E. Green
Parran, Willis and Lula	Laborer	416 N. Marion
Parker, Alfred and Martha	Laborer	409 N. Marion
Parker, Dowell	Laborer	211 E. Green
Parker, Ed	Laborer	211 E. Green
Parker, Jennie	----------	211 E. Green
Parks, Charles and Lizzie	Laborer	313 N. West
Patterson, George and M.	Laborer	421 E. Oak
Patterson, W. C. and Lydia	Barber	216 E. South
Perkins, Polly	Widow	323 E. Oak
Phenix, Cora	----------	313 N. West
Phenix, Leon	Laborer	428 N. West
Phillips, E. C.	Barber	216 E. South
Pigee, Hays and Bettie	Laborer	417 E. North
Pitts, Simpson and Gertrude	Laborer	Dudley Alley
Plumber, C. P. and Emma	Laborer	410 N. Marion
Pope, James and Lillian	Barber	214 N. West
Porter, Blaine	Laborer	418 N. Marion
Porter, Jno and Susan	Laborer	418 N. Marion
Porter, Kirby and Ollie	Laborer	Dudley Alley
Porter, Lottie	----------	418 N. Marion
Porter, Oliver and Maggie	Laborer	311 N. West
Powell, Jno and Julia	Laborer	Dudley Alley
Price, Calvin	Laborer	400 E. Green
Price, David and Sadie	Laborer	318 E. Oak
Price, D. and Lulu	Painter	426 E. North
Price, John and Mattie	Laborer	400 S. Marion
Pyles, James and Ophelia	Laborer	424 E. North
Quigley, Alex and Annie	Retired farmer	313 S. West
Ray, Charles A. and Mellissa	Miner	412 S. West
Ray, Daisy	Student	412 S. West
Redden, Frank and Margaret	Laborer	413 E. North
Reed, Gentry	Laborer	304 W. Oak
Reed, Jno	Laborer	505 Green
Reeves, Mella	Widow	504 N. East
Reliford, Ed and Ida	Laborer	319 Pecan
Rice, James and Stella	Laborer	407 S. Marion
Richardson, James	Laborer	408 N. Normal
Richardson, Richard	Laborer	430 N. West
Riley, Charles and Maggie	Laborer	304 W. Oak
Ringo, T. R. and Ana	Teamster	413 S. West
Robinson, Clem and Sallie	Laborer	423 E. Oak
Robinson, Henry and Jane	Laborer	407 E. Oak
Robinson, James and B.	Laborer	511 E. Main
Robinson, Sylvester and Ida	Laborer	419 N. West

Rogers, George and Catherine	Laborer	310 E. North
Rousey, Bart	Laborer	504 N. East
Rows, Foster and Mandy	Restaurant Proprietor	316 N. West
Russell, B.	Laborer	437 N. West
Samples, Porter	Laborer	411 E. Oak
Sampson, Malinda	----------	109 S. Marion
Sanders, Jno R. and Eliza	Laborer	322 E. Oak
Sanford, Rufus	Laborer	440 N. West
Sawell, Tom and Agnes	Laborer	215 E. South
Settler, Alex and Hannah	Laborer	504 N. Marion
Sheffie, Abe and Hattie	Laborer	408 N. Normal
Shelton, Jno and Lizzie	Laborer	216 E. Walnut
Sims, Jackson and Lizzie	Laborer	323 E. Oak
Simpson, William	Laborer	504 N. East
Sistle, Henrietta	----------	418 E. College
Smith, Anthony and Malina	Laborer	304 S. Marion
Smith, Bertha	----------	213 E. Elm
Smith, Boland	Laborer	608 S. Normal
Smith, Christina	----------	213 Elm
Smith, Daniel	Laborer	322 E. North
Smith, Hosea and Effie	Laborer	322 E. North
Smith, John and Lucy	----------	208 E. Elm
Smith, Jno	Laborer	Dudley Alley
Smith, J. A. and Lizzie	----------	Dudley Alley
Starks, Marshal and Catharine	Laborer	321 E. Oak
Stepson, Phyllis	Widow	309 E. Walnut
St. John, Westley	Laborer	Dudley Alley
Stocks, Louis	Laborer	307 N. West
Stradley, Griffin and Mary	Laborer	321 Pecan
Taylor, Elratus	Widow	613 N. East
Taylor, Isaac and Mary	Laborer	208 Birch
Taylor, S. and Effie	Laborer	427 N. West
Thomas, Levy	Laborer	502 N. Marion
Thomas, Mary	----------	502 N. Marion
Thomas, W. H.	School teacher	501 Chestnut
Thompson, Minerva	----------	323 E. Oak
Thompson, William	Laborer	504 N. East
Toney, Ada	----------	413 N. Oakland
Toney, Evelina	----------	413 N. Oakland
Toney, V. and Dorsa	Laborer	409 E. Oak
Turner, Robert and Ella	Laborer	319 Pecan
Tutt, Ben	Laborer	411 E. Oak
Tutt, Ben and Luvenia	----------	423 Willow
Utley, Henry and Daisy	Laborer	406 E. Green
Vaughn, George and Rosie	Laborer	419 E. Oak
Vaughn, John	----------	417 N. West
Vawter, Eliza	Laborer	410 S. West
Venable, John and Mary	Contractor	213 S. East
Walker, Stanley and Georgie	Laborer	406 S. Marion
Washington, Ben and May	Laborer	302 Pecan
Washington, Ed and Anna	Laborer	516 E. North
Watts, Lewis	Laborer	213 E. South

African American Residents In Carbondale, 1900-1964

Webb, Albert	Laborer	212 W. North
Welch, William and Maggie	Laborer	707 N. East
White, Charles	Laborer	703 N. East
White, Henry and Maggie	Laborer	713 N. East
White, James and Minnie	Laborer	303 E. Oak
White, Thomas and Mary	Laborer	406 E. Green
Wilkinson, Andrew	Laborer	416 W. Main
Wilson, Bertha	----------	221 E. Green
Wilson, Collins and Ora	Laborer	221 E. Green
Wilson, James	Laborer	424 E. Main
Wilson, J. H. Rev. and Millie	Minister	319 E. Oak
Wilson, Renie	----------	408 N. Normal
Wilson, Thomas and Lizzie	Laborer	424 E. Main
Williams, Al and Cora	Laborer	613 N. East
Williams, B. and Josie	Laborer	518 E. Main
Williams, Bertha	----------	319 E. Oak
Williams, Edward	Laborer	109 S. Marion
Williams, H. and Stella	Laborer	412 N. Marion
Williams, Harris and Ella	Laborer	304 S. Marion
Williams, Herman	Laborer	109 S. Marion
Williams, Henry	Laborer	109 S. Marion
Williams, Lewis and Nellie	Laborer	441 N. West
Williams, Jane	Widow	518 E. Main
Williams, John	Laborer	109 S. Marion
Williams, Jno	Laborer	406 E. Green
Williams, Rosa	----------	201 S. Marion
Williams, Thomas	Laborer	Dudley Alley
Winbush, Walker and Lizzie	Laborer	500 N. Marion
Winn, Mary Carrie	----------	428 N. West
Winfield, Julia	Widow	307 N. West
Wood, Lizzie	----------	Dudley Alley
Woods, Abe and Rhoda	Drayman	419 S. Marion
Woods, Ed and Melissa	Minister	423 N. West
Woods, Henry	Mail carrier	424 N. West
Woods, Ida	----------	424 N. West
Woods, John and Fannie	Laborer	306 S. Marion
Woods, Jno W. and Lillian	Laborer	310 S. Marion
Woods, Sadie	----------	302 S. Marion
Woolions, Arthur and Jessie	Laborer	Dudley Alley
Wright, Bob	Laborer	413 S. Marion
Wright, Carrol and Lulu	Laborer	405 N. Marion
Wright, Lettie	Widow	319 E. Oak
Wright, Virginia	Widow	313 S. West
Young, Juda	Widow	420 N. Marion

Cleo Belle Williams

Cleo Belle Williams was born in Carbondale on December 3, 1906. She was the fourth child born to Mamie Thompson Williams. Her father, Henry Williams, was a cold miner from Missouri. Mrs. Williams was a native of Tennessee.

Versa P. Hayes White

Versa P. Hayes White, the daughter of Jesse and Early Price Hayes, was born in Carbondale on December 4, 1906. Mrs. White was a retired teacher, a founding member of Gamma Kappa Omega Chapter of Alpha Kappa Alpha Sorority, and a member of the Bethel A.M.E. Church.

In 1929, Mrs. White graduated from Southern Illinois Normal University. She continued with her higher education studies and earned a master's degree in education at Southern Illinois University. She married Edward White in 1940.

Mrs. White passed away at Memorial Hospital in Carbondale on September 12, 1984. She was the mother of two daughters, Versa Lou and Georgianna White, and the grandmother of Jessica Yorama. Mrs. White was a long time resident on East Jackson Street.

Etta W. Jackson

A native of Evansville, Indiana, Mrs. Etta Waddell Jackson was the second of four siblings of John and Sallie Waddell. She was born in Evansville on December 2, 1883. Following the death of their mother, the children were separated, and Etta came under the care of Matilda Myers--a close family friend who reared Etta as her own.

Mrs. Jackson spent most of her adult life in Carbondale and was an active member of Olivet Freewill Baptist Church. She was President of the Mission Circle, a Mother of the Church, and a teacher in the Sunday School. Her marriage to Frank B. Jackson places her in Carbondale as early as 1906. The couple had one daughter, Wilma. Mrs. Jackson was a school teacher until her retirement in 1958. She was one of the early African American civic leaders of Carbondale and a dedicated businesswoman. Mrs. Jackson died on August 14, 1980 at the age of 96. She was preceded in death by her parents, her husband, a daughter, a sister, and two brothers. Among her survivors were three grandchildren, nine great grandchildren; and a great-great grandchild.

Agnus F. Woods

Agnus F. Woods was born September 5, 1908 in Carbondale. She was the second child born to Elvira Churchill Woods of Kentucky and William H. Woods of Illinois. At the time of her birth, Mr. Woods was a 38 year old mail carrier in Carbondale and the first known black to hold that particular post in the city.

Mattie Lee Hillsman

Mattie Lee Hillsman was the first child of Arizona Newbill Hillsman. She was born June 25, 1909 in Carbondale at 307 Willow Street. Her father, A.D. Hillsman, was a twenty-four year old employee with the Illinois Central Rail Road.

Allen Hillsman

Allen Hillsman was born September 25, 1909 on Willow Street in Carbondale. He was the 4th child born to Pearlie Newbille Hillsman and Edgar Hillsman.

Ella Mandy Lula Davis

Ella Mandy Lula Davis was the 5th child born to Belle Clark Davis of Henry Co., Tennessee. She was born in Carbondale May 27, 1910. Her father, James Davis, is listed as deceased at the time of her birth. James was a tie plant worker from Mississippi.

John Smith

John Smith was the 7th child of Lucinda Dolton Smith of Tennessee. He was born October 4, 1910 in Carbondale at 500 North East Street. His father, Robert Smith, also from Tennessee, worked as a day laborer.

Vivian Lucille Walker

Vivian Lucille Walker was born December 19, 1910 in Carbondale. She was the second daughter of Anna Grace Kelley Walker of Alton, Illinois and William Henry Walker, a miner, who was born in Knoxville, Tennessee.

Genoa A. R. Hillsman

Genoa Alpha Rudolpha Hillsman was the second child of A. N. Hillsman of Tennessee. Her father, Odolphus Hillsman, also of Tennessee, was employed as a day laborer. Genoa was born March 10, 1911 in Carbondale at 407 Willow Street.

Frances E. White
"Aunt Tank"

Mrs. Frances Ester White was born September 6, 1911 in Carbondale, Illinois to Val and Cecil Branch Woods. Affectionately known as "Aunt Tank," Mrs. White was educated in the Carbondale public schools and attended Southern Illinois Normal University for two years. She was married to Richard White in St. Louis, Missouri.

Aunt Tank was formerly a member of Hopewell Baptist Church. She later joined Olivet Freewill Baptist Church where she remained an active member and leader throughout her life.

Mrs. White worked as a supervisor at the Hogan Recreational Center until it became the Carbondale Teen Town. Her parents, three sisters and three brothers preceded her in death. Mrs. White was the mother of Etta Newbern and the grandmother of Vickie Simms.

At the time of her passing, family survivors included one sister, Ferne Gray; four brothers, Charles, Harold, Jerry, and Ronald Brown; and four great grandchildren; Diante, Chelsey Jr., William, and Nicole Simms.

Dorothy H. King

Dorothy Hamilton King, the wife of David King, arrived in Carbondale as a young child. When her family moved to Carbondale around 1911, Dorothy was four years old. The last of five children, she was born July 18, 1907 in Villa Ridge, Illinois to John and Mary Parks Hamilton.

Dorothy attended Attucks Grade School and Attucks High School. She received a Teacher's Certificate from Southern Illinois Normal University and taught school in the Southern Illinois area. She also attended Beauty and Cosmetology School in St. Louis, Missouri and received a beautician's license. She operated her first beauty shop in Carbondale and was married to Mr. King on June 9, 1930. Dorothy was a long time member of Rock Hill Baptist Church. She was known for her warm disposition and friendly smile.

Mrs. King died November 14, 1995 at her home at 901 North Marion Street in Carbondale. She had two sisters and two brothers who preceded her in death. She was also preceded in death by her husband, David, who died in 1989.

Delmar M. Algee, Sr.

Delmar M. Algee, the patriarch of one of Carbondale's prominent black business families of the 1900s, was born February 2, 1912 in the city at 430 East Jackson Street. He was the second of two children born to Luther and Cora Bass Algee.

Mr. Algee attended the Attucks schools, and later graduated from Southern Illinois Normal University and taught briefly in the southern Illinois area. At SINU, he was a member of the Alpha Phi Alpha Fraternity and the school Choral Club. He later attended Mortuary school and established his own funeral home service (See Black Businesses and Enterprises).

Mr. Algee also worked as a club attendant for the Illinois Central Railroad. He married Anne C. Griffin in 1945 in Carbondale. He retired in 1977 after working 38 years.

Mr. Delmar Algee, Sr. died November 13, 1994 in the town of Carbondale, the place where he spent his life and left his mark. The couple had five children and were married 49 years.

Paul Clayton Woods

Paul Clayton Woods was born in February of 1912 on E. College Street in Carbondale to Essie M. White Woods of Tennessee. His father, Joe Woods of Illinois, was a forty year old Drayman from Illinois. The birth of the baby was attended by Midwife Jennie Anderson.

William Richard Hayes, Sr.

William Richard Hayes was born to Ova and Lillian Parrott Hayes on May 21, 1912. He graduated from Attucks High School in the "Class of 1930."

Mr. Hayes became a member of Olivet Freewill Baptist Church and served as a member of the choir, a member of the Deacon Board, and in several other auxiliaries. He married Eurma Cordella Jones in St. Louis, Missouri in the late 1930s. The couple first resided on North Marion Street in Carbondale. Ten children were born to them.

Bill, as he was popularly known, joined and served in the Civilian Conservation Corps for a number of years. He then worked for the Illinois Central Railroad as a general worker and caboose supply man where he remained until his retirement in 1975. Bill's father, Ova Hayes, had also found employment with the railroad; he had earlier worked for the old Ayers-Lord Tie Plant where he was blinded in an accident on the job. He was a member of Tuscan Lodge #44, F&AM for over fifty years.

Mr. Hayes died on January 15, 1997 at the Jackson County Nursing Home in Murphysboro, Illinois. He was preceded in death by his parents; his wife, Eurma; a brother; and a granddaughter, Clinette. Survivors of his death included his ten children, Georgetta Lois Slaughter, Richard Clinton Hayes, Nettie Bell Hayes-Morgan, Ovella Mae Cooper; William "Bill" Hayes, II, Kathryn Marie Harris, Evelyn Rosemary Koine; Rev. Leland Charles Hayes; Lillian Antwoinette Peterson, and Rebecca Lynn Thomas; twenty-five grandchildren; and twenty great grandchildren.

Ezekiel Davis

Ezekiel Davis was born in Carbondale May 29, 1912 on E. Oak Street. He was born to the parentage of Jennie Rodgers Davis of Treman, Tennessee and William Davis of Pitt Co., North Carolina.

Hewitt C. Hudson

Hewitt C. Hudson was born September 10, 1912 in Carbondale to Richard and Ella Fuqua Hudson. He attended school in Carbondale and married Doris Johnson on January 31, 1933.

Mr. Hudson was a loyal and faithful member of Rock Hill Baptist Church where he served as a deacon for over twenty-nine years. He was formerly employed as a construction laborer of Local Union 227. He was later employed for over twenty years at Tuck Industries, Inc. in Carbondale where he served until his retirement in 1979.

At the time of his death on June 1, 1984, Hewitt was a resident of 425 East Sycamore Street in Carbondale. He was survived by his wife, Doris; one daughter, Marilyn Fortman; two nephews, U. L. and Archibald Hudson; and two nieces, Dorothy Jones and Charlotte Hudson.

Zanie Wimes
Born, 1912; died 1975

Nina Mae Nichols

Nina Mae Nichols was born May 7, 1894 in Rutherford, Tennessee. She settled in Carbondale in 1912. She married Thomas J. Nichols September 7, 1918 in Murphysboro, Illinois. Seven children were born to the couple. Mr. Nichols died February 26, 1939 in Carbondale.

Mrs. Nichols joined Hopewell Baptist Church under the pastorate of Rev. G. W. Dorsey. She later joined Rock Hill Baptist Church in 1921, believing that husband and wife should be together in all things. She participated in the Ladies' Afternoon Club, the Missionary Society, the Usher Board, the Homemakers' Club, the Triple Four Club, and the Delmar Devers War Mothers' Chapter.

Mrs. Nichols passed away July 1, 1981 following a lengthy illness. She was preceded in death by an infant son and her son, Joseph, who died November 10, 1979. She was survived by three daughters, Marjorie Jackson, Leota Brown, and Claudette Simon; three sons, Ted, Thomas, and Lawrence; twelve grandchildren; five great grandchildren; and one great-great grandchild.

Harry Wingo was born in Carbondale February 11, 1913 to Mattie Wilson Wingo of Saline Co., Ill and Archie Wingo of Union Co., Ill.

Charles O. White

Charles Orlando White was the second child of Maud Nance White of Illinois. He was born March 23, 1913 on E. Oak Street in Carbondale. His father, Charles White, was a native of Tennessee.

John Henry and William Henry Dalton (Twins)

John Henry and William Henry Dalton were the 3rd and 4th children born to Clara Hunter Dalton and Albert Dalton of Tennessee. The twins were born May 30, 1913 in Carbondale.

Bessie N. S. Warren

Bessie Naomi Simpson Warren was born January 16, 1898 in Hallidayboro, Illinois to Ralph and Della Grear Simpson. The family settled in Carbondale in 1912. Known for her stern discipline, Mrs. Warren was a dedicated teacher in the Attucks school system and a committed church member (See The Legacy of Attucks).

In 1914, Mrs. Warren joined Hopewell Baptist Church in Carbondale where she served as church pianist, a member of the Trustee Board, the church treasurer, Superintendent of the Sunday School, and President of the Missionary Society. She was Director of the Youth Convention in the Zion District Association. One of her favorite roles was serving as Director of the Attucks playground because, like teaching, this put her in contact with the youth of the community. She received many honors and tributes for unselfish work given throughout her lifetime.

Mrs. Warren died February 27, 1995. Her parents, stepfather, three sisters, and two brothers preceded her in death. Two very special people became as family to Mrs. Warren: Grace Boyd and Odell Robison.

Josephine L. Woods

Josephine Lincoln Woods was born October 28, 1913 in Carbondale to Essie M. White Woods of Tennessee and Joe Woods of Illinois. Josephine was the second child born to Mrs. Woods. Mr. Woods was employed as a Drayman.

Luella M. Davis

Luella McCall Davis was born April 4, 1912 in Paris, Tennessee to Lee and Crilla McCall. Her family settled in Carbondale when she was a baby in 1913.

Mrs. Davis was, herself, an icon in the city of Carbondale, standing always as a beacon for others to follow (See In Service To Their People). As a civic leader, she was a dominant force in the fight to enlighten her people on Black American culture and especially, the Black social structure of Carbondale. She was also recognized as one of the city's outstanding educators (See The Legacy of Attucks).

Mrs. Davis passed away on September 7, 1995. Among her relatives, were her two sons, Hardin A. and Otha L. Davis; two sisters, Mrs. Annabelle Jackson and Marion White; two daughters-in-law, Ida P. and Wanza A. Davis; and three grandchildren, Christy, Michelle, and Anthony Davis.

Doris N. Hudson

Doris Nancy Hudson, was born February 17, 1914 in Carbondale. She was the daughter of George and Gilberta Lawler Johnson. She was married to Hewitt Hudson January 31, 1933.

Very involved in church activities, she served in many capacities at Rock Hill Baptist Church including the Baptist Training Union, the missionary society, and the Mt. Olive Baptist District Association.

Mrs. Hudson received an associate degree in cosmetology from SIU and retired from the University of Illinois Home Extension Service, where she worked in the food and nutrition program.

Mrs. Hudson passed away Thursday May 8, 1986 at the home of her daughter in Aurora, Illinois. Surviving family members included her daughter, Marilyn Fortman; two sisters, Violet Frames and Della Lambus; and a brother, Wilber Johnson.

Edward Mason

Edward Mason, a Carbondale native, was born February 22, 1914. His parents were Nathan and Abbie Glass Mason. Ed married Willie B. Steele in 1939 in Cape Girardeau, Missouri. Mr. Mason was a construction worker and belonged to the Construction Labor Union No. 227 of Carbondale. On April 22, 1944, he enlisted in the United States Army, serving in World War II.

Mr. Mason passed away September 14, 1984 at his home in Carbondale. Among his family survivors were a son James Edward Mason; a brother, Albert Mason; a sister, Helen Green, and three grandchildren.

Clarence Ward

The sixth child of Victoria Grundy Ward, Clarence Ward, a Negro male, was born April 14, 1915 at 409 E. Oak Street in Carbondale. The birth was attended by Mrs. Marguerite Redden. Clarence's father, John Henry Ward, was a laborer from Pittsburgh, Pennsylvania. His mother, Victoria, was a native of Illinois.

William Harold Walker

William Harold Walker was the fifth child born to Anna Grace Kelly Walker of Alton, Illinois. His father, William Henry Walker was a miner and a native of New Market, Tennessee. William Harold was born in Carbondale at 306 N. Illinois Ave. on June 6, 1915. His birth was attended by Mrs. Melissa Woods.

William graduated from Attucks High School and from Southern Illinois Teachers College in 1937 with a Bachelor of Science degree in Education.

William first taught in a one room school in Perks, Illinois. He then taught in Marion, Illinois. In 1940 he enlisted in the Army and applied for the Air Corps. However, he was turned down because of his color. He finally entered the 99th Pursuit Squadron at Tuskegee, Alabama.

In 1943 he graduated as a Second Lieutenant as a fighter pilot and served in the Italian Theater of War of the 332nd Fighter Squadron. He served until the end of the war in 1946. William then returned to SIU and earned a Master's Degree in School Administration. He married Viola Crim in 1943 and the family moved to Centralia, Illinois. He was recognized as "Outstanding Citizen of the Year" and was inducted into the Centralia Historical Hall of Fame.

Harold Walker died April 26, 1999. At the time of his death, survivors included his wife, Viola Crim Walker; a son, William; and a brother, James.

William H. White

William Henry White, listed as a Negro male, was the third child born to Maud Nance White, a housekeeper from Elkville, Illinois. He was born June 9, 1915 at 303 E. Oak Street in Carbondale. His father, Charlie Nance, was a native of Union City, Tennessee. The birth was reported by O. B. Thompson of Carbondale.

Artie V. Glenn

Artie Virginia Glenn, born October 11, 1915, was the second child born to Mollie Hawkins Glenn of Missouri. Her father, William Glenn was from Jackson, Tennessee and was employed at the Round House. Attendant at the birth was Artie Hicks.

Lee Roy Jackson

Lee Roy Jackson was born in Carbondale October 14, 1915 to Mattie Tellman Harris of Mississippi. His father, Allen Jackson, worked as a laborer. Lee Roy's birth was attended by Mrs. Melissa Woods.

William F. Waters

William Floyd Waters was born February 20, 1916 at 410 E. Main Street in Carbondale. He was the seventh child born to Hattie Pricilla Johnson Waters, a forty-one year old homemaker from Carbondale. His father, Floyd Waters, was a thirty-seven year old laborer from New Madrid, Missouri.

Elna Mae Martin

Elna Mae Martin, the eldest child of Ingram and Beatrice Walker Reliford, was born August 17, 1916 in Carbondale. She was educated at the Attucks schools and was a member of Hopewell Missionary Baptist Church. Elna married Albert Martin in Jackson County. The couple had one son, Lynn. Before her retirement, Elna was employed as head cook at Thomas School. Later she worked as a nursing assistant at the Styrest Nursing Home.

Elna's parents, husband, two brothers and two sisters died during Elna's lifetime. Mrs. Martin passed away on December 4, 1995 at her home on North Marion Street in Carbondale.

Shelly M. Chappell

Shelly M. Chappell was born January 30, 1900 in Springhill, Tennessee. He was the second oldest son of Amos and Belle Chappell. Mr. Chappell moved to Carbondale in 1917, where he spent the rest of his life. He married Ida Melton on August 28, 1919 in Carbondale. Six children were born to the couple.

Mr. Chappell was active politically and worked through several organizations for the advancement of Blacks in Carbondale. He was instrumental in getting the Black voice heard at the Kopper's Plant and in bringing about changes in the town (See In Service To Their People).

Mr. Chappell died July 24, at the New Haven Nursing Home in Carbondale. He was survived by his wife Ida Melton Chappell; his six children, Jewell Harris, Ruth Brooks, Hazel Dawson, and James, Edward and William Chappell; seven sisters, Daisy Harrell, Mary Smith, Annie Perkins, Cora Cunningham, Velma Hutcherson, Pauline McDonald, and Betty Wilson. At the time of his passing, Mr. Chappell had seventeen grandchildren, and twenty-seven great grandchildren. He resided at 301 E. Larch Street

Ida A. Chappell

Ida A. Melton Chappell, the daughter of Lynn and Rilla Smith Melton, was born October 25, 1902 in West Point, Mississippi. She was married to Shelly Chappell August 28, 1919 in Carbondale. Mr. Chappell preceded her in death on July 24, 1974. Also preceding her in death were Mrs. Chappell's parents and four brothers. Mrs. Chappell was a member of the Green Street Church of God where she was a church Mother

Ida Chappell died October 13, 1978 at her home located at 301 East Larch Street in Carbondale. Her survivors included three daughters, Jewel Louise Harris, Hazel Mae Dawson, and Ruth Evelyn Brooks; her three sons, William Shelly Chappell, James Wesley Chappell and Edward Earl Chappell; two sisters, Sirmae Chandler and Minnie Hubbard; one brother, Noah Melton; and an aunt, Ethel Smith of Carbondale. At the time of her death, Ida had seventeen grandchildren; thirty-four great grandchildren; and one great, great grandchild.

Minnie H. Mooreland

Minnie Helen Mooreland settled in Carbondale September 16, 1918 and worked as a teacher at the Attucks School. She was the daughter of Anthony and Georgia Wilson Gerhardt and was born September 10, 1896 in New Franklin, Missouri.

Minnie was married to Dr. William F. Mooreland in Glasgow, Missouri. Dr. Mooreland practiced as a dentist in Carbondale until his death on December 4, 1957. Minnie was a member of Rock Hill Baptist Church and a member of the Mariam Chapter No. 17 Order of the Eastern Star where she had served as a Past Matron.

Mrs. Mooreland died November 14, 1977 in Flint, Michigan. She was survived by a son, Floyd Mooreland; two grandchildren; a great grandson; and a brother-in-law, Amos Mooreland of Carbondale.

Albert S. Reid
Born, 1918; died, 1970.

Leota Christina Nichols Brown

Leota Nichols Brown was born June 13, 1919 in Carbondale to Thomas J. and Nina Keathly Nichols. She married William H. Brown on November 11, 1943 in Cape Girardeau, Missouri.

In the 1960's, Mrs. Brown became an advocate for child care reform (See In Service To Their People). At the time of her death in 1982, Mrs. Brown resided at 212 N. 2nd St. in Murphysboro, Illinois.

Willard E. Brown

Willard Eugene Brown was born September 4, 1919 in Carbondale to John and Cecil Branch Brown. He attended the Attucks Grade School and graduated from Attucks High School with the Class of '39. While at Attucks, Willard excelled at sports and athletics.

On March 19, 1945, Willard was married to Lubertha McCoy in Murphysboro, Illinois. He was an active member of the Olivet Freewill Baptist Church and was highly active for the benefit of Carbondale's black youth (See In Service To Their People).

Willard was an Army veteran of World War II. At home, he was employed at the Veath Sport Mart and was last employed by the City Water Works Department where he worked until he became disabled.

Willard had his father, a sister, and a brother to die during his lifetime. He passed away on April 1, 1988 in Barnes Hospital in St. Louis, Missouri at age 68. His survivors included his wife, Lubertha Brown; his mother, Cecil brown; two daughters Joyce Arnette and Ethel

Welch; four sisters, Frances White; Evelyn Boykin, Betty Brown, and Fern Gray; five brothers, Jerry, Charles, Harold, Billy, and Ronnie Brown; four grandchildren; and one great grandchild.

Charles E. Harris

Charles Edward Harris was born in Carbondale on October 8, 1919. He received his educational training in the public schools of Carbondale. He served in the United States Army in World War II in France, Italy, and Africa.

Charles Harris died February 2, 1997. Family survivors included his wife, Jewel; three daughters, Twona, Hazel, and Gena Marie; a brother, James; three sisters, Imogene, Theodra, and Charlie Anne; fifteen grandchildren; and thirty-two great grandchildren.

Gary L. J. Wilson

Gary Leon J. Wilson was born to Connie Wilson and Josephine Lewis October 16, 1919 in Carbondale. He was a graduate of Attucks High School. He attended John A. Logan College and SIU where he studied Art. He was known in Southern Illinois for his writings and reading of poetry.

Mr. Wilson was a Civilian Conservation Corps graduate and an Army veteran of World War II. He was disabled while rendering service to his country in that war effort.

Mr. Wilson was an art teacher and artist. Examples of his work can be seen in the Carbondale area and in private homes. He passed away at the Veteran's Medical Center in Marion, Ill. July 11, 1996 after a lengthy illness.

Addie B. Smith

Mrs. Addie B. Smith was born November 4, 1919 in Carbondale to Louis and Beatrice Nesbitt. She received her education in the Carbondale public schools. She married Andrew Smith, Jr. in Cape Girardeau, Missouri.

Addie Smith was long employed as a cook at the Alpha Gamma Delta Sorority House at Southern Illinois University in Carbondale. She belonged to New Zion Baptist Church.

Mrs. Smith and Andrew had five daughters, Dorothy, Hazel, Lena Jean, Virginia, and Loretta; one son, Andrew Smith, Jr.; twenty-four grandchildren and twenty great-grandchildren. Mrs. Smith died September 7, 1993 in Belleville, Illinois at age 73.

Josie B. and James H. Clark

Mrs. Josie B. Clark, the wife of James Henry Clark, was born March 14, 1889 in Metropolis to Columbus and Margaret Lassiter. James, a native of Hickmon, Kentucky, was born June 8, 1885. He was the son of James and Jennie Clark.

James and Josie were married on August 23, 1906 in Union City, Tennessee. They settled in Carbondale in 1919. The couple had two daughters, Ora Holder and Virginia Clark.

The Clarks were active members of Rock Hill Baptist Church. Mrs. Clark participated in the Ladies Afternoon Club, and the Rose of Sharon Club.

Mrs. Clark was a retired beautician. She succumbed to a lengthy illness in April of 1968. She was 79 years old; she was the sister of Sarah Washington.

Mr. Clark was a retired Illinois Central Railroad laborer. At the time of his death, surviving members of his family included his two daughters, Ora Holder and Virginia Clark; a son-in-law, James E. Holder; three sisters, Rosie Davis, Amelia Clark, and Marie King; a brother, Charles; three grandchildren and six great-grandchildren. James H. Clark died in August of 1974 at age 89.

Charles E. Jackson

Charles Edward Jackson was born in the town of Carbondale March 29, 1920 to Percy and Annie Gibbs Jackson. An early funeral home document indicates that Charles was the first Negro baby born at the former Holden Hospital.

Charles was an Army veteran of World War II. He worked in civilian life operating a record shop in New York.

Mr. Jackson died January 10, 1985 in New York, New York at the age of 64. He had a daughter, Teresa Hunter of South Carolina; a son, Kevin Jackson of New York; four grandchildren; and one great-grandchild. He also had a son who died before him. Charles Jackson was the nephew of Thelma Walker of Carbondale.

African American Residents In Carbondale, 1900-1964

Top Left: William Richard Hayes, Sr. Top Right: Elna Mae Martin. Bottom Left: William Harold Walker. Bottom Right: Shelly M. Chappell

Unis Pearl Davis

Unis Pearl Davis, a native of Carbondale, was born April 14, 1920. He was the son of Elijah and Ella Lucinda Davis. He married Alfreda Nelson in Colp, Illinois. Mr. Davis worked for Sears, Roebuck and Co. He was an active community and civic leader. (See In Service To Their People; The Black Struggle.)

Mr. Davis died in Marion Illinois at the Veterans Medical Center on September 29, 1991 at the age of 71. He was the father of five sons, Maurice, Girard, Ivory, Damion, and Unis Davis II; and three daughters, Barbara Jean Phillips, Diane Harvey, and Wenetta Green. Mr. Davis had his parents, three brothers, and one sister to precede him in death.

Jewel Eugene Gibbs

Jewel Eugene Gibbs was born April 30, 1920 in Carbondale to Edward and Annie Pierce Gibbs. He graduated from Attucks High School in 1938, and later attended Southern Illinois University in Carbondale. He married Cora Fletcher February 6, 1946 in Murphysboro, Illinois.

Mr. Gibbs was employed at Veath Sports Mart in Carbondale and also worked for the Illinois Youth Commission. He was last employed as a painter at SIU-Carbondale and was a member of Painters' Local No. 352. Jewel and his family were members of the Olivet Freewill Baptist Church. He was a Past Worshipful Master of Tuscan Lodge No. 44, F.& A.M.

Upon his death, Mr. Gibbs was survived by his wife Cora; a son, Jewel Lane Gibbs; two daughters, Connie and Mary Alice; two brothers, Harrison and Theodore Gibbs; a sister, Celestine Cavitt; five grandchildren; two sisters-in-law, Anita and Jean Helen Gibbs; three brothers-in-law, Claude Fletcher, Louie Cavitt, and Lane Fletcher; and a daughter-in-law, Gloria Gaston. Jewel died on December 9, 1987 in Carbondale. He was 67 years old.

Lucy Scott

Mrs. Lucy Scott was born April 29, 1893 in Carrier Mills, Illinois to the parentage of John and Margaret Wimberly. At an early age, she joined church in Eddyville, Illinois where she served as a Sunday School teacher and sang in the choir. In 1913, she received her diploma as a teacher in Pope County and Golconda, Illinois.

Lucy married Andrew Scott in 1918, and six children were born to them. In addition to raising her children, Mrs. Scott also raised four grandchildren.

In September of 1920, the family moved to Carbondale where Mrs. Scott became a member of Olivet Freewill Baptist Church. She served as a church Mother, a member of the Missionary Society, and a member of the Eveready Club.

Mrs. Scott succumbed to illness on June 4, 1995. At age 102, she was one of four black females in the history of Carbondale to live to the age of 100 or beyond. While she was alive, she suffered the loss of many members of her family including her husband, two sisters, five brothers, three sons, one daughter, five grandchildren, and a great-great grandchild.

At the time of her death, surviving family members included a daughter, Ardelia; a son, Ora J.; nine grandchildren, including Janet Brown whom she raised; twenty-four great grandchildren; and fourteen great-great grandchildren. Mrs. Scott was the mother-in-law to Cardella Scott.

Lavern C. Thornton
Born, 1920; died, 1973.

Charles V. Anderson

Charles V. Anderson was born August 5, 1921 in Carbondale, the son of W. J. and Gladys Malone Anderson. He was a member of the Hopewell Missionary Baptist Church where he served on the Deacon Board.

Charles was educated in the Carbondale schools and at Southern Illinois University. He was employed with the Lorenzo Smith School District Number 259 of Pembroke, Illinois. At the school, he served as a teacher, a principal, a business manager, and finally as Superintendent until his retirement. He was a member of the Illinois Teachers Association.

On October 6, 1942, Charles enlisted in the United States Army. He was honorably discharged on February 22, 1946. He was married to Annie Rush on June 23, 1948 in Murphysboro, Illinois. The couple had two sons and a daughter.

Charles died January 28, 1991 in his home. He was a resident of 1209 West Freeman Street in Carbondale. He was survived by his mother and wife; two sons, Charles V. Anderson, Jr. and Kenneth Anderson; a daughter Rita Cavitt; a brother, Willie D. Anderson; and three grandchildren as well as many other relatives.

Carl Lee Stricklin

Carl Lee Stricklin was born September 10, 1921 in Carbondale to Carl Stricklin, Sr. and Ann Branch. He married Rosie Spriggs in Carbondale.

Carl was a presser and dry cleaner at Horstman's Cleaners in Carbondale. He was a United States Army veteran of World War II. His church affiliation was with Olivet Freewill Baptist Church.

Mr. Stricklin died at the age of 73 on May 31, 1995. His parents, one brother and one sister preceded him in death. Surviving his death were his two brothers, Billy and Russell; two nephews, Russell Branch, Jr. and Brian Branch; and four nieces, Karla, Sharyl, Denise, and Tamara Branch.

Robert Scott

Robert Scott was born December 4, 1921 in Carbondale to Andrew and Lucy Wimberly Scott. He married Cardella Lowery in Murphysboro, Illinois on October 18, 1948. He attended Attucks High School and later served in the U. S. Air Force where he retired after twenty years of service. He was a member of the Air Force Sergeants Association and a member of the Order of the Pyramid of Lentz Hall. In civilian life, Robert was a Food Service Manager at Lentz Hall on the campus of Southern Illinois University.

Robert passed away August 14, 1981 in Carbondale at Memorial Hospital. His survivors included his wife; a son, Bruce W; a daughter, Lea Renee Scott; his mother, Lucy Scott; two sisters, Ardelia Scott and Jeanetta Sampson; a brother, Ora J. Scott; and three grandchildren.

Monyette Rolene Mosley Penny

Monyette Rolene Mosely Penny married Ross George Penny of Alton, Illinois. She earned a bachelor's degree and began a career in the field of education. She retired from teaching after 36 years with the Alton School System.

Ross George Penny died in 1978. Monyette and Ross had one son, Ross Gerald, who became a computer analyst for the Digital Computer Corporation.

Freda O. Mosley Burch

Freda O. Mosley Burch was the second daughter born to Statsie and Inez B. Mosley. She worked as a R. N. in the city of St. Louis, Missouri.

Freda married Ray Burch, Sr. who worked for Trans Worlds Airline. The couple had one son, Ray Jr. who was Sales Manager for Mercer Cadillac Company. Mrs. Burch died in 1957, and her husband passed away in 1964. They were the grandparents of three children.

Josephine Mosley Haynes

Josephine Mosley Haynes is a retired beautician. She married Oscar Haynes, an insurance salesman, who passed away in 1991. Mrs. Mosley is currently a resident of Chicago, Illinois and is the mother of eight children, Richard, Wayne, Charles, Kenneth, Earnest, Anthony, Michael, and Orene. She is the grandmother of twelve children and the great-grandmother of four children.

Taz E. Green

A long time resident of 406 North Marion Street, Taz E. Green was born in Cherry, Tennessee on October 26, 1894. He was the oldest son of Willie J. and Amelia Green. "Grandpa Taz," as he was known by relatives, arrived in Carbondale in 1921. In 1928, he resided at 311 Larch Street. Taz married Martha Fletcher on August 2, 1931.

During the late 1930s, Taz was the only known black licensed electrician in Carbondale. He served on the

Traces In The Dust

Volunteer Police Force of Carbondale. He and his wife, Martha, were active members of Olivet Freewill Baptist Church where Taz served as a trustee.

He spent most of his life involved in community affairs and held memberships and positions of leaderships in numerous associations, clubs, and civic organizations in Carbondale and throughout Southern Illinois (See In Service To Their People).

His wife, Martha, currently resides in Chicago, Illinois; she is 93 years old. Taz E. Green was the father of James Wallace Green, popularly known as "Pinto." and the father-in-law of Ernell France Green. He was the grandfather of Sherlene Willetta Green, Debbie Kay Green, Taz Edward Green, Sidney Hibbler, and James Wallace Green, Jr. and the step grandfather of Melvin Green Macklin.

Marshall Taylor

Marshall Taylor was born to Louise McCain Taylor, a sixteen year old homemaker from Huntington, Tennessee on January 8, 1922. His place of birth is given as 707 N. Washington Street, Carbondale, Jackson Co., Illinois. His father, Frank Taylor, was a twenty-two year old farmer from Milar, Tennessee.

James Allen Smith, Sr.

James A. Smith, Sr., the son of Versus and Estella Stubblefield, was born June 28, 1922 in Carbondale. He attended the Attucks school system and was recognized as one of the outstanding Attucks High School basketball players.

James was formerly married to Ethel Florence Mathews. He married Doris Murray Brooks in September of 1975. He was a long time employee at Koppers Company Inc. in Carbondale where he worked as a high lift driver. He retired from Koppers in 1985. James passed away September 5, 1988 in Carbondale after an extended illness.

Mr. Smith was the father of three daughters and one son; Darnecea, Regina, Yvonne, and James A. Smith, Jr. At the time of his death, family survivors included his wife, Doris; his daughters and son; a brother; fourteen grandchildren; and seven great grandchildren.

James E. Anderson

James E. Anderson, a native and life long resident of Carbondale was born June 28, 1922, the son of W. J. Anderson and Gladys Malone Anderson. He married Jessie B. Gibson on October 19, 1948. He and Jessie had six children: three sons, Jeffery, James, Jr., and Mark; and three daughters, Alice, Amelia, and Valeria.

James was a deacon, a Sunday School teacher, and a trustee; he also worked for the church as its bus driver and maintenance man. He was a member of the American Postal Workers Union and was employed by the United States Post Office as a custodian until his retirement. Additionally, he was an Army veteran of World War II.

Mr. Anderson died April 1, 1988 at his home. He had two brothers, Charles V. Anderson and Willie D. Anderson of Carbondale; and twelve grandchildren.

Aubra Clay

Aubra Clay, the son of Mr. Prentice and Janie Partee Clay, was born May 1, 1897 in Tennessee. Moving to Carbondale in 1922, he worked as a porter in the hotel industry.

Mr. Clay was a member of Bethel A.M.E. Church and a veteran of World War I. He died at the Veterans Administration Hospital in Marion, Illinois April 2, 1978.

Robert Thornton

Robert Thornton, the son of Henry and Mamie Garrison Thornton, is a native of Ripley, Tennessee. He arrived in Carbondale with his family in 1922 when he was four years old. His parents settled on Willow Street. "Bob" is the nephew of the late Nealy Thornton and the brother of Mary Lee, Luvenia, Rosie, Zoda, and L.C. Thornton. Mr. Thonton is one of Carbondale's oldest living descendants of a black family from the town's early history. He yet resides in the northeast community where his family first settled.

Mamie Thornton

Mamie Thornton was born December 18, 1892 in the city of Ripley, Tennessee to the union of the late Mr. and Mrs. Garrison. She settled in Carbondale in 1922. On August 5, 1910, she married Henry Thornton. Four daughters and three sons were born to the couple.

Mamie was a member of the New Zion Baptist Church where she served on the Usher Board and the Mothers' Board. She also served as a Sunday School Teacher and was a missionary worker.

Mrs. Thornton died on July 4, 1987 in the St. James Hospital in East Chicago Heights. Before her death, she lost her husband, two daughters, and one son. Family survivors included her son, Robert Thornton; two daughters, Rosa Graham and Zoda Terry; seven grandchildren, twenty-five great grandchildren; and nine great-great grandchildren.

African American Residents In Carbondale, 1900-1964

Top Left: James E. Anderson. Top Right: Virginia Rose Hickman St. James. Bottom Left: Willie Dee Anderson ("Prof"). Bottom Right: Edward Wills.

Doris H. Smith

Doris H. Smith was the fourth child of eleven children born to Randall and Susie Murray. She was born in Carbondale on January 30, 1923. She attended Attucks High School and was a member of Rock Hill Baptist Church. Doris was married to Milton Brooks and later to James A. Smith. Doris was employed at Tuck Tape Company and later moved to San Diego California.

Doris Smith died January 23, 1996. At the time of her death family survivors included a brother, Richard W. Murray; stepchildren, Darnecea Moultrie, James A. Smith, Yvonne Drake, and Regina F. Henderson; fourteen grandchildren and eleven great grandchildren.

Willie Dee Anderson
"Prof"

Mr. Willie Dee Anderson, born May 28, 1923 in Carbondale, was the son of William James and Gladys Malone Anderson. He was a product of the Attucks school system, where he would eventually return to work.

Willie Dee married Mary Lee Smith in 1953. After receiving his education, he began a life time career in education and return to teach at the very institution from which he formerly had graduated.

Mr. Anderson was known both as a brilliant mathematician and a dedicated musician. He directed the Attucks band program for many years (See The Legacy of Attucks). At Southern Illinois University, he participated in numerous activities and organizations.

Known throughout the community as "Prof," Mr. Anderson was, in the opinion of many, one of the finest career teachers the Attucks institution had ever seen. "Prof" was also an active member of the community and a member of Hopewell Baptist Church. He was chairman of the trustee board, church musician, and choir director. A Veteran of World War II, he was the father of Alisa Anderson, Dr. Basil L. Anderson, and William James Anderson..

Mr. Anderson died in his home town of Carbondale January 14, 1992. He was preceded in death by his father, two brothers, and one aunt. Survivors included his mother, Gladys Anderson, and his children.

Virginia Rose H. St. James

Virginia Rose Hickman St. James was born in Carbondale June 15, 1923 to John and Myrtle Hickman. She married Dr. Warren St. James on July 27, 1942 in St. Louis. She had been a well known organist in Southern Illinois and was the senior pianist at Maple Park United Methodist Church in Chicago. In Carbondale, the St. James family attended the Olivet Freewill Baptist Church.

Mrs. St. James died December 14, 1986 in Chicago. She was survived by Mr. St. James; four daughters, Olivia Banks, Antoinette McAllister, June Wooden, and Sheila Townsend; a brother, Dr. John Hickman; and ten grandchildren.

Archibald P. Hudson
"Bo"

Archibald Percy Hudson was an Army veteran of World War II, serving in A Troop, 9th Cavalry. He was born August 7, 1923 in Carbondale to U.L. Sr. and Bashierdeen Johnson Hudson. He attended Attucks Grade and Attucks High Schools.

Archibald was employed at the old Holden Hospital and at the Pyramid Dormitory in Carbondale. He resided at 213 East Monroe Street.

"Bo" Hudson died at the age of 62 on October 13, 1985 at the Veterans Administration Medical Center in Marion, Ill. He was the nephew of Doris Hudson of Carbondale.

Guieula Thomas

Mrs. Guieula Thomas, a native of Carbondale, is the daughter of Marcella Criss of Missouri. She was born January 16, 1924 on Monroe Street near the present day location of Rock Hill Baptist Church. She attended the Attucks schools and graduated from Attucks High School.

Mrs. Thomas first set up household on Oak Street. She was employed for a number of years as a cook and hairdresser. Later, she worked as a baby sitter and subsequently retired as a licensed child care worker. Mrs. Thomas is a member of Bethel A.M.E. Church.

Mrs. Thomas left the city to live in Chicago and returned to Carbondale in 1954. Currently, she resides on North Pierce Street.

James W. Green, Sr.
"Pinto"

James Wallace Green was born March 23, 1924 in Carbondale to Taz Green and Allean Davis. He was baptized at Freewill Baptist Church and served on the Dining committee.

"Pinto," as he was known to his pals, was an Army veteran of World War II. He worked at the Campbell Soup Company in Chicago, Illinois and as a cook for several organizations. He was formerly married to Ernell Marie France, the daughter of James France.

Mr. Green died December 30, 1991 in Herrin Hospital in Herrin, Illinois. He was survived by two daughters, Sherlene Bowles and Deborah Onyewuchi; four sons Sidney Hibbler, Taz Green, James Green, Jr., and Melvin

Green Macklin; his sister, Gloria Dean Aiken; a devoted friend and companion, Hortense Edward; seven grandchildren; and one great granddaughter. His parents and his son, Larry, preceded him in death.

Arnold L. Ross, Sr.

Arnold L. Ross, the brother of Edna Ross and Eva Ross Buggs was born July 14, 1906 in Ward, Illinois. He passed away at his residence in Mt. Vernon, Illinois June 29, 1982 at age 82.

Aaron Brinson, Sr.

Aaron Brinson, Sr. was born February 22, 1912 in Shaw, Mississippi to John and Georgia Brinson. He spent his early life in Carbondale and was in attendence at the Attucks Grade School as early as 1924.

Aaron was married to Rose Thornton in 1932. He later moved to Chicago, Illinois where he resided until his death.

Mr. Brinson died November 17, 1981. Survivors of his death included two sons, Aaron, Jr. and Edgar; a daughter, LaVerne; and a brother, Tony.

Sadie P. Irvin

Sadie Pryor Irvin, the daughter of Henry and Dora Nicholson Pryor, was born December 22, 1892 in Madison, Mississippi. Documents indicate that she settled in Carbondale in 1924. Mrs. Irvin first married Talmadge Archie Armour in Mississippi. He preceded her in death. She later married Will Irvin who also preceded her in death. She reared her brother, William, and took responsibility for her grandchildren, Gwendolyn, Talmadge, Janice, and Tal.

Mrs. Irvin was a member of Rock Hill Baptist Church and was a Church Mother and a member of the Missionary Society in addition to participating in organizations of the church. Mrs. Irving loved fishing and working in her garden.

Mrs. Irvin passed away April 10, 1991 in the Jackson County Nursing Home in Murphysboro, Illinois. She had four grandchildren; fourteen great grandchildren; and four great-great grandchildren.

Dora Lee Armour Price

Dora Lee Armour Price was born in Madison, Mississippi in 1910, the daughter of Talmadge Archie and Sadie Pryor Armour. She arrived in Carbondale in 1924.

Dora Attended the Attucks school system and entered Southern Illinois University. She was a member of the Dunbar Society and the Sigma Gamma Rho Sorority. She united with Rock Hill Baptist Church where she sang in the church choirs.

Dora was noted for her musical talents and soprano voice; she was a charter member of the Roland Hayes Glee Club. She is also recognized as the first African American to hold a professional position at the old First National Bank in Carbondale.

Dora Armour died in August of 1980. Survivors of her family at the time of her death included her mother Sadie Pryor Irvin; a brother, Talmadge Armour; two uncles Dr. William H. Pryor and Elder Booker T. Harris; an aunt, Anna Terrell; three nieces; a nephew; and two cousins, Mrs. Ida Webb and Mrs. Maurice Shaffer, both of Carbondale.

Clarence Franklin

Clarence Franklin was born in Carbondale at 3:00 pm to Albert and Addie Franklin on January 29, 1925. The birth was attended by Dr. H. C. Moss.

Ruth H. Reliford

Ruth H. Reliford was born in Carbondale February 3, 1925 to Ingram Reliford, a native of Jackson, Tennessee and Beatrice Reliford of Carbondale. Mr. Reliford was a boiler washer, and Mrs. Reliford was a housewife. Midwife Ella Lacy attended the birth.

Imogene Young

Imogene Young was born June 1, 1925 in Carbondale, the daughter of James Lewis and Leanna Mason Young. She received her educational training from the Attucks Grade School and the Attucks High School.

Mrs. Young worked at the Attucks Day Care Center and was a substitute teacher at the Eurma Hayes Day Care Center. Imogene was united with the Rock Hill Baptist Church where she served on the Benevolence Commission. She died on July 20, 1987 in Carbondale. She was the mother of Larraine Wallace and Johnell Young.

James Jones

James Jones was born February 8, 1925 in Carbondale to Ervie and Luella Brown Jones, both of Tennessee. Luella was a housewife, and Mr. Jones was a street laborer. The birth was attended by Dr. Brandon.

Anna Beatrice Norwood

Anna Beatrice Norwood was born in Carbondale to Burna Norwood February 21, 1925. The birth was attended by Ella Lacy.

Lula Alexander Cooper

Lula Alexander Cooper was born October 21, 1925 in Carbondale to Reverend L. L. Cooper and Dora Reed Cooper. Rev. Cooper was a minister from Tennessee. Mrs. Cooper was also a Holiness Preacher from Tennessee. The birth was attended by Midwife Ella Lacy of Carbondale.

Ruth Evelyn Chappell

Ruth Evelyn Chappell was born October 21, 1925 in Carbondale to Shelly M. Chappell, a native of Hamberg, Tennessee and Ida Melton Chappell of West Point, Mississippi. Mrs. Chappell was a twenty-three year old housewife. Mr. Chappell was a 25 year old tie carrier.

Sallie Williams

Sallie Williams was born September 30, 1896 in Marianna, Arkansas to Arthur and Lucy Murdock Young. In 1914, she married Earnest Williams in Earle, Arkansas. Mr. Williams died in 1932.

In 1925, Mrs. Williams moved her family into the northeast Carbondale neighborhood, settling at the corner of Burke and Barnes Streets. There she purchased property, which then sold from $25.00 to $50.00 a lot, and built a three room house.

Mrs. Williams united with the Church of God in Christ which was then located on East Green Street. She became a missionary and a pillar of her church (See Early Black Churches and Spiritual Leadership).

Missionary Williams died August 1, 1994 at St. Joseph Memorial Hospital in Murphysboro, Illinois. She had many family members to precede her in death. Among these were her parents, a sister, a brother, a granddaughter, and one great-great grandson. Surviving family members at her death included her daughter, Marie Mason; two granddaughters, Charlesetta Lawton and Anita Gibbs; three grandsons, Raymond, Kenneth, and Jackie Mason; twenty great grandchildren; and thirteen great-great grandchildren.

Ida M. Armour Webb

Ida M. Armour Webb was born August 29, 1915. She was the daughter of Alfred and Fannie Rome Armour. Documents show that the Armour family had settled in Carbondale as early as the fall of 1925.

Ida was a product of the Attucks School system. She married Quincy Webb on March 15, 1933. The couple had one daughter, Maurice Shaffer.

Ida was a member of the Rock Hill Baptist Church. She was a former member of the Carbondale Community Club, a former election judge, and was Past Worthy Matron of Mariam Chapter No. 17, Order of Eastern Star.

Mrs. Webb died on March 13, 1983. In addition to her daughter and husband, other surviving family members included her sister, Fannie Brown; a son-in-law, Learon Shaffer; two granddaughters, Linda and Marie Shaffer; and a niece.

Jennola Green

Jennola Green was born in Carbondale December 31, 1925. She was the daughter of Charlie Green of Gravel Ridge, Arkansas and Leanne Garrison Green of Henning, Tennessee.

Osa Mae Campbell

Osa Mae Campbell was born January 3, 1926 to Jack Campbell and Nancy Kendrick Campbell. Mr. Campbell was a laborer from Hamburg, Tennessee who worked at the tie plant. Mrs. Campbell was a native of Springhill, Tennessee. The birth was attended by Dr. H. C. Moss.

Ernest Lee

Ernest Lee was born March 22, 1926, the son of John Henry Lee and Annie McBride Lee. Mr. Lee was a laborer, and Mrs. Lee was a twenty-five year old housewife. The birth was attended by Dr. W. A. Brandon of Carbondale.

Floyd A. Mooreland

Floyd Anthony Mooreland was born March 26, 1926 in Carbondale. His mother, Minnie Helen Mooreland was a twenty-nine year old housewife from New Franklin, Missouri. His father, William Floyd Mooreland, was a twenty-nine year old dentist from Carrier Mills, Illinois. The birth was attended by J. W. Barrow.

Ethel Florence Mathews

Ethel Florence Mathews was born in Carbondale April 1, 1926 to Della Griffin Mathews, a housewife from Memphis, Tennessee and Robert Mathews, who was a native of Nesbit, Mississippi. The birth was attended by Ella Lacy, who delivered the baby at 4:00 am.

Auralia Franklin

Auralia Franklin was born May 7, 1926 to Albert Franklin and Addie Boner Franklin. Mr. Franklin was a laborer and a native of Arkansas. He was employed at the tie plant. Addie Boner was a 27 year old housewife from Alabama. The birth was attended by Dr. H. Moss.

Lorene Haynes White

Lorene Haynes White was born February 14, 1919 in Gloster, Mississippi to Samuel and Matilda Brooks Haynes. She graduated from Attucks High School in 1937. She subsequently earned a master's degree and began a career as a teacher and a nutritionist. Mrs. White died on July 31, 1994 in Urbana, Illinois.

Lillie May Anders

Lillie May Anders was born May 23, 1926 in Carbondale to Willie and Vinnie Anders, both natives of Tennessee. The birth was attended by Dr. Lingle.

Billy L. Brown

Billy Larue Brown was born in Carbondale, May 23, 1926, the son of John and Cecil Brown. He attended Attucks Grade School and Attucks High School. Following the traditions of his family, he became a member of Olivet Freewill Baptist Church. He was employed as a truck driver for the Mueller Landscaping Company in Elgin, Illinois, and was a United States Army veteran of World War II.

At the time of his death, Billy resided at 1441 North 14th St. in Murphysboro, Illinois. He was 69 years old. He was the father of three children, Beverly Brown, Doris June Brown, and Billy Larue Brown, Jr.

Elcosie Bowen

Elcosie Bowen was born August 2, 1926 in Carbondale at 401 E. Willow Street to Cora Ingram Bowen of Mississippi. His father, Leonard Bowen, was a 33 year old farmer, also from Mississippi.

The birth was attended by Dr. H. C. Moss of 207 West Main Street. Elcosie Bowen is the earliest known African American baby in Carbondale to be delivered by a medical doctor.

Lane Fletcher, Jr.

Lane Fletcher was born in Carbondale September 6, 1928 to Lane Edward Fletcher and Mary Evans Fletcher, both of Mississippi. He served in the Korean War. He married Elnora Fletcher. Lane Fletcher died March 27, 1994 at the Veteran's Hospital in St. Louis, Missouri. Family survivors at the time of his death included his wife; a brother, Claude W. Fletcher; a sister, Cora B. Gibbs; and two nieces, Mary Alice Gibbs and Connie Gibbs.

Frances Marie Robertson

Frances Marie Robertson was born in Carbondale to William E. Robertson of Tennessee and Arra Brownlee of Henderson, Tennessee September 6, 1926. She was the sixth child born to the mother, who was a housewife. Mr. Robertson was a motorman at the tie plant.

William Terry, Jr.

William Terry, Jr. was born December 8, 1926 at 414 E. Jackson Street in Carbondale to Ethel Francis Terry, a housewife and native of Carbondale. His father, William Terry, Sr. of New Madrid, Missouri, was a Bell Boy at the Roberts Hotel.

Willie Dee Lilly

Willie Dee Lilly was born December 12, 1926 in Carbondale. He was the son of Charles and Hattie Bell Clark Davis Lilly. He attended the Attucks schools and was a member of Olivet Freewill Baptist Church.

Willie was married to Willie Mae Day of Colp, Illinois May 23, 1944. He served in World War II and was a member of the Tuscan Masonic Lodge, F&AM No. 44.

Willie Dee Lilly died in a swimming accident in the Mississippi River. Family survivors at the time of his death included his wife; a son, Michael, a daughter Brenda; sisters, Allean Brown Gordon, Alice Nelson, and Mary Armstead; a brother, Willard of Pulaski, and one grandson.

Anna V. P. McDonald

Anna Vera Perkins McDonald was born January 1, 1891 in Winston County, Mississippi to William and Emma Haynes. In 1911 she wedded Jacob Perkins. They had four children. Mrs. Perkins moved to Carbondale in 1926. Mr. Perkins passed away in 1962, and in 1965, Mrs. Perkins was married to James McDonald.

Mrs. Perkins first united with Bethel A.M.E. Church where she served in the missionary society and was a stewardess for fifty years. In 1987, she united with Wall Street Church of Christ in Carbondale.

Mrs. McDonald was preceded in death by her son, Woodrow, and her son-in-law, George Thornton. She died on February 28, 1992. She was survived by her daughter, Kathleen Thornton; two brothers; three grandchildren, Everett Thornton, Wayman Thornton, and Anita Green; fifteen great grandchildren; and thirteen great-great grandchildren.

Traces In The Dust

To Left: Aaron Brinson, Sr. Top Right: Dora Lee Armour Price. Bottom: Left: Lorene Haynes White. Bottom Right: Bessie N. S. Warren.

Virginia Young Gingery

Virginia Young Gingery was born March 11, 1891 in Hennings, Tennessee to Benjamin and Arminta Young. She married John Terrence Gingery in 1906. She was a member of the Greater Gillespie Temple Church of God in Christ in Carbondale. Mrs. Gingery died March 10, 1985 in Murphysboro, Illinois.

Fred and Viola Devers

Fred and Viola Pierce Devers settled in Carbondale in the year 1926. Fred was born in Birmingham, Alabama. Mrs. Devers was born in Dewmain, Illinois. The couple first established their first home on E. Chestnut Street. Mr. and Mrs. Devers had a family of thirteen children, Irvin, Eugene, Howard, Delmar, Pearl, Cecil, Dorice, Wendell, Gloria, Winona, Foice, Bobby, and Burnett.

Billy Gene Branch

Billie Gene Branch, listed as his mother's third child, was born July 25, 1927 to Alfred Branch, a laborer of St. Louis, Mo., and Anna Branch of Carbondale. The birth was attended by Mrs. Ella Lacey. Mrs. Branch was a twenty-four year old laundress at the time.

Billy was an advocate for the advancement of Blacks in Carbondale (see In Service To Their People) and a member of Olivet Freewill Baptist Church where he served in various positions.

Billy served in the United States Army and was employed for the Illinois Department of Transportation. He was married to Virginia Ellis on January 8, 1949.

Mr. Branch died March 7, 2000 in Carbondale. Surviving family members included his wife Virginia: sisters-in-law, Marilyn Branch and Clara Estinosa. His mother, father, three brothers, and one sister preceded him in death.

Johnny Harris

Johnny Harris was born August 4, 1927 to Fred Harris of Mississippi and Eliza Holland Harris, a housewife also of Mississippi. The birth was attended by Dr. Lingle.

Emma M. Ford

Emma May Ford was born in Carbondale September 13, 1927 to Robert Ford of Oklahoma and Mary M. Ford of Columbia, Kentucky.

Edna L. Cavitt

Edna Lucille Cavitt, was born October 21, 1927 in Carbondale to Ed and Beatrice Cavitt. Mr. Cavitt was a laborer from Dresden, Tennessee. Mrs. Cavitt, a native of Fulton, Kentucky, was a housewife. Midwife Ella Lacy attended the birth which took place at 3:30 p. m.

Welbert Jackson

Welbert Jackson was born in Carbondale October 24, 1927 to Louis Jackson of Tennessee and Ada Weston Jackson, a housewife of Brookville, Mississippi. Ella Lacey attended the birth.

Joe Chappell

Joe Chappell was born December 30, 1927 in Carbondale to Alice Beatrice Brooks Chappell of College Grove, Tennessee and Comodore M. Chappell, a native of Flat Wood, Tennessee. Mr. Chappell was a laborer at the tie plant. Mrs. Woods was a housewife, 33 years of age.

Grace L. Kelley

Grace Lillian Kelley was the daughter of Galveston and Leah Sumner Perkins. Born March 26, 1910 in Brownfield, Illinois, she settled in Carbondale in 1927. After receiving receiving a Bachelor of Arts degree from what was then Southern Illinois Normal University in 1931, Mrs. Kelley enjoyed a long and distinguished career as a teacher. (See, Teachers of Attucks.)

Mrs. Kelley married John Eddie Kelley, Sr. on November 25, 1946. She was a member of Olivet Freewill Baptist Church where she served as pianist.

At the time of her death on February 10, 1990, Mrs. Kelley resided on South Wall Street in Carbondale. Family members preceding her in death were a son, five brothers, and two sisters. Survivors included her husband, John Eddie Kelley, Sr.; a daughter, Katie Mae Jackson; a son, John Eddie Kelley, Jr.; a sister, Rosella Thomas; five grandchildren; and two great grandchildren.

Bernard Terry

Bernard Terry was born December 30, 1927 in Carbondale to William Terry of New Madrid, Missouri and Ethel Travis of Madison, Mississippi. The birth was attended by Dr. E. N. Neber.

Booker O'Neal, Jr

Booker O'Neal, Jr. was born January 11, 1928 to Booker O'Neal, Sr., a laborer from Tennessee and Lucy O'Neal, a housewife also from Tennessee.

Charlie Reliford

Charlie Reliford was born January 14, 1928 in Carbondale to the late Ingram and Beatrice Walker Reliford. He was employed by the Union Pacific Railroad as a laborer. He was a member of Hopewell Missionary Baptist Church. Mr. Reliford had three brothers and five sisters, Roger, Phillip, Walter, Elna, Juanita, Geneva, Ruth, and Pearlean. He died at the home of his sister, Mrs. Elna Martin, July 17, 1989.

Charles Reliford

Charles Reliford and his brother, Charlie Reliford, were born January 14, 1928 in Carbondale to Ingram and Beatrice Reliford. He married Constance Williams who preceded him in death.

Mr. Reliford was a United States Air Force Veteran and was also employed as a janitor. Charles Reliford died on July 16, 1987 at John Cochran Veterans Administration Hospital in St. Louis, Missouri. His brother, Charlie Reliford, died two years later on July 17, 1989. His survivors included his son, Charles Reliford, Jr.; two daughters, Sherry Littlejohn and Phyllis Harris; four brothers, Phillip, Charlie, Rodger and Walter; and his five sisters, Elna Martin, Juanita Thomas, Geneva Wise, Ruth Dentman, and Pearlean Gibson. Charles had sixteen grandchildren and one great grandchild.

Anna Belle Carson

Anna Belle Carson was born December 3, 1928 in Carbondale to Eddie B. Carson and Mary Alice Owen Carson, a housekeeper from Mississippi. Mr. Carson, a laborer, was born in Illinois.

Rev. Walter H. Clark

Rev. Walter H. Clark was born in Wilcox County, Alabama on December 25, 1892. He married Ethel Gladden in Alabama and moved to Pennsylvania where he worked as a coal miner. From there they moved to Michigan and then to Freeman Spur, Illinois. Rev. Clark moved his family to Carbondale in 1928.

Rev. Clark served in the United States Army during World War I. In 1927, he began his long and faithful service in the ministry (See Early Black Churches and Spiritual Leadership).

At the time of his death, Reverend Clark was survived by three sisters, Annabelle, Leona, and Bessie; a brother, William; a daughter, Lillian; five sons, Edward, Edsel, Roy, William, and Samuel; twenty-four grandchildren and eight great grandchildren.

James Arthur Valentine, Sr.

James Arthur Valentine, Sr., a long time resident and patriarch of the Valentine family of Carbondale, was born October 25, 1912 in Memphis, Tennessee. He was the son of Columbus and Annie Davis Valentine. He was a resident of Carbondale as eary as 1928. He met and married Ima Mae Sparks on June 15, 1936. The couple were married for more than fifty years and had four children. Mrs. Valentine passed away on January 17, 1987.

Arthur was employed for twenty years by the Illinois Central Railroad. He then worked as a school courier and later as a custodian for the Carbondale Elementary School District. He was an active member of Bethel A.M.E. Church where he was a trustee. He also was a member of the Tuscan Lodge #44 of Carbondale.

Mr. Valentine was a pillar of the black northeast community and was known for his wide smile and willingness to help anyone in need. He died June 26, 1996 at Memorial Hospital in Carbondale. In addition to his wife, Ima, a daughter, Arlene, also died before him.

Surviving members of his family were his son, Arthur, Valentine, Jr.; two daughters, Lovie and Janet; a brother, Columbus; and a sister, Zella Lindegren. He also had ten grandchildren and fifteen great- grandchildren. Mr. Valentine was 83 years old and resided at 417 E. Jackson Street.

Cora Chambers

Cora T. Chambers, a native of Grenada, Mississippi was born February 5, 1902. She was the daughter of Richard and Matilda Graham McCorkle. It is not certain exactly when Cora moved to Carbondale, but she had married James Chambers and had become a resident of the Carbondale Township by 1928. She was known to have two surviving cousins at the time of her death, Cornelia Holmes of Mississippi and Lawrence Brooks of Chicago, Illinois.

Mrs. Chambers belonged to Rockhill Baptist Church and served in the Missionary Society, the Pastor's Aid Society, the Senior Choir, and the Sunday School. Additionally, she was a member of the Ladies' Afternoon Club and was past president of the Rose of Sharon Social Club of Carbondale. Mrs. Chambers died January 3, 1984 at the Carbondale Manor Nursing Home.

Deloma J. Glass

Deloma J. Glass was born in Carbondale January 2, 1929 to Louis Glass of Brighton, Tennessee and Eva Lane Glass, of Covington, Tennessee. The birth was attended by Ella Lacy.

Everlina Anders

Evelina Anders was born in Carbondale January 7, 1929 to Willie Anders, a laborer from Tennessee and Verna Anders, a housekeeper, also of Tennessee.

James C. Woods

James Clifford Woods was born at 9:00 p.m. in Carbondale on March 18, 1929 to James Woods, a twenty-two year old laborer from Illinois and Ludeen Osburn Woods, a nineteen year old housewife and native of Tennessee. The birth was attended by Dr. Lingle.

James received his education training in the Attucks Grade School and Attucks High School. He married Willie B. Porter in 1946.

James was a deacon a the Hopewell Missionary Baptist Church; he also served the church in various other capacities through the years. He was a mild mannered man who was known throughout Carbondale for his winning smile and kind hearted disposition.

Mr. Woods passed away December 4, 1996 at the age of 67. He was the father of two girls, Sandra Woods and Betty Cole, and one son, Robert Woods. At the time of his death, James had seven grandchildren, Capt. Gregory Parran II, Carmen Toney, Dietra Chambers, Antonio Morgan, and Victoria, Destiny, and Charity Woods. He also had five great grandchildren; a sister, Izetta Rogers, and several nieces and nephews.

Mr. Woods had several family members who preceded him in death. These included one son, James Earl Woods; his parents and grandparents; and two brothers.

Sylvester S. R. Steele

Sylvester S. R. Steele was born to Sylvester Steele and L. C. Morse Steele March 18, 1929. The elder Mr. Steele was a forty-five year old native of Union City, Tennessee. He was employed as a general laborer at the tie plant. Mrs. Steele was a thirty-eight year old housewife from Kentucky. She is most recognized as a co-founder of the New Zion Baptist Church in Carbondale.

Homer Murray

Homer Murray was born in Carbondale April 27, 1929 to Randall and Susie Carr Murray, a coal miner and a housewife from Kentucky.

Mary Ellis

Mary Ellis was born in Carbondale June 17, 1929 to C. Willey Ellis, laborer from Tennessee and Alberta Harris Ellis, a housekeeper from Arkansas. Dr. Lingle attended the birth.

Edward E. Chappell

Edward Earl Chappell was born in Carbondale June 22, 1929 to Shelley and Ida Melton Chappell. The birth ws attended by Dr. Brandon.

Robert W. Fletcher

Robert Warren Fletcher was born at 2:30 am in Carbondale July 7, 1929 to Lane Fletcher, a laborer from Grenada, Mississippi and Mary Evans Fletcher, also of Grenada, Mississippi. The birth was attended by Dr. Brandon.

Norvell N. Haynes
"C Junior"

Norvell Nathaniel Haynes, a native of Carbondale, was the youngest of seven children born to Sam and Matilda Brooks Haynes. He was born July 26, 1929.

Known as "C Junior," Norvell became a member of Bethel A.M.E. Church at an early age, and later would become one of Carbondale's strongest black civic leaders (See In Service to Their People: The Black Struggle).

Norvell attended the Attucks Schools and Southern Illinois University at Carbondale. On April 14, 1963, he married Donna C. Basin in Chicago, Illinois. The couple had two children.

Norvell was a retired employee of the U. S. Postal Service, and had worked for the City of Carbondale Model Cities Program. He was an Army veteran of the Korean War.

Mr. Haynes died in the Jefferson Barracks Veterans' Hospital in St. Louis, Missouri after a long illness on November 14, 1990. At the time of his death, surviving family members included his wife, Donna; a son, Steven; a daughter, Earnestine; two brothers, Oscar and Irvin; a sister Lorene; and six grandchildren, Sholony L. Hughlett, Steven N. Haynes, Jr., Lance, Kamilla, Anthony and Danielle Anders.

Vernell E. Robertson
"Tater Bug"

Vernell Edward Robertson, affectionately known as "Tater Bug," was the son of William Edward and Ira Brown Robertson. He was born August 2, 1929 in Carbondale. He attended the Attucks schools.

On September 8, 1946 Vernell married Mary Francis Daniels, the couple had fourteen children. Mary Frances died in 1976. Later, Vernell married Levora Lyas who died on June 16, 1993.

Vernell was employed by the J and L Construction Company in Carbondale where he worked until he retired in 1993. He was nicknamed "Robbie" by his fellow workers. He was a member of Teamsters' Union Local 227 in Carbondale. "Tater Bug" was a member of New Zion Baptist Church.

Vernell died at the age of 66 September 12, 1995. He was a resident of 1201 North Wall Street. He was preceded in death by his son, Spence, and two brothers. Family survivors at the time of his death included five sons and three daughters-in-law, Vernell E. Robertson, Jr., Lavern Robertson, Ardell Robertson, Ronald and Margie Robertson, and Anthony Robertson; eight daughters and four sons-in-law, Brenda Pierce, Marcella and Robert Taylor, Bertha and Victor Kerrens, Francine Robertson, Sharon and Freddie Pullen, Canasta and Reuben Nesbitt, and Sandra Bursey and Lydia Robertson; five brothers and four sisters-in-law, Verzell and Evelyn Robertson, Carl and Pearl Robertson, William and Vernice Robertson, Clarence Robertson, and Joe and Elizabeth Robertson; and three sisters and one brother-in-law, Donna King, Velma Nolan, and Frances and Weldon Simpson. Vernell had fifty-three grandchildren; fifteen great grandchildren.

Francis H. Matthews

Francis Homer Matthews was born in Carbondale August 14, 1929 to Robert and Della Matthews.

John Wesley Thomas

A native of Mounds City, Illinois, John Wesley Thomas was born on September 16, 1903. He was the son of Edward and Cynthia Smith Thomas. At the age of 23, John Wesley married Hattie Viola Boykin in Dewmaine, Illinois. The exact date of his arrival in Carbondale is unknown; however, he and his wife were residents citizen of the city as early as September of 1929. The couple had eight children. His wife, Hattie, died on May 16, 1970.

Mr. Thomas was a member of Bethel A.M.E. Church for more than fifty years, where he served as treasurer of the Sunday School and wherever else he was needed.

Mr. Thomas worked for many years at the Koppers Plant. After retiring from the Koppers Company, he worked at the Illinois State Garage for a period of twelve years.

In addition to his parents, John Wesley was preceded in death by two daughters, one son, one sister, and one brother. Other family survivors at the time of his death were two daughters, Roberta Thomas and Evelyn Jackson; three sons, John, Robert, and James; two sisters, Adelle Hawkins and Edith Henry; two nieces; and a nephew. He twenty grandchildren; twenty-five great grandchildren; and had two great great grandchildren.

John Wesley Thomas was 91 years old when he died on January 13, 1995. He was a long time resident of 420 North Brush Street.

John Wesley Thomas, Jr.

John Wesley Thomas, Jr. was born in Carbondale September 8, 1929 to Wesley Thomas Senior and Hattie Viola Boykin Thomas, both natives of Illinois. The birth was attended by Dr. H. C. Moss.

Walter S. Norman

Walter Sylvester Norman was born September 27, 1929 in Carbondale to Reverend Walter D. and Willie Mae Fisher Norman. He attended the Attucks Grade School and the Attucks High School. He married Delores Brown, the daughter of Nelson and Carrie Elnora Brown Mason, on June 17, 1950 in Murphysboro, Illinois. The couple later settled at 801 North Barnes Street Carbondale.

Walter served for three and one-half years in the United States Marines, attaining the rank of Sergeant. He also worked for eleven years as a mechanic at the State Garage in Carbondale. He and his family were members of Olivet Free Will Baptist Church. He later moved to North Chicago, Illinois where he was self employed. A second move took him to Kenosha, Wisconsin.

Walter was the father of six sons; Walter DeLawrence, Max Earl, Elder John O. Norman, Joseph C., Timothy K., and Barry Stevenson. He had twenty-nine grandchildren and nine great grandchildren. Walter was 65 years old.

Eule Lee Ford

Eule Lee Ford, fondly known as "Big Euke," was born in Carbondale on December 11, 1929. His parents were Robert and Mary Mosley Ford. Eule was a graduate of Attucks High School and a member of New Zion Baptist Church. On September 11, 1957, he married Luella Scott in Murphysboro, Illinois.

For many years, Eule Lee was employed at the Koppers Tie Plant. He also worked at the Jackson Funeral Home under its previous owners, Mr. and Mrs. Frank B. Jackson, and also under its subsequent owner, James H. Walker. Eule Lee was also a United States Army veteran of World War II. In former years, Eule Lee was a member of the Friendly Five singing group in Carbondale.

Mr. Ford was the father of five daughters, Bernadette, Cozette, Joyce, Sandra, and Candice Marie; two sons, Eule Ford, Jr. and Dwaine Lee Ford; a sister, Emma Fletcher; and a brother, Robert. He died September 24, 1993 in Carbondale. He had twenty grandchildren and four great grandchildren.

William LaVoyd Blythe
"Bill"

William LaVoyd Blythe, the son of Albert Arthur and Lucille Echols Blythe, was born May 30, 1920 in LaCenter, Kentucky. He is believed to have settled in Carbondale sometime during the late 1920s and early 30s.

William was a member of Olivet Freewill Baptist Church. He entered military service in 1944 and served until 1946. Bill was a graduate of Attucks High School. Affectionately known by his friends as "Bones," Bill relocated to Chicago where he worked as a licensed barber for many years.

William died May 7, 2000 at the Veteran's Administration Hospital in Philadelphia, Pennsylvania. He was preceded in death by his parents; his stepmother, Eleanor; his sister, Lucille; two brothers, Albert, Jr. and Leon; and his sons, Richard and William, Jr. Included among his many surviving family members are his children, grandchildren, great-grandchildren, nieces and nephews.

Wendell Devers

Wendell Devers was born January 16, 1930 in Carbondale to Fred Devers, a coal miner from Village Springs, Alabama and Viola Pierce Devers, a housewife and native of DewMaine, Illinois. The birth was attended by Dr. Moss.

Joseph H. Nichols

Joseph H. Nichols was born in Carbondale January 20, 1930 to Thomas J. and Nina Keathly Nichols. Joseph graduated from the former Attucks High School where he excelled in basketball under Coach Joseph D. Russell. He received his bachelor's degree from Winston State Teachers College and his master's degree from A&T State College in Greensboro, North Carolina. He married Selena Hemphill in North Carolina.

Joseph was a teacher at the Kimberly Park Intermediate School, where he taught mathematics and physical education.

Joseph Nichols died November 10, 1979 in Winston Salem. His father and a brother died before him. Survivors included his wife Selena; a son, Joseph Jr.; a daughter, Sylvia Rene; his mother, Nina Nichols; three brothers, Thomas, Ted and Lawrence; and three sisters, Marjorie Jackson, Leota Brown, and Claudette Simon.

Lester Alexander

Lester Alexander was born in Carbodale to James and Millie Alexander January 22, 1930. Mr. Alexander was a laborer from Clarendon, Arkansas. Mrs. Alexander was a native of Clarksdale, Mississippi.

Russell Lowell Branch

Russell Lowell Branch, a native of Carbondale, was born in the city on February 6, 1930. He graduated from Attucks High School and later attended Winston-Salem Teachers College and Southern Illinois University at Carbondale.

From 1951 to 1953, Russell served his country as a member of the United States Army. He was a member of Olivet Freewill Baptist Church.

Russell was one of Carbondale's long time Black businessmen. (See Early Black Businesses of Carbondale). On July 19, 1960, Russell married Marilyn Lanton in Murphysboro, Illinois.

Russell died on in Carbondale. His parents and two brothers died before him. At the time of his death, survivors included his wife, Marilyn; three daughters, Sharyl and Denise Branch, and Karla Scott; two sons, Russell Branch, Jr. and Brian Branch; ten grandchildren; and one brother, Billy.

James W. Clark

James Wilson Clark was bonr in Carbondale May 30, 1930 to Rev. Walter H. Clark and Ethel B. Gladden Clark, both natives of Wilcox Co., Alabama. Rev. Clark worked as a miner.

David L. King

David L. King was born September 1, 1907 in Westpoint, Mississippi. On June 9, 1930 in Carbondale, he was married to Dorothy Hamilton. He was an employee of the Illinois Central Railroad for thirty-four years; he retired in October of 1972.

David was a member of Tuscan Lodge No. 44, F.&A.M. in Carbondale; a member of the International Brotherhood of Firemen and Oiler's Union, Local 931 in Carbondale, and a former member of Rock Hill Baptist Church. He was also an Army veteran of World War II.

Traces In The Dust

Top Row: (From left) James C. Woods. Vernell E. Robertson ("Tater Bug"). Walter S. Norman. Center Row: Charles R. Childress. David L. King. James Allen Smith, Sr. Bottom Row: William LaVoyd Blythe. Doris H. Smith. Andrew Smith, Sr.

Mr. King's parents died during his lifetime. He passed away in Carbondale on December 22, 1989 at the age of 82. He was a resident of 901 North Marion Street. He was survived by his wife, Dorothy King; a brother, Irving Smith; two sisters-in law, Daisy Smith and Helen Smith; and two nephews, Alard Hamilton and William Irvin Smith.

Norma Jean Greer

Norma Jean Greer was born to Horace and Truly Collie Greer September 28, 1930. The birth occurred at 7:25 a.m. and was attended by Dr. T. Leon Wallace.

Betty L. Brown

Betty L. Brown, fondly called Betty Lou, by her friends and family was the fourth daughter, and one of thirteen children, born to John and Cecil Branch Brown. She was born in Carbondale November 3, 1930. She attended Attucks Grade School and Attucks High School.

Betty was a choir member of Olivet Freewill Baptist Church and a member of the Willing Workers' Club. She was the mother of two children, Patricia, and David. She also had two brothers and one sister who died during her lifetime. Bette's daughter, Patricia, passed away in 1999.

Being part of one of Carbondale's earliest black families after the turn of the century, Betty's and her three sisters, Frances, Evelyn, and Ferne were all long time city residents, as were four of her brothers, Charles, Harold, Jerry, and Billie Brown. A fifth brother, Ronald Brown, resided in Chicago, Illinois at the time of Bette's death which occurred in Carbondale on August 13, 1989. Bette Lou had nine grandchildren. She was 58 years old.

Donnell Sanford

Donnell Sandord was born in Carbondale December 20, 1930 to Opree Sandord and Charlie Lue Fisher Sanford. Both parents came from Tennessee.

Versa Lou Crim

Versa Lou Crim was born to Alonzo Crim, Jr. and Doddridge Mary Taylor Crim January 20, 1931. Both parents were natives of Illinois. Mr. Crim was a 20 year old student at the Normal University.

Ruben A. Nesbitt

Ruben Adolphus Nesbitt was born in Carbondale to Louis and Beatrice Floyd Nesbitt February 15, 1931. The birth was attended by Dr. Lingle.

Dorothy Mae McBride

Dorothy Mae McBride was born in Carbondale to David and Earlie Mae Shoffner McBride April 4, 1931. Mr. McBride was a porter for the I.C.R.R. Both parents were natives of Ripley, Tennessee. The birth was attended by Dr. Moss.

William Lee Chambers

William Lee Chambers was born to James and Leanna Mason Chambers July 31, 1931. Mr. Chambers was a general laborer and native of Mississippi. Mrs. Chambers was a housekeeper and a native of Tennessee.

Alma Jean Farr

Alma Jean Farr was born to Noah Lee and Irene Mitchell Farr in Carbondale September 4, 1931. Mr. Farr was a general laborer from Tennessee. Mrs. Farr was a housekeeper from Mississippi.

Albert Franklin, Jr.

Albert Franklin, Jr. was born to Albert and Addie Bonner Franklin September 12, 1931. Mr. Franklin, a native of Cherry Valley, Arkansas, was a tie carrier at the tie plant. Mrs. Franklin was a housekeeper from Alabama. The birth was attended by Dr. Moss.

Jesse D. Hayes, Jr.

Jesse Doddridge Hayes, Jr. was born October 3, 1931 in Carbondale to Jesse Senior and Wilma Frances Jackson Hayes. Both parents were teachers from Carbondale. The birth was attended by A. G. Fairfax.

Quinella Anders

Quinella Anders was born December 14, 1931 in Carbondale to Willie and Vina Anders, both natives of Tennessee.

Julia Hogan

Julia Hogan, a native of Newport, Arkansas, was born January 6, 1897. She was the daughter of Emma Runion. She married Ples Hogan on April 22, 1912 in New port, Arkansas. Mr. Hogan died in 1956.

In 1931 Mrs. Hogan moved from the South to Carbondale. She was a loyal member of New Zion Baptist Church where she was a Sunday School teacher and a member of the missionary society. Her son, two daughters, one sister, and one brother, as well as her parents, preceded her in death.

Mrs. Hogan did January 30, 1985 in Memorial Hospital in Carbondale following a lengthy illness. She was 88 years old. Family survivors included her granddaughter, Hortense Edward; a great granddaughter, Agnes Medlin; a great grandson, William Edward, Jr.; and a niece, Elizabeth Runion of Coffieville, Mississippi.

Aaron H. Brinson, Jr.

Aaron Henry Brinson, Jr. was born in Carbondale March 23, 1932 to Aaron Senior, a hotel porter from Mississippi and Justine Thornton, a housewife from Ripley, Tennessee. According to available records examined, Aaron was the first known black baby to be delivered by a black doctor. His birth was attended by Jewell Lee Bass.

James E. Holder

James Emerson Holder, the son of Tom and Elizabeth Scott Holder, was Born September 6, 1907 in West Point, Mississippi. He first married Thelma Isbell in Carbondale. The couple had one child. He later married Ora Katherine Clark on June 24, 1933 in Carbondale. Mrs. Holder died June 17, 1979. Mr. Holder was a deacon at Rock Hill Baptist Church in Carbondale. As a businessman, he owned his own company (See Employment and Early Black Enterprise). James was a member of Tuscan Lodge No. 44, F. & A.M. in Carbondale. Mr. Holder was the father of three daughters and one son, Alice Ann, Margaret, Velma, and Melvin L. Holder, known by family and friends as "Pepper". Mr. Holder died on August 11, 1986 in St. Louis, Missouri. At the time of his death, his family included four grandchildren, nine great-grandchildren, and three great-great grandchildren.

Winona Jackson

Winona Jackson was born March 22, 1934 to Fred and Viola Devers in Carbondale. She attended the public schools in Carbondale and graduated with the Attucks High School class of 1952. On May 23, 1953, Winona was married to James V. Jackson, Jr. They had three children.

Winona was employed by Southern Illinois University for twenty-three years as a Library Clerk III. She was a member of Rock Hill Baptist Church, serving as an usher, a member of the Bible Class, a choir member, and in various other capacities. She was an active community and civic leader. (See In Service To Their People).

Winona's parents, husband, and seven brothers preceded her in death. Among her family survivors were three children Aloysius, Andrea, and James Vance III; two brothers and three sisters, Pearl Denton, Dorice Long, and Wendell, Burnett, and Gloria Dean Devers. She had eleven grandchildren; nine sisters-in-law; five brothers-in-law; and two aunts, Odel Devers and Mary Pierce.

Alfreda Mae Armour

Alfreda Mae Armour, the daughter of Mr. and Mrs. Alfred A. Armour was born in Carbondale January 29, 1935. She was a member of Rock Hill Baptist Church.

Alfreda was 30 years old when she passed away at her home. According to Jackson County Coroner Harry Flynn, she had been ill with a congenital heart disease. Family survivors included three sons, Michael Wayne, Steven Eugene, and Jerrold Lin; her parents; grandparents, Mary Foree and Allen Armour; and a great grandmother, Mrs. Fannie Armour.

George H. Thornton

George H. Thornton was born July 23, 1913 in Hernando Mississippi to Homer and Hattie Ackles Thornton. He was an active member of the Church of Christ of Carbondale and a former member of Gavin King American Legion Post Number 542 of Carbondale.

George was married to Kathleen Perkins on March 21, 1935 in Carbondale and was employed as a foreman in the City of Carbondale Street Department.

Mr. Thornton died January 4, 1984 at his home in Carbondale. He and Mrs. Thornton had two sons, Everett and Wayman, and one daughter Anita. Mr. Thornton was the grandfather of sixteen grandchildren and the great grandfather of two. A brother and a sister were deceased prior to his death.

Ronald M. McKinley

Born in Carbondale on April 5, 1935, Ronald McKinley was the second of three sons born to Enos and Louvenia McKinley. Like his brothers, Ronald was a graduate of Attucks High School, where his father had worked for twenty-seven years in maintenance.

Ronald received a Bachelors of Arts degree from Southern Illinois University and continued his education at Chicago State University, where he earned his Master's degree. After completing his studies in Radiology Technology at Cook County School of Medicine, Ronald was appointed Professor of Health Sciences at Malcolm X College where he remained in that capacity for almost thirty years.

In addition to his academic pursuits, Mr. McKinley was a gifted musician. When he relocated to Chicago, Illinois he became one of the city's leading tenors, performing locally and nationally in recitals, concerts, opera and oratorio. He was the featured soloist in *Saul of Tarsus* and *Requiem* by the late Betty Jackson King.

Ronald was an original member of the Betty Jackson King Artist Group and a charter member of the renowned John Work Chorale. Additionally, he was a member of the Chicago Music Association; an officer of the National Association of Negro Musicians, Inc.; and a member of Alpha Phi Alpha Fraternity.

Ronald McKinley passed away in 1998. His father, Enos, preceded him in death on February 23, 1985. At the time of his death, Ronald's family survivors included his wife, Inez Anderson McKinley; three sons, Michael, Kevin, and Patrick; his two brothers, James and Duane McKinley; his grandchildren, Tiffany, Keith, Duane, Denise, Chantae, Kevin, and Kyle.

Foice L. Devers

Carbondale native, Foice Lillard Devers, was born December 16, 1935 to Fred Gulley and Viola Pierce Devers. In 1958 he married Shirley E. Dicks in Chicago, Illinois. He attended the Attucks School system, graduating from Attucks High School in 1953. He was a member of Rock Hill Baptist Church under the pastorate of Dr. Mingo.

Foice attended Tuskegee Institute at Tuskegee, Alabama and also served in Vietnam in the United States Army. He worked as a public bus driver. He died at the age of 45 July 24, 1981 at Denver General Hospital. Two brothers and two nephews preceded him in death. Upon his death Foice Devers had two surviving sons, Foice Jr. and Eric; a daughter Cheryl Devers; six brothers, Cecil, Bobby, Burnett, Wendell, Howard Penny, and Eugene Jarnigan; four surviving sisters, Gloria, Pearl, Winona, and Dorice. He was the uncle of Brenda Devers Brandon of Chicago, Illinois.

Charles R. Childress

Charles Raymond Childress, the son of Lillian Crabtree and Raymond Childress, was born in Cook County, Illinois November 24, 1913. He received his education in the public schools of Chicago, Illinois and Indianapolis, Indiana.

Charles moved to Carbondale in 1935 while playing with the Logan Collins Jazz band. The band toured throughout the Southern Illinois area. It was a featured attraction at Junior Hatchett's establishment in Colp, Illinois. In 1936, Charles was married to Genora Jackson. He had two siblings, both of whom are deceased.

Ima Mae Sparks Valentine

Ima Mae Sparks Valentine was born December 22, 1917 in Grand Tower, Illinois to Noble L. and Cora Mae Pennick Sparks. She graduated from Grand Tower High School and attended business courses at Southern Illinois University in Carbondale. She married Arthur Valentine in Carbondale on June 15, 1936.

Mrs. Valentine worked at SIU for many years and also for the City of Carbondale in the Model Cities Program. Along with her friend and colleague, Eurma Hayes, Mrs. Valentine devoted a great part of life to improving the conditions of Blacks in Carbondale. (See In Service to Their People.)

Mrs. Valentine was preceded in death by a daughter, five sisters, five brothers, and her parents. She passed away on January 17, 1987 in Carbondale. Survivors of her death included her husband, Arthur; a son, Arthur Valentine, Jr.; daughters, Lovia Henderson and Janet McIntosh; a sister, Vester Sparks; two brothers, Arnold N. and Alonzo E. Sparks; ten grandchildren; and five great grandchildren.

Bobby G. Devers

The twelfth of thirteen children, Bobby Gene Devers was born October 23, 1937 in Carbondale to Fred and Viola Devers. He graduated from Attucks High School in 1956 and worked at the American Steel Company until his illness in 1984. Bobby was baptized in 1950 at Rock Hill Baptist Church in Carbondale. He married Vera Carter in April of 1973.

Bobby passed away on September 28, 1993. He was survived by his wife; five sons, Bobby Jr., Clifford, Vernon, Irvin, and Delmar; two daughters, Donella and Bernice; and seven brothers and sisters, Pearl Denton, Dorice Long, Wendell and Burnett Devers, Eugene Jarnigan, Gloria Dean Devers, and Winona Jackson. He was preceded in death by his parents; and his brothers Ervin Keyes, Howard Penny, and Delmar, Cecil, and Foice Devers.

James Edward and Wilma Laura Patterson Walls

James Edward Walls, Sr. was born on February 16, 1912 in Smithland, Kentucky to Walter and Mabel Hodge Walls. He grew up in Galconda, Illinois with Harrison and Florence Howard. He came to Carbondale in 1937. James was an Army veteran of World War II and a retired foreman from Southern Illinois University. He was married to Wilma Laura Patterson in 1941. He passed away February 11, 1989 in Carbondale.

Born in Duquoin, Illinois March 4, 1921, Wilma Walls was the daughter of Patrick and Isabelle Patterson. She died February 16, 1998 at her residence in Carbondale. Mrs. Walls was preceded in death by her parents; two brothers, Andrew Nelson and Delbert Merrill Patterson; and one sister, Helen Virginia Patterson Dillard.

James and Wilma were the parents of four sons; James Walls, Jr., David, Roderick and Patrick; and two daughters, Janet and Connie. They had fifteen grandchildren; five great-grandchildren; and one great-great grandchild. At his death, James was survived by a sister, Lorraine. Upon her death, Mrs. Walls was also survived by a sister, Dollie Norman Smith, and a brother, Henry P. Patterson. The Walls were members of the Monument of Hope Deliverance Church.

Edward Wills

A native of Earl, Arkansas and the son of Charlie and Mary Biggs Wills, the patriarch of the Wills family of Carbondale, Edward Wills, was born September 18, 1912. He married Pauline Harrington September 17, 1934 in Canalau, Missouri and subsequently moved to Charleston, Missouri.

Edward moved to Carbondale from Charleston in 1937 and was employed at the Koppers Company. He was a member of Bethel A.M.E. Church where he served as a steward.

Active in politics, Mrs. Wills was counted among the black men of Carbondale to advocate the black cause (See, In Service to Their People; The Black Struggle).

Mr. Wills died May 28, 1980 at Barnes Hospital in St. Louis, Missouri. At this time, he was survived by five sons, Clarence, James, Fred, Robert, and Donald; four daughters, Vera, Zelda, Paulette, and Dorothy; two sisters Elsie Cannon and Mary Wills; forty-two grandchildren and fifteen great-grandchildren. Preceding him in death were a son, a daughter, two sisters, and two brothers.

Charles "Bear" Arnette

Charles Evans Arnette, known to his friends as "Bear," was born December 15, 1923 in New Orleans, Louisiana. He was the son of George and Pinkie Lillian Netteville Arnette. The exact date of Charles's arrival in Carbondale is unknown; however, documents suggests he settled in Carbondale in the late 1930s, probably in 1937. He attended the Attucks High School where he was a member of the basketball team in 1943. On June 12, 1946 in Murphysboro, Illinois, he married Ella Marie Brinson of Carbondale, the daughter of Eddie and Lenora Robinson Brinson.

"Bear" completed his career training at the Decatur Barber College, Decatur, Illinois, graduating August 8, 1947 and acquired the ownership of a barbering business in Carbondale (See Black Business and Enterprise).

"Bear" was affiliated with Tuscan Lodge No. 44, Carbondale, and Gavin King American Legion Post No. 542, Carbondale. He was a member of Bethel A.M.E. Church. He passed away on August 13, 1984. Family survivors included his sons Keenan and Charles Arnette, Jr. and three grandchildren.

Jordan Daniels

Jordan Daniels, a native of Tulsa, Oklahoma was born October 12, 1891 to William and Matilda Henderson Daniels. He married Bertha Miller December 24, 1910 in Lonoke, Arkansas. They had twelve children. Mrs. Daniels died on September 4, 1978.

Mr. Daniels was a farmer in his early years in Arkansas. After moving to Carbondale in 1939, he worked for the railroad at the Roundhouse. He was a member of Bethel A.M.E. Church in Carbondale.

Mr. Daniels passed away on January 21, 1985 in Carbondale after a long illness. Among his family survivors were two sons, George and Harold; six daughters Beatrice Reid; Bernice Sutton, Claudia Scott, Everlene Chambers, Ercie Sumner, and Bennie Reynolds; two sisters, Catherine Parks and Charlotte Paxton; forty-two grandchildren; seventy-nine great grandchildren; and three great-great grandchildren.

George Daniels

George Daniels was born February 10, 1919 in Lonake, Arkansas to Jordan and Bertha Miller Daniels. He received his educational training in the public schools of Arkansas. He worked for several years in the Civilian Conservation Corps. He served in World War II and received medals for his service during this period.

Mr. Daniels, along with other members of his family, was an active community worker and a concerned citizen of Carbondale. At the time of his death, Mr. Daniels was a resident of 638 East Searing Street. He was 72 years old.

Bernice Sutton

Bernice Sutton was born to Jordan and Bertha Daniels on October 12, 1923 in Lone Oak, Arkansas. The family later moved to Carbondale in 1939, and Bernice became a member of Bethel A.M.E. Church.

Bernice attended Attucks Community High School in Carbondale. She worked for Southern Illinois University for approximately 20 years.

Bernice married Wayne Sutton in August of 1941. They couple had four children. One infant son and her husband preceded Mrs. Sutton in death. Bernice was known for her pleasant personality and kindness toward others.

She passed away on July 30, 1991 at the home of her daughter, LaBarbara Crowley. In addition to her daughter, Mrs. Sutton was survived by two sons, Lawrence and Daryl Sutton; her sisters, Beatrice Reed, Everlene Chambers, Ercie Sumner, and Bennie Reynolds; and her brother Harold Daniels.

Charles H. Mitchell
"Peachem"

Charles Hamlet Mitchell, Jr., affectionately known as "Peachem," was born to Bertha and Charles "Blue" Mitchell in Fulton, Kentucky January 11, 1940. He was a graduate of Carbondale Community High School and the first African American to sign up for the football team at the school.

Upon graduating from CCHS, "Peachem" entered the United States Army where he served for twenty-three years. He served in the 1st Armored Division, and later he became a supply sergeant. His tours of duty took him to Korea, Vietnam, Germany, and numerous other cities and countries of the world.

Charles was married to Gaye Fitzpatrick. He later married Mary Silas in 1980. He had one daughter, Stephanie Mitchell, and was a member of Bethel A.M.E. Church.

Charles died August 21, 1999. Family survivors included his mother, Bertha Mitchell; his six brothers Dana, Aaron, Tyrone, Earl, Leonard, and Anthony; his daughter, Stephanie, and two grandchildren. Charles was predeceased by his father, "Blue" Mitchell, and one brother, Curtis Mitchell.

William D. Fletcher, Jr.

William Donald Fletcher, the son of William Donald Fletcher, Sr. and Dorothy R. Allen Fletcher, was born in Carbondale April 9, 1940. He graduated from Attucks High School in 1958 and attended Southern Illinois University in Carbondale where he played basketball. He was baptized at Hopewell Baptist Church under the pastorage of Reverend W. H. Clark.

In 1959, Donald entered the Unites States Air Force where he served his country for eight years. He was a MEDIC in the Vietnam Conflict, and for his service, he was honored with several recognitions. Among these were the National Defense Service Award, the Air Force Longevity Service Award, and two Good Conduct medals. After his tour of duty, Donald returned to Chicago and worked at Chicago Alls Company.

Mr. Fletcher died December 23, 1997 in Chicago, Illinois. He had three children, Corey, Erica, and LaToya. A sister, Martha Etta, died earlier during his lifetime. Other family survivors included his mother, Dorothy A. Thomas; his sister, Nancy McDonald; two nieces, Tamara and Leah; and several aunts.

Louis E. Cavitt

Born to the parentage of Louie and Celestine Gibbs Cavitt, Louis Edward Cavitt was born in Carbondale September 14, 1940. Mr. Cavitt attended Attucks High School and received his diploma from the American High School In Germany. He worked as a chef for Southern Illinois University in Carbondale and the Marriott Motel in Dallas, Texas. He also worked as an Admitting Officer at the Veterans' Administration Admitting Office in Marion, Illinois. He was a member of Olivet Free Will Baptist Church.

Louis was an Army veteran of the Vietnam War and was awarded the Bronze Star Medal for meritorious service against the enemy. Louis died February 19, 1992 in Irving, Texas. His grandmothers and two grandfathers preceded him in death. Among the relatives surviving Mr. Cavitt's death were his parents; Louie and Celestine Cavitt; six aunts, Edna Mann, Cora Gibbs, Beatrice Cavitt, Louberta Cavitt, Anita Gibbs, and Jean Helen Gibbs; three uncles, U. L. Hudson, Jimmy Cavitt, and Harrison Gibbs; and a devoted cousin, Rodney Cavitt.

Nathaniel Smith

Nathaniel Smith, the son of Arthur and Mattie Lewis Smith, was born in West Point, Mississippi January 14, 1912. He moved to Carbondale in the early 1940s. He worked as a construction laborer of Local Union 227. He was also a veteran of World War II.

Nathaniel had a sister and a brother who died before him. Survivors of his death were a son, Michael Armour; two sisters, Mable Boyd and Erma Lee Carr; a brother, Raymond Smith; and two grandchildren. Nathaniel died October 2, 1984 at his residence at 404D South Marion Street in Carbondale. He was 72 years old.

Rev. U. P. Penn

The seventh child of twelve children, Rev. U. P. Penn was born to Charles Robert Penn and Mattie Fowler Penn in Mounds City, Illinois on April 12, 1905. He came to Carbondale in 1940 and joined Bethel A.M.E. Church.

U. P. first married Jewell Thompson, and later he was married to Alee Crook. He was married to Millicent Welch on April 12, 1976 in Edwardsville, Illinois.

Rev. Penn was an active community leader in Carbondale, always following his often quoted motto, "I'm going to work until my day is done." (See In Service To Their People).

Rev. Penn worked for the Illinois State Highway Department and was a former mail contractor. He formerly was pastor at the White Chapel A.M.E. Church.

Rev. Penn had his parents, six sisters, and four brothers to precede him in death. He died on December 1, 1991 in Carbondale. Surviving family members included his wife, Millicent Penn; three daughters, Dorothy Douglas; Jean Penn, and Jacqueline Hamilton; two sons, Robert and David Chambers; one sister, Sylvia Haynes; one brother, Jasper Penn; a son-in-law, Dwayne Hamilton; a daughter-in-law, Angie Chambers; and seven grandchildren.

Marlee Wooley

Long time resident of Carbondale, Mr. Marlee Wooley, was born July 5, 1926 in Brent, Alabama. He was the son of Raymond and Mattie Duff Wooley. Marlee moved from Brent, Alabama, to Murphysboro, Illinois where he married Francis Louis. As early as 1940, he was attending the Attucks grade school.

Mr. Wooley worked fifteen years for the Illinois Central Railroad, the Missouri Pacific Railroad, and the G. M. & O. Railroad. He was also a World War II Navy Veteran attaining the rank of Seaman 2nd Class. He was last employed at Southern Illinois University at Carbondale where he spent twenty years in maintenance.

Mr. Wooley residence was located at 313 East Chestnut Street in Carbondale at the time of his death on July 29, 1999. He was 73. He had fifteen children.

Aaron Brooks, Sr.

Born to the parentage of Reverend Moses and Minnie McDonald Brooks, Sr., Aaron Brooks, Sr., was born May 3, 1927 in Levings, Illinois. He settled in Carbondale in 1944.

A veteran of World War II, Mr. Brooks was formerly employed at the Veterans Administration Hospital in Battle Creek Michigan and worked for the Missouri Pacific Railroad. He was last employed at the Student Center at Southern Illinois University at Carbondale. Aaron was a member of New Zion Baptist Church.

Mr. Brooks lost his father, two sisters, and two brothers during his lifetime. He was survived by a son, Aaron, Jr.; his mother, Minnie McDonald Brooks; six sisters, Florence M. Harris, Minnie Hall, Rose Speller, Edna Mason, Shirley Cooper, and Mildred Hunter; three brothers, Moses Brooks, Jr. and Joseph and Robert J. Brooks; one granddaughter, Cilina Marie Brooks; and several nieces and nephews.

Mr. Brooks, Sr. died July 9, 1983 in the Veterans Administration Medical Center in Marion, Illinois.

African American Residents In Carbondale, 1900-1964

Top Left: Minnie B. Brooks Hall. Top Right: Julia Hogan. Bottom Left: Bernice Sutton. Bottom Right: Bobby Gene Devers.

Traces In The Dust

Estelle D. France Chappell
"Aunt Rich"

Estelle Doretha France Chappell, was born on August 29, 1929 in Roanoke, Virginia, the second daughter of James Abe and Luvenia France. She came to Carbondale with her family in August of 1941. She completed her education in the Attucks public schools and graduated with honors in the class of 1946. She received a Bachelor of Science degree from Southern Illinois University at Carbondale. Estelle was working toward a master's degree when she was stricken with bad health.

"Aunt Rich," as she was affectionately known to her nieces and nephews, was active in many civic and community organizations in Carbondale. For a number of years, she headed a local day care program (See In Service To Their People). She also worked for the Carbondale Public School system and at SIU. She was an active member of Rock Hill Baptist Church.

Estelle married William Chappell in 1947 in Murphysboro, Illinois, and four children were born to them. In 1982, she eventually returned to Roanoke where she remained with her daughter, Hazel Chappell Law, and sister, Ernell France Glasby, until her death on August 5, 1982. Among Mrs. Chappell's many survivors were her mother, Luvenia M. France; her stepmother, Mrs. Madeline A. France; her three daughters and son, Hazel Jane Law, Iva Lynette Ewing, Patricia Jean Hubbard, and Arthur Alexander Chappell; four sisters, Ernell Glasby, Vivian West, Virginia Mae Lane, and Phyllis France; four brothers, James, George, Jeffrey, and Michael France; a son-in-law, Frank Ewing; and a daughter-in-law, Fern Chappell. At the time of her death, Mrs. Chappell had seven grandchildren.

James Abe France

Mr. James Abe France was the son of William France of North Carolina. He was the grandson of Moses Hatcher, a white slave owner, and Judy France, a Black slave. His father, William, was married three times and had twenty children. Abe France was one of nine children from the first marriage.

James Abe was born in St. Louis, Missouri April 23, 1898. He settled in Carbondale in August of 1941 after living in Roanoke, Virginia. He was first married to Louvenia Martin of Roanoke in December of 1923. He later married Madelene Allen and settled with his family at 308 East Chestnut Street in Carbondale.

Mr. France was the father of ten children, James, Ernell, Vivian, Estelle, Virginia Mae, George, Jeffrie, Michael, Wilma and Phyllis. He worked as a porter for the Illinois Central Railroad, and he was a barber. He was employed for a number of years at the Halstead Barber Shop on Halstead Street in Chicago. Mr. France died May 4, 1973. He was survived by his wife, Madelene; his daughters, Ernell France Green, Vivian West, Estelle Chappell, Virginia Mae Lane, and Phyllis France; his sons, James Arthur France, George "Buck" France, Jeffrey France, and Michael France. James was predeceased by his daughter Wilma France Dixon, who passed away June 1, 1970.

James Arthur France

James Arthur France was born December 24, 1924 in Roanoke, Virginia, the oldest son of James Abe and Luvenia Martin France. James was educated in the schools of Roanoke and Carbondale. He arrived in Carbondale with his father and siblings in August of 1941. He attended the Attucks School system and graduated from Attucks High School in 1943.

James subsequently made his home in Philadelphia, Pennsylvania. James married Mary Louise Tilley on December 12, 1953. He and Mary had two children, Reggie and Michele. James entered the United States Marines and also served in the Marine Reserves. He retired from the Reserves as a Master Sergeant in December of 1985.

James pursued a second career in law enforcement following his distinguished tour of active military duty. He spent twenty years in the Philadelphia Police Department as a Detective. Prior to his retirement, he received numerous recognitions for service rendered to the department. He was a co-founder of the Montford Point Marine Association and held memberships in several civic and professional organizations including Toastmasters, the Fraternal Order of Police, Men of the Sea, and the Compliance Officers of the Department of Labor.

James died July 30, 1994 in Philadelphia. He was survived by many family members who included his wife, May; his son and daughter, Reginal and Michele France; four sisters, Ernell, Vivian, Virginia Mae, and Phyllis; and three brothers, George, Jeffrey, and Michael France. James was predeceased by his mother, Luvenia France; his father and stepmother, James Abe and Madelene France; and two sisters, Estelle France Chappell and Wilma France Dixon.

Madelene France

Madelene France was born October 7, 1914 in the community of Thompsonville, Illinois to the parentage of Henry and Matilda Stewart Allen. She attended the Pleasant Grove School of Corinth Township, Illinois. She met James Abe France in Roanoke, Virginia. They later married in Marion, Illinois. The Frances settled in Carbondale in August of 1941. Four children were born to them, Jeffrie, Wilma, Wilma, and Phyllis.

Mrs. France was a homemaker. Later in life, she was employed as a cashier for the Church Women United Thrift Shop of Carbondale. Her church affiliation was with Bethel African Methodist Episcopal Church. At Bethel she was a member of the Rose of Sharon and the Lilly of the Valley clubs. In 1983 the church presented her with a Valuable Service Award for her dedication and support. Mrs. France was also a member of the Duchess Club of Carbondale.

Mrs. France died October 14, 1985 in Carbondale. She was a resident of 811 North Washington Street. Among Mrs. Frances many surviving family members were her two sons, Jeffrie Lynn and Michael Wayne France; her daughter, Phyllis France; two stepsons, James Arthur and George France; three stepdaughters, Ernell Glasby, Vivian West, and Virginia Mae Lane; five brothers, Charlie, Walter, James Bowman, and Roy Allen and Carl Jones; and two sisters, Nellie Mae Powell and Grace Edwards. Survivors also included Mrs. France's seventeen grandchildren (and step grandchildren) and nine step great grandchildren.

Mrs. France was preceded in death by her husband, her parents, her daughter, Wilma France Dixon, four brothers, two sisters, and one stepdaughter, Estelle France Chappell.

Estella Kelley Parker

Born the second daughter of five children, Estella Kelley Parker was born in Torrence, Mississippi on December 26, 1915 to Ed and May Belle Kelley.

Moving to Carbondale in 1941 from Coffeeville, Mississippi, she joined the New Zion Baptist Church where she served as a member of the Young Adult Choir, a Sunday School teacher, and a participant in the Baptist Training Union.

At the time of her death, she had two daughters, Loretta K. Harris and Edna E. Kelley; two brothers, John E. and William Kelley; three grandchildren, Sheila, Melanie, and Troy; an uncle, Daniel Kelley; seven great grandchildren; eight nieces; and six nephews, in addition to many other relatives. Mrs. Parker's funeral services were held on April 23, 1990.

Wayne Sutton

Wayne Sutton was born on June 1, 1920 in Brownfield, Illinois. He moved to Carbondale as a young child and resided with his grandparents, Galveston and Leah Perkins, He was a member of Olivet Freewill Baptist Church when it was located on Illinois Avenue in Carbondale.

In 1941 Wayne was married to Bernice Daniels, and they had four children, one of whom was deceased as an infant.

Mr. Sutton was a veteran of World War II, and he was employed for thirty-four years at Southern Illinois University. He retired in 1983.

Mr. Sutton died July 14, 1987 at Memorial Hospital in Carbondale. Among his family survivors were his wife, Bernice Sutton; a daughter LaBarbara Crawley; two sons, Lawrence and Darryl; and two grandsons, Kevin and Justin.

Minnie E. Hinton

Minnie Etta Hinton, a native of Clarksdale, Mississippi was born September 4, 1923, the daughter of Henry and Hattie Adams Hogan. She attended the Attucks school system, graduating from Attucks High School in 1941. She continued her education at Southern Illinois University in Carbondale. Minnie married Lloyd Hinton in Carbondale February 15, 1945. She was a member of Bethel A.M.E. Church for many years. For thirty-eight years, Mrs. Hinton was employed at the Physical Plant at SIU-Carbondale. She retired in 1990.

She was an active member of various organizations and played key roles in several of these. She was a former member of Semper Fidelis; Past Matron of Mariam Chapter #17, O.E.S.; Past Deputy of Area VI, O.E.S.; Past Loyal Lady Ruler, Hiram Assembly #54; Past State Grand Loyal Lady Ruler; a Deputy of Oasis, Daughters of Isis.

At the time of her death on November 7, 1992, a son, Lloyd Hinton, Jr. and three grandchildren were among her family survivors. Mrs. Hinton died at her home at 317 East Oak Street in Carbondale. Eleven sisters preceded her in death.

Ora Lee Jacobs

Ora Lee Jacobs was the daughter of Zechariah and Samella Branch Cawthon. She was born December 20, 1897 in Dyersburg, Tennessee. Ora moved from Dyersburg and settled in Carbondale in 1942. She married Tommy Jacobs in 1947; he died in 1962. Mrs. Jacobs was a member of New Zion Baptist Church and the owner of a family business (See Early Black Businesses).

Ora Jacobs, a mild and pleasant woman, was the mother of two sons who had died earlier. Also three sisters preceded her in death. Mrs. Jacob's death occurred on August 2, 1982 in Carbondale. Her family survivors included a son, Leroy Ridley; two brothers, Rev. R. C. Cawthon and Leroy Cawthon; two grandchildren; a sister-in-law, Lillian Cawthon; one great-grandchild; and five great-great grandchildren.

Willie Mae Day Lilly Thomas
"Aunt Duck"

Willie Mae Day Lilly Thomas was a long time resident of 1201 North Robert Stalls Street, (formerly Barnes Street) in Carbondale. She was the daughter, and one of ten children, born to Willard and Beatrice Lewis Day. She was born June 20, 1924 in Colp, Illinois. She moved to Carbondale about 1942. She was formerly married to Willie Dee Lilly in the early 1940s and later married Lee Thomas, Jr. in 1978.

"Aunt Duck, " as Willie Mae was fondly called by family and friends, joined Olivet Freewill Baptist Church under the pastorate of Reverend Loyd Sumner. She was formerly employed at Southern Illinois University in Carbondale. Later, she was employed by the Consolidation Coal Company where she worked until she retired. Willie Mae died May 9, 1999. She was the mother to four stepchildren, Mike Lilly, Brenda Gibbs, and Eric and Pamela Green.

Earl Alexander, Jr.

Earl Alexander, Jr., the son of Earl and Nettie Alexander, Sr., was born November 3, 1944 in Carbondale. He attended the Attucks School system and graduated from Attucks High School with the Class of '63. In high school, he was one of the many star basketball players of the Attucks Bluebirds. He was a former member of Hopewell Baptist Church.

Earl passed away July 18, 1991 in the UCLA Medical Center in Carson City, California. He was preceded in death by his father. Earl's family survivors included his mother, Nettie Alexander; two brothers, James and Charles; three sisters, Betty Foree, Margaret Passmore, and Donna Alexander; a sister-in-law, Alberta Alexander; three uncles, Willie D. Campbell, and William and Mervin Alexander; and several nieces and nephews.

Hardin A. Davis

Hardin Allen Davis, the son of Louella Davis was born in Carbondale on December 9, 1944. He met Ida Pattin of Blue Heaven, Missouri after she arrived at Southern Illinois University in 1966. The two were married November 19, 1967 at Ward Chappell A.M.E. Church in Cairo, Illinois. The couple first settled across the street from the Davis family homestead at 307 E. Green Street.

Mr. Davis, attended the Attucks school system and--following in the footsteps of his mother--devoted his life to the education of generations of Carbondale's children. He is the second graduate of the Attucks institution who became a principal in the public schools of Carbondale (See In Service To Their People).

Hardin and Ida are the parents of two girls, Christy Ann Davis and Michele Denyce Davis. They currently reside in Carbondale.

Michael W. France

Michael Wayne France was born November 26, 1944 in Carbondale, the son of James Abe and Madelene Allen France. Michael had a special flair for life, preferring the "do it my way" approach. This tenacious yen for independence earned him the nickname "The High Plains Drifter."

"Uncle Mike," as he was called, worked for many years in the construction industry, working first on projects for the early Model Cities Program in Carbondale and in later years as an independent contractor.

In his high school years at Attucks, Michael was an active participant in sports and especially enjoyed playing on the Bluebirds basketball team.

Michael graduated from Southern Illinois University in Carbondale and taught for a while at the City Colleges of Chicago at the Dawson Skill Center. He spent several years working on a book relating the history of Afro-Americans in Southern Illinois which he desired to have published. However, Michael was beset with illness before this dream could be fulfilled; he died on March 16, 1999.

Michael had one daughter, Danielle Monique Henry. His parents, two sisters, Wilma Jean France Dixon and Estelle Doretha Chappell, along with his brother, James A. France, preceded Michael in death. In addition to his daughter, among Michael's surviving family members were two brothers, George A. and Jeffery France; four sisters, Mrs. Ernell F. Glasby, Vivian West, Virginia F. Lane, and Phyllis France as well as several nieces and nephews.

Beverly Gween Wise

Beverly Gween Wise, the daughter of Arthur Louis Morgan, Sr. and Jessie Mae Williams Morgan, was born May 9, 1957 in Ripley, Tennessee. She received an Associate Degree in Marketing from John A. Logan College. She was a transcription secretary in the School of Medicine at Southern Illinois University. She also worked in the School of Social Work at SIU.

Beverly married Bryan Wise on August 22, 1987. She was a member of Faith Temple Church of God in Christ in Carbondale. She died March 6, 1991.

Beverly Gween Wise

Moses Brooks, Jr.

Moses Brooks, Jr. was born May 10, 1925 in Charleston, Missouri to Rev. Moses Brooks, Sr. and Minnie McDonald Brooks. Mr. Brooks married Rosetta Scott Jefferson on July 17, 1968 in Carbondale.

Moses was employed as a custodian at Southern Illinois University until he was stricken with illness. He died on July 1, 1990 at the Jackson County Nursing Home in Murphysboro, Illinois. His father, two sisters, and three brothers preceded him in death.

Among Moses's surviving family members were his wife, Rosetta; three sons, Moses Brooks III, Derek Brown, and Eddie Irby; a daughter, Patricia Brown; his mother, Minnie Brooks; six sisters, Florence Harris, Minnie Hall, Rosie Speller, Edna Mason, Shirley Cooper, and Estella Hunter. He was also survived by two brothers, Joseph and Robert Brooks; and five grandchildren. Mr. Brooks resided at 505 North Washington Street.

Lucius Cooper

Lucius Cooper, "Uncle Buddy," was a native of Yellow Bush County in Mississippi. He was born March 28, 1906 to Robert and Hannah Cooper Booker. He attended Pleasant Grove Public School in Mississippi. "Uncle Buddy" settled in Carbondale in 1944.

Mr. Cooper was a former employee of the Missouri-Pacific Railroad Company. He retired after twenty-five years of service. He married Laura Mae Kelley in Torrence, Mississippi. Mrs. Cooper died in 1956. Mr. Cooper died September 2, 1987. He resided at 422 East Willow Street.

Linda Marie Moore Woods

Linda Marie Moore Woods was born in Carbondale April 13, 1946 to Iray and Finas Williams. She attended Attucks High School from 1960 to 1964. She served in the United States Army from 1964 to 1966.

In 1967 she entered Southern Illinois University at Carbondale continuing through 1969. She then entered Warsham college of Mortuary Science in Chicago, attending the institution from 1974 to 1976. Linda owned and operated Arnold A. Woods Memorial Funeral Services in Chicago, Ill.

Linda was formerly married to Levon Porter. She was later united in marriage to Reverend David Moore and had a son, Jonathan David Moore. She was a member of Olivet Freewill Baptist Church in Carbondale and later united with Evening Star Baptist Church in Chicago where she was Superintendent of Sunday School, Trustee and Financial Secretary.

Mrs. Woods was preceded in death by her father Arnold A. Woods, Sr. She died on May 17, 1995. She was survived by many family members including her mother, Iray Williams Woods Tisdale; her son, Jonathan; her stepfather Frederick Douglas Tisdale; her seven brothers Arnold Woods, Jr., Kendall, Bradford, and Donnell Woods, Frank and Vernon Williams, and Finas Williams, Jr.; five sisters Raydeane Woods, and Shirley, Laverne, Francis, and Virginia Williams; three aunts and two uncles.

John Eddie Kelley

John Eddie Kelley was born June 17, 1917 In Bryant, Mississippi to Ed and May Bell Wilson Kelley. May Bell died when John Eddie was a young child. Ed Kelley later married Myrtle Ingram Kelley who raised John Eddie and his siblings.

John Eddie attended school in Coffeville, Mississippi. He moved to Carbondale in 1946 and joined New Zion Baptist Church where he served on the Usher Board for a number of years. He married Grace Perkins Kelley November 29, 1946. Mrs. Kelley preceded him in death.

Mr. Kelley worked for the Mssouri-Pacific Railroad as a trackman for thirty years and retired in June of 1980. He worked an additional twelve years at the Wall Street Car Wash. He also served in the United States Navy from 1943 to 1946.

Mr. Kelley died March 19, 2000 at his home in Carbondale. He was survived by his son, John Eddie Kelley, Jr.; three daughters, Barbara Jean Byox, Katie Mae Jackson and Brenda Greer; nine grandchildren; four great grandchildren; nine nieces; two nephews; and many cousins and other relatives. In addition to his wife, Mr.

Kelley's parents, step-mother, two sisters, and two brothers also preceded him in death.

Larry E. and Wilma McDaniel, Sr.

Larry E. McDaniel, Sr. was born June 13, 1947 in Carbondale to Mr. and Mrs. Lloyd McDaniel. He attended Attucks Grade School and Attucks High School.

Larry served in the United States Army for over four years, and he has worked twenty years for Southern Illinois University where he is an assistant supervisor in the Central Receiving Department.

Wilma McDaniel was born October 31, 1948 in Carbondale. She is the granddaughter of Minnie Brooks. She grew up in Carbondale and attended the Attucks school system where she was a Cheerleader in both the junior high and the high schools. She was also a basketball Sweetheart Queen, a member of the Future Homemakers of America, and a participant in the drama club. She played clarinet in the Attucks school band.

Wilma completed her education at Carbondale Community High School, and attended cooking school for two years. She has been employed at SIU for twenty-three years in the food service department as head cook. She is a member of Bethel A.M.E. Church where she serves on the Usher Board. She has four sisters and three brothers.

Larry and Wilma are the parents of three girls and two boys. They also have nine children.

Edward Fletcher, Jr.

Edward Fletcher, Jr. was born in Carbondale December 21, 1947 to Edward, Sr. and Emma Ford Fletcher. He attended Attucks Grade School and Graduated from Carbondale Community High School. He was a member of Bethel A.M.E. Church.

Eddie married Carolyn Patterson in 1983 in Murphysboro, Illinois. He worked as an employee of the Jackson County Housing Authority and also as an independent carpenter and laborer.

Eddie, as he was affectionately called, served in the navy from 1966 to 1968. He received the National Defense Service Medal, the Vietnam Service Bronze Star, and the Vietnam Campaign Medal.

Eddie died October 30, 1983 at age 35. He had one son, Edward III, and one daughter, Yolonda. He was the nephew of three aunts, Cora Gibbs, Luella Ford, and Arminta Fletcher and five uncles, Jewel Gibbs, Eule Ford, Robert Ford, Claude Fletcher, and Lane Fletcher.

Minnie B. Brooks Hall

Minnie B. Brooks Hall settled in Carbondale in 1947 with her family and husband, Ira Hall, whom she married in 1938 in Villa Ridge. Illinois. Born in Marianna, Arkansas on April 12, 1921, she was the daughter of Rev. Moses Brooks, Sr. and Minie McDonald Brooks.

Mrs. Brooks was employed as a housekeeper at the old Franklin Hotel in Carbondale. She worked for the E. W. Vogler family for thirty-five years and for the Harriet Day family for twenty-six years. Minnie and Ira had five children. Her husband passed away in 1960. Minnie was an active member of New Zion Baptist Church. There, she held an active leadership role including serving as a teacher in the Baptist Training Union and as a member of the church's choir.

Mrs. Hall died at her home at 507 East birch Street on September 7, 1997. Among her surviving family members were two sons; Alfred and Alphonso Hall; five sisters, Florence, Shirley, Edna, Vernice and Idella; two brothers, Joseph and John; fourteen grandchildren; and thirteen great-grandchildren. A son, two daughters, three brothers, and three sisters were deceased prior to Mrs. Hall's death.

Charles E. Hall

Charles Edward Hall was the son of Ira and Minnie Brooks Hall. He was born January 5, 1939 in Mounds, Illinois and moved to Carbondale with his family in 1947. He attended the Attucks schools and completed his secondary education and training in the United States Navy, where he served from 1956 to 1962.

Charles worshipped at New Zion Baptist Church and was baptized during the pastorage of Rev. W. H. Clark. He first married Ruth Combs in 1958 in Carbondale. They had five children. He later married Alva Lois Wilkins in Battle Creek, Michigan. They had two children.

Charles was formerly employed as a truck driver by the Raymond Jones Construction Company in Harisburg, Illinois and was a member of the International Brotherhood of Teamsters, Local No. 347. He was also a former empoyee of Southern Illinois University-Carbondale.

Charles was the father of four daughters and three sons, Roxanne Charlotte, Sharon, Patina Mae, Darryl Wayne, Douglass and Earl Quincy. He had two sisters and two brothers, Frances, Florence, Alfred, and Alphonso. He was the grandson of Minnie Brooks of Carbondale.

Frances Hall Sanders

Frances Hall Sanders, the daughter of Ira and Minnie Brooks Hall, was born June 30, 1940 in Mounds, Illinois.

She arrived in Carbondale with her family in 1947. She attended the Attucks Schools, graduating from Attucks High School in 1958. She subsequently attended John A. Logan College and Southern Illinois University in Carbondale.

Frances was a member of New Zion Baptist Church, joining the congregation under the pastorage of Rev. W. H. Clark. She married John I. Willis in Battle Creek, Michigan. She later married William Locke and was last married to Robert Sanders on April 2, 1981 in Murphysboro, Illinois.

Frances was formerly employed as a secretary at the Southern Illinois University Morris Library. She also worked for Tuck Industries, Inc. and the General Telephone Company. She was a receptionist for the Carbondale School District 95. She was a member of the Carbondale branch of the N.A.A.C.P.

Mrs. Sanders passed away on March 24, 1985 in Carbondale. She lost her father and a brother during her lifetime. She was survived by her husband, Robert; a daughter, Elizabeth K. Willis; her mother, Minnie Hall; a sister, Florence Evelyn Blythe; two brothers, Alfred and Alphonso Hall; and a granddaughter, Jasmine Rudder.

Florence Hall Blythe

Florence E. Hall Blythe was born in Mounds, Illinois June 4, 1942. She was the daughter of Ira and Minnie Brooks Hall. Florence was a graduate of Attucks High School with the Class of 1962; she, along with her family, was a member of New Zion Baptist Church.

She held a secretary position at SIU and was employed as a proof reader for the Southern Illinoisan. She was also a former employee at Tuck Industries, Inc. She died in Carbondale on December 28, 1985.

Robert Cole, Jr.

Robert "Bubba" Cole, Jr. was born August 12, 1929 in Ripley, Mississippi to Robert, Sr. and Natalie Vernor Cole. He moved to Carbondale in 1948 where he worked for the City of Carbondale in the Sanitation Department. He belonged to Laborers' Local No. 347.
Robert was a member of Rockhill Baptist Church.

Mr. Cole married Betty Woods in 1970 in Pinckneyville, Illinois. He was the father of three daughters and seven sons, Carmen, Diedra, Michelle, Anthony Lewis, Lamont, William, Gregory, Michael, Anthony, and Darryl.

Robert Cole died May 28, 1990 at the age of 60. He resided at 1204 North Barnes Street.

Jewel Lane Gibbs
"Huckie"

Jewel Lane Gibbs, known to his family and friends as "Huckie," was the son of Jewel Eugene and Cora Fletcher Gibbs. He was born May 5, 1949 in Carbondale. He received his educational training in the Attucks school system.

While in high school, "Huckie" worked after school at the former Ben Franklin Store in Carbondale, his first job. He later worked in maintenance at the former Holden Hospital. He also worked at the Memorial Hospital and Styrest Nursing Home in Carbondale.

"Huckie" was a member of Olivet Freewill Baptist Church and a resident of East Fisher Street.

Jewel passed away on September 9, 1993 in Carbondale. His father and grandparents died before him. Jewel's survivors included his two daughters, Gloria and Kimberly; a son, Jewel Lane, Jr.; his mother, Cora Gibbs; two sisters, Mary Alice Gibbs and Connie Gibbs; and several aunts and uncles. "Huckie" was 44 years old.

Frank and Mary Liza Shird

Frank Shird was the son of Dane Shird and Mari Magie of Jackson, Tennessee. He was born in Little Rock, Arkansas in Cross County February 1, 1873. His wife, Mary Liza Lilly was born in Pulaski, Illinois Arpil 25, 1911. She was the daughter Charles F. Lilly, Sr. and Rosie Thompson.

Frank and Mary were married in Pulaski on September 5, 1932 and Mary settled in Carbondale in 1949. The Shird family had homes on East Willow Street and at 503 E. Birch Street. Mary and Frank had eight children: Mayetta, Loretta, Frankie Susie, Wesley, Martha Ella, Ellena Ann, Naomi Marie, and Doris Jean Moore, all of whom, except for Doris resided in Carbondale.

Mr. Shird was employed in Pulaski for the W.P.A. Company. Mary Shird attended Bannaker School District 10 in Pulaski and graduated from the 8th grade in 1928. Mrs. Shird remained at home as a homemaker. The couple attended the St. John Baptist Church of Pulaski from 1911 until 1949 when Mary relocated to Carbondale. Upon arriving in Carbondale, the Shirds united with the New Zion Baptist Church where they retained their membership until well into the 1960s.

Mary Liza Lilly's second marriage was to Henry Armstead, the son of Madora Bodnocke Hudson and Joseph Hudson. He was born May 15, 1892 in Greenwood, Mississippi. Seven daughters and a son were born to them: Madora, Esther Lee, Shirley Alice, Pamela Joyce, Carolyn Marie, Malinda Kay, Connie Derrand, and

Henry Raymond Armstead, Jr.

Historical records indicate that the Armstead family is most likely Carbondale's oldest African American family. Sam Armstead, a 30 year old day laborer from Alabama, was residing in Carbondale in 1870. Shelton Armstead (believed to be a cousin) was a 35 year old farmer from Tennessee. He also had arrived in Jackson County by 1870; he settled in Murphysboro.

Henry Armstead died March 19, 1981 in Milwaukee, Wisconsin. He had a brother named Lewis Armstead who resided in Carbondale. Lewis died in Carbondale about the year 1966. Frank Shird passed away October 5, 1939 in Pulaski, Illinois. Mary Lilly Armstead died October 6, 1987 in Peoria, Illinois.

Robert L. Cavitt, Jr.

Robert Lewis Cavitt, Jr. was born to Ethel Lee Moore Cavitt and Robert Cavitt, Sr. April 30, 1950 in Carbondale. He was employed as a correctional officer for the State of Illinois Prison System for fifteen years and was a member of the American Federation of State and County Employee's Union. Robert was married to Rita Anderson on June 7, 1970. He was a member of Hopewell Baptist Church.

Mr. Cavitt, who resided at 200 East Larch Street, died August 19, 1991. He had two sons, Dana R. and Reginald L. Cavitt. In addition to his wife and sons, he was survived by his father, Robert Cavitt Sr.; his mother, Ethel Lee Rockett; a sister, Sherry Ann Norman; three brothers, Bobby and Ruben Cavitt, and Aaron Dooley; and his grandmother, Daisy Koonce.

Judy Ann McKinley

Judy Ann McKinley, the daughter of Augustus, Sr. and Lena Mckinley, was born December 14, 1950 in Carbondale, Illinois. She attended Thomas Grade School and Lincoln Junior High School. At the time of her death, she had two aunts living in Carbondale, Mrs. Louberta Cavitt and Mrs. Louvenia McKinley. Judy Ann died June 18, 1999 in Anna, Illinois.

Henry Lee Carter

Henry Lee Carter was born in Cruger, Mississippi February 12, 1945. He is the great grandson of Lee Andrew Ollie, who was a slave. Henry's grandfather, Henry Ollie, was a share cropper on the Egypt plantation which was purchased in 1834 by the city of Cruger, Mississippi when Henry Carter was born. Henry's birth occurred on the plantation where his mother, Lizzie Mae Ollie Carter, worked from dawn to dusk picking cotton to help her father feed his family.

Henry moved to Carbondale in 1950 and attended the Attucks school system. He graduated with the Senior Class of 1963. He was an avid sports player and was widely recognized as one of Attucks's most talented basketball players of the sixties. At the State Track and Field Competitions in Champaign, Illinois, Henry was the 1st black in Southern Illinois of the time to break the two minute half mile (880 yards).

Henry participated actively in the civic and community affairs of Carbondale and held memberships in several African American organizations.

Delmar G. A. Hoyt

Delmar George Albert Hoyt arrived in Carbondale in 1950. He was born October 26, 1919 in Bakersfield, California to George Sherman and Lily Long Hoyt. In 1958 he married Lillian Miller, who died in 1969.

Mr. Hoyt was a construction worker in Carbondale and a member of the Laborers' International Union of North America, Local 227. He was a former member of Rockhill Baptist Church where he served as an usher.

At the time of his death on July 10, 1985, Mr. Hoyt resided at 300 South Marion Street. He was 65 years old. Family survivors included a step son, Benjamin Walton; a step daughter, Edna Marie Armour; a step granddaughter, Ilona Armour; and an aunt, Fannie Long.

Willie Phelps

Mrs. Willie Phelps was born September 8, 1898 in Fulton, Kentucky to Mr. James W. Bell and Carrie Caroline Bell. She was one of eight children. In 1917 she married Rev. George Phelps of East St. Louis, Illinois. She moved to Carbondale in 1950 and united with the Rock Hill Baptist Church. She died March 3, 1975. Family survivors included her three sisters, Mittie Longon, Gladys Surrett, and Sadie Smith; and three brothers, Charlie, Raymond and Clifford Bell. Rev. Phelps passed away in February of 1954.

Carbondale, Illinois--Jackson County

Where it all began...

The township of Carbondale sprang up along the spot where, according to John Wright, city founder, Daniel Harmon Brush, saw "a wilderness of forest and dense undergrowth of hazel bushes, wild grape and running rose vines." This was an area, Wright comments, which "had not been worth clearing." Noticing the potential for a booming metropolitan area, Brush wanted to settle a vicinity which was along the established railroad lines and, at the same time, accessible to Murphysboro and other "major" cities at the time. Foreseeing a great business from the abundance of carbon (coal mines) throughout the area, Brush christened the settlement, "Carbondale."

Downton Carbondale (the early 1900s).

Courtesy of the Jackson County Historical Society. (Photo source: Wright, John W. D.; *A History of Early Carbondale, Illinois, 1852-1905.*

Traces In The Dust

The Crossroads

The crossroads of downtown Carbondale (the intersection of Main and Illinois Streets) and the hub of the city's central business area, c. 1949.

Photo Courtesy of The Southern Illinoisan.

African Americans in Carbondale, 1900-1964

William R. Mattingly

William Rudolph Mattingly was born in Whittenburg, Missouri to William and Louise Bufford Mattingly. He attended school in Whittenburg. Rudolph was residing on N. Allman Street in Carbondale in the early fifties with his sister Lacey Fowler. He worked at the Illinois Central Railroad, the Kopper's Tie Plant, and with the Civilian Conservation Corps.

"Uncle Rudolph," as he was called by the neighborhood children, had his parents, two sisters, and two brothers to precede him in death. He died February 10, 1989 at the Carbondale Manor Nursing Home. Survivors included two sisters, Etta O'Neal and Lacey Fowler of Carbondale; one sister-in-law, Ethel Lee Mattingly of Ohio; three nieces; and four great nephews.

Patricia Ann Brown

Patricia Ann Brown was born in Carbondale on February 10, 1951, the daughter of Bette Lou Brown and Isiah Simmons. She attended Thomas Elementary School in Carbondale and graduated from Carbondale Community High School in 1969. Patricia earned a bachelor's degree and a master's degree in Special Education at Southern Illinois University at Carbondale. She spent twenty years teaching in Park Forest, Illinois.

Patricia, who was a member of Olivet Freewill Baptist Church, was blessed with an extraordinary musical talent. She was recognized as one of the lead female vocalists for the Inspirational Singers--the churches youth choir prominent during the early 1970s. On tour or at home, Patricia's gifted voiced was truly inspiring.

In August of 1986 Patricia was married to Byron D. Collins. She was the mother to one stepson, Byron Collins, Jr. Patricia Collins died February 3, 1999 in Carbondale.

Gerlean M. Hayes

Gerlean Matlock Hayes, a native of Benton County, Tennessee, settled in Carbondale with in April of 1951 and resided on E. Willow Street. She is the mother of Pauline Hayes Dixson.

Connie Elaine Cole Holmes

Connie Elaine Cole Holmes was born on the 18th of September, 1951 in the city of Carbondale, Illinois to the union of Melvin Lovelace and the late Laura Cole. A member of the Hopewell Missionary Baptist Church of Carbondale, Connie was a 1969 graduate of Carbondale Community High School.

Connie was employed for more than twelve years by the Central Illinois Public Service Company of Carbondale and was formerly employed by the Wal-Mart corporation.

Mrs. Holmes passed away June 16, 1996 at her residence. She was the mother of Contrice and Keith Kendall.

Alice M. Gardner

Alice Marie Gardner was born in Carbondale on January 12, 1952. She was the daughter of James and Jessie B. Gibson Anderson. Alice was a graduate of Carbondale Community High School. She was a member of Hopewell Baptist Church. Later, she became a member of the Monument of Hope Deliverance Church. She served as an usher and a choir member.

Alice Marie married Earnest Gardner on June 7, 1970 in Carbondale. She was employed as a Home Health Aide and was an Aide at the Styrest Nursing Home. She was also an employee at Southern Illinois University.

Mrs. Gardner succumbed to a lengthy illness on April

Traces In The Dust

26, 1994 at Memorial Hospital in Carbondale, Illinois. Her father preceded her in death. In addition to her mother, Jessie B. Anderdon,
surviving family members included her husband, Earnest Gardner, an assistant principal with the Carbondale Elementary School District; a son, Darrell Gardener, a Corporal in the Unites States Army; a daughter, Tyesha; two sisters, Valeria and Amelia; three brothers, Jeffery, James, Jr., and Mark David; and several nieces, nephews and cousins.

Charlie and Lonnie C. Scott

Born in Canton, Mississippi on July 2, 1906, Charlie Scott was the son of Felix and Rosetta Luckett Scott. Mr. Scott was a retired employee of the Laborers Construction Union, Local 227 of Carbondale; a member of Tuscan Lodge F. & A.M. No. 44, Carbondale, Illinois; and a member of the Citizens Community Development Steering Committee of Carbondale.

Mr. Scott was a devoted family man and one dedicated to his religious beliefs. He was a member of the New Zion Baptist Church in Carbondale where he served as a deacon since 1952, and he was President of the Brotherhood and financial secretary.

Mrs. Lonnie Cole Scott, a long-time resident of Carbondale, was born May 11, 1909 in Philadelphia, Mississippi. Her parents were Will and Mary Ann Cole. Lonnie was married to Charlie Scott on December 25, 1925 in New Madrid, Missouri. The Scotts relocated to Carbondale in November of 1952, and made their home at the corner of Larch and Barnes Street. Mrs. Scott was a member of New Zion Baptist Church where she served as a Church Mother.

In December of 1975, Mr. and Mrs. Scott observed their 50th wedding anniversary. Mr. Scott succumbed to a short illness at the age of 74 on September 1, 1980. During his lifetime, he lost this parents; three sons, Charlie, Eugene, and Leonard; a sister; three brothers; and one grandson. He was the brother of Ophelia Tyler and Nancy Cole Monroe.

The Scotts were the parents of eleven children, Velma, Beatrice, Luella, Christine, Eugene, Charlie, Leonard, Calvin, Minnie, Hazel, and Kenneth.

Mrs. Scott passed away on December 29, 1993. She was 84 years old. She was preceded in death by three of her sons and one daughter, along with her parents, three brothers, two sisters, two grandchildren, and one great grandchild.

Mrs. Scott was also survived by a foster daughter, Bennie Simmons of Indiana, and two brothers, Roscoe and Willie Cole. Mr. And Mrs. Scott had twenty grandchildren, twenty great grandchildren, and five great-great grandchildren.

David E. Chambers

David E. Chambers was the son of U.P. Penn and Paquita Chambers. He was born May 15, 1953 in Carbondale. He received his educational training in the Carbondale public schools system and attended Paducah Community College in Paducah, Kentucky.

David was employed by the Illinois Department of Transportation for over sixteen years as an Engineering Technician in the Bureau of Project Implementation. He was a member of Olivet Freewill Baptist Church. David was the father of one son James, and one daughter, Maria.

Amos Mooreland

Amos Mooreland was born January 2, 1911 in Carrier Mills, Illinois to Moses and Annie Allen Mooreland. He attended the public schools of Carrier Mills. He married Emma Mooreland in Carbondale May 19, 1953. He formerly worked at the Green Mill and Hub Cafes in Carbondale. His last employment was at the Gardens Restaurant in Carbondale.

Amos succumbed to a lengthy illness in Carbondale at the age of 71 on June 29, 1982 at his home. He was a resident of 205 East Birch Street. Mr. Mooreland's parents, three brothers, and one sister preceded him in death. Survivors were his wife, Emma; a nephew, Floyd Mooreland; a niece, Lucille Mooreland; a great nephew, Anthony Mooreland; and one great niece, Nikki Moss of Detroit, Michigan.

Emma M. Mooreland

Emma M. Mooreland, wife of Amos Mooreland, was born in Perry County, Missouri to William and Louise Burford Mattingly on August 2, 1904. She attended school in Perry County.

Emma passed away October 1, 1984 in Carbondale at the Styrest Nursing Home. She had six brothers and sisters, three of whom died during her lifetime. Two sisters and one brother were her surviving family members, along with three nieces and four nephews. The three surviving siblings at the time of Emma's death were Etta O'Neal, Lacy Fowler, and Rudolph Mattingly. Mrs. Mooreland was 80 years old.

Sylvester Miles Walker

Sylvester Miles Walker, Jr., was born on October 25, 1953 in Carbondale. He was the son of Sylvester, Sr. and

Mary Gibson Walker. He attended the Carbondale public schools. He was a member of the New Zion Baptist Church under the pastorage of Reverend W. H. Clark.

Sylvester was a Navy veteran of the Vietnam War. At the time of his death, he was a student in the SIU School of Technical Careers, majoring in tool and manufacturing.

Sylvester died January 10, 1986 in the St. Francis Medical Center in Cape Girardeau, Missouri. He was 32 years old. Family survivors included three sisters, Mary Alice Mayfield, Cassandra, and Wanda Walker; two brothers, Otis Lee and Daniel Craig Walker; four nieces; and five nephews.

Alvest Broadnax
"Axe"

Alvest Broadnax was born September 19, 1934 in Fort Pillow, Tennessee. In 1953, he moved to Carbondale where he later married Etta Garrett in 1955.

Known to his friends as "Axe," Alvest subsequently relocated to the West Coast and was last married to Josephine Daniels October 24, 1987 in San Diego, California. He was employed as a Correctional Officer for the Department of Justice-Bureau of Prisons and was a Captain at the San Diego Federal Prison. He was a member of Calvary Baptist Church in San Diego.

Alvest passed away at age 56 September 8, 1991 in Kaiser Hospital in Elcajon, California. He was preceded in death by this father, three sons, a sister, and a stepdaughter. Included among his survivors were his wife, Josephine; a son, Michael; a daughter, Rosemary Smith; his mother, Elsie Napper; three sisters, Loretta Napper, Dolly Owens, and Cora Barbee; four brothers, Fred, Willie, John, and Montell Jackson; and four stepsons, Vincent, Dereck, and Tracey Daniels, and Louis Glover.

John Wesley Jackson, Jr.

John Wesley Jackson, Jr., known as "J. W.," was born October 29, 1935 in Boliver, Tennessee. His parents were John Wesley, Sr. and Cora Jackson. He was married to Berleen Haley Johnson in Murphysboro, Illinois.

John moved to Carbondale where he grew up attending the Attucks Schools. He graduated from Attucks High School in 1953. He was a member at Rock Hill Baptist Church.

A Marine Corps veteran of the Korean War and a member of the Marine Corps Reserved, "J.W" received the Korean Service Medal, the National Defense Service Medal, and the United Nations Service Medal.

John worked as a custodian in the housing department at Southern Illinois University at Carbondale and was a member of Local Union 316.

John was the nephew of Carrie Jackson and the stepson of Flossie E. Rice. He was the stepfather of Nelda Ross and Michael Johnson. He died in Carbondale on September 10, 1987; he had nine grandchildren and ten great grandchildren at the time. He was 51 years old, and he resided at 1046 North Barnes Street.

Roosevelt Turley
"Rose"

Roosevelt Turley, the wife of Reverend Lenus Turley, was born March 21, 1904 in Brookport, Illinois to Lewis Thomas and Nola Elizabeth Kendall Sims. She attended the public schools in Brookport and later graduated from Wilberforce University in Wilberforce, Ohio.

"Rose" Turley was married to Rev. Turley July 21, 1925 in Paducah, Kentucky. Three children were born to them. Rev. Turley died November 8, 1969. Mrs. Turley, who came to Carbondale in 1954, was active in the community as well as in church (See In Service to Their People).

Mrs. Turley attended courses at Southern Illinois University and worked as a substitute teacher for the Carbondale School District 95 until her retirement.

Mrs. Roosevelt Turley died July 2, 1991 in Carbondale at the age of 87. She was a resident of 405 East Larch Street. In addition to her husband, Mrs. Turley's parents, her son, Louis, and three brothers also died during her lifetime.

Included among the many survivors in her family were two sons, Lowell and Melvin Turley; a niece and nephew, Nola and Maurice Pullen; seven grandchildren; and thirteen great grandchildren.

Jesse Albert Chappell

Mr. Jesse Albert Chappell was born May 6, 1927 in Flatwoods, Tennessee to Nimrod and Mary Alexander Chappell. On September 16, 1950, he married Bertha L. Mays in Corinth, Mississippi. The Chappells moved to Carbondale in 1954.

Mr. Chappell was a member of Bethel A.M.E. Church where he worked on the Trustee Board and served in other capacities. He was a United States Army veteran of the Korean War. In civilian life, he was employed as a custodian at Southern Illinois University at Carbondale where he worked until he retired. Mr. Chappell was active in the community and was involved in providing activities for the neighborhood youth.

Mr. Chappell died June 19, 1994; he was 67 years old. Preceding him in death were his parents, three sisters, and one brother. Survivors included his wife; two daughters, Regina and Delores; two sons, James Andrew and Wallace; nine grandchildren; two great grandchildren; and four sisters, Minnie Cole, Hazel Swiney, Laney Mays, and Sarah Chappell.

Queen Esther Higgins

Queen Esther Higgins was born March 15, 1927 in Macon, Mississippi, the daughter of Richard and Ella B. Reed Barber. She was formerly married to Lester Higgins and later to Leroy Dentman. Mrs. Higgins was formerly employed at the Selmier Peerless Laundry in Carbondale. She was also employed as a cook at "U.D.'s" (the former University Drug Store Cafeteria).

Mrs. Higgins resided in Murphysboro, where she attended the Morning Star Baptist Church. She was a resident of Carbondale as early as 1956.

Mrs. Higgins died on January 1, 1994. Preceding her in death were her parents, two sons, three brothers and a sister. Surviving family members included six daughters, Eunice Higgins, Cherry, Carla, Sharon and Debra Dentman, and Regina Kay Cole; and three sons, David Dentman, Leonard Higgins, and Lester Higgins, Jr.

Geneva Mason

Geneva Mason, born July 26, 1926 in Mt. Vernon, Illinois. She was the daughter of Henry Lee Sawyer and Dorothy McCuley. Geneva was employed as a cook at Southern Illinois University and in the Carbondale public schools. She also worked for a while at the Thrift Shop. She married Albert Mason in 1956 in Carbondale.

Mrs. Mason was a member of Rock Hill Baptist Church. She was active in the BTU and in the Mt. Olive District. She died January 28, 1987 in Carbondale.

Mrs. Mason was the mother of three daughters, Angel, Vicki Lynne, and Shirley; a stepdaughter, Melissa; two sons, Donald and Phillip; and two stepsons, Mark and Michael. She was a sister to Virginia White of Mt. Vernon. At her death, Mrs. Mason had fifteen grandchildren and two great grandchildren. Her daughter and brother, Verla and Lester, were deceased prior to Mrs. Mason's death.

Carla Denise Allen Schauf

Carla Denise Allen Schauf was born in Carbondale August 11, 1957 to James Bowman and Barbara Shoffner Allen. She attended the public schools in Marion and graduated from Marion High School. She then attended Southern Illinois University at Carbondale and graduated with a degree in marketing in 1989.

Carla married Harry L. Schauf in Paducah, Kentucky May 19, 1989. They had two daughters, Amber Vantrece and Veronica BeAnn. In 1986, she became Vice-President of J&W Allen Construction Company of Marion, Illinois, a black owned and operated business begun in 1977.

Carla was a life long member of Bethel A.M.E. Church in Marion where she served as Church Treasurer, Treasurer of the Building Fund, and a member of the Missionary Society and choir.

Carla passed away May 24, 1995 at Marion Memorial Hospital. A sister, India LaJean Allen, preceded her in death. In addition to her two daughters, Carla was the mother of two stepsons, Vernon and Steven Schauf, and a stepdaughter, Jennifer Schauf. Carla had four sisters and five brothers, Carmen, Grace, Dorothy, Elaine, Craig, Walter, Garry, Donald, and Jerry Allen. She also had several grandchildren and great grandchildren.

Hattie B. Thomas

Hattie B. Thomas, the daughter of Tom and Susie Carr Roberts, was born August 3, 1910 in West Point, Mississippi. She died October 15, 1983 in Memorial Hospital in Carbondale.

Hattie married James Thomas on December 28, 1931 in Cairo, Illinois. James died on March 3, 1979. The family resided in Mounds, Illinois for over twenty years and settled in Carbondale in 1957. For over twelve years, Mrs. Thomas was employed as a housekeeper at the former Van Natta Funeral Home in Carbondale.

Mrs. Thomas had several members of her family to pass away before her including two sons, a sister, and two brothers. Survivors of her death included five daughters, Annie Mae Willis, Marie Mayfield, Hazel Burns, Dorothy Neal, and Christine Thomas; five sons, Jessie, Samuel,

Arthur, Robert, and Wayne; three sisters, Beatrice Morris, Elnora Miller, and Rosella Jones; two brothers, Samuel Roberts, and Willie C. Roberts of Chicago, Illinois; twenty-eight grandchildren; and two great grandchildren.

Frances Van Hook

Frances Van Hook, the daughter of Cordell and Lucy Green Shepard, was born May 1, 1917 In Elaine, Arkansas. She married Louis Van Hook, Sr. in June, 1932 in Elaine, Arkansas. Mr. Van Hook died in August of 1952. The family moved to Carbondale in November of 1959 where Mrs. Van Hook worked for the Robert E. Feigenbaum family. She also worked at the Levelsmier Insurance Company as an office attendant. She was last employed at the Sudzy Dudzy Laundromat in Carbondale.

Frances had one son to precede her in death. At the time of her passing on November 25, 1985, she had one daughter, Corrine Hughlett; two sons, Louis Van Hook, Jr. and James Green of Decatur, Illinois; four sisters, Magnolia Wiley, Letha Shepard, Irene Morris, and Lenora Shepard; three brothers; twenty-five grandchildren and five great grandchildren.

Erma C. Clemmer

Erma Christine Clemmer was the second daughter of Namon and Annie Ruth Howard Clemmer. She was born January 5, 1960 in Carbondale. Christine, as she was commonly known, graduated from Carbondale Community High School and attended Southern Illinois University. She worked in the Human Development office at S.I.U. as a transcribing secretary.

Christine died on November 12, 1983. Her parents, one brother and one sister had died earlier. Christine was 23 years old and had resided at 413 North Brush Street in Carbondale.

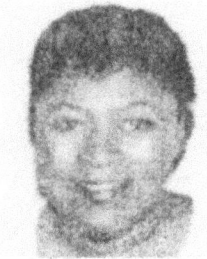

Felica C. Powell

Felica Charlene Powell, was the daughter of Odell, Jr. and Bertha Mosley Powell. She was born January 15, 1961 in Carbondale.

Felica graduated from the Carbondale Community High School. She was a member of Rock Hill Baptist Church and participated in the Exemplary Youth Program operated by the Illinois Farmers' Union-Training, Inc.

Felica was the mother of Calvert Luther Johnson, III. She passed away on September 10, 1988 in Memorial Hospital in Carbondale. She was preceded in death by her paternal grandmother. Survivors included her son; her parents; two brothers, Reggie Miller and Gerron Powell; her maternal grandmother, Lula Mae Rowe; paternal grandfathers, Carl Mosley and Odell Powell, Sr.; her stepmother, Shirley Powell; a stepsister; Maria Branch; and two stepbrothers, Ricky and Gerald Branch.

James Wallace Green, Jr.

James Wallace Green, Jr. was the son of James "Pinto" Green and Marian "Shorty" L. Hutcherson. He was born June 4, 1961. He attended the Carbondale Public School System, and he was a member of the United States Army National Guard.

"Jimmy Junior" and two of his brothers, Taz Green, and the author, Melvin Green Macklin, was brought up under the stern guidance and love of his grandmother, Allean Brown Gordon, known to all as "Momean." It was in 1965, following the death of their mother, Mariam, that Jimmy Junior, age four, and his brother, Tazz Edward Green, age two, went to live with "Momean". She saw to it that all her grandchildren were raised in the church, and Jimmy Junior was baptized at Olivet Freewill Baptist Church at an early age.

"Jimmy Junior" died March 7, 1997 in Murphysboro, Illinois. He had three children, James W. Green, III, Marlon, and Angel Green; three brothers, Tazz, Melvin, and Sidney Hibbler; and two sisters, Sherlene Willetta Green Bowles and Debra Kay Reese. He was the nephew of several aunts, Gloria Dean Aiken, Gladys Johnson, Geneva Brown, Vaughn Carter, Elmira Phillips, Remonda Chambers, and Eugenia Robinson of Murphysboro. His uncles were Russel, Charles, and Elmer Hutcherson.

Ora P. Lilly

Ora P. Lilly was born September 6, 1915 in Pulaski, Illinois, the daughter of Napoleon and Callie Thorpe Mackons. Mrs. Lilly was married to Edward Lilly, Sr., in Pulaski in 1933. She moved to Carbondale in 1961 where she became a member of the Church of Christ Church and worked in the area nursing homes.

Ora and her husband were married thirty years and had twelve children. Mr. Lilly died August 27, 1966. Mrs. Lilly died April 17, 1995 in Cape Girardeau, Missouri. Her son, Joseph Lilly, and five brothers and three sisters, were deceased prior to her death. Surviving members of her family were four sons, Edward, John, Marcus, and Napoleon, and seven daughters, Geraldine, Edna, Carol, Delois, Callie, Rose, and Gloria. She had forty-two grandchildren. Ora was the sister of Luvesta Givens.

Gregory Clint Bell

Gregory Clint Bell, the son of Flassie and Clifford Bell Jr. was born June 7, 1956 in Ullin, Illinois. He came to Carbondale with his family in 1962 and attended the Carbondale elementary and high schools. He was married to Janice Caves on July 9, 1980.

At the time of his death, Gregory was an employee of the C.I.P.S. Company and worked at the power plant in Grand Tower. He was a member of Faith Temple Church of God in Christ.

Gregory died at age 34. Family survivors included his wife Janice; two daughters, Diedre and Arika Bell; his parents; four sisters, Glenda Cawthon, Gita Doss, Gwanda Tribbett, and Gina Kemp; three brothers, Gardeth, Gabriel, and Gaylon Bell, and his mother-in-law and father-in-law, Mr. and Mrs. Tyler January. Mr. Bell's was preceded in death by his maternal grandparents

Willie Elmo Eanes

Willie Elmo Eanes was born July 6, 1917 in Blytheville, Arkansas to James and Cora Harris Eanes. He married Geneva Massie November 18, 1939 in Charleston, Missouri. The Eanes moved to Carbondale in 1964 from Ullin, Illinois.

Mr. Eanes was a World War II Army veteran and was a former maintenance laborer at Southern Illinois University at Carbondale.

Mr. Eanes passed away July 22, 1982 in the Veterans Center in Marion, Illinois. His parents, one son, and three daughters died before him. Family survivors included his wife, Geneva Eanes; three sons, Elmo, Jr., Jesse, and James; six daughters, Flossie, Charlotte, Betty, Carol, Cora, and Catherine; three brothers, Robert, Napoleon, and Roscoe; three sisters, Rosie Eanes, Maxine King, and Malinda Seahorn; twenty-six grandchildren; and two great grandchildren.

Lovie Geneva Massie Eanes

Lovie Geneva Massie Eanes was born in Ullin, Illinois October 15, 1920 to Thomas and Lydia Greer Massie. She attended the public schools in Ullin and in Mounds, Illinois.5 She was married to Willie Elmo Eanes November 18, 1939 in Charleston, Missouri. Mr. Eanes died July 22, 1982.

Upon settling in Carbondale, Mrs. Eanes became a member of Faith temple Church of God in Christ, serving as a church Mother and Sunday School teacher until her health prevented her from rendering further service.

During her lifetime, Mrs. Eanes witnessed the deaths of many of her family members, including a son, three daughters, three sisters and three brothers. Lovie Eanes passed away at age 67 at the St. Joseph Memorial Hospital in Murphysboro, Illinois on June 13, 1988.

Among her surviving family members were five daughters, Charlotte Eanes, Flossie Bell, Carol Eanes, Cora Marable, and Catherine Israel; a son, Elmo Eanes, Jr.; two brothers, Leonard and Thomas Massie; two sisters, Vera Marshall and Edith Carpenter; and an aunt, Irene Gaines. Mrs. Eanes had, at the time of her death, twenty-four grandchildren and fifteen great grandchildren.

Earl Farmer

Earl Farmer, born March 13, 1929 in Wolf Island, Missouri, was the last known African American to settle in Carbondale in the year 1964, moving into the city in late December of that year. He was the son of Harry and Luejune Rowden Farmer.

Earl married Luberta Mims April 16, 1976 in Clinton, Kentucky. He worked as a private mail route contractor in the Postal Delivery Service. He retired after 19 years of service.

A former member of Shiloh Baptist Church in Murphysboro, Illinois, Mr. Famer died March 21, 1994 in Carbondale. He was the father of seven sons and four daughters, Earl, Danny, Sherman, Randy, Tony, Timothy, and Patrick, Doris, Linda, Velma, and Sherry. He was also the father of five stepchildren Rubye, Larry, Frank, Howard, and Gary. Upon his death, Mr. Farmer had thirty-two grandchildren and twenty-one great-grandchildren. He was 65 years old.

Wardell L. Armstrong

Wardell L. Armstrong was born May 21, 1923 in Terre Haute, Indiana. He was the son of Herman and Bertha Roby Armstrong.

He married Ida Nance who preceded him death. Later he married Louise Bolden of Daytona Beach, Florida. Wardell lived and worked much of his life in New Jersey.

Wardell died on February 13, 1986 in Rahway, New Jersey. At the time of his death, family survivors included his wife, Louise Armstrong; three daughters, Brenda Walker, Dorothy Daniels, and Gwendolyn Edwards; a son Wardell London Armstrong; three brothers, Willie J., Elbert Armstrong, and Walter Neal; his step-parents, Mr. and Mrs. Willie Neal; his sister, Lula Mae Rowe; his uncle, Julius Armstrong; and seven grandchildren.

Ella Arnette

Mrs. Arnette graduated from SIU, receiving both her Bachelor and Masters degrees, and began a lengthy teaching career. She became a member of Olivet Free Will Baptist Church and served as a mother of the church, a Sunday School teacher, church pianist and choir member, and as a church announcement clerk. She was a member of Mariam Chapter No. 17, Order of Eastern Star as well as a member of the Carbondale Community Club.

Mrs. Arnette and her husband, Charles, Sr., were the parents of two sons, Keenan and Charles E. Arnette, Jr., "Chuck." They had three grandchildren. Charles preceded his wife in death on August 13, 1984. Mrs. Arnette passed away July 21, 1986.

Grace Boyd

Grace Boyd was born February 15, 1896 in Levings, Illinois. She was the daughter of Chris and Nannie Woods Boyd. She attended Attucks school system. After completeing her education at SIU, she began a teaching career which spanned over forty years, first in Southern Illinois and later in Evanston and Chicago, Illinois.

Mrs. Boyd was a life long friend to Mrs. Bessie Warren. The two scholars made many journeys to over thirty countries in five continents in their life time. At Hopewell Baptist Church, Mrs. Boyd was a Sunday School teacher, Director of Vacation Bible School, Missionary Society member, and treasurer of the Sunday School. Mrs. Boyd died April 23, 1995.

Leota Christina Nichols Brown

Leota Nichols Brown was born June 13, 1919 in Carbondale to Thomas J. and Nina Keathly Nichols. She married William H. Brown on November 11, 1943 in Cape Girardeau, Missouri.

In the 1960's, she became involved with the development of the Head Start Program in Southern Illinois. She served as a social worker for the newly established organization and as SIU-C undergraduate trainer for child development. Later, she became lead teacher. At the time of her death in 1982, Mrs. Brown resided at 212 N. 2nd St. in Murphysboro, Illinois.

Ronald Brown

Ronald Brown, the son of Cecil and John Brown, is the father of two children, Alecia and Ronald Jr. Ronald has two grandchildren.

Alice Scott Davidson

Alice Scott Davidson, a homemaker, was born May 15, 1939 in Fulton, Tennessee. She was the daughter of Nellie Scott of Carbondale.

Alice was educated in the schools of Carbondale and was married to Nick Davidson. The couple had a son named Kevin. Mrs. Davidson died August 31, 1984 in Zion, Illinois at age 45. Her father and an uncle preceded her in death. Survivors at her death included her husband Nick; one son, Kevin D. Davidson; her mother, Nellie Scott; a brother, Harold D. Scott; an aunt, Sudie Scott; and an uncle, Joe Johnson.

John H. Dodd

John H. Dodd was born June 8, 1908 in Rhoma, Missouri and was reared by his grandmother, Martha Dodd, in Grand Tower, Illinois where he attended the Grand Tower Schools. He last married Marie Speers in 1949 in Murphysboro, Illinois.

Mr. Dodd was a member of the Olivet Freewill Baptist Church. He worked at the former Selmier-Peerless Laundry in Carbondale and also for the Illinois Central Railroad.

Mr. Dodd passed away at the age of 86 on October 30, 1994 in Carbondale He was a resident of 418 East Willow Street. He had one son and his parents who died before him. Survivors included his wife, Marie; four sons and one daughter-in-law, Charles Noble, Lester, Joe Louis, and Donald Gene and Jessie Dodd; twelve grandchildren; and seven great grandchildren

Vivian A. Douglas

Vivian Arlene Douglas was born on March 3, 1924 in Sedalia, Missouri to Benjamin and Sallie Isaac. She was a member of Bethel A.M.E. Church of Carbondale.

Vivian was employed at the Carbondale Community Correctional Center. In 1947, she was untied in marriage to Emanuel Douglas in Columbia, Missouri. Mr. Douglas predeceased his wife.

Mrs. Douglas died October 21, 1994 at her residence in Carbondale. She was the mother of three sons, Emanuel, Norman, and Bruce Douglas; and two daughters, Camellia Jackson and Velvetta Brooks.

Charles E. Foster
"Pancake"

Charles Edward Foster, affectionately known as "Pancake," was born March 22, 1928 in Metropolis, Illinois to Henry Foster and Gladys Watson Crim. He attended the public schools in Metropolis. He married Pearl Robinson in Carbondale on November 16, 1962.

"Pancake" served his country as a soldier in the United States Army being honorably discharged December 10, 1946 at Camp Lee, Virginia. He was employed at Southern Illinois University in the food service department for more than thirty-five years and belonged to Olivet Freewill Baptist Church.

Charles Foster died April 11, 1997 at the Jackson County Nursing Home in Murphysboro, Illinois. He had three daughters, Mary Joiner, Vickie Sue Dickson, and Louise Johnson; three sons, Willie Cannon Robinson, William Robinson, and Racine Robinson; fourteen grandchildren and six great-grandchildren.

Reginal Glispie

Reginal Glsipie, Sr. was born September 27, 1943 in Salt Lake City, Utah. He was the fifth child of John Henry and Hazel Blake Glispie.

Reginal received his educational training in the Mounds City, Illinois public schools; he also attended the former Attucks High School in Carbondale.

He was united with the Church of Christ in Carbondale, Illinois. Reginal married Rosa Liddell in Carbondale on October 7, 1961. Two children were born to them, Reginal, Jr. and Timothy Wayne.

Mr. Glispie was employed by the Carbondale Senior Citizens organization for seven years. He was also employed by the Dallas Transit Office. He worked for the Jackson County Sheriff's Office until he became ill.

Reginal's parents, two sisters, paternal and maternal grandparents, and grandson preceded him in death. Family survivors at the time of his death included his wife, Rosa; his sons, Reginal and Timothy; a mother-in-law, Lucille Beard; six grandchildren; a great grandchild; two sisters, Charlene Dyson and Helen Cooper; a brother, Robert Glispie; and an uncle, Buford Lewis.

Milton G. Harkins, Sr.
"Hawk"

Milton G. Harkins, Sr. was born August 21, 1921 in Hallidayboro, Illinois to the late Anthony and Jennettie McAllister Harkins. He was married to Louise Anderson on April 14, 1946 in Cairo, Illinois. Mr. Harkins was a former coal miner and owner of his own business. (See, Early Black Business. Known to many as "Mr. Hawk," he was also affiliated with Illinois Police Association, the Jackson County Sheriff Department as a Deputy, and the Illinois Sheriff's Association. He was a member of the Mt. Zion Baptist Church in Hallidayboro.

During his lifetime, "Hawk" lost his parents, a daughter, two sisters, and one brother. He passed away August 17, 1983 at his home in Carbondale. Among surviving family members were his wife, Louise Anderson Harkins; a son, Milton G. Harkins, Jr.; two daughters, Viola and Jackie Harkins; two brothers, Ben and Roscoe Harkins; a sister, Marguite Anderson; and six grandchildren.

Milton G. Harkins, Jr.

Milton G. Harkins, Jr. was the son of Milton, Sr. and Louise Anderson Harkins. Born April 4, 1948 in DeQuoin, Illinois, Milton received his early education in the DuQuoin schools. He continued his secondary education at Carbondale Community High School. He was one of only a few Blacks participating in sports at the school during the late 1950s and early 1960s.

Milton was formerly married to Deborah Passmore. The couple had three children. Milton was preceded in death by his father and one sister. He died on February 26, 1993. At the time of his death, surviving family members included his mother; a son, Scott Baxter; three daughters, Kimberly, Tara, and Shanon; four grandchildren, Bianca, Aaron, Cala, and Seth; two sisters Viola and Jackie; an aunt, Marguerite Anderson; two uncles, Ben and Roscoe Harkins; and two nephews, Lamont and Damon Harkins.

Pearl Hudson Foster

Mrs. Pearl Hudson Foster, known to her friends as "Tee Pearl," was born November 10, 1922 in Blytheville, Arkansas to Wille and Tinia Hudson. She received her educational training in the Carbondale public schools and Southern Illinois Normal University in Carbondale where she received an associate degree in art. On November 16, 1971, she married Charles E. Foster in Carbondale, Illinois.

Mrs. Foster was an accomplished Pianist. She played the piano professionally, for fifteen years, in various places and in Chicago, Illinois. She served as pianist for many churches throughout the state including New Zion Baptist Church in Carbondale, Illinois.

Mrs. Foster was a member of Zion Temple Church of God in Christ in Murphysboro, Illinois where she served as a church Mother. Her parents, two sons, and three grandchildren preceded her in death.

Pearl Hudson Foster, departed this life on June 21, 1995. She had made her home in Murphysboro, Illinois. She was 72 years old. At the time of her death, surviving family members included her husband; three daughters, Mary P. Joiner, Louise Johnson, and Vickie Sue Dickson; three sons, Willie Cannon, William, and Racine Robinson; fourteen grandchildren; and six great grandchildren.

Henry and Vastulia Slaughter

Henry and Vastulia Slaughter were married in Philadelphia, Mississippi. They settled in Carbondale on the old Walker's farm (property that was owned by the James Walker family northward beyond Oakland Cemetery). Henry and Vastulia were the parents of ten children: Wardell, James, Willie, Henry, Jewel, Bonnie, Jeraldine, Lauretha, Charles, and Barbara.

Dewitt Haynes

Dewitt Haynes, the son of Sam E. and Matilda Hinton Haynes, was born March 13, 1922 in Gloster, Mississippi. He arrived in Carbondale around 1923. After receiving his education in the elementary and secondary schools in Carbondale, Dewitt completed graduate and post-graduate work at Southern Illinois University at Carbondale earning both a bachelor and master's degree. He then began teaching in the Carbondale Elementary District 95 at Parrish and Thomas Schools.

Dewitt married Wanda Perkins Garrison December 19, 1976 in Carbondale. He was a member of Bethel A.M.E. Church in Carbondale where he served as a trustee. An Army veteran of World War II and the Korean War, Mr. Haynes, served in Europe, Alaska, and the South Pacific. In Carbondale, he was a representative and active participant in the political arena (See In Service To Their People; The Black Struggle).

Mr. Haynes was preceded in death by one brother, one sister, and his parents. In addition to his wife, Wanda, survivors of his family included a sister, Lorene White; three brothers, Oscar, Irving, and Norvell; three step-children, Beverly Gardner, Isadore Garrison, Jr., and Reginald; seven grandchildren; eight nephews; three nieces; three aunts; and an uncle.

Ellis L. Hudson

Ellis Lee Hudson was the son of Richard James and Ella Fuqua Hudson. He was born January 16, 1903 in Trezevant, Tennessee. In 1942 in Cape Girardeau, Missouri, he was married to Zula Atkins, who died on May 14, 1978.

Mr. Hudson was a member of Rock Hill Baptist Church. As a soldier, he was a veteran of World War II, serving from September of 1942 until March of 1943. In civilian life, Ellis worked for many years with the Illinois Central Railroad in Carbondale. He also worked at the Don Raines Barber Shop in Carbondale.

Mr. Hudson died July 30, 1978 in Carbondale. His family survivors included a sister, Pauline Webb; a brother, Hewitt Hudson; two sisters-in-law, Bashierdeen and Doris Hudson; two nephews, U. L. and Archibald Hudson; and three nieces. He also had two brothers who died before him.

William Archie Jones

William Archie Jones, a native of Illinois, was born March 20, 1901 in Carrier Mills. He was the son of Radford and Malissa Jones. He received his early education in the public schools of Carrier Mills, Illinois and later attended medical school. Archie changed majors and received a Bachelor degree from the University of Illinois. He came to Carbondale in 1955 with his new bride and last wife, Mae Miller. Prior to his marriage to Mae Miller, Archie was married to Thelma Cason.

Archie Jones died November 16, 1988 in Carbondale. He resided at 1030 North Wall Street. He was preceded in death by his parents and three wives, Thelma Cason, LaVada Lamton, and Mae Miller. Mr. Jones was the father of Wanda St. James, Winona Wysinger, and Mariam Perkins. He was also survived by his step-son, Harry Clingman, and grandchildren, Duane and Marie Perkins.

Thomas C. Kelly

Thomas Ceaser, the son of Ed and Mary Bell Wilson Kelly, was born April 27, 1922 in Torrance, Mississippi. He married Etta Greer February 5, 1954 in Murphysboro, Illinois.

Thomas was a World War II United States Navy veteran, and served from 1939 to 1946. In civilian life, he was a member of the American Legion Post No. 542 and also a Carbondale precinct committeeman.

Thomas was formerly employed at Century Sports in Carbondale, the State HIghway Department, the sheriff's department, and the Urban Renewal Program in Carbondale.

Thomas died November 13, 1983. He had a son, Dewayne, and two daughters, Trudy and Sharon. He was the brother of Estella Parker.

Hal McCroy, Sr.

A native of Hamburg, Tennessee, Hal McCroy, Sr. was the son of Richard and Bessie Armstrong McCroy. He was born April 7, 1907 and settled in Carbondale in 1924. He was later married to Lillie Forest on May 29, 1939 in Jackson, Missouri. For 46 years, Hal was an employee of the Koppers Division Plant in Carbondale.

Mr. McCroy succumbed to an extended illness on March 20, 1984. His parents, one daughter, one sister and one brother died during his lifetime. Family survivors included his wife, Lillie; two daughters, Odessa Meeks and Bessie Bowers; his son, Hal McCroy, Jr.; fourteen grandchildren and seven great grandchildren.

Reverend Shedret McQueen

Rev. Shedret McQueen, was born April 13, 1914 in Desha, Arkansas. He was the son of Martin and Amelia Griffin McQueen. He married Exie Hamilton November 25, 1947 in Sikeston, Missouri.

Rev. McQueen was a former pastor of the Mt. Pleasant Missionary Baptist Church of Harrisburg, Illinois. He was employed as a truck driver for the city of Carbondale.

Rev. McQueen died March 13, 1991 in St. Joseph Hospital of Murphysboro, Illinois. He resided at 648 East Searing Street in the Carbondale northeast community.

Evelyn Morgan

Evelyn Morgan was born April 5, 1897 at Fort Pillow, Tennessee. She was the daughter of Christly and Aline Jones Wallace. In November of 1957. At that time, she joined the Gillespie Temple Church of God in Christ, now the Greater Gillespie Temple Church of God in Christ where she served as President of the Home and Foreign Mission Department and as a church Mother for many years.

Mrs. Morgan died in Carbondale on June 1, 1980. She was survived her daughter, Julia Mae Wynn; her sons, Earnest Morgan, Major Lewis Morgan, and Gilbert and Henry Morgan; a sister, Lucy O'Neal; seventeen grandchildren; and twenty-six great grandchildren. Mrs. Morgan had one son, one daughter, and her husband who preceded her in death.

Wiley Morris

Wiley Morris haled from Batesville, Mississippi, where he was born on September 8, 1908. He was the son of St. Rainey and Lile Gooch Morris.

Mr. Morris was an elder at the Green Street Church of God. He was employed as a laborer in construction; he also worked at Kopper Industries. In 1930, he was married to Beatrice Roberts in Wyatt, Missouri

Wiley Morris died on February 26, 1991 in Carbondale at Memorial Hospital. Mrs. Morris died earlier in 1987. The Morris family resided at 1110 North Barnes.

At the time of his death, Mr. Morris's surviving relatives included his sons, Richard, Ernest, Tom B. Morris, Morris Abrams, Willie and Harold Morris; a daughter, Dorothy Jones; a brother, Rainey Morris; a sister, Reatha Taylor; twenty-seven grandchildren and several great grandchildren.

Thomas V. Morris

Thomas Vesto Morris was born February 5, 1934 in Charleston, Missouri. He was the son of Wiley Morris, Sr. and Beatrice Roberts Morris. Thomas attended the Attucks school system and graduated from Attucks High School in 1952. He was a member of Olivet Freewill Baptist Church.

Thomas was the father of three daughters, Cynthia, Danette, and Teresa, and he was the father of four sons. Thomas died November 28, 1966 in Carabondale.

Tom Mason

Tom Mason, the son of Leonard and Mary Jane P. Mason, was born on October 2, 1908 in Jackson, Tennessee.

Mr. Mason moved to Carbondale and united with the Rock Hill Baptist Church.

In 1947, he married Carrie E. Hodge in Murphysboro, Illinois. He was a retired construction laborer and concrete finisher; he belonged to the laborers Local 227 of Carbondale.

Tom died at his residence October 6, 1981. His parents, a son, and a brother died before him. He was survived by his wife; a son, Tom Jr.; a daughter, Rita Dolores Norman; seven grandchildren and six great grandchildren.

Charles H. Mitchell
"Blue"

Charles H. Mitchell was born September 17, 1917 in Alamo, Tennessee to Henry and Mattie Moore Mitchell. On may 8, 1938, in the city of South Fulton, Tennessee, Mr. Mitchell was united in marriage to Bertha Johnson.

Traces In The Dust

The couple had ten children.

Charles, known by his friends and family as "Blue," was employed with the Illinois Central Railroad as a Coach Attendant. He was a member of Bethel A.M.E. Church where he was leader of Class #9, a church trustee, and Treasurer of the Men's Club. He was also a member of the Layman's Club and the Hiram Lodge No. 56 of Chicago, Illinois.

"Blue" Mitchell died July 5, 1986 in Carbondale at the Memorial Hospital. Three sons, his parents, a sister, and a brother died before him. Among his surviving relatives were his wife, Bertha Johnson Mitchell; seven sons, Charles, Aaron, Leonard, Earl, Tyrone, Anthony, and Dana; thirteen grandchildren; and five great grandchildren. Bertha and Charles Mitchell were married 48 years. Mrs. Mitchell currently resides at their homestead in Carbondale.

William Clyde Perkins

William Clyde Perkins, son of Aaron and Lucy Perkins, was born March 16, 1913 in Brownfield, Illinois. "Clyde," as he was known to family and friends, attended Southern Illinois Normal University where he met Geraldine Browning. They were married December 26, 1938. The couple had three children, Delores, Gloria, and William Jr.

During his high school years, Clyde was a 6'2' center for the Attucks Bluebirds. At Rock Hill Baptist Church, he served as a trustee and church treasurer. He was a longtime member of Tuscan Lodge No. 44, Prince Hall Mason. He retired from SIU after more than twenty-five years of service. He also worked as a barber.

Mr. Perkins passed away January 5, 1995. He was predeceased by his wife, Geraldine Perkins. Family survivors included his children; a brother, Everett Perkins; three sisters Veachie Robinson, Etta Hayes, and Wanda Haynes; four grandsons and a granddaughter, Amanda Perkins.

Woodrow W. Perkins

Woodrow W. Perkins was born Feb. 9, 1916 in Louisville, Miss. to Mr. and Mrs. Jacob K. Perkins. He moved to Carbondale at a very young age with his parents and united with Bethel A.M.E.

Woodrow attended Attucks School and was later married to Cleva Mae Bradley. In 1943 he Joined the Unites States Army and received three Overseas Service Bars, the American Campaign Medal, The Bronze Star Battle Medal with three Stars, the Good Conduct Medal, the World War II Victory Medal, and the European African Middle East Campaign Medal. He received an Honorable Discharge in 1947. Woodrow died on April 7, 1984. Surviving family members included his mother, Vera Perkins McDonald, and a sister, Kathleen Thornton, both of Carbondale.

Irma L. Gibbs Price

Irma Lee Gibbs Price, daughter of Edward and Annie Pierce Gibbs, was born August 22, 1914 in Fulton, Kentucky. She first settled in Carbondale in the early 1920s. She received her educational training in the Attucks schools. She was a member of Olivet Freewill Baptist Church.

Irma married Clarence Price February 23, 1937 in Chicago, Illinois. She and her husband returned to Carbondale November 11, 1978. Irma became an active member of the Carbondale Model Cities Senior Citizens Program.

Irma was preceded in death by her parents. Among her survivors were her husband, Clarence; a sister, Celestine Cavitt; three brothers, Harrison, Jewel, and Theodore Gibbs; and seven nieces; and seven nephews.

George H. Reid

George Henderson Reid was a native of South Fulton, Tennessee. He was born January 4, 1902. On May 8, 1950, he was married to Lizzie B. Douglas in Arkansas. She and Mr. Reid raised Charles Ferrell.

Mr. Reid was a member of New Zion Missionary Baptist Church in Carbondale where he served as Church Clerk, a deacon, and teacher. He was a past member of the Jackson County Sheriff Association. He retired from the First National Bank and was a member of the Tuscan Lodge #44, F.&A.M., Prince Hall Affiliate at Carbondale.

Mr. Reid's parents, five sisters, and his wife died before him. Survivors included his son Charles; a daughter-in-law, Marinda Ferrell; five grandchildren; three great grandchildren; and two sisters, Hattie Williams and Georgia Hudson. Mr. Reid died March 8, 1992.

Rev. Will A. Reid

Reverend Will A. Reid was born March 30, 1895 in the city of Ripley, Tennessee to the union of William and Mattie Reid. He met and married Isbella Whitelow, and the couple had four children. Mrs. Reid passed away on August 16, 1956. Will later married Beatrice Daniels on October 29, 1959.

Rev. Reid accepted the call into the ministry and became the pastor of the New Zion Baptist Church in Carbondale during its early history (see Early Black Churches and Spiritual Leadership). He was employed as a custodian for the Carbondale School District Number 95 for twenty-seven years.

Rev. Reid died on September 21, 1980 at the Memorial Hospital in Carbondale. Surviving family members at the time of his death included his wife, Beatrice Daniels Reid; a son, Willie Reid; a step son, Louis Johnson; a step daughter, Ruby Brown; two brothers, Alvin and Clifton Reid; three sisters, Florine, Mary Sue, and Elnore; eleven grandchildren; and ten great grandchildren.

Willie H. Reid

Willie H. Reid, the son of Rev. Will A. Reid and Isabella Whitelow Reid, was born in Ripley, Tennessee and spent most of his life in Chicago, Illinois.

Willie H. Reid was the father of six children: Hildegarde Thames, Anthony Reid, Gus Reid, Wanda Hobson, Renita Bonner, and Stephanie Reid. He was the father-in-law of Virginia Reid and Willie Bonner.

Robert Lee Ross

Robert Lee Ross was the son of Thomas and Mary Eddington Ross and the brother of Eva Buggs and Edna Ross. He was born March 21, 1921 in DeSoto, Illinois. Robert graduated from Elkville High School in 1939 and resided in Hallidayboro, Illinois and in Chicago, Illinois.

Robert returned to the Southern Illinois area in the late 60s and went to work at Southern Illinois University in food service. He died at the Veterans Administration Medical Center in Marion, Illinois at age 65 on February 2, 1987. At the time of his death, he was a resident of 1425 West Main Street in Carbondale. Mr. Ross was survived by his son, Anthony J. Ross; his two sisters, Eva and Edna; one brother, Arnold Ross; and three grandchildren.

Lula Mae Rowe

Lula Mae Rowe was born March 6, 1925 in Terre Haute, Indiana to Herman and Bertha Armstrong. She attended the Carbondale public schools and worked in the Styrest Nursing Home as a C. N. A. She also worked at the Carbondale Care Center and at Southern Manor. She was last employed as a housekeeper at Memorial Hospital in Carbondale where she worked for over thirty-three years, retiring in August of 1986. Mrs. Rowe was first married to Carl Mosley and later to Dan Roseman, Jr. She last married Brown Rowe.

Rock Hill Baptist Church was Lula's church home where she served as a Mother of the Church, participated in the Sunday School and choir, and was a member of the Good Samaritan Circle of the Missionary Society.

During her lifetime, Mrs. Rowe lost several members of her family including two of her former husbands, a sister, two brothers, a granddaughter, Felicia Powell, and her grandparents. Lula died August 5, 1996 at Memorial Hospital where she had worked for so many years.

Mrs. Rowe had six daughters, Bertha Powell, Delores Smith, Zora Oglesby, Diane Tipton, Evelyn Roseman, and Sharon Hyche; two brothers, Willie James Armstrong and Walter Neal; fourteen grandchildren; twenty-six great grandchildren; and three great-great grandchildren. She was the niece of Vera Small and Julius Armstrong.

Shedrick Spriggs

Shedrick Spriggs was born in Brusly, Louisiana February 22, 1898 to Thomas Spriggs and Mary Griffin. He was married to Beaulah Haynes in Gloster, Mississippi on February 24, 1923. He retired from the B&O Railroad Freight Department on June 3, 1963.

Mr. Spriggs died at the age of 79 in Carbondale on January 10, 1978. Family survivors included his wife, Beaulah; six children, Verna, Rosie, Mary, Lillie, Napolean, and Franklin; one sister, Sadie Light; eighteen grandchildren; and eight great grandchildren.

Elsie Steele

Elsie Steele, the daughter of Richard and Katie Norse, was born March 22, 1891 in Lovesvill, Kentucky. Elsie married Sylvester Steele, Sr. November 16, 1916 in Murphysboro, Illinois. Mr. Steel died March 3, 1970.

Mrs. Steele was one of the founders and a charter member of one of Carbondale's oldest churches (see Early Black Churches and Spiritual Leadership). In addition to her spiritual pursuits, "Mama Steele," as she was known in the community, also was the proprietor of a small store which was a part of her home on Allman Street in Carbondale. Two daughters, five sisters, and three brothers preceded Mrs. Steele in death.

Upon her death, which occurred in Carbondale on January 20, 1990, Mrs. Steele's surviving family members included two sons, Sylvester Steele, Jr., and Walter Steele; nineteen grandchildren; thirty-six great grandchildren; and five great-great grandchildren. Mrs. Steele was 98 years old.

Traces In The Dust

Top Left: Ora P. Lilly. Top Right: Pearl Hudson Foster. Bottom Left: Milton Harkins, Sr. Bottom Right: Dewitt Haynes.

Henry Cornelius Thomas

Henry Cornelius Thomas was born June 4, 1904 in New Orleans, Louisiana, the son of Emile and Julia Thomas. He was educated in the public schools of Louisiana, and he attended the Catholic Church. He married Dorothy Allen Fletcher September 4, 1952. He worked as a general laborer.

Henry Thomas died in Carbondale December 23, 1995 at Memorial Hospital. He was survived by his wife, Dorothy Thomas; stepdaughters, Nancy McDonald; and Jackie Armstrong; and a stepson, William Donald Fletcher.

Ruben Valliant
"Jack"

Ruben "Jack" Valliant was born August 15, 1921 in Clay County, Mississippi To Ruben, Sr. and Annie Lou Buchanan Valliant. He attended public school in Mississippi and was a member of the Locust Grove Baptist Church in Mississippi. In 1948, he married Mary Frances Morrow in Aberdeen, Mississippi.

After leaving Mississippi, "Jack" and his family moved first to Marion, Illinois and later to Carbondale. He was last employed by the Carbondale School system as a crossing guard.

Ruben died in Carbondale August 12, 1983. Among his family survivors at the time of his deaath were his mother, Annie Lou Valliant; five daughters, Diane, Georgia Ann, Annie, Lou Ann, and Mary Faye; four sons, Lee Clay, Jack, Jessie, and Kenneth; three sisters, Anna Spratt, Lucille Buchanan, and Mary Hudson; a brother, Henry Valliant; and eleven grandchildren.

Willie J. Brooks Wilson

Willie Joe Brooks Wilson was born December 7, 1897 in Ripley, Mississippi, the daughter of Joseph and Fannie Lowery Brooks. She attended the public schools of Carbondale and was an L.P.N. at the former Holden Hospital. She was married to L. V. Wilson on June 18, 1923.

Mrs. Wilson was a member of Hopewell Baptist Church, serving for many years as Church Clerk, supervisor of the Kitchen Committee, and pianist for the Sunday School. She was a member of the Trulight Club and the Community Club.

Funeral services were held for Mrs. Wilson in July of 1988. Family survivors included cousins, Mr. and Mrs. Alonzo Palmer and Mr. and Mrs. Moses Palmer.

Bobby J. Wimberly

A native of Grantsburg, Illinois, Bobby J. Wimberly was born December 19, 1939, the son of Newton and Estella Wimberly. He attended the Attucks Schools and married Richard Ann Dent in Murphysboro, Illinois.

Bobby worked for the City of Carbondale Street Department for more than twenty-six years and was a member of Faith Temple Church of God in Christ.

When he died, Mr. Wimberly had two daughters Wilma and Ghada and a son, Robert. One son and five brothers died during Bobby's lifetime. He was the brother of Violet McCombs of St. Louis, Missouri, and Quincey and Donnell Wimberly of Carbondale.

Curtis W. Wimberly

Curtis Westley Wimberly, the son of Newton and Estella Wimberly was born March 5, 1928 in Brownfield, Illinois.

Curtis was a construction laborer and an Army Veteran of World War II. He was married to Velma Stevenson on November 13, 1973. She passed away on April 14, 1989.

Curtis died August 8, 1989. His parents and two brothers also died before him. Survivors included two daughters, Vivian Walker and Robin Spiller; one stepdaughter and stepson, Cathy Stevenson and James Stevenson; one sister Violet McComb; five brothers, Quincey, Joe, Bobby, Luther, and Donnell; an aunt and uncle, Lucy Scott and Henry Scott; four grandchildren; and ten step grandchildren.

Luther Leroy Wimberly

Luther Leroy Wimberly was born January 14, 1944 in Merment, Illinois to Newton and Estella Scott Wimberly. He was married to Loretta Murphy, and the couple had two children.

Luther was formerly employed as a construction worker. He died September 28, 1990 in Carbondale. His parents and three brothers preceded him in death.

At the time of death, Luther's survivors included a son, Tracey Wimberly; a daughter, Vickie Wimberly; four brothers, Donnell, Quincey, Bobby, and Joe; a sister, Violet McCombs; two grandchildren; an aunt, Lucy Scott of Carbondale; and an uncle, Henry Scot of Merment, Illinois.

Ernest Williams

Ernest Williams was born January 21, 1920 to Farmer and Ella Williams. Ernest enlisted in the U.S. Air

Force in July of 1941. In 1945, he was honorably discharged.

While in the military, Ernest earned the AP Theater Ribbon, two Bronze Service Stars, the Good Conduct Medal, the World War II Victory Medal, and the American Defense Service Ribbon.

Ernest died November 26, 1985. He was survived by a son, David Dean Williams; two daughters, Sharon Williams Hutcherson and Stephanie L. Williams; a brother, Rogie Williams; a sister-in-law, Willie Bea Williams; four grandchildren; and a niece and six nephews.

Leora Hamilton Watkins

Leora Hamilton Watkins, the second oldest child in a family of five, was born to John and Mary Hamilton in Villa Ridge, Illinois. She was born in 1903. She lost an older brother, Roosevelt, who died October 22, 1982 and a second brother, Fairbanks, who died November 22, 1982. She was left with two sisters, Dorothy Hamilton King and Daisy Hamilton Smith.

She attended the Attucks Schools. She also attended Southern Illinois Normal University and earned a teacher's certificate. She taught in Pulaski County before moving to St. Louis, Missouri where she married Joel Watkins on February 23, 1932. Mr. Watkins died in 1980.

In Carbondale Leora was a member of Rock Hill Baptist Church, working in the Sunday School, the choir and other departments of the church.

Leora died in 1983. Among her survivors were her two sisters and two nieces.

Estella K. Parker

Born the second daughter of five children, Estella was born in Torrence, Mississippi on December 26, 1915 to Ed and May Belle Kelley. Moving to Carbondale in 1941 from Coffeeville, Mississippi, she joined the New Zion Baptist Church. She served as a member of the Young Adult Choir, Sunday School teacher, and worked in the Baptist Training Union. At the time of her death in 1990, she had two daughters, Loretta K. Harris and Edna E. Kelley; two brothers, John E. and William Kelley; three grandchildren, seven great grandchildren; eight nieces; and six nephews.

Samuel Fowler

Samuel Fowler, known as "Sam," was the son of Calvin and Dora Murdock Fowler. He was born February 12, 1905 in Hardin County, Tennessee. He married Loraine Clark in Egypt, Mississippi. Sam was formerly employed at the Koppers Plant. He was a World War II Army veteran, serving in the 984th Quartermaster Service Company from 1942 to 1945. He was retired at the time of his death.

Samuel died on February 18, 1982 in St. Louis, Missouri. He had five sisters and five brothers who died before him. Sam was the father of a daughter, Doretta Scott, and two sons, Glennie and Samuel, Jr. He had a brother, Chester, a sister, Josephine Farr, and several nieces and nephews.

Mack McCutchen

Mack McCutchen, a resident of 647 East Searing Street, was born September 9, 1902 in Mound Bayou, Mississippi. He was the son of George and Mattie Lewis McCutchen.

Mr. McCutchen was a life long member of the New Zion Missionary Baptist Church; a member of the Laborers Construction Union Local 227; and a member of the Masonic Lodge #44.

Mr. McCutchen married Savannah Warr on May 24, 1943 in Lovejoy, Illinois. Mr. and Mrs. McCutchen, were among the first of Carbondale's Blacks to organize committees and work to improve conditions in the city; particularly on behalf of the black children of the northeast community (see In Service To Their People).

The McCutchens were the parents of five children, Gloria, Norma, MacFredrick, known as "Mac," William, and Hazel. At the time of Mr. McCutchen's death on May 11, 1992, he had ten grandchildren and three great-grandchildren.

Willie C. Hughlett

Willie C. Hughlett was born July 14, 1946 in Covington, Tennessee to Rosevelt and Pauline Hughlett. He attended the Attucks school system and graduated from Carbondale Community High School. He subsequently attended the School for Building Maintenance - Technical Careers Program at Southern Illinois University and was formerly employed at the Stotlar Lumber Company and the Prairie Farms Dairy. He was last employed by the City of Carbondale, Code Enforcement Division.

On July 10, 1965, Willie married Corrine Van Hook in Carbondale, and in 1977 he began in the Ministry. He became the pastor of the House of Prayer Apostolic Church in April of 1987.

Elder Hughlett passed away in Carbondale February 4, 1993 at age 46. The Hughletts had three children, Carl, Christine, and Cynthia; and four grandchildren.

Arthur Louis Morgan, Sr.

Arthur Louis Morgan, Sr. was a native of Fort

Pillow, Tennessee. He was born June 11, 1933 to William and Leona Reed Morgan. He married Jessie Williams September 12, 1953 in Ripley, Tennessee. Arthur was an associate member of Faith Temple Church of God in Christ. He was a supervisor for the Illinois Youth Commission and a veteran of the Korean War from 1953 to 1955.

Arthur Louis died October 1, 1978 in Carbondale. He was survived by his wife; two sons, Keith and Arthur, Jr.; three daughters, Beverly, Mary Beth, and Sue; his mother; and four brothers, Glenn, Lynn, William, and Lorenzo. His father preceded him in death. Louis was the grandson of Mrs. Sarah Bonds of Ripley.

Levora D. L. Robertson

Mrs. Levora D. Lyas Robertson was a native of Carbondale, the daughter of Uslessious, Sr. and Rosa Lee Hawkins Lyas. She attended the Attucks school system and received a Bachelor of Science Degree from Southern Illinois University. She studied in the College of Human Resources and in Child and Family Services, earning the honor of having her name on the Dean's List in 1974.

Lavora was first married to Matthew A. Harper; the couple had four children. She later married Vernell Robertson on September 22, 1978.

Levora was an active leader and organizer, earning numerous awards and recognitions for services to her job and to her community (See In Service To Their People). She worked deligently at the New Zion Missionary Baptist Church, serivng as pianist of the Sunday School and Secretary of the General Missionary Society.

Mrs. Robertson was the mother of three daughters and a son, Darlene, Cathy, Susan; and Abram. She died at her home June 16, 1993 at 1201 North Wall Street.

Lillie Hayes

Lillie Bell Hayes was born August 26, 1880 in Makanda, Illinois. She was the mother of William R. Hayes.

Joe L. Wimberly

Joe L. Wimberly was born in Brownfield, Illinois to Newt and Estella Scott Wimberly on September 26, 1937. Joe was a steel foundry worker in Milwaukee, Wisconsin, and he was employed as a construction laborer in Carbondale. He was a member of the First Church of God in Christ in Mt. Vernon, Illinois. He had four brothers, along with his parents, who died during is lifetime.

Other relatives living at the time of his death included a sister, Violet McCombs; his three brothers, Quincey, Bob, and Donnell; and his aunt, Mrs. Lucy Scott of Carbondale.

Andrew Smith, Sr.

Andrew Smith, Sr. was a native of Milan, Tennessee. He was born there March 18, 1913 to Versus and Lena Simmons Smith. He married Addie B. Nesbitt June 6, 1936 in Cape Girardeau, Missouri. Mrs. Smith died on September 7, 1993.

For thirty-three years, Andrew worked for the Kopper's Tie Plant. He also worked for more than ten years as a school crossing road guard for the Carbondale Police Department. He was also a veteran of the United States Navy.

Mr. Smith was a member of the New Zion Baptist Church in Carbondale .Andrew lost his parents and one brother during his lifetime. Surviving his death were his five daughters, Dorothy, Hazel Johnson, Lena Jean Scott, Virginia Edwards Aiken, and Loretta Scott; a son, Andrew Smith, Jr.; twenty-four grandchildren, and twenty great grandchildren.

Daisy L. Smith

Born on March 7, 1910 in Villa Ridge, Illinois, Daisy L. Smith was the youngest of five children of John and Mary Parks Hamilton.

Daisy received her educational training in the Attucks schools of Carbondale. She received a Teacher's Certificate and taught in Mound City, Illinois for several years.

Daisy became a member of Rock Hill Baptist Church where she served as pianist for the choir and a teacher in the Sunday School. She was a member of the Missionary Society as well and was president of the Good Samaritan Missionary Circle at the time of her passing.

Mrs. Smith operated her own business in Carbondale (see Early Black Businesses in Carbondale). Later, she worked at Southern Illinois University-Carbondale in Food Services. She died April 29, 1990 in her home at 901 North Marion Street in Carbondale.

James Arthur Sykes

A native of Jackson, Tennessee, and the son of James Brittan and Estella Sykes, James Arthur Sykes was born May 9, 1926. He was educated in the Tennessee public schools and worked as a general laborer. James also served in the United States Navy.

Mr. Sykes died May 22, 1995 in Carbondale at age 68. Surviving family members included two daughters, Agnes Medlin and Katherine Sykes Robinson; a son Delbert Sykes; his mother, Estella Bryant; three stepsons, Melvin Foster, Fred Foster, and Cary Brooks; three sisters, and six brothers.

Traces In The Dust

James E. Wills

James Edward Wills was born on August 13, 1937 in Matthew, Missouri. He attended the former Attucks Grade School. He was also a student University High School.

James attended the University of California at Los Angeles and served in the United states Marine Corps for four years. He was employed as an Aeronautical Engineer for McDonnell Douglas Air Craft of St. Louis, Missouri and the Hughes Air Craft in Los Angeles, California.

In Carbondale, James was a member of Bethel A.M.E. Church. James passed away in the Veterans Administration Medical Center in Marion, Illinois July 12, 1989. He was preceded in death by his father, two brothers, and two sisters. Among his surviving family members were his mother, Pauline Wills Kenner, and stepfather, George; his four brothers, Clarence, Fred, Donald Ray, and Robert; his three sisters, Vera, Paulette, and Zelda; and his son and two daughters, Carlos, Leslie and April. He also had nine stepsisters and two stepbrothers. Mr. Wills was 51 years old.

Corrine Van Hook Hughlett

Arthur Yarbro

Mr. Arthur Yarbro was born in Clarksdale, Mississippi August 29, 1909. He was the son of Daisy Whittaker Corthen.

Mr. Yarbro was raised in Wardell, Missouri and previously lived in the Illinois cities of Chicago and DuQuoin. He spent the majority of his adult life in Carbondale.

Arthur Yarbro was a retired employee of Southern Illinois University at Carbondale where he worked as a laboratory assistant in the Life Science Building for more than twenty years. He was a member of the Jehovah's Witnesses faith.

Mr. Yarbro's stepfather, Lemon Corthen, his mother, and four brothers were deceased during his lifetime. Arthur Yarbro died January 21, 1997 at age 87. At the time of his death, surviving family members included a brother, Aaron Corthen; two sisters, Ester Williams and Sarah Corthen; three nieces and five nephews.

Elder Willie C. Hughlett

Louis Van Hook, Jr.

Louis Van Hook, Jr. was born May 5, 1947 in St. Louis, Missouri to Louis Sr. and Frances Shepard Van Hook. He attended the public schools in Carbondale and was an army veteran of the Vietnam War.

Louis died April 16, 1986. He was the father of Eudora Armstead and Latisha Smith and the brother of Corrine Hughlett and James Green.

African American Residents in Carbondale, 1900-1964

Top Left: Charlie Edgar, affectionately known as "Po Charlie," the husband of Ida Edgar and stepfather of Imogene Washington. Top Right: Mamie Thornton. Bottom Left: Evelyn Boykin. Bottom Right: Ellen Martin, wife of Joseph Martin.

Traces In The Dust

Top Left: Alice Stayton. Top Right: Evelyn Morgan. Bottom Left: John Eddie Kelley. Bottom Right: Lucy Scott.

African American Residents in Carbondale, 1900-1964

Top Row: Thomas Vesto Morris. Eule Ford. James E. Holder. Bottom Left: Gregory Clint Bell. Bottom Right: Hattie B. Thomas.

Traces In The Dust

Top Left: Arthur James Valentine, Sr. Top Right: Queen Esther Higgins. Bottom Left: John Wesley Thomas. Bottom Right: Jesse Albert Chappell.

The Way It's Spozed To Be
        by
    "Grandtee"
  (Dorothy Sykes)

Woke up this mornin
Nobody in dis bed but me
Wonder where in this world
Can my good man be?

Down in the Bottoms
Playing Georgia Skin
Women all round him
Cause dey know he gonna win

Gonna Git up from here
Pistol in my pocketbook
Going down to the Bottoms
Drink me some moonshine
Walk aroun and take a look

Went into the backroom
What did I see?
Young big leg yallow woman
Sittin on my man's knee

Said Big Momma's here now
Don't want no trouble, but
If you ain't offn Lil Joe's knee
By the time I counts to three
Gonna blow you to hell and
Take my man back home with me

Woke up this mornin
Nobody in dis bed but me
De Good Lawd knows
Dat ain't th way hits spozed to be.

Traces In The Dust

Top Left: Joseph Ivy. Top Right: Bessie Brown, sister of Arthur Brown. Bottom Left: Stella Ivy. Bottom Right: Ruben "Jack" Valliant, Jr.

African American Residents in Carbondale, 1900-1964

Top Left: Anabelle Jackson. Top Right: Eva Ross Buggs. Bottom Left: Arthur Brown, first husband of Allean Brown Gordon. Bottom Right: Charles Brown.

Traces In The Dust

Top left: Robert Scott. Top Right: Thelma Steed. Bottom Left: Mary "Priss" Bell, 1942. Bottom Right: Willie Joe Wilson.

African American Residents in Carbondale, 1900-1964

Top Left: Ora Holder. Top Right: Lit Simon. Bottom Left: Truley Louise Greer. Bottom Right: Louvenia Fletcher, 1943.

Traces In The Dust

Top Left: Virginia Clark. Top Right: Helen Waters Jones. Bottom Left: Emma Ford Fletcher. Bottom Right: Shedrick Spriggs.

African American Residents in Carbondale, 1900-1964

Top Left: Gieula Thomas, Age 16. Top Right: Louie Cavitt. Bottom Left: Elizabeth "Liz" Mason. Bottom Right: Vance Mason.

Traces In The Dust

Top Left: Claudia Daniels, 1944. Top Right: James "Doc" Denton, 1944. Bottom Left: Lola Belle Williams, 1943. Bottom Right: James Henderson, 1944.

African American Residents in Carbondale, 1900-1964

Top Left: Lula Mae Mosley Roseman Rowe. Top Right: Bob Thornton. Bottom Left: Isola Garrison, 1942. Bottom Right: Ernell France.

Traces In The Dust

Top Row: Ida M. Armour Webb. Robert Shoffner. Center Row: George Henderson Reid. Marlee Wooley, Sr. Bottom Row: Minnie Etta Hinton (1923-1992). Wayne Sutton.

African American Residents in Carbondale, 1900-1964

Top Left: Earl Farmer, the last known African American to settle in Carbondale in the year 1964. Top Right: Lovie Geneva Massie Eanes, mother of Flossie Bell. Bottom Left: James Abe France. Bottom Right: Charles "Blue" Mitchell and son, Tyrone.

Traces In The Dust

Top Left: Louis Van Hook, Jr. Top Right: Emma M. Mooreland. Bottom Left: Irma Lee Gibbs Price, sister of Celestine Cavitt. Bottom Right: Robert Louis Cavitt, Jr.

African American Residents in Carbondale, 1900-1964

Top Left: Louise Miller. Top Right: Claude Fletcher and Marie Johnson. Bottom Left: Gladys Malone Anderson, mother of Edward, Charles, James, and Willie Dee Anderson. Bottom Right: Doris Howard Mitchell.

Traces In The Dust

Top Left: Henry Carter. Top Right: Milton G. Harkins, Jr. ("Hawk"). Bottom Left: Clinette Yavonne Hayes-Steele. Bottom Right: Reginal Glispie, Sr.

African American Residents in Carbondale, 1900-1964

Top Left: Nettie Hayes, daughter of Eurma and William Hayes. Top Right: Gay Fitzpatrick Mitchell, daughter of Francis Armour. Bottom Left: Wilma France, daughter of Madelene and James Abe France. Bottom Right: Julia Ann Jamison, daughter of Willie Mae and James Arthur Jamison.

Traces In The Dust

Top Left: William Donald Fletcher, Jr. Top Right: Robert Cole, Jr. Bottom Left: Michael Wayne France. Bottom Right: William Battle.

Traces In The Dust

Top Left: Margaret Laster Mayberry, daughter of Atlas and Rose Laster. Top Right: Marilyn Brown-Tipton, daughter of Charles and Beulah Brown. Bottom Left: Darnella Wakefield-Morrison, daughter of Annie Mae Dunlap Wakefield. Bottom Right: Leatreasa M. Lilly, daughter of John and Janet Lilly.

Part V

Around the Town

The "Big House"

The home of John and Cecil Brown ("Mama Cecil") was known as "the Big House" within the area of the northeast community called "The Hoodlums." This same area was also known, at various times, as "The New Addition or the "Renfro Addition." Another section of the northeast community in the 1940s and 1950s was referred to as "Plum Nelly" (Plum Alley) because of the large amounts of plum trees that at one time grew along the back roads of the wooded areas just north of the present day location of Thomas School and also along Fisher Street.

The "Big House," with its pot-bellied coal and wood burning stoves and upstairs rooms, stood just off the corner of Allman and Burke Streets. Its huge front yard and driveway area provided the "playground" for generations of Carbondale's black children. Of particular importance were the neighborhood baseball games. These games were watched with enthusiasm by the many adults who staked their claims to prized spots of the Big House's spacious steps and porches. From such vantage points, mothers and fathers and aunts and uncles roared out their raucous support and loud "pearls of athletic wisdom" and advice to their children as the young ones engaged in one of their most beloved sports. Many a time, however, an overly worked-up parent would find himself confiscating the bat from some unfortunate and disgruntled child as the adult instructed him on the finer points of the game. Moreover, it was not uncommon for the adults to get so carried away that it wasn't too long before the entire playing field consisted of all grown-ups, and the children found themselves occupying the porches.

Traces In The Dust

Lucinda Ollie, Clarence "Tat" Ward, Unis Pearl Davis, Faye and Annie Mae Fisher, daughters of Helen Fisher, Wendell Bowers, Helen Fisher, and others in early group photo, early 1900s.

Around The Town

History of Woods Park

Based on information from the Woods Field Diary of Alice Woods Stayton and Reprinted by Raydeane Woods Routen, July 10, 1991. Printed by permission of Raydeane Woods Routen.

Woods Field, later named Woods Park was purchased February 1, 1928 by Abe and Alice Woods From Ada Caldwell. This included 20 acres that is presently known as Eastgate Shopping Center.

Immediate construction began to include the park, a house for the grounds keeper and a Dance Hall. Numerous Carbondale residents were employed to complete the construction. A few being listed as Clyde Hayes, Taz Green, Jim Wilson, Titus Jones, Mr. Kelley, Dean Hinchcliff, Henry Davis, and a Mr. Rendlemen.

Woods Park was famous for its multitude of annual activities, political rallies and, of course, its ball games. Many local and state orchestras also played at the Dance Hall.

Woods Park and the Dance Hall were frequently leased to others for special activities. These included: the Carbondale Elks, local churches, civic groups, as well as individual residents.

From 1928 to 1941, teams from companies and businesses, as well regular ball clubs, played at Woods Park. Such teams representing businesses were from the Prince Cleaners, the Hilton Cubs, and the Elks Lodge. The Carbondale Merchants and the West Frankford Athletic teams were other local groups who played at the park. The East St. Louis Giants, the Kentucky Cardinals, the DuQuoin Indians, the East Chicago Reds, and Westelen College came into Carbondale to compete as well as teams from Johnson City, Maple Grove, and other areas. On Thursday, October 6, 1932, the following persons were a few of the Major League players to play on the West Frankfort Athletic Team, or the Van Natte Aces: Benny Tate, Ray Starr, "Dizzy" Dean, Jimmy Wilson, and Pepper Martin.

The first orchestra to play in the Dance Hall was Coco Cola and the Silver Slippers. They were followed by the Snow Birds, King Oliver, Jimmy Waters, Piny Woods, and the Plantation Cotton Pickers.

The first Frank B. Jackson Picnic was held at Woods Park on August 2, 1928. It included an array of festivities for the community. This day is presently known as the "Emancipation Day."

Numerous descendants of Abe and Alice Woods continue to reside in Carbondale. Woods Park was sold around 1945.

Traces In The Dust

Top: Bob Thornton, Henry Traylor, Homer Malone, and Clayton Greer enjoy a day of rabitt hunting at Campbell Hill near Ava, Illinois. Bottom Left: William Archie Jones. Bottom Right: Leonard Bostic and William R. Hayes.

Around The Town

Friends
Clara Maddox Barnett, mother of Odell Robison, and best friend, Ella Watson.

Traces In The Dust

Top Left: Beverly Garrison and father on Oak Street; sitting on the porch is Vivian France West (left), daughter of James France, 1948. Top Right: Vernell Robertson and family. Bottom Left: Juanita Thomas, Beatrice Hudson, and Celestine Cavitt. Bottom Right: Bertha Mitchell and Estelle Chappell.

Around The Town

Top: Virginia Mae Hawkins (2nd row; 2nd from left) and Anna Ruth Clemmer (2nd row; 4th from left) at Southern Illinois Normal University, 1941. Bottom Left: Ida Chappell and Cora Cunningham. Bottom Right: Gloria Haynes.

Traces In The Dust

Good Times!

The best of friends share a moment of camaraderie during the heyday "The Levee" of "uptown" Carbondale. Pictured are (from left) James "Pinto" Green, Charles Young, William Edward, Dee Lilly, and George Kenner.

Around The Town

> We always had plenty of hogs, ducks, and chickens. We didn't have to worry about going hungry.
>
> --Della Matthews, 1997

The Old Homestead of Robert and Della Matthews

Robert and Della Matthews settled their family homestead at 511 E. Sycamore Street.

Janet Johnson

Around The Town

Top Left: Priscilla Love, Darnecea Smith and Friends. Top Right: Charles Lilly at the home of Ernell and James Green on North Washington Street, 1952. Bottom: The Cobras Little League baseball team; Willard Brown, Sponsor.

Traces In The Dust

Top Left: Frances Robertson. Top Right: Ronnie Brown at Jones Cafe.
Bottom Left: Cozette Bell and Shirley Boykin get ready for the school prom.
Bottom Right: Naomi Glispie.

Around The Town

Top: Melvin Green Macklin and Gaye Fitzpatrick at the home of Mr. Charles "Papa" Lilly on Barnes Street, 1952. Papa Lilly (background right) is pictured sitting in his favorite spot, the front porch of his house. Bottom Left: William Cole and Charles King, 1961. Bottom Right: Gary Mason and David Dean Williams.

Traces In The Dust

Top Left: Lucy and Aaron Perkins. Top Right: Vivian France West and James "Swig" Anthony. Bottom: Carbondale residents. Among the group are J. C. Penn; Lovia Penn; Jean Penn, daughter of U.P. Penn; LaVidas Hillsman; and Janet Valentine (little girl).

Top Left: Rev. Will Reed's home at the corner of Wall and Green Streets. (Children in foreground) Francine Robertson, Canasta Robertson, and Norma Jean Brown. Top Right: Diana Gilmore, daughter of Edna Mason. Bottom: Children at Attucks Playground: Among those in the group are Mary Holder, Virginia Smith, Diane Roseman, Cozette Bell, Betty Sue Parran, Janice Bell.

Traces In The Dust

Versa Lou White, daughter of Versa Hayes White, at Attucks Picnic, 1963.

Around The Town

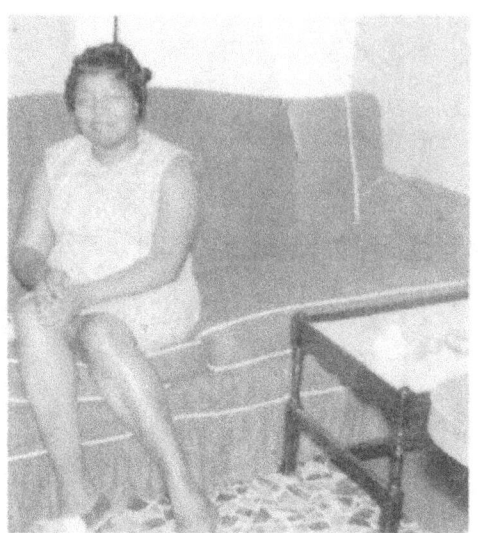

Top Left: Mable Evelyn Meredith Favors. Top Right: Carl Mosley. Bottom: Brenda Devers and Jackie Armstrong attend a Spirit of Attucks Reunion.

Traces In The Dust

William Duane and Marie with son, Darren, and daughter, Monica

Top: Earl Alexander and Alfred Hall on the Attucks School campus, 1960. In background is the Attucks High School. Bottom: Curtisteen Colbert relaxes on the front porch of her home on East Larch Street.

Traces In The Dust

Top Left: Rosemary Fitzpatrick. Top Right: Milton Miller. Bottom Left: Abram Matthew Harper (1960-1994). Bottom Right: Linda Butler (1939-1981).

Around The Town

Top: Wilbert Bowers, Jr., Doretta Smith Bowers, Robert E. Gilleylen, Sandra L. Smith Gilleylen. Bottom Left: Vyonne Lynette Johnson. Bottom Right: Julia Ann Thomas Brown, daughter of Lucille Bradley Thomas.

Above: Proclamation of Senior Citizen Day. Mrs. Stella Ivy is honored at the celebration of Senior Citizen Day, an Honorary Official Day so designated on February 26, 1994 at the University Mall. Mayor Neil Dillard proclaimed Senior Citizen Day to recognize and show appreciation for "the valuable human resources in the community and the significant contributions Carbondale Senior Citizens have made to the overall quality of life." Pictured with Mrs. Ivy are the Honorable Mayor and Mrs. Neil Dillard. Below: A group of Carbondale citizens. The identified are Mr. Shelly Chappell, Mrs. Ora Holder, and Mr. Rayford Perkins

Around The Town

Top Left: Sherlene Willetta Green, daughter of Ernell and James Green. Top Right: Darnell Johnson, son of Gloria Dean Aiken and grandson of Allean Brown Gordon. Bottom Left: Etta Garrett White, daughter of Annie Mae Dunlap Wakefield. Bottom Right: Edward Blythe.

Top Left: Gloriastene and James Edward Chappell. Top Right: Raydeane and Robert James. Bottom Left: Vicky Lynn White Simms, daughter of Etta White Newbern. Bottom Right: Alvin Davis, son of Dorcas Cunningham Davis.

Around The Town

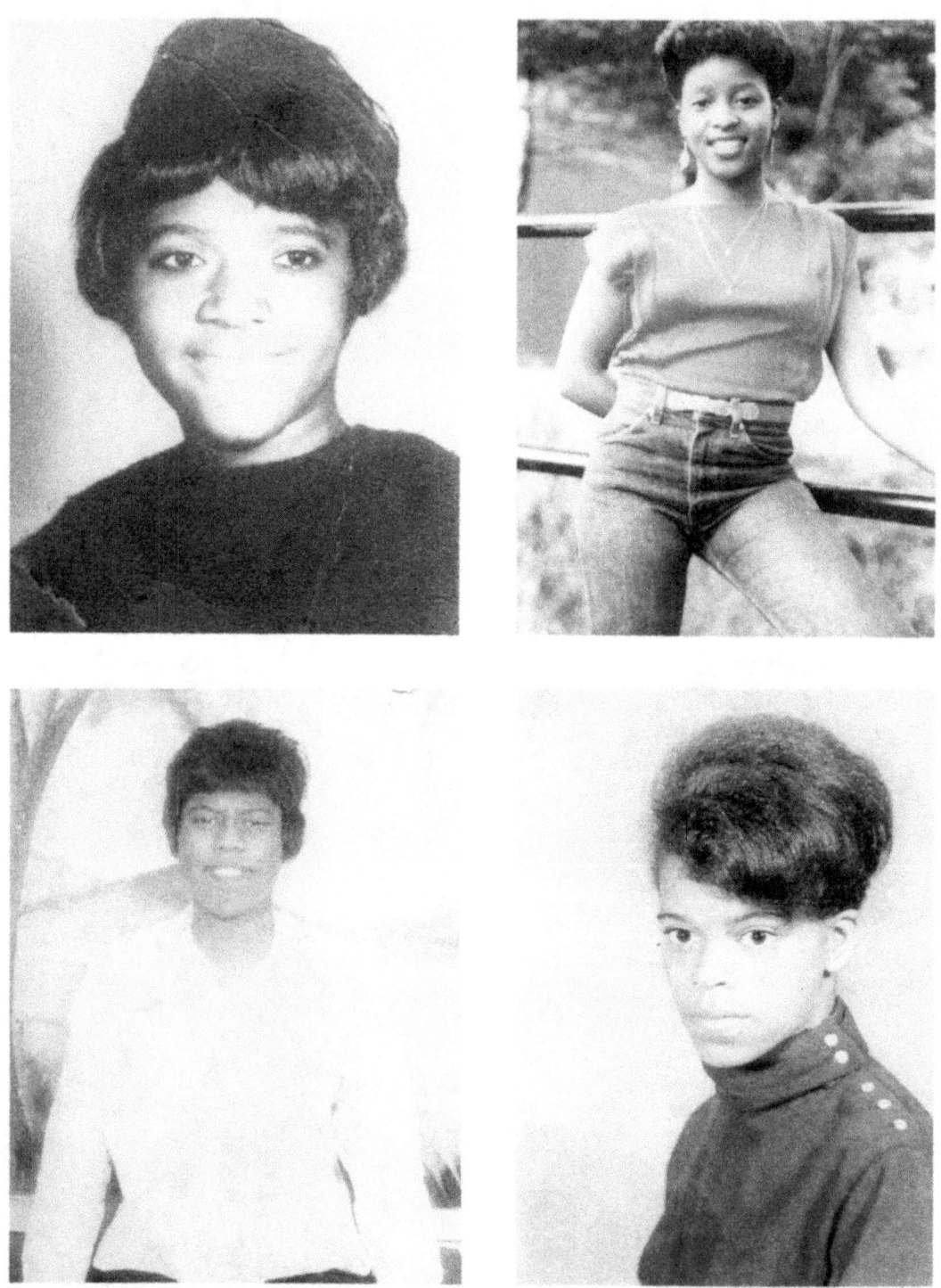

Top Left: Joann Gilmore, daughter of Edna Mason. Top Right: Judy O'Neal, daughter of Erie and Booker O'Neal, Jr. Bottom Left: Barbara Tender. Bottom Right: Barbara Scott, daughter of Robert and Cardella Scott.

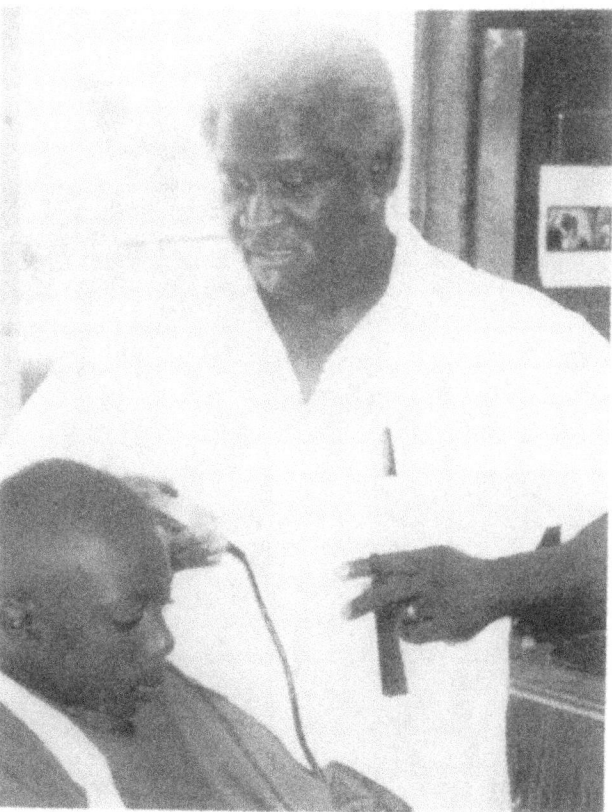

Top Left: Janice Bell Humphrey and Gwendolyn Cavitt Gails. Top Right: Delores Lilly Hill. Bottom Left: Willie Carl Westley, Sr., keynote speaker at the Spirit of Attucks Reunion, Rock Hill Baptist Church, 1998. Bottom Right: Kent Mason, owner of the former Arnette's Barber Shop.

Around The Town

Top: At "The Stand" on Gum Street, Dorcas Cunningham, Harry Mitchell, and Dara Smith, c. 1950.
Bottom: Eula James and Stella Ivy.

Part VI

African American Families

1900-1964

H. Gloria Dean Brown Aiken
Daughter of Arthur and Allean Davis Brown

Top Left: Darnella Johnson Pierce, daughter of Darnell Johnson, with husband Tony and son, Tony Darnell Eugene Pierce. Top Right: Wendell James Johnson, oldest son of Gloria Aiken. Bottom Left: Larone Reliford and children, Jennifer, Keenan, and Marva. Bottom Right: Casandra Aiken, daughter of Columbus Aiken and Gloria Dean Brown Aiken.

African American Families, 1900-1964

Chester and Delores Albritton

Chester and Delores Albritton, the daughter of Raymond and Opal Alexander, were married in Paducah, Kentucky in 1960. Delores's parents settled in Carbondale in 1910 at 423 E. Jackson Street. Her father was born in Fulton, Kentucky on June 13, 1897 and her mother, Opal, was born in Makanda, Illinois on March 17, 1910. In addition to Delores, the Alexanders had two other children, Ramona and Georgette.

Delores and Chester were the parents of three children, Chester Ray Albritton, Jr.; Penny, and April. Chester, Sr. and his daughter Penny are deceased. Mrs. Albritton is the director of the Eurma Hayes Center in Carbondale.

Above: Chester and Delores Albritton and children, Penny, April, and Chester, Jr.

Left: Penny and April Albritton.

Traces In The Dust

Frances L. Johnson Armour

Frances Louise Johnson Armour was born November 8, 1920 in Carbondale, Illinois, the daughter of Sergent Johnson of New Orleans, Louisiana and Mable Sykes Johnson. She grew up in the northeast community of Carbondale, residing on Jackson, Brush, Willow and E. Main Streets.

Mrs. Armour received her education at the Attucks schools and is a long time member of the Olivet Freewill Baptist Church where she has served in various capacities through the years, including committee work and serving in the former Willing Workers Club. Now retired, she formerly worked at the old Jabo's Barbecue stand on "The Levee."

Mrs. Armour is the mother of two daughters, Rose Mary Thornton Watson and Gabrielle Fitzpatrick Mitchell. She has two granddaughters, June Rose Watson and Stephanie Mitchell Jones, and she also has two great granddaughters, Sparkle Mitchell and Nancy Scherril. Frances is the sister of Charles Johnson and Mildred Anderson Harrington; a second sister, Bernice Johnson Mitchell, is deceased.

Flossie and Clifford Bell

Flossie Evelyn Eanes Bell is the daughter of Willie Elmo and Lovie Geneva Massie Eanes. She received her education in the public schools of Ullin, Illinois and moved to Carbondale in August of 1962. She is the sister to five siblings, Elmo Jr., Charlotte, Carol, Cora Faye, and Catherine.

Flossie attended John A. Logan College, earning certification in early child care and development. She was employed in child care for twenty years and retired in March of 2000. She has been a member of Faith Temple Church Of God In Christ since 1962 where she serves on the Mother's Board. She is president of the youth department and a Sunday School teacher.

Flossie was married to Clifford Bell, Jr. in August of 1956. They are the parents of seven children, Gina Kemp, Geta Doss, Glenda Cawthon, Gaylon, Gaideth, Gwonda Tribbilt and Galinee. They also are raising their grandson whose father, Greg, was killed in an auto accident in 1991. The Bells also lost a daughter-in-law who passed away in 1998. The Bell's have twenty-one grandchildren and two great grandchildren. Their family has been featured in several articles in the Southern Illinoisan.

Above: Flossie and Clifford Bell and children.

Henry W. and Mary "Priss" Bell

Mary Elizabeth Flowers was born June 23, 1915 in St. Louis, Missouri. She was the daughter of Thomas Flowers and Mary Brown Flowers. She arrived in Carbondale with her mother on October 16, 1916 when she was sixteen months old and received her educational training in the Attucks schools. Mary Elizabeth, who became known as "Priss," was married to Henry W. Bell on April 20, 1934. The couple settled at 313 E. Birch Street, and "Priss" began to work and help support her family.

Mrs. Bell became a member of Olivet Freewill Baptist Church, and always held a deep, abiding belief in her faith in God. Along with her husband, she became one of the long standing pillars of Olivet, forever aiding in its growth and development.

Henry Bell was born July 15, 1910 in Clarksville, Tennessee. His mother, Mattie Bell, was the fourth wife of John Henry Bell, who had been born a slave in Adairville, Kentucky about the year 1831. The elder John Bell was a Slave House boy, and later, after being set free, he became a farmer. He served in the Civil War and was wounded in battle between December 1861 and January 1862. Henry W. Bell, always the independent spirit, was self employed as a truck driver in Carbondale.

Henry and Priss were married 66 years before the death of Mrs. Bell on July 5, 2000. They were the parents of four children, Henry, Jr., Thomas Eugene, Cozette Regina, and Janice Marie--all of whom have followed their parents' footsteps through dedicated service to their communities and faithfulness to their religious upbringing. Mr. Bell has twelve grandchildren and seven great grandchildren.

African American Families, 1900-1964

Top: The Bell Family. Pictured with the Bells is family friend, Jessie Miller. Bottom Left: Grandchildren of Mary and Henry Bell, Sr.: (From left) Brian, Carol, Henry Bell III, and Paula Bell.

Frances Sadberry Bowers

Frances Sadberry Bowers was born November 17, 1911 in DuQuoin, Illinois to Henry and Emma Stewart Sadberry. She graduated from high school in Kansas City, Missouri and attended Southern Illinois University. Miss Sadberry married Wilbert D. Bowers, Sr. on May 5, 1931. She was a member of Rock Hill Baptist Church and an active participant in the Carbondale Community Club, the Attucks School P. T. A., and the Senior Citizens Programs. She was honored for her contributions to the community on Senior Citizens Appreciation Day, February 29, 1992. She was employed many years at Southern Illinois University and worked several years at the Senior Adult Center.

Mrs. Bowers passed away on July 13, 2000 in Aurora, Illinois. Her family survivors included a daughter Doris June; a son, Wilbert Bowers, Jr.; grandsons, John Thomas, Jr., and Wilbert D. Bowers, III; a son-in-law, Lowell Turley; a daughter-in-law, Doretta Bowers; and two great grandchildren, Brandon and Adam Thomas.

Evelyn and Everett Boykin

Everett Boykin was born in Dewmaine, Illinois July 10, 1913. He was the son of Robert and Cora Flippin Boykin. He was a guard at the Stateville Penitentiary in Joliet, Illinois and at the Menard Correctional Center in Chester, Ill. He retired from the Central Illinois Public Service Company in Carbondale after seventeen years of service. He served as a deacon and a choir member at Olivet Freewill Baptist Church, and Mrs. Boykin served as a Church Mother, a member of the senior choir, and a member of the Willing Worker's Club of Olivet.

Evelyn V. Boykin was born August 1, 1914 in Carbondale to Val and Cecil Branch Woods. She received her educational training in the Attucks schools. She was formerly employed at UD's Cafeteria. Mr. and Mrs. Boykin were married July 15, 1934 in Carbondale. The couple raised a family of seven children.

Everett preceded his wife in death on October 5, 1991 at age 78. Evelyn was also predeceased by her parents, two sons, one daughter, three brothers and two sisters. Mrs. Boykin passed away November 2, 1995 at Carbondale Memorial Hospital. At the time of her death, family survivors included her two daughters, Barbara and Shirley; two sons, Everett Jr. and James; three grandchildren, Anthony, Kerwin, and Nicole; one great grandson, Braison; two sisters Francis White and Ferne Gray; four brothers, Charles, Harold, Jerry, and Ronald Brown; two sons-in-law, Oliver Wheeler and James Watson; and one daughter-in-law, Gloria Boykin.

Minnie M. Brooks

Minnie McDonald Brooks was born February 10, 1901 in Marianna, Arkansas. Her parents were James Edward and Florence Breathett McDonald. Mrs. Brooks married Rev. Moses Brooks in Forest City, Arkansas. The couple had fourteen children. In 1944 Mrs. Brooks moved to Carbondale, and became a member of New Zion Baptist Church. She was active as a Church Mother and a member of the Missionary Society.

Mrs. Brooks was a homemaker and possessed a strong belief in the family unit. As such, she was a very devoted mother and care giver to her husband and children. Mrs. Brooks formerly resided at 510 East Chestnut Street. At the time of her death, she was a resident at 300 South Marion St. Mrs. Brooks died November, 4 1996. She was preceded in death by four sons, three daughters, one brother, and two sisters. Her surviving children included Florence Harris, Minnie Hall, Rosie Speller, Edna Mason, Shirley Cooper, Wilma McDaniel, and Joseph and Robert Brooks. Mrs. Brooks had forty-seven grandchildren and many great grandchildren and great-great grandchildren.

Buelah Mae Brown

Traces In The Dust

Top: John Brown, husband of Cecil Brown, and grandchildren, James "Jasper" Boykin, Alisa Brown, Marilyn Brown and Ronald Brown, Jr. Bottom Left: Stephanie Love, daughter of Priscilla Brown Love (bottom Right).

Lillie and Cornelius Brown

Carl and Eva C. Ross Buggs

Mr. Carl Buggs and his twin sister, Lena Buggs, were born March 7, 1902 in Greenville, Tennessee to Dee and Nancy Buggs. Lena died at age eighteen.

Mrs. Eva Ross was born in De Soto December 19, 1904, the daughter of Thomas A. and Mary L. Eddington Ross. She perceived it an honor that in 1924 she was one of the three students in the first class to ever graduate from the old Attucks High School in Carbondale. She was also the last surviving member of that class. Prior to her marriage to Mr. Buggs on March 7, 1946 in Carbondale, she was the former wife of Ulysses Garrison.

Mr. Buggs was a former employee of the Illinois Central Railroad. For many years he worked as a porter at the old Roberts Hotel in Carbondale. He was an Army veteran of World War II and a member of the American Legion Garvin King Post no. 542.

Mrs. Buggs died in Carbondale on February 15, 1991 at age 86. Her husband succumbed to a lengthy illness at Memorial Hospital in Carbondale on November 23, 1984. He was 82. The couple was married 38 years and resided at 416 East Willow Street. They were the parents to one daughter, Isola Hart, and a son, Isadore Garrison. Eva was the sister of Edna Ross who then resided in Springfield. She was preceded in death by four sisters and eight brothers. Carl Buggs was preceded in death by four sisters and three brothers. He was survived by one brother, Ulysses Buggs of Mounds, Illinois. At the time of her death, Mrs. Buggs had twenty-four great-grandchildren and four great great-grandchildren.

A. D. and Louberta C. McKinley Cavitt

Louberta Catherine McKinley Cavitt was born on August 22, 1907 in Hargrove, Alabama to Edward McKinley of Macon, Georgia and Lula Alexander McKinley of Eutaw, Alabama. She was the only girl and the third child in a family of six children. Four of her brothers are deceased, Edward, William, Enos, and Augustus. She is the sister-in-law of Louvenia McKinley. The McKinleys settled in Carbondale from Dewmaine, Illinois in 1925. Louberta's mother, Lula McKinley, was a licensed evangelist in the A.M.E. Church and a minister in the Church of God.

Louberta graduated from University High School in 1926 and completed a two-year degree program in 1930 at Southern Illinois Normal University. On November 10, 1930, she married Alfred Donald Cavitt of Carbondale. The couple had seven children, Bernadine, Vernita, Edward, Gwendolyn, and Rodney. Two of the children, Alvin and Alfred are deceased. Mr. Cavitt died in 1969. Mrs. Cavitt has seventeen grandchildren, twenty-one great grandchildren, and a great-great grandchild.

Traces In The Dust

Louberta Cavitt and Children

Seated: (from left) Vernita, Gwendolyn, Louberta Cavitt, and Birnadyne. Standing: (from left) Rodney, Alvin Dean, and Edward.

Louie and Celestine M. Cavitt

Celestine and Louie Cavitt are one of the few early African American couples in Carbondale today. Mrs. Cavitt's parents, who were natives of Kentucky, settled in the Carbondale Township in the 1800s.

Celestine Cavitt, fomerly Celestine Gibbs, is the daughter of Edward and Annie E. Pierce Gibbs. She was born in Carbondale on July 10, 1921. She graduated from the former Attucks High School in 1940, and in the same year, she married Louie Cavitt on the 6th of May. They have been married for over sixty years. The Cavitts were the parents of one son, Louis Edward Cavitt, who passed away in 1992 following a distinguising military career.

Mr. Cavitt was born in March of 1920 in Carbondale. In the 1940s, he was employed with the Scott and Greer's Taxi Company, but his last twenty years were spent working at Southern Illinois University. Mrs. Cavitt was formerly employed at the Carbondale Health Care facility. She also worked on the Southern Illinois University campus a number of years for the Sigma Sigma Sigma Sorority.

While a student at Attucks, Mrs. Cavitt held a strong interest in music and was recognized for her exceptional sporano voice. An event at which she excelled was the annual musical contest held during the School Intellectual Competitions. She traveled throughout Southern Illinois consistently taking first place in Solo Competitions.

Her ability and talent caught the attention of her music professors at SIU. She entered one of the institution's major musical events and after taking first place over a white student (something unheard of at that time), she earned the opportunity to debut in New York City.

Mrs. Cavitt continued with her music at Olivet Freewill Baptist Church. Throughout the years, her melodic soprano voice could be heard ringing out in the church choirs. She served on the Mother's Board and was a former member of the Willing Workers Club. Like her mother before her, she is a member of the Mariam Chapter No. 17 Order of the Eastern Star. Throughout the years, Mr. and Mrs. Cavitt have remained residents in their hometown community of northeast Carbondale.

John and Everlene Chambers

Top: William Chappell and children, Hazel, Arthur, Iva, and Patricia. Bottom Left: Louvenia France, mother of Ernell, George, James Arthur, Virginia Mae, Vivian, and Estelle France Chappell. Right: Corrine Robinson, sister of Louvenia France and aunt of Estelle France Chappell.

Traces In The Dust

Josie Belle Clark

Anna Ruth Clemmer

Known by her friends simply as "Anna Ruth," Mrs. Anna Ruth Clemmer was born August 20, 1920 in Ripley, Tennessee. Her parents were Samuel and Erma Thornton Adams. Anna Ruth was a devoted mother and long time community worker (See In Service To Their People).

Mrs. Clemmer joined Rockhill Baptist Church early in life and served in many positions throughout the years. Included were her roles as announcement clerk, her memberships in the Missionary Society, and the Senior Choir, and her leadership role as member of the Scholarship Commission. She also was a pianist for the Sunday School.

Anna Ruth was first married to Melvin Howard, Sr. and later to Namon Clemmer. Mrs. Clemmer was the mother of four children, Melvin Howard, Jr., Betty Anne, Erma Christine, and Felix. Mrs. Clemmer's death occurred on June 29, 1983 in Carbondale. She was 62 years old.

Above: Anna Ruth Clemmer and Family, Veronica Powledge, granddaughter; Christine Clemmer, daughter; and Alan Bauldin.

Traces In The Dust

Mary Francis Daniels

Attucks graduate Dorcas Cunningham Davis and sons, Alvin and Leo. Alvin is pictured graduating from Southern Illinois University in 1981 with a Bachelor's of Science degree in Computer Programing.

Traces In The Dust

Top Left: Crilla Davis, grandmother of Hardin Davis, and Luella Davis. Top Right: Porter McCall, Luella Davis, and Annabelle Jackson. Bottom Left: Christy Ann Davis, granddaughter of Luella Davis. Bottom Right: Elizabeth Davis ("Aunt Lizzie") and Lee McCall ("Grand Papa"), grandfather of Otha and Hardin Allen Davis.

William and Hortense Edward

William Edward, Sr., known affectionately as "Popeye," was born December 11, 1929 in Birmingham, Alabama to George and Chinnie Coleman Edward. He married Hortense McCallister on December 11, 1954 in Carbondale. Before taking up permanent residence in Carbondale, "Popeye" resided in Colp, Illinois where he attended school. In Carbondale he was a member of Rock Hill Baptist Church where he served as a trustee and an usher. "Popeye" was also a member of the Mount Olive Baptist District - Camp Turley Committee, which was responsible for maintenance and improvements to the camp grounds and facilities.

Mrs. Edward, a housewife, is a member of the Olivet Freewill Baptist Church where she has worked for many years on the kitchen committee. "Popeye" was employed for twenty-five years at Southern Illinois University where he served as foreman of grounds maintenance at the physical plant. He was a member of the Laborers' International Union of America and was also a veteran of the Korean War in the United States Army. Mr. Edward was known for his friendly disposition and willingness to help others whenever possible.

William Edward died at age 54 of heart failure at Memorial Hospital in Carbondale August 2, 1984. He was preceded in death by his parents. At the time of his death, family survivors included his wife, Hortense; his son, William Edward, Jr.; his daughter, Agnes Medlin; and his mother-in-law, Mrs. Julia Hogan. Mrs. Edward currently resides in Carbondale.

Pictured above: Hortense, William Edward, Sr., and son, William Edward, Jr.

Mable Evelyn Meredith Favors

Mable Evelyn Meredith Favors is the daughter of Joseph and Teeny Meredith and the sibling of four sisters, Frances, Leona, Beatrice, and Vivian. Mable was the first of her sisters to move to Carbondale from Chester, Illinois. She arrived in 1941 and resided with relatives. She attended the Bethel A.M.E. Church and graduated from Attucks High School in 1944. She is a resident of East St. Louis, Illinois.

George and Ann Harriston France
Son and daughter-in-law of James Abe France

Traces In The Dust

Top Left: Sons of James Abe France, George "Buck" France and James Arthur France. Top Right: Devin and Alexis, grandchildren of George and Ann France. Bottom: The family of James Arthur France (standing). Seated are daughter, Michelle; wife, Mary; and son, Reginald.

African American Families, 1900-1964

Above: Samuel and Jean Helen Gibbs. Samuel Harrison Gibbs was born July 29, 1907 in Carbondale. He and his wife, Jean Helen English, were married April 7, 1955. They established their first family residence on Walnut Street. Samuel and Jean are the parents of five children, Linda, Herschel, Brenda, Edward, and Dennis. Below: Jewel and Cora Gibbs with her father, Lane Fletcher, and children, Jewel, Mary Alice and Constance.

Cora L. Fletcher Gibbs

Cora Lee Fletcher Gibbs was born March 29, 1922 in Grenda, Mississippi to the union of Lane and Mary Evans Fletcher. The Fletchers had settled in Carbondale by 1928, and Cora was one of four children born to them. In 1941 Cora was a senior at Attucks High School and on February 6, 1945 she was married to Jewell E. Gibbs. Jewell and Cora had three children.

Cora accepted Christ at an early age and was a member of Olivet Freewill Baptist Church. After completing her education at Attucks, she attended Southern Illinois University. Cora was the first known Black student from the area to attend the Cook County Medical School. She worked as a nurse at Holden Hospital and Memorial Hospital. She was a member of the Lamplighter's Club and the Marion Chapter No. 17 Order of Eastern Star.

Cora died August 16, 2000 at her home. Her parents, two brothers, her son, and husband preceded her in death. Surviving family members included two daughters, Constance and Mary Alice Gibbs; a brother Claude of St. Louis, Missouri; grandchildren, Gloria Cora Gibbs, Jewel L. Gibbs, Jr., and Kimberly Volner; step grandchildren Lionel and Anthony Gaston; sisters-in-law and brothers-in-law Celestine and Louie Cavitt, Emma Fletcher, S. Harrison and Jean Gibbs, Anita Gibbs, and Eleanor Fletcher; a daughter-in-law, Gloria Jean Gaston; and great-grandchildren, Gloria Shanece and Simeon.

Above: Cora Gibbs and son, Jewel ("Huckie").

Allean Davis Brown Gordon
"Momean"

Ferne and Jeffrey Gray

Ferne Gray was the daughter of John and Cecil Brown. She was born in Carbondale on September 4, 1921. She married Jeffrey Gray in Milwaukee, Wisconsin in 1948. Mr. and Mrs. Gray had five children, Priscilla (dec.), Jeffrey, Jr; Cheryl, Mayola; and Terrie Lynn.

Ferne and Jeffrey were long time members of Olivet Freewill Baptist Church. For many years she served faithfully on the kitchen committee preparing meals and dinners for various events. She was also a member of the Willing Workers Club of Olivet and a long time member of the church choir. She worked in the Sunday School and organized youth groups and young peoples' programs of the church. Ferne was a graduate of Attucks High School. She was employed at the Home Health Care facility. Jeffrey Gray was born in Monroe, Louisiana. He was a past employee of Vogler Ford. Mr. and Mrs. Gray passed away in 2001.

Ferne Gray passed away January 17, 2001. She was preceded in death by her husband Jeffrey Gray, Sr., a daughter, a grandson, a great grandson, four brothers, and five sisters.

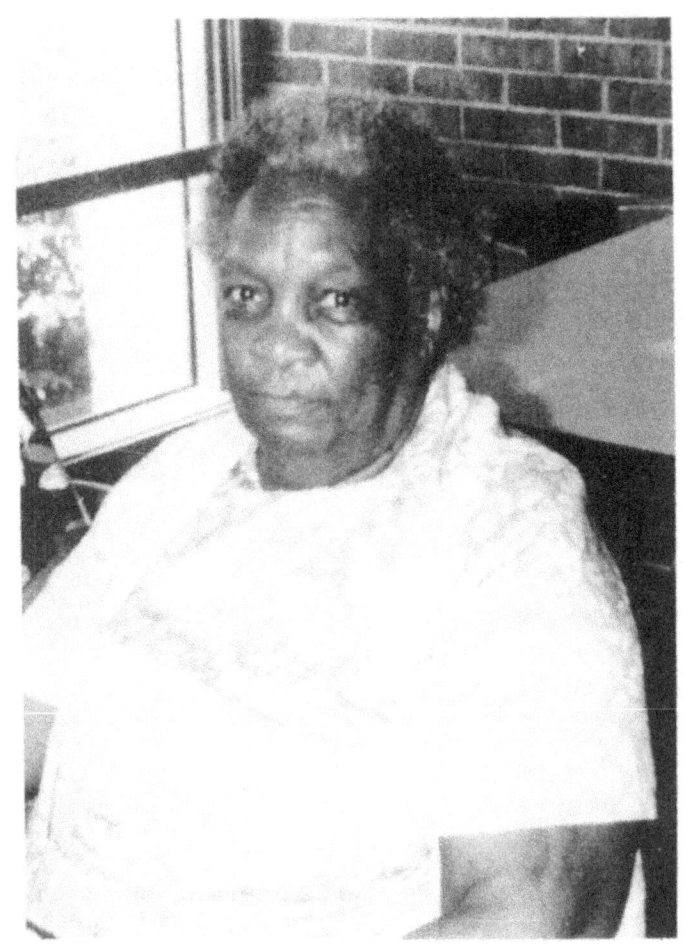

Mary Helen Greene-Jennings

Mary Helen Greene-Jennings was born in Carbondale August 4, 1921 to Archie Judge and Ella Smith Greene of West Point, Mississippi. Archie and Mrs. Greene settled in Carbondale in 1918 where Mr. Greene found work at the Kopper's Tie Plant. He served as a precinct Captain of the 2nd ward under the Roosevelt Administration.

Helen Greene grew up in Carbondale where she attended the Attucks Grade School and the Attucks High School. She was a member of the class of 1939.

Mrs. Greene-Jennings united with the Hopewell Baptist Church under the pastorship of Rev. Joseph Peterson in 1929. She was a member of the National Association for Young Colored Girls under the leadership of Hannah Woods. She was also a member of the Camp Fire Girls under the directorship of B. B. Brown.

Mrs. Greene-Jennings was employed as a cook for the Kappa Alpha Kappa Fraternity house at Washington University in St. Louis, Mo for three years. She was a Housekeeper for the MacIntosh family in Palestine, Illinois for thirty years. After working a total of fifty-five years, Mrs. Greene-Jennings retired in 1986.

Helen Greene-Jennings is the mother of Shirley Mason Moore and the sister of Cassie McNulty, Lydia Stewart, and Dorothy Lou Devers. Two of her sisters, Beulah Mae Brown and Marguerite Greene, are deceased. She has three grandchildren, Tracey Sims, and Victor and Matthew Moore. She also has three great grandchildren, Pierre, Tiffany and Nicolas Moore.

Irene Rice Hayden

Irene Rice Hayden, affectionately known as "Mamarene," settled in Carbondale in 1933 from Brookport, Illinois. She married Simon Hayden in 1934. The late Mr. Hayden retired from the railroad; he worked at both the round house and the tie plant.

Above: Mrs. Irene Hayden with her four daughters, Doris, Christine, Mardell, and Thelma Maretha.

William Hayes with mother, Lillian, daughter, Nettie and grandchildren.

Traces In The Dust

Wanda Perkins Garrison Haynes

Wanda Perkins Garrison Haynes was born in 1927, the youngest of eight children of Aaron and Lucy Perkins. Wanda attended Attucks Elementary and Attucks High Schools. She graduated from high school and married Isadore Garrison in 1945. The couple had three children, Beverly, Is adore, Jr., and Reginald. In 1976, Wanda married Dewitt Haynes, who passed away in 1982.

Wanda has been an active member of Rock Hill Missionary Baptist Church since 1940. She retired from the choir in 1999 after sixty years of service. Currently, she serves as a Church Mother.

Wanda retired from GTE in 1981 where she was a telephone operator. She has given much effort to the civic affairs of the community (see In Service To Their People). In her spare time, Mrs. Haynes enjoys participating in the Carbondale Community Club. She also enjoys spending time with her grandchildren and great grandchildren.

Above: Wanda Perkins Garrison Haynes is shown with her mother, Mrs. Lucy Perkins, and children, Beverly and Reginald. Not pictured is the eldest son, Isadore Garrison, Jr.

Beatrice and U. L. Hudson, Jr.

U. L. Hudson, Jr., the son of Bashierdeen and U. L. Hudson, Sr., was born in Carbondale. He was the brother of Charlotte Hudson (dec.), Dorothea Jones of Milwaukee, Wisconsin, and Archibald Hudson (dec.). He graduated from the Attucks school system and was a member of Rock Hill Baptist Church.

Beatrice Cavitt Hudson is the daughter of Edward and Beatrice Cavitt, both of whom are deceased. She was also born in Carbondale and is the sister of Louie Cavitt. Like her husband, Beatrice is a former student of the Attucks Grade School and a graduate of the Attucks High School. She is a member of the Olivet Freewill Baptist Church where she serves in the Senior Choir and sits on the Mother's Board. Mrs. Hudson is a former member of the Willing Workers Club of Olivet and a member and Past Matron of the Order of the Eastern Star, Mariam Chapter No. 17.

U. L. Jr. and Beatrice Hudson were married on February 15, 1942. U. L. Passed away on October 2, 2001. Mrs. Hudson is the mother of two daughters, Claudette and Lorraine. She has two grandsons, K. Tyrone Spann and Rodney D. McConnell, and she has one great granddaughter.

Lorraine Hudson and son Rodney

Alice Isbell

Stella Ivy and granddaughter, Rebekah Everage

African American Families, 1900-1964

Top Left: Stella Ivy and son, Jesse Euell Ivy; holding Jesse Euell is Mrs. Ivy's niece, Betty Jean Smith. Top Right: Owen Ivy, son of Stella Ivy. Bottom Left: Callie James, daughter of Stella Ivy. Bottom Right: Stella Ivy, Roberta Smith, and Rosetta Cole attend a family reunion.

Willie Mae and James A. Jamison

James A. Jamison, the son a of a Baptist Minister, was born on June 25, 1916 in Macon, Mississippi. His parents were Reverend Gilbert and Dora Ferguson Jamison. James married his childhood sweetheart, Willie Mae Cooper, the daughter of Forest Cooper and Freddie B. Metz Cooper, on June 21, 1937 in Macon, Mississippi. They settled in Carbondale in November of 1938.

Mrs. Jamison was a Film Librarian at Southern Illinois University in Carbondale from 1950 to 1988. She served in the Carbondale Community Club and the Triple Four Community Club and has been honored for her work in these organizations. Mr. Jamison was a leader at his church and the founder of one of Carbondale's most successful spiritual musical groups.

Mr. Jamison was a United States Army veteran of World War II and a former Worshipful Master of Tuscan Lodge #44 F. & A.M. of Carbondale. He was employed at Southern Illinois University as a maintenance technician where he retired after more than thirty years of service. In 1987, Mr. and Mrs. Jamison celebrated their Golden Wedding anniversary in Carbondale. They raised a family of eight children: James, Forest, Charles, Willie James, Julia Ann, Ginger, Nadine, and Michael.

James Jamison had five brothers and five sisters who preceded him in death. He died August 12, 1995 in Peoria, Illinois at St. Francis Medical Center. Mrs. Jamison has twenty-two grandchildren and twenty-eight great-grandchildren.

Top: Daughters and granddaughters of James and Willie Mae Jamison. (From left, back row) Nadine, Ginger, and Julia. (From left, front row) Jamie Jamison, daughter of Forrest Jamison; and Ebonee, daughter of Ginger and Abraham Westley. Bottom: Sons and grandsons of James and Willie Mae Jamison, James, Jr.; Charles, Michael, Forrest, Donald, Damien, Charley, Jr., and Willie James.

Mildred Mable Anderson Harrington Jordan

Mildred Mable Anderson Harrington was born August 12, 1929 at 424 E. Jackson Street in Carbondale and grew up on East Brush and North Barnes Streets. She is the daughter of Mable Sykes Johnson Anderson and Charles Anderson of Quincy, Illinois.

Mildred attended Attucks Grade and Attucks High Schools. She worked as a supervisor at Tuck Tape and retired after 28 years of service. She is an active member of Olivet Freewill Baptist Church where, through the years, she has served in several capacities. Additionally, she has worked in the quest for the betterment of the Carbondale Community (see In Service To Their People).

Mildred is the sister of Charles Johnson and Frances Johnson Armour. One sister, Bernice Johnson Mitchell, is deceased. She has two step-sisters and one step-brother, Iray Franklin Tisdale, Mary Franklin Hersey, and Albert Franklin, Jr.

Mildred is the mother of seven children, Willie Carl Westley, Abraham Westley, Jr., Don Harrington, Sherrie Lee Harrington Duncan, Clarence Harrington, III, Anthony Harrington, and Angela Lorraine Harrington Jackson. On June 30, 2001, Mildred married Edward Jordan, Sr. Mrs. Jordan has twenty-one grand children and seventeen great grand children.

Maggie L. Steele Kenner

Maggie L. Steele Kenner was born in Carbondale on June 7, 1914 to Harrison and Natalie Rice Steele. She attended the Attucks schools and was married to George Kenner on July 1, 1933 in Carbondale. The couple established their home at 413 1/2 Brush Street where their twelve children grew up.

Mrs. Kenner worked as a housekeeper for Dr. Fred Lingle, and she retired from Southern Illinois University as a cook. At the time of her death, family survivors included her children, Patsy Dean, Gwendale, Joyce, Delilah, LaDonna, Rhonda, Janice, Yvonne, Larry, Carlos, Basil, and her husband, George.

Traces In The Dust

Top: The Kenner Sisters, (from left) Janice, Rhonda, Patsy Dean, Gwendale ("Baby Sis"), LaDonna, and Delilah. Bottom Left: Margaret Michelle Margrum. Bottom Right: Janice Kenner Bailey.

Rose and Atlas Laster

Atlas Laster, Sr. was born October 8, 1919 in Edmondson, Arkansas to Early and Hattie Griffin Laster. He entered the United States Army on September 7, 1942 and received an Honorable discharge on September 23, 1945. He was awarded three Bronze Stars and the Good Conduct Medal for campaigns in France, the Rhineland, and Normandy. Atlas married Rose Ella Brown in Blytheville, Arkansas, and the family moved to Carbondale in 1952. They united with the New Zion Missionary Baptist Church. Mr. Laster was employed by the Carbondale School District 195 in the maintenance department. He also worked for Drs. Hugh and John McGowan of Carbondale and was a member of the Service Employees International Union Local 316, AFL-CIO of Carbondale.

Rose Laster was born July 26, in Marston, Missouri to Frances Valliant Brown and Nelious Brown. She was employed by Church Women United Day Care Center, which later came under the directorship of Model Cities and eventually was taken over by the City of Carbondale. Mrs. Laster retired from this job in the position of Support Services Assistant. Atlas Laster died September 13, 1985 at the Jackson County Nursing Home in Murphysboro, Illinois. He was preceded in death by a brother and two sisters. He was survived by his wife, Rose; three sons, Atlas, Jr., Early, and John; seven daughters, Margaret, Frances, Phyllis, Kathleen, Rhonda, Annie Louise and Gloria; thirty grandchildren; and five great grandchildren. Mrs. Laster, a long time worker in the community, continues to be involve in community affairs and with various civic organizations (See In Service To Their People).

Traces In The Dust

Top: Rose Laster and Family. (Back row, from left) Atlas Laster, Jr., Kathy Laster, Margaret Laster Mayberry, Early Laster, Phyllis Laster Khaalig; and Frances Davenport. (Seated, from left) Rhonda Laster, Mrs. Rose Laster, and John Laster Bottom Left: Lashaunda Laster, granddaughter of Rose Laster. Bottom Right: Grandsons of Rose and Atlas Laster, Tony, Early II, and Austing Laster.

Frances Rachel Meredith Lee

Frances Rachel Meredith Lee, the daughter of Joseph and Teeny Meredith, arrived in Carbondale from Chester, Illinois in 1943 to live with an aunt and her husband, Jessie and Bob Lewis, at 313 E. Oak Street. She graduated from Attucks Junior High School and completed her education in East St. Louis, Illinois. She eventually became a resident of Cahokia, Illinois.

Frances attended Bethel A.M. E. Church, where she worked with youth groups and the youth choir. At age 12, she worked at Allean's Cafe, and she is a former employee in Janitorial Services at Southern Illinois University. Frances is currently employed at the St. Clair County Court Building in Belleville, Illinos, where she had worked for 32 years. She is the mother of seven children and the grandmother and great grandmother forty-six grandchildren combined.

Charles Lilly, Jr.
Son of Hattie Belle and Charles "Papa" Lilly, Sr.

Geraldine Lilly and Family

(From left) Cynthia; Ronoda Moore; Wilbert; Mrs. Geraldine Lilly; Michael, grandson of Geraldine Lilly; and Tiffany Moore, daughter of Ronoda Moore.

Traces In The Dust

The Family of Ora P. and Edward Lilly, Sr.

The children of Ora and Edward Lilly, Sr.: (From Left) Edna Bradsfield; Napoleon Lilly; Geraldine Lilly; Cecil Edward Lilly, Jr.; Carol Lilly-Brown; John Lilly, Sr.; Rose Johnson and Callie Lilly.

Willie Dee Lilly
Son of Charles "Papa" Lilly

Edna and Thomas Mason

Edna and Thomas Mason were married on June 30, 1975 in Cairo, Illinois. Thomas, a native of Jackson, Tennessee was born on October 16, 1930. He worked for the E. T. Simon Construction Company in Carbondale and retired from the firm at age 62.

Edna Mason retired from the Eurma Hayes Child Care center when it was under the administration of the City of Carbondale. Mr. and Mrs. Mason are members of Olivet Freewill Baptist Church. Mrs. Mason serves on the Mother's Board and is active in other areas. She serves on the kitchen committee, helping in the preparation of meals at various church functions. The Masons have four children, Dyanna F. Van Laré, Willie JoAnn Reed, Candice M. Wilson, and Torrence L. Westbrook. Two children, Larry D. Gilmore and Robert T. Gilmore are deceased. Mr. and Mrs. Mason are current residents of the Carbondale northeast community.

Gladys and Warren Grigsby and Family

Gladys Mae O'Neal Grigsby was born in Carbondale on January 3, 1934. Warren Grigsby, Sr. was born April 11, 1940 in New Madrid, Missouri. The couple married on December 23, 1960 and settled in their first home on East Brush Street. The Grigsbys attended the Attucks school system in Carbondale and have worked faithfully through the years in the ministry. Warren and Gladys organized the Grigsby Family Singers and have given concerts throughout the Southern Illinois area.

The Grigsbys are the parents of six children: Anthony, Daphne Lorraine, Darlene Denise, Darron, Erica Elaine, and Warren Grigsby, Jr.

Traces In The Dust

Top Left: Delores and Anita, daughters of Vance and Marie Mason. Top Right: Vance Mason and grandson, Jimmie. Bottom Left: Raymon Mason, son of Vance and Marie Mason. Bottom Right: Anita Mason Gibbs and son, Gary.

Reverend James and Charlesetta Mason Moore

Della and Robert Matthews

Christine and Cleveland Matthews

Traces In The Dust

Top: Della Matthews and neighborhood children at the birthday party given for Darnecea Smith who turned two years old; among the children are (foreground) Darnecea Smith, Janet Johnson, Connie Walls, Diane Roseman, Gloria Perkins, and James Corthen; (background) Zoro Roseman, Delores Perkins, and Willis Gibson. Bottom Left: Della Matthews. Bottom Right: Ethel Florence Smith, daughter of Della Matthews, dons evening attire for the annual Mardi Gras, January 1966.

Beaudenual Virginia and Earnest Mayfield

Beaudenual Virginia Millner moved to Carbondale from Hickman, Kentucky in 1948. She is the daughter of Ruby Millner of Little Rock, Arkansas and Locie Millner of Fulton, Kentucky. Mrs. Millner, better known by friends and family as "Virginia," had sister and three brothers who are deceased.

Earnest, the son of March and Earnestine Mayfield, arrived in Carbondale in 1946 from Hermandale, Missouri. He and Virginia met in 1962 when Virginia moved back to Carbondale from Charleston, Missouri. They were married Oct 18, 1964.

The couple made their first homestead in "The Fields" (the area immediately north of Fisher Street and to the east of Barnes Streets) in a house owned by Rev. Reed. Mrs. Mayfield did housework cleaning four homes a day for eight years. Mr. Mayfield work as a janitor at the Varsity Theater, the Varsity Cafe, and the Varsity Barber Ship. He also supported his family by working at the Sobery Bakery where he remained for 16 years until its closing. The couple moved to Marion Street in 1962. Mr. and Mrs. Mayfield raised seven children: Barbara Jean, Maxine, Melvin, Earnest Jr., Wanda Sue, Marylyn, and Mary.

Traces In The Dust

Top Left: Ahsanti Elcrilla Foster, daughter of Robert McCall Foster. Top Right: Robert Lee McCall Foster. Bottom Left: Clarence and Elner Jane Johnson with Robert Lee McCall, Jr., son of Robert Lee McCall Foster. Bottom Right: Terrill Travis son of Robert Lee McCall Foster.

Hal and Jessie McCroy

Hal McCroy, was born in Carbondale on Ashley Street on April 15, 1940. He is the son of Lillie McCroy, a native of Mississippi, and Hal McCroy Senior of Corinth, Tennessee. He was delivered by Dr. Jewel Bass, who at one time resided on Jackson Street in Carbondale. Hal attended Attucks Grade School and graduated from Attucks High School.

Hal was first married to Geraldine Greer who passed away in 1967. The couple had two daughters, Angela Denise and Phyllis Delores. Hal and Jessie Clare McDaniel were married June 14, 1968 and three children were born to them: Rhonda, Julian, and Richard.

Jessie McCroy is a native of Mt. Vernon, Illinois. She arrived in Carbondale in 1958 and attended the Attucks Schools. She is a long time, active member of Olivet Freewill Baptist Church. Hal is the brother of Bessie McCroy Bowers and Odessa Meeks. He is a Maintenance Technician for the Jackson County Housing Authority. Hal and Jessie have seventeen grand children and two great grandchildren. The couple resides on Robert Stalls Avenue (the former North Barnes Street).

Odessa McCroy Meeks

Odessa McCroy Meeks was born in Carbondale on February 12, 1942. She graduated from Attucks High School in 1960 and married Raymond Mason in 1961. She later married Billie Meeks of Centralia, Illinois. Affectionately known as "Rabbitt," Odessa is the mother of four children, Jason Meeks, and Lowell, Twanda, and Tanya Mason. Odessa has worked tirelessly on behalf of the African American Community of Carbondale and is the recipient of several awards and recognitions (See In Service To Their People).

African American Families, 1900-1964

Top Left: Tanya Mason and daughter, Ajisha. Top Right: Lowell and Kathi Mason with sons, Cameron and Raymond. Bottom Left: David McCroy and Wife, Benita, and daughter, Deandre. Bottom Right: Lillie McCroy with grandson, Jason Meeks.

Enos and Louvenia McKinley

Enos James McKinley was born November 22, 1910 in Hargrove, Alabama, the son of Edward and Lula Alexander McKinley. His family moved to Illinois in 1915, where he attended public school in Dewmaine and Colp, Illinois. Enos settled in the city of Carbondale in 1929 and attended Southern Illinois Teachers college. His wife, Louvenia Bell of Mounds, Illinois, was born March 14, 1914, and came to Carbondale in 1931.

The McKinleys were married on January 17, 1933 in Murphysboro and settled at 305 East Chestnut Street in Carbondale. They remained married for over fifty years and were the parents of three sons James, the oldest; Ronald, the second born; and Duane, the youngest son, known by friends and family as "Skip." All of the Mckinley sons were graduates of the old Attucks High School.

Enos was a long time employee at Attucks High School where he worked as a custodian, painter, and mechanic for twenty-seven years. He retired in 1975. Mrs. McKinley was a housewife and a long time community leader (See, In Service to Their People).

In 1943 Enos became a member of Bethel A.M.E. Church where he took pride in providing maintenance for the church and served in various capacities over the years. He passed away in February of 1985. At the time of Mr. McKinley's death, family survivors included four grandsons, Michael, Kevin, Steven, and Patrick; one granddaughter, Carla; and three great grandchildren, Ronald Michael, Tiffany, and Keith. Mr. McKinley had two brothers, Edward and Odell, and one sister Louberta Cavitt. He had several brothers and sisters by marriage.

Lee Anna Miller

Lee Anna Walls Miller first settled in Carbondale in 1941 after living in Clarksdale, Mississippi. Her husband, Joe John Miller, was born in Tupelo, Mississippi. The couple was married at 1118 N. Allman Street in Carbodale. The Millers had twelve children: Johnny, R. E. Berry, Joe, Oliver, Richard, Leon, Louise, Gloveree, Early, Georgia Ann, Valerie, and J. W. Williams. They had eleven grandchildren: Dorothy, Ella Mae, Bud, Luster, Earnestine, Milton, Eanner, Harlee, Danny, Thornlee, and Leo.

Traces In The Dust

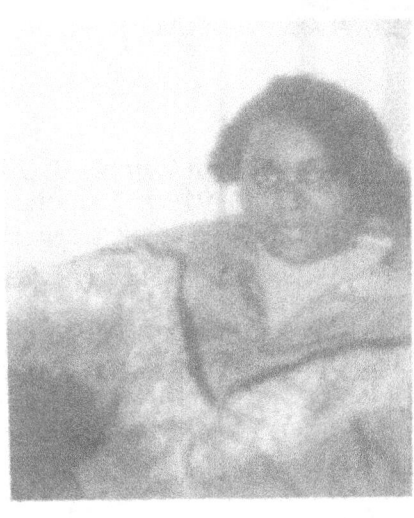

Top Left: Eanna Miller. Top Right: Early and Gloveree "Huncie" Miller, children of Lee Anna Miller. Center Left: Richard Miller, son of Lee Anna Miller. Bottom Left: Levett Johnson, daughter of Dorothy Miller. Lower Right: aunt of Dorothy Miller, Louiese Miller; and Dorothy Miller Lewis.

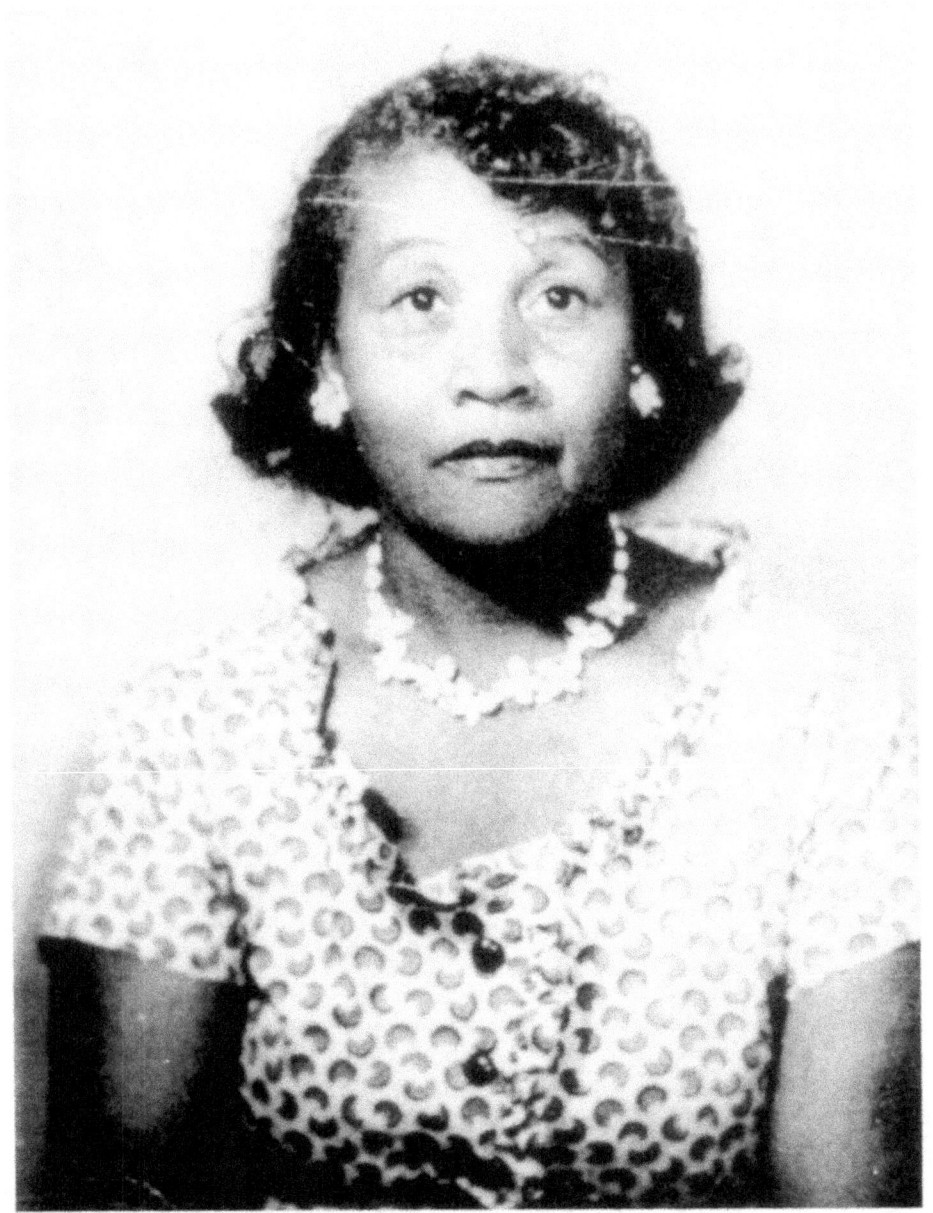

Ida A. Chappell

Ida A. Melton Chappell, the daughter of Lynn and Rilla Smith Melton, was born October 25, 1902 in West Point, Mississippi. She was married to Shelly Chappell on August 28, 1919 in Carbondale. Mr. Chappell preceded her in death on July 24, 1974. Also preceding her in death were Mrs. Chappell's parents and four brothers. Mrs. Chappell was a member of the Green Street Church of God where she was a Church Mother.

Ida Chappell died October 23, 1978 at her home on East Larch Street in Carbondale. Her survivors included three daughters, Jewel Louise Harris, Hazel Mae Dawson, and Ruth Evelyn Brooks; her three sons, William Shelly Chappell, James Wesley Chappell, and Edward Earl Chappell; two sisters, Sirmae Chandler and Minnie Hubbard; one brother, Noah Melton; and an aunt, Ethel Smith of Carbondale. At the time of her death, Mrs. Chappell had seventeen grandchildren; thirty-four great grandchildren; and one great, great grandchild.

Bernice and Sola B. "Mitch" Mitchell

African American Families, 1900-1964

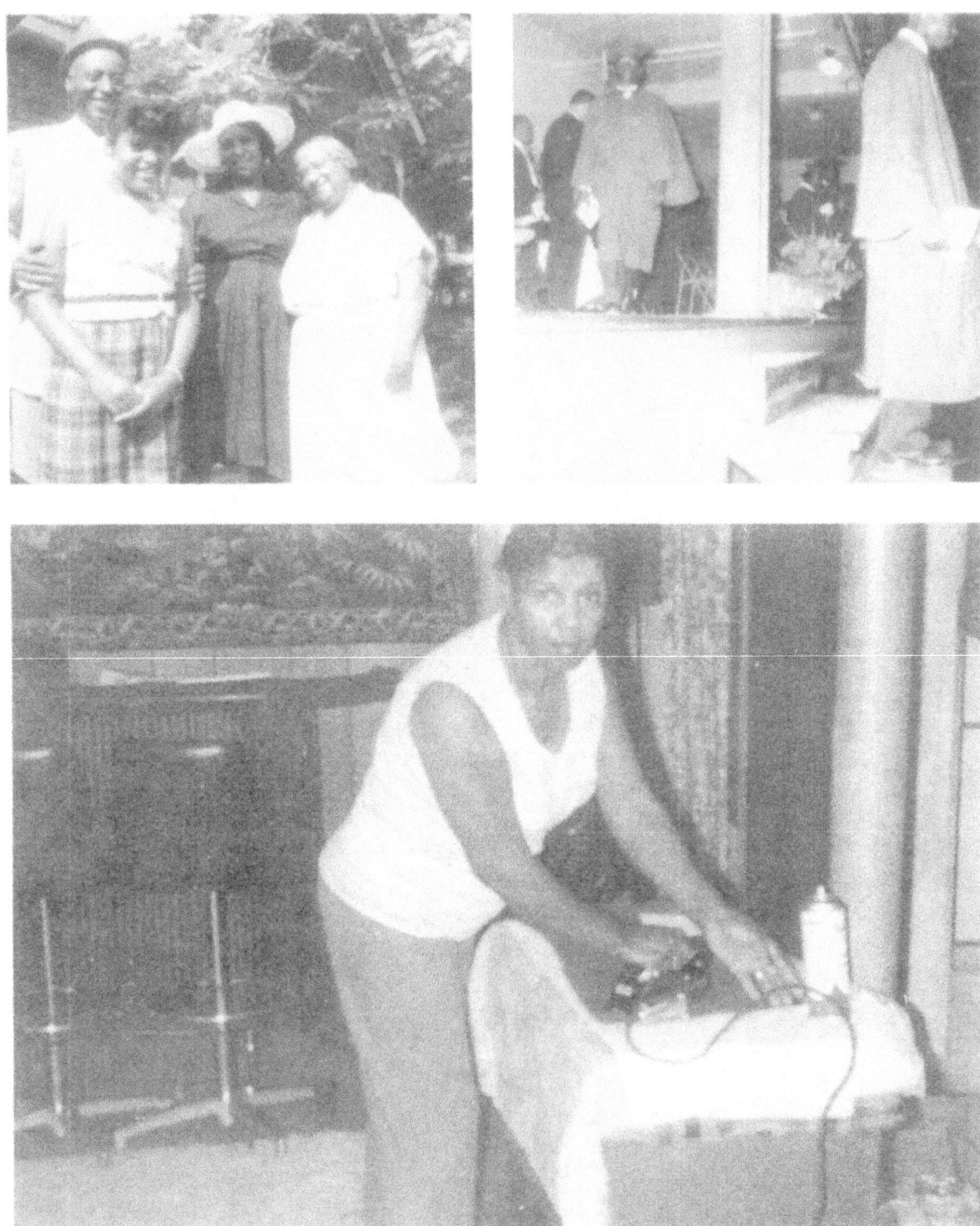

Top Left: Three generations, Mrs. Mabel Franklin (right) with daughter, Bernice Mitchell; granddaughter, Sandra Sue Greer; and "Mitch." Top Right: David Dean Williams marches across the stage at his Attuks Junior High School 8th grade graduation ceremonies, 1961. Bottom: Mrs. Bernice Mitchell at her home on North Barnes Street.

Bertha Mitchell

African American Families, 1900-1964

Statsie C. and Bertha I. Mosley

Statsie Carl Mosley was born in Mounds City, Illinois on November 22, 1890. In 1909 he married Bertha Inez Meeks of Pulaski, Illinois in East St. Louis, Illinois. Mrs. Mosley was born August 8, 1891. The Mosleys moved to Carbondale in the year 1921 and settled at 309 Willow Street. Mr. Mosley was employed as a boiler maker for the Illinois Central Railroad. His wife was an educator. Mr. Mosley died on January 9, 1962. Inez Mosley passed away on April 30, 1967. Mr. and Mrs. Mosley were the parents of seven children, Monyette Mosley Penny, Freda Mosley Burch, Josephine Mosley Haynes, Carl Mosley, Geneva Mosley Lang, Archibald Mosley, and Clifford Mosley.

Dr. Archibald and Jerolene Mosley

Reverend Doctor Archibald Mosely, a minister and a retired educator, was born in Carbondale May 25, 1925 to Statsie and Inez Meeks Mosely. He is the husband of Jerolene Thomas Mosley. Rev. Mosely pastored for a number of years in Carbondale at Bethel A.M.E. Church (See In Service To Their People). He later worked as the Public Relations Director for the city of Pontiac, Michigan. Rev. and Mrs. Mosley are the parents of four daughters, Elizabeth, Vickie, Susan, and Theresa. They have five grandchildren.

Thomas and Margaret Nesbitt

Thomas and Margaret Jean Nesbitt, lifelong residents and civic minded innovators of Carbondale, were among the early builders of the Northeast community. Thomas was born in Carbondale on July 31, 1926, the son of Beatrice Floyd Nesbitt of Cotton Plant, Arkansas. His father, Mr. T. Nesbitt, a laborer from Mississippi, was a worker at the tie plant. The birth was attended by midwife Ella Lacy.

Margaret Jean Simon, a native of Tennessee, was born in Memphis in 1929 and arrived in Carbondale with her family in 1940 when she was eleven years old. Thomas and Margaret were married June 15, 1948 and first set up household on East Willow Street. The Nesbitts were the parents of four children, Carol Jean, James Darnell, Debra Joyce, and Ulysses Carl Marshall. Mr. Nesbitt was employed for more than twenty years at the United States Post Office. Mrs. Nesbitt was a former employee at Southern Illinois University and is currently the owner of D's Restaurant. The Nesbitt family has been united with Rock Hill Missionary Baptist Church since the late 1940s, the children following in the footsteps of their mother, Mrs. Jeanetha Simon. Mrs. Nesbitt serves in the Senior Choir and the BYPU. She also serves in the Usher Board and the Dining Hall Committee.

Mr. Nesbitt passed away August 11, 1992 at the Veteran Administration Medical Center in Marion, Illinois. Preceding him in death were his parents, a daughter, a sister and two brothers. Surviving relatives included two grandchildren, Miya and Hasani Nesbitt; three sisters, Addie Smith, Frances Morgan, and Alberta Blythe; and a brother, Reuben Nesbitt. Mrs. Nesbitt currently resides in Carbondale and--following in the footsteps of her mother and husband--remains actively engaged in the continuous struggle to help improve conditions for Blacks in the city (See In Service to Their People).

Traces In The Dust

John and Rosetta O'Neal

John Milton O'Neal, Sr. was born July 2, 1912 in Mound City, Illinois, the son of Rev. William and Myrtle Harper O'Neal. In 1939 he married Rosetta Crenshaw of Rives, Tennessee. The couple lived in Mound City where their three children were born. The O'Neals moved to Carbondale in 1958.

Mr. and Mrs. O'Neal were both career educators and active community leaders Mrs. O'Neal developed a strong interest in Black culture and eventually took measures to research and preserve the traditions and history of the black community of Carbondale (See In Service To Their People).

John O'Neal passed away November 23, 1992. At the time of his death, family survivors included his wife; a daughter Pamela Moody; two sons, John Jr. and Wendell; two brothers, Angelo and Robert O'Neal; two sisters, Kate Meeks and Laverne Cozart Robinson; and seven grandchildren.

Erie and Booker O'Neal

Traces In The Dust

Top: Walter and Delores Norman and Sons. Bottom: Three Generations: Carrie Mason (left) with daughter, Delores Norman and granddaughter, Sunday, daughter of Johnny Norman.

Emily Palmer Lyles and Mother, Mrs. Thelma Palmer

Traces In The Dust

Galveston and Leah Perkins

Galveston and Leah Perkins were the parents of Aaron Perkins. Aaron was the oldest of his siblings. The Perkins settled in Carbondale from Brownsfield, Illinois in 1922. Clyde Perkins was the eldest child of Aaron and Lucy Perkins.

Top: Galveston and Leah Perkins.

Bottom: The Perkins family: (Standing, from left) Clyde Perkins and wife, Geraldine Perkins: Joseph Hayes; Henry Perkins; Marion Perkins; Iva and Walter Neal and granddaughter, Angie; Robert Perkins; and Dallas Perkins. (Kneeling, from left) Ottie Perkins; Veachie Robinson; Etta Delores Hayes; Rubye Perkins, Wanda Haynes and Grace Perkins Kelley. In absentia are Mattie Perkins Webb; Roselle Perkins Thomas; Rayford Perkins; Elva Perkins; and Mable Perkins Lyles.

African American Families, 1900-1964

Clyde and Geraldine Perkins

Russell and Veachie Perkins Robinson

Russell Robinson, a native of West Point, Mississippi, was born January 12, 1918 to George and Louise Robinson. He attended St. Augustine Catholic School in East St. Louis, Illinois. Russell came to Carbondale where he met and married Veachie Perkins.

Russell had an illustrious military career. Entering the United States Army in 1941, he spent 18 1/2 years of active duty with the 93rd Division. His tours of duty included Germany, Korea, the Pacific, and other areas of Asia. He was a squad leader of thirteen men, all of whom were killed. After being wounded, Russell spent one year in Gardner General Hospital. He was discharged as a disabled veteran at Fort Knox, Kentucky. He received several awards including the Korean Service Medal with seven Bronze Service Stars, the United Nations Service Medal, and the National Defense Service Service Medal.

Upon returning to civilian life, Russell worked at the Statesville Correctional Institution in Joliet, Illinois and at the Koppers Company in Carbondale where he retired as the first black supervisor at that establishment. Russell served as an usher and a trustee at Olivet Freewill Church.

Mr. Robinson died April 7, 1997 in Marion, Illinois. Surviving his death were his wife, Veachie; a son and daughter-in-law, Robert and Jackie Robinson; a daughter, Nedra Taylor; four grandchildren, Brandon Robinson, Andrea Elliot, Garland Taylor, II, and Brian Taylor; and two great-grandchildren, Ashley and Briane Elliott.

Bottom: Daughters and son of Clyde and Geraldine Perkins. Left: Delores Perkins Rhodes and Gloria Perkins Oglesby. Right: William "Billy" Perkins.

Russell and Veachie Robinson

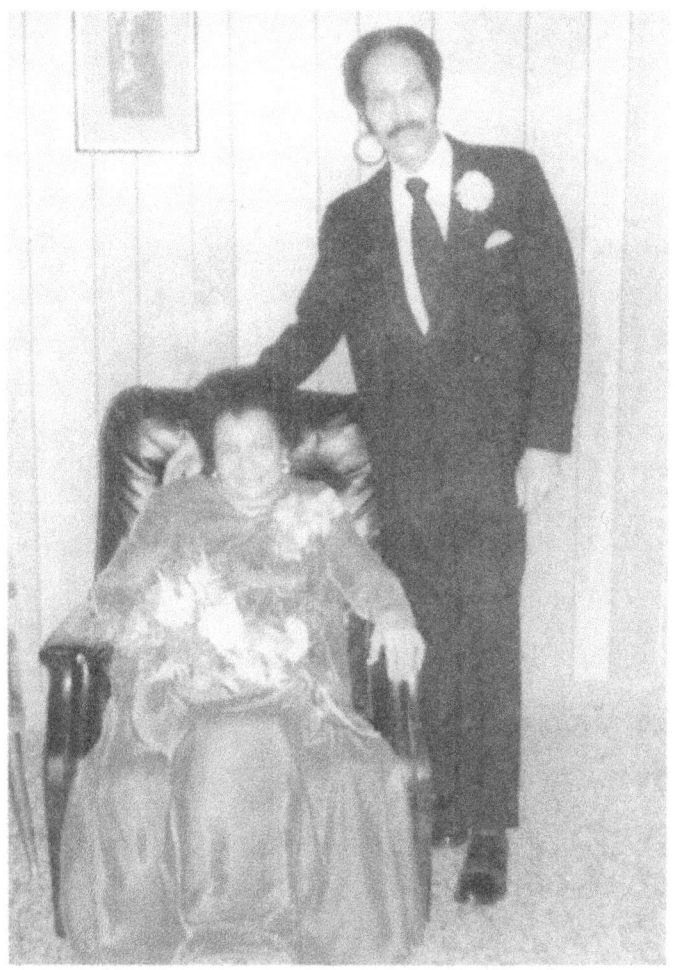

Grace and Milton Roberts

Grace Jones Roberts was born in Chicago, Illinois on December 10, 1924. She attended school in Chicago and came to Carbondale in 1959 to join her aunt and uncle, Cora and Henry Benningham, who were already residing in the city. She first resided on Fisher Street and later moved to Searing Street.

Mrs. Roberts is a retired social worker, a position she held under the Carbondale Model Cities Program. She and her family have been members of Olivet Freewill Baptist Church since she first moved to Carbondale. She currently serves as President of the Mothers Board.

Mrs. Roberts first married Adolphous Jones in 1942; she married Milton Roberts in 1972. She has been blessed with nine children, twenty-one grandchildren, and four great grandchildren.

Above: The marriage ceremony of Grace and Milton Roberts, 1972. Mrs. Grace Roberts wears a weding gown which was designed and created for her by the author.

Top and Bottom: The Family of Grace Jones Roberts. Above photo: Children of Grace Robert Jones (Kneeling, from left) Ruby, Mrs. Grace Jones Roberts, and Robin. (Back row, from left) Adolphus, Adele, Judy, Steven (oldest son), Sala, and Ramon.

Frances Robertson

African American Families, 1900-1964

Odell Barnett Robison

Traces In The Dust

Top: Seven sisters (from left) Mary Smith; Daisy Harrell; Cora Cunningham, mother of Dorcas Cunningham Davis; Dove; Annie Perkins; Betty Wilson; and Velma Hutchinson. Bottom Left: Verna Roseman and daughter, Patricia Brown. Bottom Right: Rosie Stricklin graduating from Beauty College.

African American Families, 1900-1964

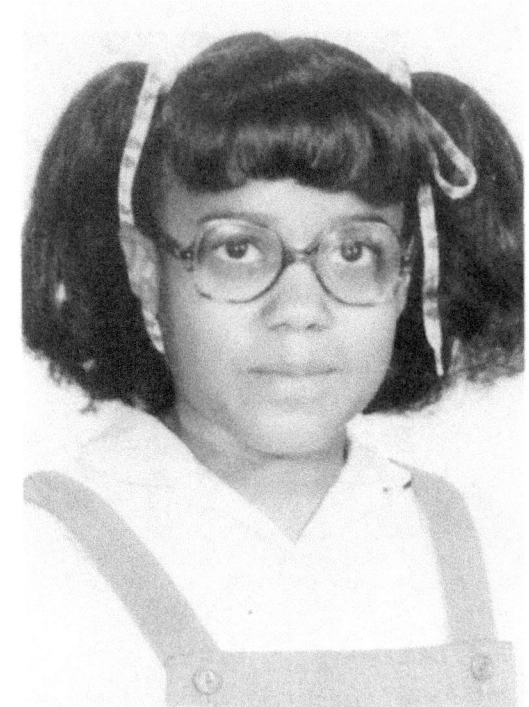

Top Left: Tracey and B. J., grandsons of Verna Roseman. Top Right: Tanya McCoy, daughter of Greg McCoy; granddaughter of Verna Roseman. Bottom Left: Montell Brown, son of Patricia Brown, and sons, Sherard Delano and Jordan Montell Brown. Bottom Right: Pauline and Franklin Spriggs.

Beulah Spriggs
Mother of Verna Roseman

Julia and James Rowe

James Rowe, a native of Carutherville, Missouri, was born October 9, 1927 to James Lawson Rowe and Mary Ella Rowe. He is the brother to Ercie Anderson, Robert Rowe, Oliver Rowe and Geneva Churchill. James worked as an orderly at Memorial Hospital in Hayti, Missouri and at the Koppers Tie plant in Carbondale in the 1960s. He also worked as a janitor for thirteen years and spent another thirteen years at Southern Illinois University. He has been a crossing guard for Carbondale School District for 20 years.

Julia Rowe was born in Greenwood, Mississippi March 28, 1928. She and James were married June 24, 1962. They established their household on Green Street in Carbondale where they currently reside. Julia received her education at Swift Grade School and Hayti Central High School in Hayti, Missouri. She earned certification as a Nurse's Aide and worked in Home Health Care at several facilities including the Jackson County Nursing Home in Murphysboro. She was employed with the Food Service Department at SIU and has been a cook with the Jackson County Sheriff's Department and Carbondale School District 95.

Mrs. Rowe is a member of the Community Club and the Friendship Club of Carbondale. She has been a member of New Zion Baptist Church since 1967 where she serves as an usher and as Vice president of the Mission. She is the sister of twelve siblings, Henry Gamble, Sampson Gamble, Florence Gamble, Catherine Brown, Leroy Lockridge, Wille Lee, Willie Mae, Martha J., Rosie Lee, Robert Lee, L. G. Gamble, and Bernida Hill. Two of her siblings are deceased. Julia and James are the parents of ten children, Jackie, Dwight, Sharon, Eunice, Lequeita, Roderick, Broderick, Katrina, Tishunda, and LaToya. They also have twenty-five grandchildren and seven great grand children.

Above: James and Julia Rowe with granddaughters, LaTona Bryant, Jacinta M. Gamble, LaKisha Bryant, and Shoneedra Cole.

Traces In The Dust

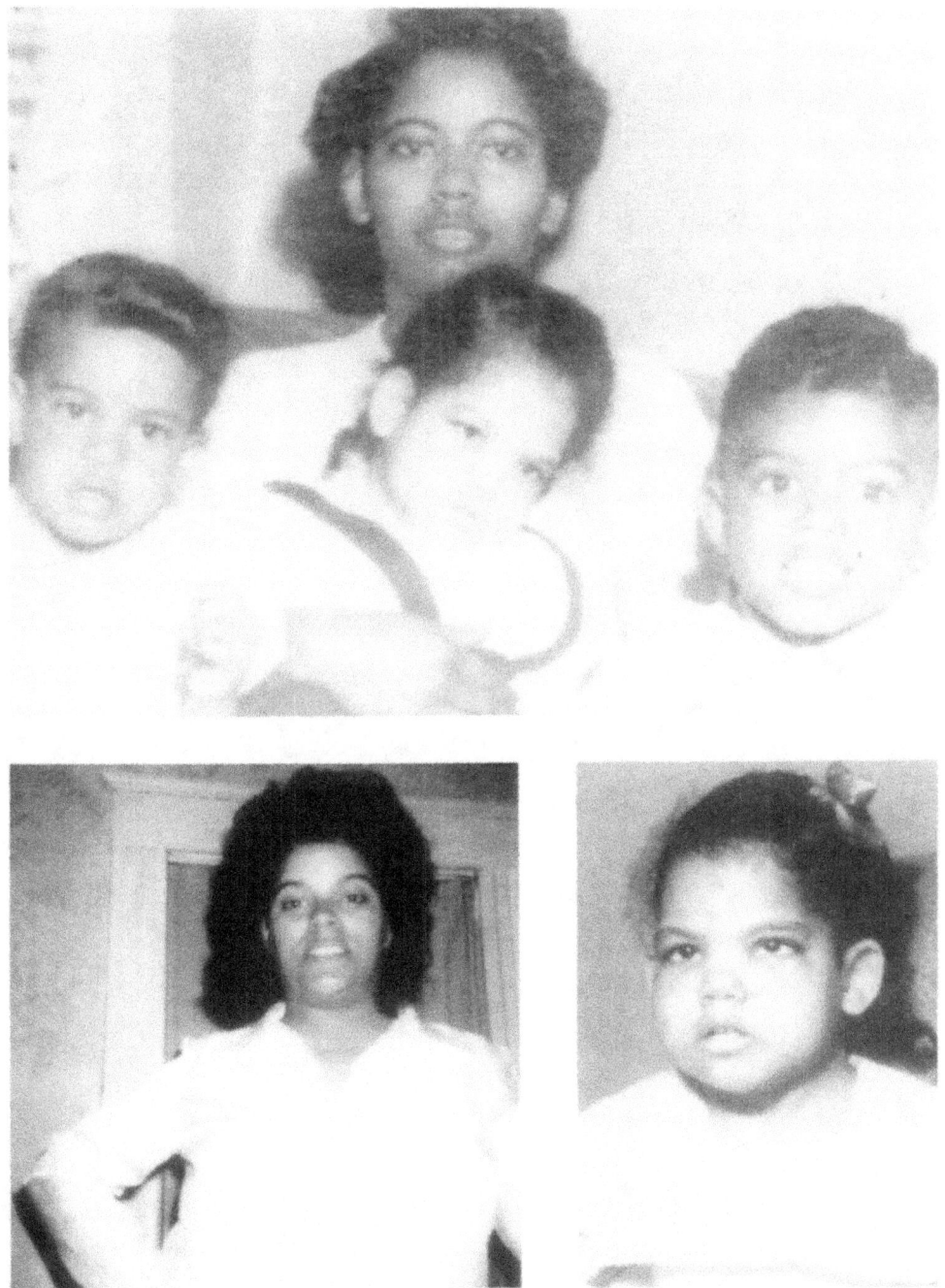

Cardella Lowery Scott

Cardella Lowery Scott was born March 15, 1928 in New Madrid Missouri, the daughter and only child of Manervia Barnett and Theoe Felix Lowery. She attended the Attucks Schools and married to Robert Scott on October 18, 1948. Robert died in August of 1981. Cardella, an active leader of the Black community (See In Service To Their People), died in Carbondale May 23, 1999. She was the mother of three children, and was also preceded in death by her daughter, Brenda.

Top: Cardella Scott and children, Barbara, Brenda, and Bruce. Bottom Left and Right: Sisters, Barbara and Brenda Scott, daughters of Robert and Cardella Scott.

African American Families, 1900-1964

Top Left: Leo Scott, son of Lonnie and Charlie Scott. Top Right: Charlie and Lonnie Scott celebrate their 50th wedding anniversary, 1975. Bottom: The family of Lonnie and Charlie Scott.

Ora and Grace Scott

Pervie and Lillie Scott

Mr. Pervie Scott was born in Canton, Mississippi September 19, 1905. He was the son of Mr. and Mrs. Fellix Scott. He married Lillie Cole September 1, 1924. Pervie and Lilly arrived in Carbondale from Earl, Arkansas in 1949. They were the parents of twelve children, Janet Ree, Rosetta, Mary Lee, Christine, Fannie B., Teresa, Katherine, Robert, Pervie Scott, Jr., Cleo, Leon, and Bennie. The couple had a daughter, Janie, who died in September of 1973. Mrs. Scott passed away earlier that same year in January of 1973. A son, Leon, passed away on September 9, 1999.

Mr. Scott was a deacon at New Zion Baptist Church in Carbondale. He retired from Koppers plant. He had one brother, Charlie Scott, who lived in Carbondale. Mr. Scott died September 6, 1974 in Carbondale. He was 68 years old.

Above: The family of Pervie and Lillie Scott in Earl, Arkansas, late 1940s. (From left) Pervie Scott, Jr.; Janet Ree Scott; Mr. Pervie Scott, Sr.; Mrs. Lillie Scott; Katherine Scott (being held by Mrs. Scott); Leon and Bennie Scott; Christine Scott (sitting on fender of car); and Mary Scott.

Traces In The Dust

Left: Leon Scott and sons, Tyree and Chevel.
Right: Bennie, Robert, Mary, and Leon, children of Pervie and Lillie Scott.

Top: Daughters of Pervie and Lillie Scott: (from left) Teresa, Fannie, Mary, and Christine and Tony (infant), son of Christine Scott.

Mary Silas and daughter, Kim

Traces In The Dust

Lit and Jeanether Simon

Lit Simon was born in 1900 in Memphis, Tennessee. Mrs. Simon, formerly Jeanether Bland, was born February 6, 1900 in Kerrville, Tennessee. She was the daughter of Dan and Lillie Sherill Bland. Lit and Jeanether were married in 1918 in Tennessee. They settled in Carbondale in 1940 at 417 E. Oak Street.

Mr. and Mrs. Simon professed a strong belief in God and instilled this belief in their children. Mrs. Simon was a life-long leader at Rock Hill Baptist church. She passed away Novermber 13, 1992. Mr. Simon died in 1966.

Lit and Jeanether had seven children, Lit Simon Jr., Beatrice, Margaret, Charles, and Elbert. Two of their children, James and Gertrude, preceded their mother in death. Also preceding Mrs. Simon in death were her parents, six sisters, and four brothers. At the time of her death, Mrs. Simon was survived by five children; a sister, Nancy Price; two brothers, Russell and Arnez Bland; thirteen grandchildren; and fourteen great grandchildren.

African American Families, 1900-1964

Top: Henry and Jean Slaughter with daughters, Alicia and Angela. Bottom: Isalee and Henry Morgan with daughter, Evelyn.

Traces In The Dust

Irvin and Helen M. Hillsman Smith

Helen Smith was born March 9, 1913 in Carbondale to Edgar B. and Pearlie Newbill Hillsman. She joined Bethel A.M.E. Church in 1928 where she was a member of the Senior Choir, Class Leader #10, Stewardess Board, Missionary Society, Rose of Sharon Club, Semper Fidelis Club, and Sunday School. She worked for fifteen years in child care and was a member of Memorial Hospital Volunteers. She worked for many years in Hillsman store, an enterprise established by her father. She married Irvin Smith on May 10, 1934. Irvin Smith worked for the IC Railroad for many years. Mrs. Smith departed this life February 25, 1992. Mr. Smith currently resides in the family homestead in the northeast community of Carbondale.

Ozell and Carrie Smith

Mary Minnie Smith
Mother of Ozell Smith, Sr.

Rosetta Smith
Age 16
Easter Sunday, 1943

Mary Spriggs, Age 16
Sister of Verna Roseman

Top Left: Glenice Steele and son, DeAngelo Miguel Macklin. Top Right: Wendell James Johnson, son of Gloria Aiken, and Faye Steele, daughter of Walter and Doris Steele. Bottom Left: Walter, Jr., Kim, and Tracey Steele, sons of Doris and Walter Steele. Bottom Right: Doris and Walter Steele. Photo of Mr. Steele was taken during the period of his illness and two months prior to his death which occurred in November of 1998.

Traces In The Dust

Juanita Thomas and daughters, Judy and Mary.

Top: The Family of John and Juanita Thomas. Bottom: The Reliford brothers: (From left) Walter (youngest), Phillip, Charlie, Charles (oldest), and Rodger.

Rose B. and Robert A. Thomas

Top Left: Hattie V. Boykin-Thomas, mother of Robert Thomas. Top Right: Harold Edward Thomas, brother of Robert Thomas. Bottom: A Reunion of the Robert Thomas Family.

Rosella Pearl Thomas
"Aunt Rosell"

Rosella Thomas, known to all as "Aunt Rosell," was the daughter of Galaveston and Leah Sumner Perkins. She was born February 25, 1903 in Brownfield, Illinois. She was first married to Will Neal. They had two children. She later married John L. Thomas. They had three children.

Mrs. Thomas was a pastry cook and supervisor at the University Drug Store and Cafeteria in Carbondale. She, along with Allean Brown Gordon and Julia Mae Thompson cooked meals at the establishment for more than thirty years. She was a member of Olivet Freewill Baptist Church and served in the Willing Workers' Club, the Sunday School, the senior choir, and the Missionary Society. She was also a member of the Carbondale Community Club and the Carbondale Senior Citizens organization.

Mrs. Thomas was known for her bright smile, her wonderful, sparkling personality, and her ability and willingness to bring laughter and encouragement to all she met. She was one who truly touched the heart.

Mrs. Thomas died in Murphysboro, Illinois at St. Joseph Memorial Hospital. She was survived by two daughters Berdena and Hazel; two sons, John Jr., and Linford; and fifteen grandchildren. She was preceded in death by a daughter, three sisters, and five brothers.

Archie Dean and Jewel Thompson

Archie Dean Thompson, the son of Julia Mae Morgan Thompson, and Jewel Slaughter Thompson, the daughter of Vastula Slaughter, are both natives of Carbondale and both graduates of Attucks High School. Archie Dean was born April 28, 1940. Jewel was reared by her step parents, Henry and Alene Slaughter. She was born Sept 4, 1941 Slaughter.

Jewel and Archie Dean were married in Carbondale June 26, 1960. They had three children, Archie Dean, Jr., Margo Delisa, and Julia Louise; their daughter, Margo, passed away September 16, 1999.

The Thompsons were among the first young families of the 1960s era who chose to remain in Carbondale and build their homes, when many of Carbondale's younger African Americans were seeking to move to the larger cities of the United States. They continue to reside in their family home in the northeast community.

Traces In The Dust

Julia Mae Morgan Thompson

Known by friends and relatives as "Aunt Julia Mae," Julia Mae Morgan Thompson is the matriarch of one of the oldest black families in Carbondale. She was born July 23, 1916 in Hennings, Tennessee and arrived in the township of Carbondale in 1930 at the age of 14. She married Dossie Thompson, the son of a Tennessee slave, in 1942. In 1951, Julia Mae purchased what was then a three room house on Green Street. To pay for the home and support her two kids and her sister's two kids, she took on various jobs. Eventually, at a cost of thirty-five hundred dollars, she added a new roof and three additional rooms to her home.

Mrs. Thompson worked until she was 78 years old when was forced to quit her job because of a "white woman from Ziggler." At the time, Mrs. Thompson was the only Negro cook at a small group housing on the Southern Illinois University campus, and the white boss saw to it that the work was too hard for her to do by herself.

Mrs. Thompson is the mother of two sons, Joe and Archie Dean Morgan. Joe was among the few black students who attended the all white University High School in the 1950s before segregation.

Iray Franklin Woods Tisdale

Traces In The Dust

Top: Fred and Iray Tisdale and granddaughter, Jameca Routen. Bottom Left: Linda Woods Porter, daughter of Iray Tisdale. Bottom Right: Bradford Lamont Woods and wife, Annis.

Annie Mae Dunlap Garrett Wakefield

Annie Mae Dunlap Garrett Wakefield was born in Carbondale June 14, 1917 behind Rock Hill Baptist Church at South Marion and E. Walnut Streets in the location where the former Red Carpet Filling Station once stood. She was born to the parentage of Mattie Jones Dunlap and Robert Dunlap, both of Henry, Tennessee. The family moved to East Willow Street when Mrs. Wakefield was three years old.

Mrs. Wakefield attended the Attucks schools and graduated from Attucks High School in 1936. She worked as a cook with the Carbondale School District 95 and is a member of Olivet Freewill Baptist Church where she is a Church Mother. She is a member of the Carbondale Community Club and was a member of the former Triple 4 Club which was organized by Mrs. Bessie Waren. She is also a member of the Mariam Chapter #17 Order of the Eastern Star.

Mrs. Wakefield is the mother of six children, Orvid Garritt, Etta White, Sherry Garrett, Darnella Morrison, Verlena Greer, and Andrew Wakefield, Jr. Mrs. Wakefield has several grand children and great grandchildren. She has one sister and four brothers, Wittie Mae Dunlap, and James, William, George, and John Dunlap. Mrs. Wakefield resides in the Carbondale northeast community.

Thelma and James Walker

Backyard at Mrs. Imogene Washington's parents home at 409 East Green Street, c. 1947. Imogene Harris Washington is shown holding daughter, Ida Marie Washingtron; Charlie Edgar, father of Imogene Washington; and Samuel Charles Washington, son of Imogene Washington, accompany her.

Patsy Dean Kenner Watson

Patsy Dean Kenner Watson was born March 17, 1935 in Carbondale to George and Maggie Steele Kenner. She was born at home in the house on Barnes Street now owned by the Taylor Family. Her father later built a house at 413 1/2 Brush Street next to her great grandparents. Patsy Dean, as did many of her brothers and sisters, attended the old Attucks Grade School and Attucks High School. The younger siblings, Carlos, Jolene, Rhonda, and Yvonne attended Carbondale Community High School.

Patsy Dean finished high school May 26, 1953 and was married to Robert Morgrum. The couple had five children, Karen, Tyrone, Carmen, Yolanda and Margaret. Patsy decided to return to school in 1970 and enrolled in Southern Illinois University Vocation Technical School as a nursing student. She was also attending John A. Logan College. After graduation in 1972, she went to work for the Jackson County Health Department as a Public Health outreach worker. Additionally, she was working at Doctors Memorial Hospital, in her spare time, as a private duty nurse.

Patsy Dean lived in Du Quoin, Illinois for 26 years. She married Robert E. Watson on December 24, 1980 in Elkville, Illinois at the home of her father and stepmother, Pauline Wills Kenner. The Kenners became members of Smith Memorial A.M.E Zion Church were Mr. Watson serves on the Trustee Board and as church treasurer. Mrs. Watson serves as a deaconess, a class leader, a Sunday school teacher and a choir director. In the Conference year 2000, she was appointed by Bishop Enoch Rochester to serve as Chairman of the Life Member Council of the Women's Home and Overseas Missionary Society. Locally, she is chairperson of Church Women United.

Mrs. Morgrum relocated back to Carbondale in December of 1999 where she came out of retirement and is currently with the Department of Human Services. She is the sister to Gwendale, Joyce, Delilah, LaDonna, Rhonda, Janice, and Yvonne. She has three brothers, Larry, Carlos, and Basil.

Mary Lee and George Westley

Traces In The Dust

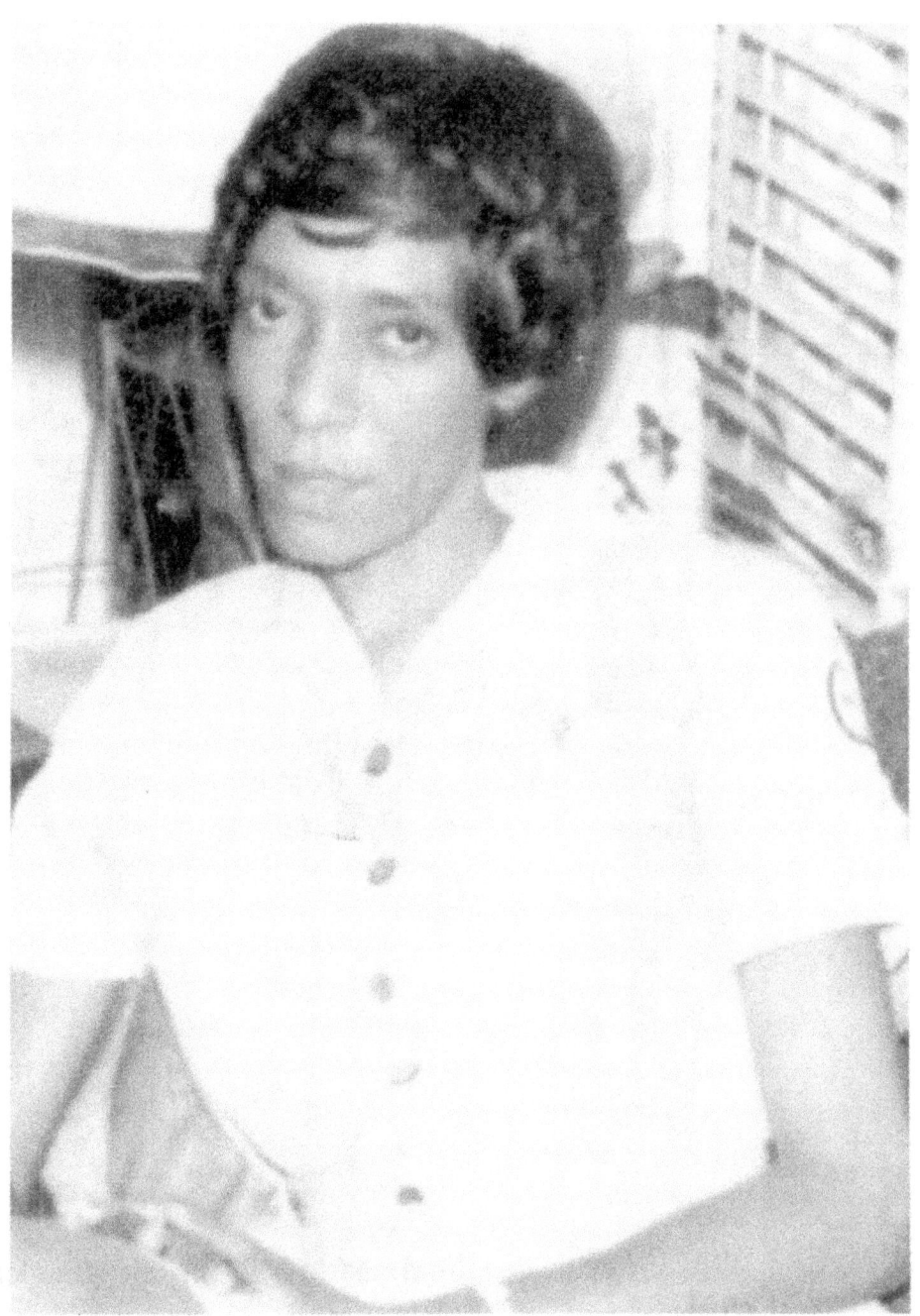

Etta White Newbern

African American Families, 1900-1964

Missionary Sallie Williams with daughter, Marie Mason, and grandchildren, Anita and Kent Mason

Mrs. Pauline Wills Kenner and Family
(From left) Fred, Vera, Zelda, Donald, and Robert. In absentia are Paulette, Clarence, and James.

Top: Clarence Wills on patrol. Bottom: Children of Pauline and Ed Wills (from left) Donald, Paulette, Bob, Mrs. Pauline Wills Kenner, Zelda, James, Vera, Clarence, and Fred.

Candice Gilmore Wilson and Children

Lillian Louise Woods

Lillian Louise Woods, a native of New Madrid, Missouri, was born February 26, 1927 to Sylvester and Thelma Steed Love. She graduated from Attucks High School in 1946 and attended SIU in Carbondale. She married George Woods in Carbondale September 25, 1948.

Lillian was baptized under the pastorate of the Rev A. A. Crim in 1944 and joined Olivet Free Will Baptist Church. An active participant in the affairs of the community, Mrs. Woods was among those civic leaders who advocated for better conditions for Blacks in Carbondale (See In Service To Their People).

Lillian Woods passed away January 22, 1976. She was the mother of three children, Gregory, Deborah, and Louise. She was preceded in death by her father and her husband, who died in in 1976. At the time of her death, surviving family members included her mother, Thelma Steed; her children; and four aunts, Alberta Jordan, Lessie Hawkins, Hazel Mitchell, and Martha Holmes.

Above: Left: Lillian and George. Above Right: Louise Woods, daughter of Lillian Woods.

Traces In The Dust

Thelma Steed

Thelma Steed came to Carbondale around the mid 1940s. She was born in New Madrid, Missouri on April 13, 1908. She came to Carbondale to be with her half sister Hassie Farr. She worked as a domestic for the Shryock family of Carbondale, as a maid at Holden Hospital, and as a janitor at Good Luck Glove Factory during the late 1950s. During the 1970s, she worked as a maid and cook for Southern Illinois University in Wilson Hall. She retired at the age of 78 in 1986.

Top: Mrs. Thelma Steed, mother of Lillian Woods, and Janae Townsend.

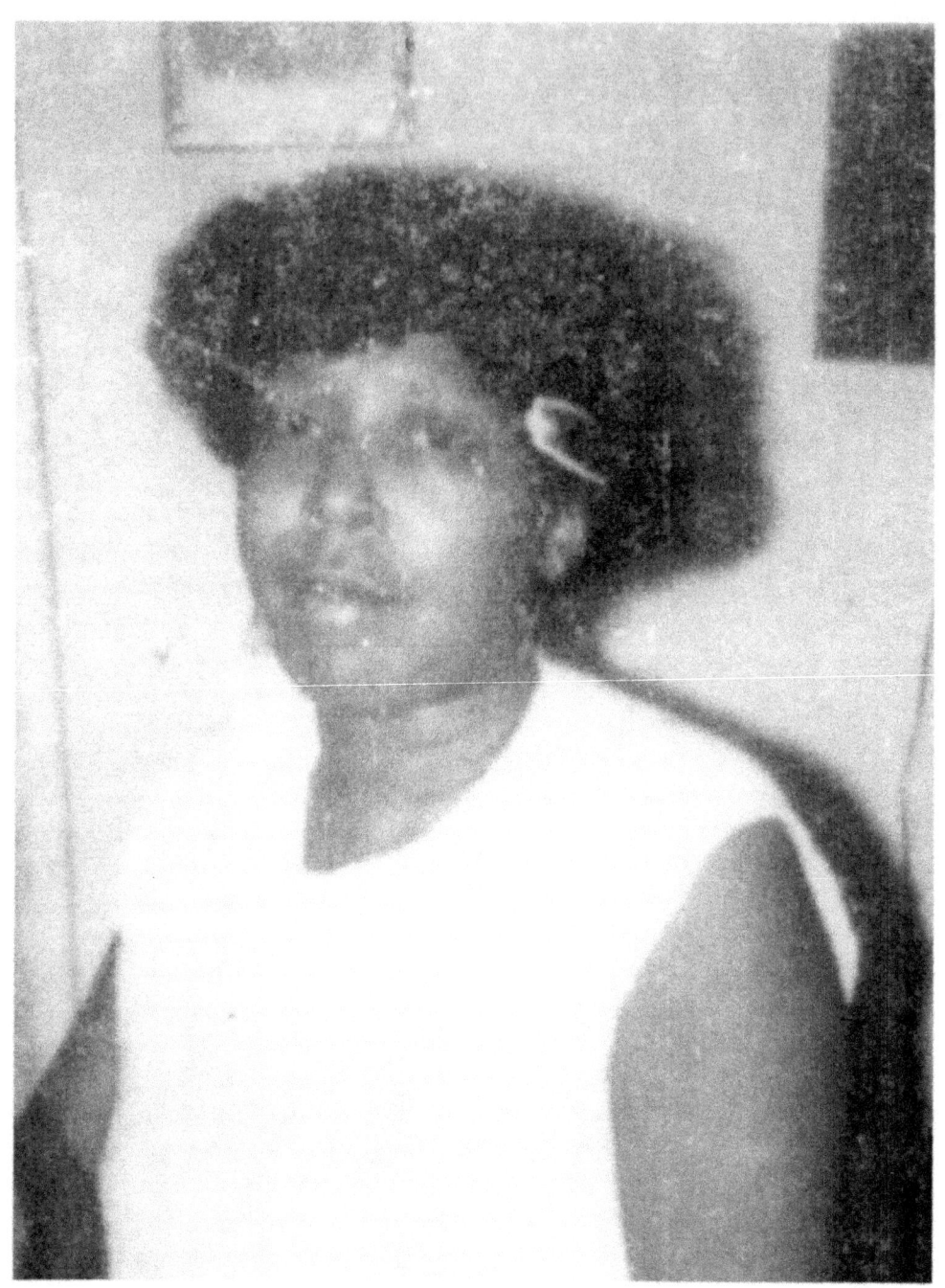

Francis M. P. Louis Wooley

Francis Marie Pauline Louis Wooley, the daughter of William and Celia Louis, was born on August 1, 1929 in Murphysboro, Illinois. She married Marlee Wooley, Sr., a native of Brent, Alabama, on July 21, 1947. She and Marlee had fifteen children. Mrs. Wooley was a housewife. She passed away on June 27, 1981 in Carbondale. Mr. Wooley died in July of 1999.

Family members of Francis and Marlee Wooley, Sr.

(From left) Jerry Lewis, son-in-law; Penny Lewis, daughter; Joanne Cole, daughter; Kenny Quinn, son-in-law; Kelly Cole, grandson; Patricia Wooley, daughter; Jerome Wooley, son; Deborah Quinn, daughter; Wendell Wooley, son; Norma Wooley, daughter; Kenneth Wooley, son; Tammy Wooley, daughter; Danny Wooley, son; Cinton Wooley, son; Barbara Dewalt, daughter; David McCory, grandson; Lawrence Wooley, grandson; and Matez Wooley, great grandson. In absentia is Larry Wooley, son of Francis and Marlee Wooley, Sr.

Mr. and Mrs. Tyler Young, Sr. and Children
(From left) Tyler Young, Sr., Mrs. Virginia Mae Young, Delores Young, and Tyler Young, Jr.

Virginia Mae and Tyler Young, Sr.

Tyler Young, Sr. came to Carbondale around 1920 with his grandparents, Sherman and Emma Reatheford when he was about three years old. He attended Attucks Elementary and Attucks High School, and completed his high school education while in the military. Tyler sang with two local gospel groups: the Kings of Harmony and the Pilgrim Travelers. With the Pilgrim Travelers, he sang with Albert Reed, Willie Reed, and Vernon Williams. Hassie Williams Farr, a long time resident of Carbondale (who was also Vernon's mother and Virginia's aunt), was Manager of the Pilgrim Travelers.

From 1936 to 1939, Tyler Sr. served in the Civilian Conservation Corps (CCC Camp) at Fort Isaac Walton near Peoria, Il. With assistance from Virginia's cousin, he began corresponding with Virginia Hawkins. The two met when The Pilgrim Travelers sang in New Madrid, Missouri in the 1930's. In the fall of 1940, when Virginia enrolled at Southern Illinois Normal University, the couple became closer and were later married in Jackson, Missouri.

Tyler and Virginia's first child, Virginia Delois, was born when the couple resided at 1103 North Barnes. Tyler worked as a laborer for the Kopper's Tie Plant and Culp's lumber yard. At this time, it was not easy for young married couples of that vicinity since Barnes Street was an unincorporated area that was outside of the Carbondale Township and homes had no indoor water, electricity, or plumbing. The Youngs had to pay to have their water hauled to them at twenty-five cents a barrell. Since there were no paved roads in that area of town, during severe inclement weather, the streets often became impassable and families who didn't have wells had to find other means of getting water.

In November of 1943, Tyler enlisted in the military, and Virginia moved with her daughter to New Madrid where she resumed teaching. Tyler Jr., Virginia's second child, was born in 1945. Virginia returned to Carbondale in August of 1960. Returning to Carbondale with Mrs. Young's family was her 66 year old mother, Lessie Irene Steed Hawkins; her nephew, Russell Hawkins; and her nieces, Versie Marie Murray and Stephanie Diahann Murray. Delois had arrived in Carbondale several weeks earlier to register at Southern Illinois University. On April 15, 1964, Keith Alan, the Young's third child, was born in Carbondale.

Tyler Sr. served in World War II, the Korean Conflict, and the Vietnam War. During his military career, he sustained injuries in Warold War II and in the Korean War. He attended Military Police School and served as an MP in the United States and overseas. After a 30 year military career, Tyler Sr. was honorably discharged in June of 1973. He then worked as a security guard in Columbia, South Carolina. Mr. Young currently resides in Carbondale. Mrs. Virginia Young died in September of 2001.

Below: (Left) Russell Hawkins. (Right) Keith Young celebrates his 8th grade graduation.

Part VII

In Service To Their People: Labors and Achievements

Political, Social, and Economic Development

The Black Struggle

In the daily fight to eke out a living for themselves and their families, black men faced discrimination in almost every situation imaginable in the early days of Carbondale, practices that did not really face any public challenge until the early 1960s when public awareness began to grow, and the age of desegregation saw protests, marches, sit-ins, and demonstrations forced all segments of American to take a hard look at the effects of social separation and neglect. It wasn't until decades later--after the first Black families had established themselves in Carbondale--that "the better things in life" began to come their way. Until this time, conditions for the blacks in Carbondale had not really been that much of an improvement from those circumstances black families had escaped in the South.

In Carbondale, as in the South, black family men, trying to support their families, still had to accept conditions and certain indignities that their white counterparts didn't have to endure. Men like William Hayes and Irvin Smith, who worked long years at the railroad, had to concede to the lower ranking positions with less pay, even though their jobs were often more arduous than that of the higher paid white workers. Although his title was that of a brakeman, Mr. Hayes worked more as a general laborer, stocking and replenishing the caboose and getting supplies to the other workers. Pushing a wheelbarrow stocked with paper cups and ice for the water cooler, and other items for the caboose, he often had to walk from Carbondale to as far as De Soto to make his deliveries. In the cold and ice of the Illinois winters, or in the heat of summer, Mr. Hayes still had to make the long trek on foot simply because the company would not supply him a truck.

During the 1930s and throughout the late 1950s, women like Julia Mae Thompson, Roselle Thomas, and Allean Brown, who spent decades preparing meals at the University Drug Cafeteria for the white students, still had to go outside in back of the cafeteria and eat their lunch sitting on the stoop because they were colored, and colored people couldn't eat with whites. It didn't seem to matter to anyone that it was the "coloreds" who had cooked the food in the first place. Nor did it seem ironic that the colored cooks couldn't even eat their own food in the very establishment where they cooked it.

Even the black students at Southern Illinois Normal University were not allowed to be housed in the dormitories with the white students in the early years of the institution--a situation that did not change until the school decided to project a new and more tolerant image, changing its name to Southern Illinois University and instituting new and gradual policies of reform in the early 1950s. Until then, black students had to find off-campus lodging with families throughout the town--which in those times usually meant residing within the black neighborhoods of the northeast community since only a few blacks lived "across the tracks." Also, it was generally not acceptable for blacks to be in the white sections of town after nightfall unless they were working for the white families. The Hamilton House on Marion Street, owned and operated by the Hamilton family, was recognized as the first black dormitory for Black students in Carbondale. Other black families also rented rooms and small, makeshift apartments for blacks coming to SIU for an education.

With the advent of desegregation in 1963 and with the closing of the black Attucks High School in 1964, conditions for blacks in Carbondale began to change; however, the process was slow and some of the chances themselves, from the black perspective, were not necessarily always for the better. The loss of Attucks brought a loss of individualism and closeness that blacks had always known. It brought a kind of friendly alienation. While it opened the doors for equal educational opportunities, it dissipated the kindred spirit that had existed in the northeast community and the strength of unity blacks had always held dear. Blacks could now attend movies at the white Varsity Theater, but could no longer hold on to their sense of common independence. Blacks could now walk through the serving lines at different eating establishments and could move into the dormitories at SIU, but they could not recapture their "wholeness."

Men like Archie Jones, U. P. Pen, Reverend Lenus Turley, and Rev. Crim, and William Hayes, fought for the needs of Black Carbondale in the early years, and were followed by such leaders as Bob Stalls, Norvell Haynes, Reverend Archibald Mosley, and Richard Hayes, Jr., and who would carry on the fight for decades to come. While the men were on the "front" lines, women like Eurma Hayes, Louberta Cavitt, Kathleen Thornton, Jennie Jones, Marie Johnson, and Luvenia McKinley continued the battle by paving the way to bring in new programs such as model cities and Head Start. In support of their efforts, women like Margaret Nesbitt, Delores Mason, Cardella Scott and many other of Carbondale's unsung black heroines, continued with innovative ways to directly meet the needs of the people and to remind them of the need to stick together.

Mrs. Francis White, Estelle Chappell, Anna Ruth Clemmer, Martha Green, Winona Jackson, and Beulah Mae Brown were but a few of the women who threw themselves into the cause of raising the status of the city's African American women through the participation in clubs and organizations which promoted unity while women like Ima Valentine, Luella Davis, and Rosetta O'Neal sought to bring attention to the history of the Blacks of Carbondale and the contributions they made to the progress of the city as a whole.

In today's "modern era" of black Carbondale, the quest for racial equality and equal opportunity yet continues. New generations of leaders--sons and daughters of the earlier vanguard--have now taken up the torch. Perhaps, in time, such diligence will result in a coming together of hearts and minds and a restoring of that strong pride and universal, community dignity the people of the northeast community once shared and so preciously clung to. Perhaps, in spite of all, it may yet be possible to "return home again."

The African American children of Carbondale's northeast community were able to explore new and creative activities due to those adult mentors who unselfishly volunteered their time and efforts. Below, a troop of Boy Scouts, under the leadership of Mr. U. P. Penn, pays a visit to Everett Boykin, Jr. (center). Among the troop members identified are David Dean Williams, Alfred Hall, James Thomas, and Duane McKinley, c. mid-1950s.

Labors and Achievements

Sources: Southern Illinois Achievers Bulletin. The Southern Illinoisan. Corporate, private, and family owned documents. Southern Illinois University files and records printed by permission of the university. Church records and documents printed by permission of the religious institutions.

Wanda Perkins Haynes
Club President

Mrs. Haynes enjoys serving as a member of the Carbondale Community Club, one of the oldest black civic organizations of Carbondale. She has been a member for approximately years. As a former president of the organization, Mrs. Haynes sought to improve the conditions of Blacks in Carbondale through positive social change.

Mildred Harrington Jordan
Community Involvement

Mildred Mable Anderson Harrington Jordan has worked long years in church activities and has been a tireless worker in the community. She has served in the Willing Workers Club of Olivet Freewill Baptist Church; is a past President of the Usher Board; and a member on the Mothers' Board.

In civic affairs, Mildred been a volunteer with the American Cancer Society, where for twenty-seven years she has conducted door-to-door campaigns. Her most recent endeavors include serving as a volunteer with the "I Can Read" program initiated by the Attucks graduating class of 1948.

Magnolia Maggie Martin
Community Involvement

Mrs. Magnolia Martin, an active community leader, became a member of New Zion Baptist church in Carbondale in 1958 and served as a teacher in the Sunday School and Vacation Bible School in addition to holding several other positions.

Mrs. Martin was a long time member of the Attucks Parent Teacher Association and one of its staunchest supporters. Mrs. Martin received many recognitions for her unselfish service to her people. She was honored with The Finer Womanhood Award in 1988 by Zeta Phi Beta (Mu Zeta Chapter) in 1988. Earlier, in 1985 she was honored for faithful service at New Zion Baptist Church where she was also recognized as the institution's oldest Mother.

Jeraldine Brown
First African American at City Hall

Jeraldine "Jeri" Brown, a thirty plus year veteran with the City of Carbondale, attended John a. Logan, majoring in clerical administration. Her unique experience in working for the city of Carbondale as its first black woman in City Hall has been both rewarding and trying. During her tenure, she has encountered many setbacks, but has always managed to move forward. This is evidenced by her motto: "Perseverance is the key to success."

Mrs. Brown is the wife of Jerry Brown, one of Carbondale's long time African American law enforcement officers. She advises today's youth, "Education is the ultimate goal, but if you cannot acquire a formal education or receive a college degree, take pride in whatever you do and do it well."

Reverend Lenus Turley
Human Relations Commission and Activist

Born in Brookport, Illinois, the son of Cullen and Biddie Silvers Turley, Rev. Turley was interested in all facets of life. He emphasized the "positive approach" to solving life's problems as he engaged in the struggles for the rights of Blacks in Southern Illinois. He led protest marches in Carbondale and was instrumental in organizing a group of black citizens who participated in the reknown March on Washington in support of the efforts of Dr. Martin Luther King in 1963. Always and inspiration and a role model, Rev. Turley encouraged honesty, energy and determination.

Over the years, Rev. Turley received a myriad of acknowledgements and recognitions for his services including awards from the city of Carbondale given posthumously. Apart from the many duties of his ministerial work, two specific events mark what may be his most outstanding

Traces In The Dust

accomplishments: substantially increasing the membership of the Rock Hill Baptist Chruch and acquiring a 60 acres plat of land which was used as a campsite for the inspirational and recreational life of young people. The camp, which was complete with playground equipment and separate buildings was used largely by the Mount Olive District Association, near Herrin, Illinois. It was named Camp Turley in honor of Turley's devotion to public service. The city of Carbondale dedicated Lenus Turley Park in his honor in October of 1980.

Davis: Gave 100 percent to community.

Unis Pearl Davis
Community Leader

Unis Pearl Davis was the founder and president of the Southern Illinois Reunion Picnic. After relocating to Southern Illinois, Unis became President of the No. 9 Community Development Corp. He fought for a sewer extension in the unincorporated area in Williamson Co. west of Colp, Illinois. Davis advocated for improvements in services, not only in Carbondale, but in all of the Southern Illinois area. He was especially concerned for and worked tirelessly on the behalf of the area's senior citizens. Unis Davis died at age 71.

Cleveland Matthews
Community Leader

Cleveland Matthews was responsible for writing the first Comprehensive Affirmative Action Program for the city of Carbondale. His primary focus was to implement steps to help eliminate barriers of race, sex, handicap and national origin which might be used to prevent a person from joining the work force. He recruited minorities for City jobs and worked to convince other employers to hire minorities. Mr. Matthews was selected by the Illinois Department of Commerce and Community Affairs to serve on the Technical Advisory Committee to develop the State's Community Development Assistance Program guidelines. He has also been honored by the Illinois Department of Human Rights.

Mrs. Veachie Perkins Robinson
Volunteer and Supporter

Mrs. Robinson is a former student of Attucks. She was an ardent supporter of Attucks students and an accomplished seamstress. For many years, she was responsible for creating majorette outfits, cheerleader uniforms, and formals for the young ladies of the school.

Hattie A. Hogan
Early Church Advisor and Organizer

Hattie Adams Hogan was born December 25, 1894 in South Carolina to Henry James and Nancy Ann Adams. She married James Henry Hogan February 12, 1911 in Clarksdale, Mississippi.

Mrs. Hogan, a professional seamstress, was a member of Bethel A.M.E. Church in Carbondale for over fifty years and was recognized as one of the church's early female leaders. Among her many positions were her former roles as president of the Stewardess Board, president and treasurer of the Golden Leaf Club and a member of the Illinois Conference Laymen's Organization. She helped in planning and developing the Layment's Camp in Colp, Illinois. Other memberships held by Mrs. Hogan included seats in the Carbondale Federated Women's Club, The Foreign Wars Mother's Organization, and the Rose of Sharon Social Club. The former James Henry Hogan Recreational Center in Carbondale was named for her son who was killed in World War II.

Robert Alvin Stalls
Community Activist

Born in 1921, Robert Alvin Stalls, graduated from high school in Metropolis, Illinois. He enrolled at Southern Illinois University in Carbondale and later served in the United States Army. He attained the rank of Staff Sergeant and ended his tour of service with an Honorable

Discharge. He was awarded two Bronze Stars, the American Theater Ribbon, the EAME Theater Ribbon, the Good Conduct Ribbon, the Victory Medal, and the Asiatic Pacific Theater Ribbon.

Mr. Stalls is remembered for his years of dedicated service as director for the Carbondale Model Cities Program. The former North Barnes Street was renamed in his honor.

Hazel Scott

Hazel Scott became the first African American crowned as Homecoming Queen at Southern Illinois University.[1]

Shelly Chappell
Union President

Mr. Shelly Chappell was a past president of the United Mine Workers Union of the Kopper Plant in Carbondale. He was instrumental in bringing about beneficial changes at the work place for black workers. He also held the position of City Auditor. He was a Past Worshipful Master of Masonic Tuscan Lodge No. 44 and a Past Patron of Mariam Chapter No. 17 Order of the Eastern Star. He was an active member of Bethel A.M.E. Church.

Rosetta O'Neal
Educator and Author

Rosetta O'Neal graduated from Lane College with a degree in Elementary Education. She was Principal of Colp Elementary School and ended her teaching career in the Carbondale elementary system in 1973. She was one of two teachers in District 165 responsible for developing a Remedial Reading Program which was ranked among the top programs in the state of Illinois.

A former member of the Bethel A.M.E. Church, Mrs. O'Neal served in the Carbondale Preservation Association and was President of the Afro-American Historical and Genealogical Society. Under her direction and guidance, the organization produced the first major published work on the history of Blacks in Carbondale:

Roosevelt "Rose" Turley
Community Leader

Mrs. Roosevelt Turley, the wife of Reverend Lenus Turley, was an advocate of better community relations and an active participant in the religious affairs of the church. At Rock Hill Baptist Church, she assisted and supported her husband, the Reverend Lenus Turley, by serving as president and teacher in the Missionary Society and working in the Mt. Olive Baptist District Association. She also served in the Illinois State and in the National Baptist Conventions.

Mrs. Turley was a quiet, mild-mannered woman and a highly civic minded citizen. She served as president of the Carbondale Community Club, and she worked diligently with the Church Women United organization. Her works went far in helping to improve and promote racial harmony.

Taz E. Green
Community Involvement

Taz E. Green was a life-long active participant in community affairs and civic activities. He was Past Commander of the American Legion Garvin King Post No. 542; Past Worshipful Master of Tuscan Lodge No. 44 F&AM; and Past Patron of Mariam Chapter No. 17 O.E.S. Statewide, he served as a member of Peter Clark Elk's Lodge No 483, Peoria, Illinois and led several organizations as the chief officer. These include tenures as Past Commander in Chief of Hiram Consistory No. 51, Cairo, Illinois; Senior Steward of Prince Hall Grand Lodge of the State of Illinois (and its affiliates); Past Raban of Shriner Bagdad Temple No. 104 of Cairo, Illinois; and Past High Priest of Royal Arch Tuscan Lodge F&AM No. 44. He also served the local community as a former President of the Double Six Club. Taz was a licensed electrician and a member of the Auxiliary Police of Carbondale.

---
[1] See Hazel Scott. In Unity There Is Strength. A Pictorial History of the African American Community of Carbondale, Illinois. Little Egypt Chapter; Afro-American Historical and Genealogical Society, 1999.

Mrs. Savannah McCutchen
Early Community Organizer

Mrs. Savannah McCutchen, the wife of Mack McCutchen, was one of the original organizers to coordinate local efforts to provide activities for the young black children of Carbondale in the early forties. As president of a neighborhood committee, she spearheaded a drive to get park and playground equipment for children on the northeast side of Carbondale. She was a role model for other Blacks who wanted to improve conditions for Carbondale's black youth.

Norvell N. Haynes
"C Junior"
Community Leader

Norvell "C Junior" Haynes was a long time fighter and one of the most forceful voices for the black people in Carbondale. He was a member of the Tuscan Lodge No. 44, F.& A. M. in Carbondale and an active leader in the Carbondale Branch of the NAACP.

Mr. Haynes traveled throughout Jackson County in his efforts to effect changes for his fellow residents. He was a precinct committeeman for Ward I in Carbondale, and he was one of the organizers of the Carbondale unit that participated in the 1963 Civil Rights March in Washington, D.C. where Dr. Martin Luther King, Jr. delivered his immortal speech, "I Have A Dream." Mr. Haynes also served his country as an Army veteran of the Korean War.

Thomas Nesbitt
Political Leader and Youth Mentor

Thomas Nesbitt, along with his wife Margaret, was one of the early pioneers in the fight for a better life for the Blacks of Carbondale. He was a role model for the young black children, coaching and managing the first Little League Team in Carbondale. Thomas, himself, was a pitcher for a professional softball team in Jacksonville, Illinois.

Mr. Nesbitt was a former manager at Veath (Century) Sport Mart and a retired postal worker from the U.S. Postal Service in Carbondale. He belonged to the American Postal Union of Carbondale, Local 944, where he held the position of Union Steward.

Mr. Nesbitt was a member of Tuscan Lodge No. 44, F.&A.M. and a member of the Veterans of Foreign Wars, having served his country in World War II. However, his greatest contributions to northeast Carbondale no doubt resulted through his political involvement and affiliation with the local branch of the N.A.A.C.P. and his direct contact with the people through the various community organizations and programs such as the Double Six Club and the Attucks P.T.A.

Cardella Lowery Scott
President of the Northeast Congress

Mrs. Scott was one of the early leaders in the struggle to improve conditions for Blacks in Carbondale. She operated the first low income energy program in Jackson County. As president of the Northeast Congress, she helped bring awareness and solutions to the problems of the northeast section of town. Additionally, Mrs. Scott was a former member of the Spirit of Attucks Reunion Committee and a volunteer for the Senior Citizens Program of Carbondale.

Winona Jackson
Political Leader

The late Winona Jackson was active in getting her people to the polls in the fifties and sixties, and she served as a judge on the State Voters Board. She was a board member of the Attucks School "Spirit of Attucks" reunion committee and a volunteer with the Memorial Hospital Auxiliary. Mrs. Jackson was a strong supporter of her Alma Mater, Attucks High School, and, as an alumni and parent, took an active part in the Attucks PTA. Because of her efforts and ideas, the northeast community benefited greatly.

In Service To Their People: Labors and Achievements

Grace Boyd
Educator and Founder

Mrs. Grace Boyd, educator and world traveler, was a co-founder of the Psi Chapter of Sigma Gamma Rho Sorority, Inc., which, according to local history, was the first black sorority at Southern Illinois University (1934). She was also a member of the Zion District Association, a member of the Southern Illinois Retired Teachers' Association, and a charter member of the Southern Association Chapter 504 of Jackson County.

John L. Thomas
Educator and Community Leader

Mr. Thomas, educator and principal, received numerous awards for decades of services rendered to the community. However, he is, perhaps, best remembered for his wise council and stern guidance given to countless of Carbondale's Black youngsters throughout his long and distinguished career.

Mr. Thomas earned a two year teaching certificate from Southern Illinois Normal University in Carbondale in 1929. He began his career at Attucks in 1931 after spending the previous year in Cairo, Illinois. He earned a bachelor's degree in 1939 and a master's degree in 1947.

Mr. Thomas became the first black member of the Jackson County Housing Authority in 1968. He served on the board for ten years and served for over twenty-five years in the Sunday School Department of Rock Hill Baptist Church.

Mr. Thomas spent over four decades in education, including serving as teacher, a principal, and sitting on the Board of Education for District 95. He was recognized by the city of Carbondale with the declaration of John L. Thomas Day on May 25, 1974.

Mr. Thomas was the recipient of numerous other awards including the CCHS Service Award in 1977, the IEA Service Award in 1957, the Carbondale PTA Award for Distinguished Achievement in 1974, and the Southern Illinois Reunion Council Bicentennial Award in 1977. He received the NAACP Award Portrait in 1978 and The Award of Merit for 43 years of service from the Carbondale Elementary District 95 Board. Additionally, Mr. Thomas was the first principal of Thomas School, which was named in his honor in 1955. "Professor Thomas," as he popularly known throughout the community, retired in 1974.

Rev. Loyd C. Sumner
Religious and Civic Leader

Rev. Loyd Sumner began pastoring at Olivet Freewill Baptist Church in 1961. He is perhaps best remembered for reviving the church through the introduction of innovative programs and reforms. Under Pastor Sumner's leadership, Olivet experienced a period of growth and development unparalleled in the history of the institution.[2]

Jeraldine Brown

---

[2] See Loyd C. Sumner in "Black Churches and Spiritual Leadership" in Generations--A Pictorial Review of African Americans in Carbondale, Illinois by Melvin L. Green Macklin.

John Louis Thomas

Estelle Doretha France Chappell
Day Care Director

Estelle Doretha France Chappell completed her education in the Attucks public schools and graduated with honors in the class of 1946. She received a Bachelor of Science degree from Southern Illinois University in Carbondale. Estelle was studying for a master's degree when she was stricken with bad health. Estelle was active in many civic and community organizations in Carbondale. For a number of years, she headed a local day care program and worked for the Carbondale Public School system and at SIU.

Right: Estelle Doretha France Chappell.

News photo of local historians Mrs. Louberta Cavitt, Mrs. Luvenia McKinley, and the late Mrs. Kathleen Thornton categorizing photos and articles of Black history in Carbondale.

Traces In The Dust

Top Right: Lillian Woods, Organizer and Board Member. Top Right: Early Child Care Pioneer and Day Care Organizer and Teacher, Leota Christina Nichols Brown. Bottom Left: Winona Jackson, Community Involvement. Bottom Right: Hardin Allen Davis, Educator and Principal.

Leota Christina Nichols Brown
Head Start Organizer

Leota Nichols Brown served as Executive Secretary in the Zion District Baptist Association. Mrs. Brown, who was born June 13, 1919 in Carbondale to Thomas J. and Nina Keathly Nichols, married William H. Brown in November of 1943 in Cape Girardeau, Missouri.

In the 1960's, she became involved with the development of the Head Start Program in Southern Illinois. She served as a social worker for the newly established organization and as an undergraduate trainer at the Southern Illinois University Child Development Center. Later, she became a lead teacher.

Levora D. L. Robertson
Community Board Member

Mrs. Levora D. Lyas Robertson attended the Attucks school system and received a Bachelor of Science Degree from Southern Illinois University. She studied in the College of Human Resources and in Child and Family Services. She was named to the Dean's List in 1974. She also received several awards during her 27 year career with the Social Security Administration.

She was a member of the Alpha Kappa Alpha Sorority, Inc. and the Gamma Kappa Omerga Chapter of Carbondale. She was Vice-President of the International Toastmistress Club and served on the Attucks Community Service board.

Vantrece Russell Shoffner
Business Owner

Vantrece Russell Shoffner was born in 1912 in Dewmaine, Illinois. She was the daughter of David and Mary Catherine Wilkes Russell. She married Robert Shoffner November 28, 1932 in Murphysboro, Illinois. Vantrece was one of the early Black Carbondale residents to first attend SIU and was also one of the first Blacks to own her own business, Russell's Grocery Store, which she inherited from her parents. As an active community leader, she was a member of several organizations including, the Semper Fidelis Club of Bethel A.M.E. Church, the Lamplighters Social Club, and the Mariam Chapter No. 17 of the Order of Eastern Star.

Margaret Jean Nesbitt
Community Leader and Entrepreneur

Margaret Nesbitt, a renowned activist for civil rights in the city of Carbondale, has devoted many years to enhancing the quality of life of the African Americans of Carbondale. A life member of the National Association for the Advancement of Colored People, Mrs. Nesbitt has been active leader in the civil rights movement since the early 1960s. Her involvement with the Students Non-Violent Freedom Council led the way for the first federal housing for low income people being built in Carbondale. In 1969, while working at Southern Illinois University, she was a member of the NAACP committee which eventually led to the establishment of an Affirmative Action office in city government.

As president of the Northeast Community Development Congress in 1972, Mrs. Nesbitt headed the governing body charged with overseeing the Model Cities Program. It was during her leadership that the Eurma C. Hayes Day Care Center was established. In 1988, Mrs. Nesbitt was honored by the Carbondale Branch of the NAACP for her commitment to the community, receiving the Community Service Award. Mrs. Nesbitt has been a member of the Attucks Community Service Board for over twenty years; has served as a Jackson County Registrar at Large; and she was the first African American woman of Carbondale to run for City Council. Still an active businesswoman and community leader, Mrs. Nesbitt is the owner of D's Quick Shop in Carbondale and the director of the "I Can Read" program. This program--designed to promote literacy and develop reading skills--was initiated by the Attucks graduating class of 1948 of which Mrs. Nesbitt is a member.

Lillian L. Woods
Board Member and Organization Leader

Lillian Louise Woods was a member of Local 994, Laborers' International Union of North America, A.F.L.-C.I.A., and a member of the Union Executive Board of Tesa Tuck, Inc. She last worked at Tesa Tuck Industries, Inc. where she received her Twenty-Five Years' Plus Service Award. She also belonged to the Zeta Amicae Auxiliary and Mariam Chapter No. 17, Order of Eastern Star, holding each of the organization's positions during her membership.

Prior to going to Tesa Tuck, Inc., Mrs. Woods was a former employee of the Elk's Club in Carbondale and the Sangamon Electric Company. At Olivet Free Will Baptist Church, she served as treasurer and usher.

Margaret Jean Nesbitt

Willard Eugene Brown
Youth Leader and Communtiy Worker

Willard Eugene Brown was recognized as a leader and mentor for Carbondale's black youth. He was the organizer and coach for one of the first Little League baseball teams for black children in the city. At Attucks High School, Willard himself was very interested in sports and was an active participant in the athletics program.

Willard was a member of the American Legion Garvin King Post no. 542 in Carbondale. After becoming disabled, Willard helped to organize and was president of "The Loafers' Club," an organization for retirees and senior citizens.

In 1987, Willard Brown was presented a Sports Hall of Fame Certificate by the Spirit of Attucks organization citing him as an Outstanding Athlete of the former Attucks Bluebirds. Willard was 68 years old when he died on April 1, 1988.

Roosevelt "Rose" Turley
Community Leader

Mrs. Roosevelt Turley, the wife of Reverend Lenus Turley, was an advocate of better community relations and an active participant in the religious affairs of the church. At Rock Hill Baptist Church, she supported her husband, the Reverend Lenus Turley, by serving as president and teacher in the Missionary Society and working in the Mt. Olive Baptist District Association. She also served in the Illinois State and in the National Baptist Conventions.

Mrs. Turley was a quiet, mild-mannered woman and a highly civic minded citizen. She served as president of the Carbondale Community Club, and she worked diligently with the Church Women United organization. Her works went far in helping to improve and promote racial harmony in the city in the days preceding the era of legalized integration.

Annie Ruth Clemmer
Community Worker and Board Member

Through her role as a member of the Board of Governors of the Northeast Congress, Anna Ruth Clemmer was instrumental in bringing many improvements to the black community. She was an ardent supporter of the Attucks PTA and held memberships in the Ladies' Afternoon Club and the Friendly Eight Social Club. Having both a gifted voice and a talent for oratory, Mrs. Clemmer was often called on to perform solos and to speak at various functions throughout the area.

Anna Ruth also operated a barbecue business in Carbondale and was one of the first black employees of the Day Care Program sponsored by the Church Women United organization.

William Archie Jones
Educator, Political Leader, and Humanitarian

William Archie Jones received a Bachelor of Arts degree from the University of Illinois and a Master of Arts degree from Southern Illinois University. He was an educator for forty-six years until his retirement at age 65. After his retirement, he continued to teach in other areas such as the Man Power program.

An active church leader, Mr. Jones served as a steward, treasurer and Sunday School teacher. Additionally, he served as the Sunday School Superintendent of the Illinois South District which, at the time, consisted of some thirty different churches.

As a civic leader, Archie Jones spent many years in service to the people of Carbondale and received many awards, citations and recognitions for his efforts. Archie Jones Street, located in northeast Carbondale, stands in testament and memorial to his outstanding and illustrious efforts.

Luella McCall Davis
Educator, Civic Leader and Humanitarian

Mrs. Davis was recognized statewide for her leadership abilities. She was a founding mother of the Carbondale Chapter of the Alpha Kappa Alpha Sorority. Her service record of 38 years at both segregated and integrated schools is one of the longest in the history of Carbondale educators.

At Bethel A.M.E. Church, Mrs. Davis served for over fifty years in almost every capacity of the church including pianist, church clerk, superintendent of the Sunday School, secretary of the Trustee Board, and choir member. She was a member of the Rose of Sharon Club and the Missionary Society. She also sat on many panels including committees to raise finances for various church functions.

One of Carbondale's finest humanitarians, Mrs. Davis unselfishly gave of her time to administer to the needs of others. She was frequently asked to be the keynote speaker at community affairs, and she directed numerous civic functions as well. At Attucks, she always admonished her students, "Don't just think about it; always think it through."

Traces In The Dust

"The hardest thing about facts is to face them."

--Archie Jones, from *Facts, Facets and Consideration of Life*, by William Archie Jones.

Archie Jones: Carbondale's 'Citizen of Year'

By Dave DeWitte
Of The Southern Illinoisan

The Carbondale Chamber of Commerce Citizen of the Year has done more things in one lifetime than many people could do in two, but he's not ready to call it quits yet.

City Councilman Archie Jones, 83, was honored by the chamber of commerce Saturday night for 30 years service to the city — first as an educator and later as a city leader.

A Carrier Mills native, Jones did not come to Carbondale until he had served as an educator for 30 years in Saline County Schools. He came to Carbondale in 1955 to work as Principal of the Attucks High School for the next 11 years.

In future years, Jones "served on nearly all city commissions and committees," according to Matt Maier, the 1983 Carbondale Citizen of the Year, who introduced Jones at the chamber's annual winter social event.

Currently wrapping up his fourth city council term, Jones has already begun to seek a fifth four-year stint on the council. In addition to his usual activities, Jones serves as mayor pro-tem in the absence of Mayor Helen Westberg. he is treasurer of the Bethel AME Church in Carbondale, a member service in membership recruitment. He expressed hopes that the chamber would become more of a unifying force in the community during the upcoming year.

"We all know we need some unity in this town and I think we're moving in that direction," he said.

Other service awards were presented to Nancy Sorgen, Pat Burley, Maier, Dick Hunter, Robert Ratcliffe, Greg McMillan and 1985 President Sue Herron for outstanding work in the chamber.

The chamber's record for 1984 was a good one, according to chamber Executive Director Jim Prowell.

Archie Jones: Honored by chamber

Archie Jones
Educator, Political Leader, Humanitarian, and Author

Above: A portion of one of many news articles written about the life and work of William Archie Jones in the city of Carbondale. The article recounts many of his accomplishments in and out of the political area.

Courtesy of the Southern Illinoisan.

In Service To Their People: Labors and Achievements

Luella McCall Davis

Traces In The Dust

Community Leaders. Top Left: Rev. U. P. Penn. Top Right: Norvell "C. Jr." Haynes. Bottom Left: Ima Mae Sparks Valentine. Bottom Right: Educator and Civic Leader, Wilbert Bowers, Sr.

In Service To Their People: Labors and Achievements

Reverend Dr. Archibald Mosley
Educator and Religious Leader

Dr. Archibald Mosley, an Attucks graduate, became pastor at Bethel A.M.E. Church in 1958 and served in that capacity until 1962. Dr. Mosley earned undergraduate and graduate degrees from Wilberforce University, Payne Theological Seminary, Southern Illinois University at Carbondale, and the University of Detroit. He received a Ph.D at Wayne State University in 1976.

Dr. Mosley was a leader in Carbondale community affairs and throughout the Southern Illinois area. He served as Pastor and Presiding Elder in the Illinois Conference and as Pastor in the Michigan Conference. He was a teacher and coach at Douglas Junior High School in Murphysboro, Illinois and an instructor and dean at Shaw College in Detroit, Michigan. Dr. Mosley's works and deeds impacted the lives of many in the city of Carbondale.[3]

---

[3] See Archibald Mosley in "Black Churches and Spiritual Leadership" in <u>Generations--A Pictorial Review of African Americans in Carbondale, Illinois</u> by Melvin L. Gre Macklin.

Eurma C. Hayes

Eurma C. Hayes, the wife of William Richard Hayes, Sr., was born on May 1, 1918. She was employed in the Home Economics Department at Southern Illinois University and as a cook for one of the institution's sorority houses. She also worked as a seamstress and domestic housekeeper. Mrs. Hayes is most remembered for her devotion to the advancement of the black race in Carbondale and for her efforts in the development and expansion of the African American northeast community. In recognition of her tireless endeavors, the Eurma Hayes Center was named in her honor. This multi-purpose facility is one of two public buildings located in the northeast community named for a black citizen of Carbondale.

Above: A portrait of Mrs. Eurma C. Hayes on permanent display at the Eurma Hayes Center. Printed by permission of the Eurma Hayes Center.

In Service To Their People: Labors and Achievements

Southern Illinois University and Student Housing

Many enterprising individuals received income both directly and indirectly from the early Southern Illinois Normal University campus located in Carbondale, which eventually became Southern Illinois University-Carbondale. Since Negro students were prohibited from living on Campus in the early years of the institution, they had to find lodging with other colored families and residents of the city. This blight of discrimination wrought by the white community ironically proved to be mutually beneficial for the African American students and the Negro families of Carbondale who provided shelter for them.

Above: Mrs. Ida Edgar of Carbondale is visited at her home on Green Street by her sister, Mrs. Arzenia Brown of Waukegan, Illinois. Ida and her husband, Charlie, were among the first African American families who rented rooms in their northeast side home to college students. Other Negro couples who boarded students in their homes included the Hamiltons (owners of the Hamilton House) and Taz and Martha Green. Dick Gregory, national civil rights activist, roomed with the Greens while attending Southern Illinois University. The Edgars rented rooms to male students at the university for more than twenty-five years.

Traces In The Dust

Breaking The Barriers

In 1947, Mrs. Jeanether Simon fought unsuccessfully to have her children enrolled at the white Carbondale Community High School. Below (left) is one of several letters Mrs. Simon received from the office of the Superintendent of Public Instruction. The letter claimed local school boards had the power to determine which schools children could attend, and the Superintendent's office in Springfield, in effect, had no authority to overturn local policy regarding the issue. The letter advises Mrs. Simon against seeking any type of legal action since, according to district policy, the local school board has "a right to make reasonable rules and regulations with reference to where children shall attend school." The letter is signed by N. E. Hutson, Assistant Superintendent in charge of Legal Matters. Below (right) Carbondale African American citizens participate in the national civil rights sruggle, 1963.

VERNON L. NICKELL
SUPERINTENDENT

State of Illinois
Office of the Superintendent of Public Instruction
Springfield

September 17, 1947

Mrs. Jeanether Simon
209 East Oak Street
Carbondale, Illinois

Dear Mrs. Simon:

Your letter of September 3rd, addressed to Honorable Vernon L. Nickell, Superintendent of Public Instruction, has been referred to my desk for reply.

The Board of Education of your district has a right to make reasonable rules and regulations with reference to where children shall attend school. This office has no power to require the Board to permit the pupils to go to different schools than those designated by the Board.

In other words, the Board's decision is final in these matters and if you feel that there is discrimination against your children, the only way such a question could be settled would be by action of the courts. We do not advise legal procedure except in cases where an injustice is being done and where it cannot be rectified otherwise.

I hope you may be able to work out your problem with your local school board without the necessity of resorting to court action.

Yours very truly,

N. E. Hutson
Assistant Superintendent
in charge of Legal Matters.

NEH:RHL

Above: Mr. William Hays stands in front of one of several buses from Carbondale headed for the now famous "March on Washington," led by Dr. Martin Luther King, Jr. in September of 1963. The march was a crucial event in the nation wide movement to end segregation in the United States.

In Service To Their People: Labors and Achievements

Robert A. Stalls
Director of Model Cities
City Demonstration Agency

Traces In The Dust

Below: An excerpt from "Toward A Model City," the Summary Progress Report, delivered by City Demonstration Agency Director Robert A. Stalls after the second year of operation of the Model Cities Program. In his speech, Mr. Stalls recognizes the Northeast Congress as instrumental force in the improvement of the quality of life for the citizens of the northeast community.

Mid-way through the Second Action Year we can point to clearly recognizable results of our efforts to improve the quality of life in the Model Neighborhood. Over one hundred fifty residents of the target area have employment and are receiving training and continued education as a result of the Model Cities effort. One hundred ten low income families now have all of their health care needs fully paid for. A full-time dentist and a half-time physician and supportive staff are serving the neighborhood. Over thirty new housing units have been constructed in the Model Neighborhood. Social Service Delivery is being coordinated and facilitated. Transportation is available to assure access to services. Youth and senior citizens are stimulated by a variety of educational, recreational, and cultural activities. Finally and most importantly the Model Neighborhood is gaining a stronger voice in the total community as a result of the citizen participation organization, the Northeast Community Development Congress.

Robert A. Stalls
Director
City Demonstration Agency
(Model Cities)

In Service To Their People: Labors and Achievements

Top Left: Odessa Meeks receives the Lindell W. Sturgis Award for service to the community, state, or nation. At the time of the presentation, Odessa was the second African American ever to receive the honor. Odessa is secretary and a charter member of the Spirit of Attucks organization and a member of the Attucks Community Service Board. She is also a member of the Executive Board of the Civil Service Union at Southern Illinois University. Top Right: Louberta Cavitt, Early Carbondale Community Leader. Bottom Left: Carbondale Affirmative Action Leader Cleveland Matthews, son of Della and Robert Matthews, is pictured with national political figure Jullian Bond. Bottom Right: Dr. Elizabeth Inez Mosley-Lewin, the daughter of the Reverend Dr. Archibald and Jolene Mosley, is the first native African American of Carbondale to become Superintendent of the Carbondale Elementary School District.

Traces In The Dust

Top Left: Educator and Higher Education Program Director, the Reverend Dr. Lovenger Hamilton Bowden. Top Right: Attucks High School teacher, Arthur Newbern. Bottom Left: Community Leaders, Willard and Harold Brown, sons of John and Cecil Brown. Bottom Right: Recreational Center Director, Frances White.

In Service To Their People: Labors and Achievements

Fred Wills, "Salesman of the Year."

Mr. Fred Wills, the son of Pauline and Ed Wills, is honored as the top saleperson in automotive sales at Ike Buick in Carbondale. Mr. Wills, a former business enterpreneur, is a graduate of the former Attucks High School and has been the president of The spirit of Attucks Reunion Organization for the past twenty years. Photo courtesy of the Southern Illinoisan.

Left: Former Community Club President, Wanda Perkins Haynes. Right: Annie and Arthur Jones, owners of Jones Cafe. Photo courtesy of Betty Woods.

Epilogue

**Voices
Past and Present**

Voices Past and Present

The Early Black Families
by
Albert "Flat Top" Mason

The first families who I can remember, the Carbondale folks who built Carbondale was people like George Green, John Brown, Tom Holder, Taz Green, the Parrons, the Bowers, the Thomases who stayed on North Wall and The Gibsons. The Gibsons left Carbondale during the depression. The Gibsons belonged to Rock Hill. Taz Green was an electrician. He was the only black man at that time who I know that had a license for electrical work. He taught me how to wire a house. Also there was Eunice Davis, the Chappells, the Clarksons, "C. Junior" Haynes, and the Scott family--Ora Scott was born and reared on Wall Street. Two other early families were the Kenners and the Cavitts. George Kenner's grandfather was a switchman who worked in the Tower at the Round House. He switched all the Illinois Central trains that came through here. He switched every train that was going and coming. Also there was the Banks and the Housers--and the Nelsons who lived on Oak Street. Joe Houser lived in Puppy Tail, at the end of Jackson Street. Then you had the Armours, Tom Jacobs, and the Gibbs. And Hannah Gentry. There was a lot more families; there were the Relifords, the Crims and a man called John Crisp.

To my knowledge, the first black person was born on East Main. He was Boston Williams. There was some slaves way back before then, but I don't know about them. But I know that they were buried in the southwest corner of Woodlawn Cemetery.

Now, when I was born in 1913, there was about 800 some black folk here in Carbondale. It was a sign that used to be right out on Illinois when you were coming into town from the North. It had how many people were in the town, and I remember the sign said the number of Whites and the number of Blacks. It was a hold lot of Black folks. The city limits was out on North 51 where the IC tracks curved to go to St. Louis. When I got up some size, Hannah Woods's husband was the only black mail man. Another Woods was a photographer.

The first blacks working at the railroad in the twenties were my daddy, Nathan Mason, William Hayes, and Mr. Hillsman. There were a lot of others that came along soon afterwards. We couldn't go in a restaurant in the front at all; we could go in the back. We could go in the front only at the Illinois Central restaurant. All the hotels, restaurants, and bus lines had black cooks and black workers.

Now, there was a lot of black folk in the thirties and forties who had land all over Carbondale, just about everywhere you could think of. On the white side of town, from Oakland Avenue on the west side running clear on back South (and to the north), Blacks owned all those farms. The Murrays, The Woods, The Gibsons. Blacks had land on Illinois that ran from Hickory Street to Route North Illinois. It was Mr. Alfred Ray that sold his land to the white man where the Varsity Theater is now. He owned a big house right in the spot where the theater sits, and he owned two more lots across from the movie. He used to fish in a creek that ran from the old train depot down to where Rock Hill Church is now. Mrs. McCracken stayed on West Pecan; she had a lot of land. And there was an old black lady named Dodd[1] who lived on Pecan and had about four or five acres of asparagus. The white man cheated her out of all her land and property. On the east side, Mr. Woods owned Woods Park. The Woods had all that farm land where the Fox Theater is. All that land from South Wall and Main Street going on back like you go toward Marion. I don't know how far east it went, but I can tell you he had a lot of acres out there. All the land that the black folks had somehow or another ended up in the white folks' hands.

After a while, things got so most of the Blacks was mostly living over here in the northeast side, and then it got so if you were Black, you bet' not be caught on the white side of town at night. If you didn't have business over there, they might stop you and want to know, "Hey, Boy! What'cha doing over here?" And you had to be careful around white people. Some of the blacks would step aside if a white person came walking by. And you couldn't look too hard at a white woman. That was all right here in Carbondale. You didn't have to go down South. All that happened right here in *this* town. I know what I'm talking about because I was here!

And another thing I didn't like at that time was Community High School got all the new school books; we got the old, second-handed books that they had used and torn up. I *can* say we had good teachers. They taught us black history.

---

[1] Documents indicate that the reference,"old black lady named Dodd," most likely refers to Mrs. Marie Dodd--the wife of John Dodd--who resided in Carbondale in the late 40s.

Traces In The Dust

Everybody talks about how good things are and how it is now. But I tell you, Carbondale used to be something else! At one time, the police was scared of some of the places around here. You couldn't get a white police to go back out in the woods of the "hoodlums." They would say right quick, "I ain't going out there up in them woods after no nigger!" And they didn't go either! Ask some of these old timers around here; they will tell you if I'm lying or not.

Oh, Yeah! Those were the good days. People nowadays don't know what "good times" are. Those were *really* the good old days! Anything you wanted, you could find--liquor, home brew--it didn't matter. Whatever you wanted, you could get! That area of woods back out there was the place to be I tell you. That was where the Blacks gathered.

It was one joint what we called the "Good Time Place" up there in those woods--like going out to the old junk yard. It would be fights and killings and all kinds of stuff going on out there. That was where I got my name "Flat Top," but I can't put that story down in a book.

But, back to how it used to be. It was my mother and a few of the other black women that first demanded police protection for the Negro citizens and for black people to serve as police officers. The white man set up a volunteer police department with a few of the town's Black men on it so they would have somebody to go after the blacks--'cause like I say, you couldn't get a white police to go up in there. Those fellows (the black police) were tough too! Taz Green was one of the first blacks that worked on that force. Quincy Webb and Bill Hayes served on it too. Now, Lee English, he was the first real black policeman in Carbondale; then came Hosey Howard. Taz Green and A. D. Cavitt were Deputy Sheriffs.

Lee English was hired on the regular force. And one thing, I can say about Lee: he didn't take no stuff! When he said something, that was it! He was a big man; plus, he carried a big "billy club." Every black man in town knew Lee English. And when he came driving up, they had sense enough to get out of the way--some of them Negroes would leave town if they heard Ole Lee was hunting them! But he was fair. Just because he was Black, that didn't go to his head. He treated everybody fair, the blacks and the whites.

Carbondale has really changed now. Now, you got a whole lot of new people, and I don't hardly know many folks now. Now, since I got sick, I just mostly sit here in my home and think about the "good times." Most everybody I knew are just about gone. This whole street is changed; there are only a few of us old heads left. They always come to us when they want to know about the old Carbondale.

--July, 1998

Cousin Jenny, the Healer

As told to the author by Mrs. Irene Haydene ("Mamarene")

You talk about Cousin Jenny giving your mama cow manure tea to give you--I remember the time I was real sick, suffering from ovary problems.

I was home sick, and Aunt Babe called the doctor. The doctor came and looked at me and examined me and everything. The told me I had to have an operation right then or I was going to die. I told him if I had to have an operation, I would just die right then before them. They wouldn't be cutting on me. Well, Son called another doctor, and he told me, "Mrs. Hayden, if you don't get to the hospital in fifteen minutes, you want be here by nightfall." I told that doctor the same thing I told the other one--that I was just going to have to die. Well, then, it was Grace . . .Grace Kelly came down and her and Aunt Babe tried to get me to go to the hospital. Aunt Babe (Mrs. Barner) told me, "Irene, they said if you don't get to the hospital in fifteen minutes you'd be dead. You have to go!" Still I wasn't going. And I mean I was hurting! It wasn't playing at hurt either; I was deathly sick!

Well, Miss Jenny came down and come on in the house where I was. She looked at me and said, "What's the matter with you, Rabbit?" Miss Jenny always called me "Rabbit." Well I told her everything and about what all the doctor had said. And about that time, Aunt Babe said, 'Yeah, if she don't get to the hospital, she's going to die." Well, Miss Jenny looked at them and said, "Ya'll hush. Ain't nobody going to die today!"

Well, Miss Jenny looked at me and said she'll be right back. Miss Jenny came back and she took camphor and rubbed it in her hands. Then she took two pieces of cotton clothes and put camphor all on the rags, and laid one over each side of my stomach over the ovaries. She told Son, "Now, when they dry out, wet them down real good and lay them back over her. I'll be back later and check on her to see how she's doing. She'll be up and out sitting on the porch by the time I get back." By the time Miss Jenny got back, I had got up, done cooked supper, and cleaned the house, and hadn't had no ovary trouble since.

One time I had a real bad cold. Some times we took Vic salve. Everybody gave it to their kids. But Miss Jenny didn't want that. She said Vic's salve made you sweat and that only lifted the cold for a while, but it could come back on you. So, instead of that, she took some goose grease and gave me. I said I couldn't take that, but Miss Jenny said, "Yes you can. Be quiet and take it." Well, I swallowed it down. Then Miss Jenny said, "Now, you spit up all that fluid and that cold will be gone. She was right.

Another, time she asked Son if he had some hog hooves. Son said, "No." "You young people ain't got nu'thng!" Miss Jenny told him. Well, Miss Jenny went home and directly, she come back with some strong black tea. "Here she said. I made you dis heah hog hoof tea. You just keep drinking dis tea. You'll be fine." Again, she was right.

Another remedy Miss Jenny used was mutton grease. She would rub it all on you and give you that goose grease. That would take care of it, all right. You better believe it! Now-a-days everybody go to the doctor, and half of them die. If your Cousin Jenny around, a lot of people wouldn't have to go to no doctor--you know she lived to be well over a hundred and something!

--July, 1996

Growing Up in Carbondale
by
Barbara Greer Lemons

Growing up in the '50s and '60s in Carbondale was fun. We didn't have a lot of different places to go, but in the summer time we went to Attucks Park where we went to find all kinds of different things with which we created toys to amuse ourselves with.

Many times our parents could not afford to buy new bikes, so we went to the city dump and found old parts and built our own bikes. We also played in cow fields which were at that time located on Wall Street.

We used empty coffee cans to make walking stilts. Also, we hooked two small cans together with a long string and pretended to talk on the telephone.

I attended Thomas School from kindergarten through the sixth grade. I attended seventh and eight grades at Attucks Junior High School. I completed my education at Carbondale Community High School where I attended ninth through the twelfth grades.

The Recreation Center, which was run by Mr. Bill Hayes and Mrs. Etta White, was where we went for relaxation and to enjoy recreational activities. We could listen to music and dance, play pool, ping-pong, and cards. There was a five dollar fee for dues which paid members up for one full year.

Growing up in Carbondale was really a lot of fun for us kids!

--August, 1998

Dedicated Teachers
by
Cleveland Matthews

The teachers of Attucks were committed to seeing their students succeed in spite of segregation. The word segregation was never a part of the dialogue during training and teaching for Attucks school students. The teachers felt that there was no need for the children to have segregation become a distraction from learning. Children were admonished to succeed in spite of segregation.

Although there was blantant racial discrimination all over, the parents preachers, and teachers discussed it among themselves. The children were protected from the agony of it all. Later, as they grew up and matured, they were strong enough and knowledgeable enough to deal with it intelligently. They could now fight it themselves. Before then, they had to simply survive.

--July, 1997

Memories
By
Marilyn Brown-Tipton

I have so many fond memories of growing up on the far northeast side of Carbondale. The area that I grew up in was commonly called, "The Hoodlums". We had rock roads and no streetlights. In fact, our address was RR 3. We were not included in the city limits.

I lived next door to my grandparents and my aunts and uncles lived down the street. We all lived in a three-block radius of each other. My cousins, Patricia and Billy and my uncle Johnny lived next door with Mama Cecil and Papa John and everyone thought Patricia and Billy were my brother and sister.

John and Cecil Brown had 13 children and a tribe of grandchildren. Needless to say, they needed a farm to raise enough food to feed them all. We raised hogs for market. We also owned a cow, goat, many chickens, rabbits, dogs, and cats. We grew most of our vegetables and fruit. The only thing we really had go buy at the store was sandwich bread and soda. Mama Cecil churned her own butter made the best apple butter I ever tasted. She canned fruits, jellies, and vegetables. We smoked the meat to preserve it.

Papa John worked for the Kopper's Tie Plant. They made cross ties for the railroad. Mama Cecil took in ironing for white people. One of her customers I could remember was Dr. Stelzie. He was an eye doctor and had an office on University Avenue, next to Horstman's Cleaners.

Papa John owned one of the two horse and buggies in town. Mr. Tate owned the other one. I got such joy out of riding to the junkyard with him and Mr. George Rice. Later a man name Mr. January had a horse and buggy. He rode it until the early 1980's.

Our neighborhood was a close knit neighborhood. Some of the families were the Morgans, Partlows, Jordons, Gordons, Browns, Edwards, Scotts, Steels, Haydens, Beards, Boykins, Masons, Lilly's, Fletchers, Gibbs, Fowlers, Jacksons, Millers, Rices, Thompsons, Williams, Mitchells, Franklins, Spriggs, and we had 3 white families in our neighborhoods named Woods and Greenwalts. Tommy and Pauline Woods, and his brother, Walter Woods and his family lived the closest to us. They lived right next door to the Partlows and Jordons. We played with there kids and we all got along well.

Every evening all the neighborhood kids would gather at the corner of Burke and Allman Street and have a big softball game. We would use anything we had for bases, (cereal boxes, cans, notebook paper, etc) The games would go well until I got mad and took the ball and bat. You see the ball and bat belonged to me! Everyone would get so mad at me.

During the summer months around 6:00 PM all my family members would gather at the "Big House" and we would snap beans, shell peas, pick greens or take are of whatever was harvested from the garden that evening. My dad raised a big garden and would share with all our family members and neighbors.

The "Big House" did not have a furnace, running water, or a bathroom. We had an outhouse behind the barn and would take a bath in a No. 3 tub in the kitchen. It would be so cold in the winter and we would all gather around the coal stove to keep warm. It was Billy's job to get coal and chop the kindling to start the fires. Next door we had oil stove, so I didn't have to get in any coal, but I would help Billy sometimes. Billy also had to gather the eggs. He would take a stick and knock all the chickens off their nest and then get the eggs. Sometimes the rooster would get after him. I can remember messing with our cow and he broke loose and almost trampled me. After three trips around the Big House, and Trish yelling jump on the porch, I finally got out of his way.

I attended Thomas School from K-6th grade. All of my teachers were African American except my 5th grade teacher. Mr. Thomas was my principal and Mrs. Ella Mae Martin was the cook. She sure could cook good. We have great meals everyday. There were not special education classes at Thomas. Everyone learned together. The teachers cared and made sure you learned it. There were also severe consequences if you didn't. They would whip you and call home and have a whipping waiting on you when you got home.

Church was a big part of our lives. I attended Hopewell and Olivet Freewill Baptist Church growing up. I sung in the Inspirational Choir at Olivet. We had such good times. We even made an album. Rev. Sumner had us singing at two churches per Sunday in different towns. We stayed on the road. Kay Pace was our choir director, Darvell Samuels played drums, Ron Scott played the organ, and Charles Slaughter played the Bongo's. We had it going on! We even sang with James Cleveland at the Keil Auditorium. Aunt Tank (Frances White) was our Sunday school supt. She ran a tight ship. She always took us out of town for conferences in Lovejoy, Brooklyn, East St. Louis, and St. Louis. I remember traveling to Slater, Mo. one year. We would rent a room in a church member's house.

--September, 1998

Family Life in Carbondale
by
Louvenia McKinley

In Carbondale when we were raising our children, one of the main priorities of the parents was always knowing where our children were and whom they were with. There were about twelve of us ladies who organized "Mothers Clubs" so we could always be available to take care of our kids. Our children were not to be running around unsupervised all over the neighborhood, and they were not to be out at all hours of the night. It was very different then.

We instructed our children to always let us know where they were. We taught them this because children have to be instructed and they have to be treated firmly. We were fair with our children, and we were firm. The mothers and the fathers stood in agreement, and they didn't go against one another. That way, the children always knew just what was expected of them. They knew that if the mother said "No," then that was it; they didn't go running off after the father.

We had different projects to keep our children busy. When they went out play, they knew how to behave and conduct themselves. They knew when to go, and they knew when to come home. When they were small, the parents went with them. Sometimes it was the mother, sometimes it was the father. We accompanied them until they were too old to follow. Later, when they grew up and went to social affairs, they were timed when to come home. We planned meetings at such times that one parent would be home most of the time. We attended the parent-teacher programs at school each time their was a meeting of the PTA. Not only did we help out at the school, we also monitored our kids at Attucks. We helped chaperone the "soc hops" and the homecoming dances. We prepared the gym for the Miss Attucks contests and the junior-senior proms. We were always nearby when our children needed us. That is what it means to be a parent.

The children had three basic rules they were expected to follow: one, they had to attend their classes and activities at school; two, they had to do their work and chores at home; and three, they were taken to church. We raised our children by talking with them and praying with them. Sometimes, some of them needed a little swat from time to time. We did this because we loved them and--like all parents--we only wanted the best for them. We had parents who really loved and cared for their children.

--July, 1998

Pulling Together
by
Everlene Chambers

Back in the late forties and early fifties, there was not much in the way of activities for blacks; especially for the black children. Except for playing with each other in their yards, there was nothing. There was no entertainment for them--absolutely nothing. So some of the adults in our community formed a committee to get something going so that our kids would have somewhere to go and something to do, particularly when school let out in the summer months.

Mrs. Savana McCutchen served as president. Jewell Gibbs was instrumental in helping us, since he worked for the city. He knew what we needed in the northeast part of town. What resulted was that we approached the City Park District and asked them to give us some equipment for the young Black boys and girls. So the Carbondale Park District at that time gave us items like balls and bats and other equipment. And the ball games started. We also began something that the kids just absolutely loved: we began showing movies in this big field we had located out on Burke Street. The kids and adults would come from all over the neighborhood, and in the middle of this big field we would show the films that we got from the city. The event came to be known by the kids as the "free movies" because they could watch the movies from the bleachers, completely free of charge. Some would sit on the ground; others would sit on table tops when the bleachers were full; the larger teenagers would sometimes just lean against the cars. They would be everywhere. This was a proud and meaningful moment for us-- this was something we began for our kids!

We would sell Kool Aid, pickles, and pop corn to raise money to pay for the lights and to get funds to do other things for the people in the neighborhood. It took a lot of work from a lot of different people, but those of us who are still around can remember and now, nearly fifty years later, we can say we did something that helped to make a difference. Those little kids now are all grown and have kids and grand kids of their own. But they still talk about the "free" movies Mr. "Jelly" Gibbs would have for them.

Other men like John Jones worked extensively with the youth. Willard Brown, and a group of neighborhood men working with him, got the baseball teams going. I would sell the candy and pop corn to the kids. There was so much to do. Everyone just sort of pitched in, and wherever we saw the need for something to be done in the "Hoodlum" (that was what our area was referred to for a long period of time), we tried to take care of it. Others in our neighborhood who worked actively in these endeavors included Reverend and Mrs. Shedrac McQueen; Mrs. Beatrice Reed, the wife of Rev. Will Reed; Cora Gibbs, George Coins, and the Chappell family. Bertha and Jessie Chappell did a lot for the kids, as did everyone else.

These turned out to be some of the best times and most joyous events--just having the people together, you know--and all the neighborhood working together. In those times, it was a matter of just being together and doing things together. It was simply the joy of being in touch with one another and knowing that you always had friends, neighbors, and family around you could count on. It was all about togetherness. We don't have that today. Somehow, over the years, we have lost touch with one another. Today, folks don't even know who their neighbors next door are. We don't know the kids by name like we once did. The closeness is gone.

Life in the Church

A brief enlightenment of the Black Churches in Carbondale, Illinois as witnessed by Cozette Bell Spinner, former Choir Director and Minister of Music at Olivet Freewill Baptist Church.

"Cozette," whispered the switch as it lay ominously on the big piano which stood like a sentinel in the empty choir stand of Rock Hill Missionary Baptist Church. That is what I imagined I heard as I sat watching that switch along with its thin, slinky mean brothers and sisters who were all laughing at us six year olds in our primary class. One, with its eyes in narrow, Chinese-like slits, whispered, "I want Brenda's back first." Ooh, I just hated that Bible School! It seemed as if Mrs. Mingo could find the keenest, greenest, longest lasting, stingingest switches in town. Rock Hill was "down" with the switches. All of the churches had strong discipline policies because they didn't play! Just as in regular school, no Bible School staff would tolerate foolishness, especially in the house of our Lord and Savior Jesus Christ. In essence, you could get "torn up" in church.

Rock Hill set out to prove that fact over and over, in my humble opinion. Sister, mother, her majesty, Mingo was a master at disciplining. She could find the keenest switches on any tree. It seemed to me that the trees could talk, and they would be saying to her, "Hey, come and get me; I can sting any little legs and backs. Oh yes, I can straighten up any slumping shoulders, take any grin off any face, and banish any tickle in a flash. I even know some names. Let me think. Yes. I know Cozette, Freddie, Eddie, Odessa, and even Janice. I, however, am most familiar with Cozette. My brothers and sisters always tell me abut how much she likes to talk. Well, we will take care of her in short order."

In Carbondale in the late forties to early fifties, there were only about 2,500 Blacks who lived exclusively on the east side of Carbondale, separated from the white community by railroad tracks and Conner Street. We had a representation of just about every popular faith Black folks ascribed to and nice looking, to stately built churches to prove it. There was Bethel A.M.E. on Jackson Street near our Attucks School complex. Almost directly across from the school was Hopewell Missionary Baptist Church. Sandwiched in between was a C.M.E. Church, a small, plain, cinder-block building that looked like "real" church was never held in it. That was where my Father, Mr. Bell, who didn't go to anybody's church, said he belonged. (We younger Bells didn't believe him.) New Zion Baptist Church was located down the street from my house, which, at that time, was located on Willow Street. Gillespie Temple was located on Wall Street, that was where my second brother joined in his teen years to meet girls. "Jumping" Faith Temple was on North Marion Street, north of my church, Olivet Freewill Baptist. There were the Jehovah's Witnesses, but I'm not sure where they met; yet, they were there in Carbondale when I was a child. Our church is one of the oldest organized African American churches in Illinois. We held a special place in town because of that fact; only Bethel was older.

But this did not motivate our parents, nor did they care about the age of a particular church, where it was located, who pastored it, or even how well the choir sang. All they cared was that it was open during the summer. As soon as school was out and we children had barely had a chance to forget the faces of our teachers, we found ourselves in a line in some basement of one of these churches, waiting on that ever present treat of Kool Aid and two, count them, two cookies. Most of the time they were the dried up coconut kind. Lord knows I hated coconut, but they were free! So, I was in line with the rest of the "Attucks children" because that's who were there. Every kid who was in my class at school was also in my Bible School class. I'm telling you, we had some smart parents! A few kids always begged off, I guess, but for the most part, my class went from church to church all summer long right along with me.

When we went to New Zion, the New Zion Kids in our class were the "big Jocks" because we were, of course, in their church. They had "dibs" on us. They got in line first for the Kool Aid and (Lord help) two, count them, two cookies. No one at any church ever gave out three cookies, not even accidentally! I guess parents got together in groups, in their secretive planning meetings, to plot how to stagger each Bible School so as to make sure we were occupied all summer long! At least up until the middle of August. They were smart, I tell you! Any way, I could imagine a conversation among my mama and a few other ladies. "Priss, as soon as we over here at Bethel finish our two weeks (never under two weeks--absolutely no mercy), New Zion can be ready to go the following Monday of the 3rd." "Well, we here at New Zion had planned our church picnic for that week, and it might push us a bit. How about Rock Hill going ahead of us this year?" "Absolutely not! We want to be last because we have conference early this year; we can't miss Reverend Turley's appreciation." This, I believe, is how we got ushered from church to church all summer long until Attucks was ready to begin anew. It didn't matter what the faith of the church was or what the doctrine of the church was; if it had a Bible School program, we had to go!

It got to be that we identified Bible Schools by specifics. I especially remember that Bethel was the killer church in the Kool Aid department. After we had sung our songs, prayed our prayers, learned our scriptures, read our little stories, and played our games, it was time for treats. Lord help, if the Bethel parents had known how we hated their Kool Aid, they would have killed us. They would march the whole Bible School down to the basement, and on the big table near the kitchen would be a big shiny pot, sweating on the outside. There would be a smiling Bible School helper slowly dipping into the pot and pouring the red liquid into small white cups, handing them to the entire thirsty student body, who took them eagerly and walked away. Yes, we walked to the outside of the building, where, with disgruntled faces, we choked down that drink. It was as sour as an over ripped lemon! Somebody there absolutely hated sugar! I envisioned one of those elderly women mixing the Kool Aid: she couldn't have put in more than a few teaspoonsful of sugar at best! All right, maybe a couple of tablespoons! One thing was certain: there couldn't have been one diabetic at Bethel! When I was about twelve years old, I wanted to march into the kitchen and say, "My mama could lend you all some sugar if you just ask!" However, that would have been insolent, and one of the truths we were taught in these same Bible Schools was that you never, never intentionally hurt someone's feelings. "Jesus was a compassionate person, we were taught. Always use His life as an example." So, we drank that sour Kool Aid and went one.

New Zion was the church that had the great choirs. We knew we were going to have a great time musically when we went there for Bible School. We were never disappointed. New Zion also had a young membership, and young leaders as well. We enjoyed going there because of their youth oriented programs. Their pastor, Rev. Clark was a great speaker.

Freewill, my church, was all right, but that was just it. It was my church, so things were just "regular" when we attended our Bible School. However, we did have our specialty too. Freewill was known for the good cooks. Many of the black women at Olivet were professional cooks on the campus of Southern Illinois University and were known for their special dishes. Therefore, not only were we a popular church because of our cooks, but we maintained that status at our Bible School--we had SUGAR. The cookies were the same, but the Kool Aid was delicious! Hopewell, my good friend and classmate's church had the same Kool Aid problem as did Bethel. They were located only a block apart, so they must have had the same kind of "diabetic-minded" mothers.

Faith Temple and Gillespie Temple were the Apostolic faiths in Carbondale. We loved to attend their convocations. They held services outside in the summer. They had the most wonderful musicians. One of them, Mrs. Pullen, astounded me with the way she could "whip" a piano. When she played, it was pure magic! The church had several talented pianists, but she was the known master of the instrument--all others bowed to her extraordinary talent. I loved watching her fingers go up and down the keys. All the music seemed unplanned and spontaneous. Her music could be heard blocks away, long before you got to Faith Temple. I would always try to sit where I could see her playing the instrument (or riding it like like it was a wild bronco)! Every night she tamed that piano into sweet submission to her will. She was an inspiration for me.

Gillespie Temple held the same kind of convocations. This was where I learned to "Testify." I loved to hear the "Saints" who would sing songs and stand speaking of the goodness of God far into the evening. Their voices and instruments could be heard for blocks, just like Mrs. Pullen's piano. Gillespie Temple, under the strong, loving direction of Bishop C. W. Gillespie, had a large, dedicated and sanctified membership. There church services were lively and filled with excitement. During their convocations, over half of the people attending would be guests from the other black churches in town. Their preachers also had a great drawing appeal. So, with the singing, the instruments, the preaching, and the "fellow shipping," it was a joyous time when these sessions were held.

We, my Bible School classmates and I, were masters at attending the churches in Carbondale. Today, as I reflect on these pleasant memories which make me shake with laughter--and smile when I think of all of those old people, now long gone--my heart fills with love. For it is these same people who were my teachers, my scout leaders, my role models, my friends, and, in actuality, my everything. These people from all of the churches cared for us; they taught us, guided us, led us, held on to us, and demonstrated and modeled for us the ways of living that Blessed our Heavenly Father and eventually formed us young'uns into resourceful adults. It was these people who meant that we were going to be productive, happy, useful member of a society that rejected us in every way and on one every level simply because we were of a different color and of a different race. It was these parents who counted on the churches to be an integral part of that village that was needed to help raise us so that we could eventually take their places and continue their legacy.

I believe I voice the sentiment of many Carbondalians when I humbly thank all of those responsible for helping to teach us the strong Christian standard by which we live today. We are now the Bible School teachers and Superintendents. We are the Conference speakers and leaders--the Choir leaders and directors. We are the church organizers--the preachers and pastors. We are the deacons and trustees, the chairpersons and instrument players. We are the tithers and givers--the movers and the shakers. We are now the builders of young minds and the molders of young souls. The legacy has been passed down from those of so long ago to us whom they molded into the the minds and souls they meant us to be.

Those Were The Days
by
Hal McCroy

Attucks, we loved old Attucks with her buildings, grounds and skies of blue.

Yes, those were the days. When we treated people with respect and not neglect.
Yes, we had some of the nicest black business people here in Carbondale. Mrs. Carter and her husband, Mr. Cliff, had some of the best hot dogs and chili, not to mention their Mac sodas.

This was our little paradise back then. And Mrs. Clark had some of the best chili, too. We would go there at lunch time to listen to some rhythm and blues. People like Lavern Baker, the Spaniels, and the Moonglows, Frankie Lymon were real popular back then.

Yes, those were the days. And each time I think about them. I love them in so many ways.
There was Fat's place across the street from Mrs. Clark where we would go and talk.
And my cousin, Phillip Kendrick, would do the greasy walk.

Oh yes, we were cool!

On Wed., Fri., and Sat. we would go to the Recreation Center and congregate with Mr. Crim and Mrs. Frances White--and shoot some pool.

Yes, we treated each other with respect and not neglect.
When Baby Ruths and Butter Fingers were a nickel.
And people took a peppermint stick and stuck it in a pickle.

Yes, those were the days. And each time I think about them,
I know I loved them in so many ways.

Like Miss Campbell's grocery store,
To be around her was a treat--because she was always so neat.

She had her little store on the corner of Green and Barnes Street
and on Asley Street there was Mrs. Emma Banks.

I'm not trying to be in a rush. This other street is called Brush.
Where another little store could be found--owned and operated by Mr. Slaughter Brown.

Now back to Barnes Street, Where Rev. Thomas had his store.

There was Mr. Johnson, who had his store. Mr. Johnson had some of the best penny candy.
To me that was just dandy!

Across the street there was Mrs. Taylor with her little establishment.

Where we all hung out. Night and day--was a place we called Jones Cafe.
He had some of the best hot dogs and fish.

Farther down on Willow Street, we had Mr. Henchey's Store.
And on the corner we had Mrs. Hillsman.

Traces In The Dust

And around the corner on Marion Street
Was Mrs. Russell's grocery store.

Let's skip to the Levee where we had Mrs. Daisy Hanilton's Barbeque stand.
And Mr. Lee English's Barbeque stand.

Yes, those were the days! And when I think about them,
I loved them in so many ways.

We also ad Mr. Ben Isom's store, and Mr. Fletcher's. There was Mrs. Jacobs, and Mr. George
Johnson who had his own Sanitation Business.
There was Mr. Charles Edwards, who had his own cleaner on Washington Street.
And, oh yes before I stop.
Thommy Morris had his own Record Shop! And Bear had his Barber shop.

Yes. Those were the black business men here in Carbondale.
Also, I remember when the lower end of Oak Street was called Puppy Tail.

And after you passed Fisher Street, it was the Hoodlum.
And past Miss Williams's home, it was called the New Edition.

Yes, those were the days when we had lots of fun.
Yet, it fills my heart with joy to have grown up in Carbondale when I was a boy.

Yes, I can shout it from the highest steeple.
I thank God for letting me know all those wonderful people!

Yes, those were the days!

The Good Times!
by
Della Matthews

When I was a little girl, in the olden times, everybody was happy and people were neighborly toward each other. Now, sometimes you just don't know the people who are around you. Everything is strange these days--half of your children are gone. You got these grandchildren, and half of them don't mind you at all. Well, everything is just changed. That's all you can say.

You know, back then, people would come to your home and bring you dinner. And you'd do the same. My husband would cut the young'uns hair. He started cutting in the shop; he was one of the first colored men that I know of to cut in the white man's shop, but then they got so to where they had to have a liscnece. Well, the folks found out he didn't have a licsence. After that, he started cutting at home. He charged twenty-five cents a head. If the kids didn't have the money, he'd cut their heads for nothing. My husband cut anybody's head--he didn't care if you was colored or white. It didn't make no difference to him. He just cut hair--period!

Like I say, people helped each other back then. Mrs. Thornton (Mamie) would come in and help deliver my babies--then she'd cut the cord. We didn't always have money and the folks didn't always have it, so we just dealt in trade. If you needed some meat and I needed some sugar or anything like that--well, we'd just swap out. They called it "Bartering." Same thing if you needed some help with something. The men would do barn raising and they would help one man build his barn or house or whatever he needed. Then they would go around to somebody else. Everybody pitched in.

And another thing you can put down, we didn't go to no nursing home either--our children would take care of us. They moved the old folks right into their homes and gave them their own room and cooked for them. Now, the young folks put the old folks in the nurshing home--they don't won't to be bothered with you. Your children will do for you, but that's about all.

We raised our own food. We would go fishing in the Big Muddy. We would each some of the fish--we would sell some and give some away if somebody really needed it. I used to feed the hoboes that came through on the train. They would work for a meal, and they never hurt anybody. Wasn't no such thing as them stealing or robbing folk. They just wanted a meal. They did some work and you fed them, and off they went.

Me and my husband had ducks, chickens, geese, hens--some of everything you could name. We raised our own. One thing about it, we didn't have a lot of money, but me and my husband--we made it. And all the other old folks my age made it. And I taught all my children how to make it. They all have made good. They have nice homes and good husbands and wives. I had a lot of children, and not one of my kids ever went hungry. I didn't do like a lot of women and throw my husband's money away. Whatever Robert gave me for the house, that's what I used it on. I'd pray and asked to Lord to show me what to do as a wife. I tried to stick with him (Robert) all the way. I'd see to it that we had enough clothes and food. Me and my husband, well we weren't nothing special. We just tried to do the best we knew how.

--Della Matthews. June 28, 1998.

Growing Up in The Hoodlums
Compiled by
Frances Armour and Mildred Harrington Jordan

When we were growing up in the northeast Carbondale community on North Barnes Street, which was called--at that time-"The Hoodlums," (once you crossed Fisher Street on Barnes, now called Robert Stalls Avenue), our mother Mabel married our step father, Albert Franklin. I was about seven years old, and we lived at the corner of Barnes and Burke Streets. My sisters were Frances and Bernice, and my brother was Charles. We had three step sisters, Iray, Orene, and Mary and one step brother, Albert, Jr.

At that time, there was no running water, no indoor plumbing, and no electricity. We burned kerosene lamps and carried water from Koppers Tie Plant. We walked from Barnes Street to East Jackson to attend Attucks School. There were no buses and no such thing as "snow days." You went to school regardless--in bad weather or good. Additionally, you walked home for lunch and then back to school afterward, and you were never late.

To entertain ourselves, we had minstrel shows in a vacant lot, and we found other means of entertainment among ourselves. Some of the families of our community at that time were the Steele family, the Masons, the Fletchers, the Youngs, the Fords, the Carvins, the Haydens, the Browns, the Spriggs, the Haynes, and the Westleys.

In The Hoodlums, everybody helped each other raise their children; any of the adults would correct you or spank you if you were doing something wrong. Then, when you got home, your parents got you also.

Across the street lived Sister Williams. She was a stern Christian lady who went to the Church of God In Christ. Sister Williams would take us to the Tent meetings, and it was really something to be a part of. We went fishing in a creek behind the dump yard called Crab Creek, and they also went swimming in Crab Creek. For fishing, we had long cane poles ten or twelve feet long, sometimes longer. We didn't have rods and reels until later. The Westleys had a lunch business and sold piesand sandwiches, and later, they had a grocery store. The Fletchers also owned a grocery store--these were all in The Hoodlums.

Growing up in northeast Carbondale was a struggle for our parents, yet it was very rewarding for the siblings. In spite of the hardships and disadvantages, our parents saw to it that we had food and whatever we needed to make it. And, eventually, we did make it. We grew up and had families of our own. Charles had a daughter named Betty. Frances had three daughters, Louise, Rosemary, and Gabrielle. Bernice had three boys and three girls, John, Michael, David, Bernadine, Jeweldine, and Sandra. I had five boys and two girls, Willie, Abraham, Jr., Don, Clarence, III, and Anthony, Sherrie, and Angelia.

Those were some wonderful days. Mrs. Allean Brown and Mabel Franklin, my mother, were the cooks of the Hoodlums. They could cook the most wonderful foods, and they cooked for everybody!

"My Years at Attucks"
by
Virginia Mae France Lane, Class of 1950

Attucks, I loved Ole Attucks, her grounds and her building, too. Yes, I loved her teachers all brave and true!

What I gained from Attucks as a student in the 1940s can never be measured or replaced. I gained values, morals, and principles that carried me, molded me and helped to form and shape my entire life, thus far, in a positive manner. This is largely due to the education I received at Attucks.

On the other side of the coin, however, when I saw cardboard boxes filled with the second-handed material being discarded from the schools on the other side of the tracks, I wished that our books and equipment could have been brand new like the ones the white kids received. I feel new books and materials would have impacted the quality of education I received. Yet, it was not all inferior coming from a completely segregated school. For the most part, our teachers were prepared. However, I felt that they did not have all the tools to work with that the whites had and that made it more difficult to teach what should have been taught.

We had lots of white educators to come to our commencement exercises and tell us what a marvelous system we had, even though they knew that the money did not reach us; and they knew that the foundation of our academics was not built on as solid grounds as their system was. When we left Attucks and entered Southern Illinois University, we had a rude awakening into the real world of higher education and learning. We found out that we were missing something that, had we gotten it in high school, could have prevented us from struggling so hard to receive that "A" or "B" at SIU or being always just on the edge with that "C" and "D." It was most difficult. To be frank and truthful, a lot of students coming out of Attucks just couldn't cut it at Southern. But this is not an indictment against our former teachers; but more so, it is an indictment against the system we were under. Our teachers did the best with what they had.

Granted, not all segregated schools were falling through the cracks back in the forties. Even if they didn't have a superior academic program, they had others areas in which they measured highly. Attucks, itself, excelled in many such areas. We had the best sports teams (our bluebirds) that couldn't be beat. We had the best social life. There were always activities being put on. In a way, it could be said that we had the best of many worlds; we just didn't have the new books. Take it from me, as the saying goes, "I loved ole Attucks."

Lucille Walker, Mother of Us All
by
Hortense "Tootsie" Edward

When I was in the eighth grade, I went to work for Mrs. Walker. I would take care of her house on Illinois street. Whatever she needed done, I would do it. This involved mostly cleaning, washing a few things, dusting the furniture, and just general housekeeping.

What I remember particularly most of all was that Mrs. Walker had this wide, huge table in the dining room, and on that table she had papers everywhere--stacks and stacks of papers. This table was not to be touch under any circumstances. On this point, she had been unquestionably clear: do not touch that table or her papers. "Hortense," she informed me, "Now, I don't want you to bother this table because these are my papers I'm checking, and I don't want anything to happen to them. I'll take care of this myself when it needs straightening up."

Well, knowing Mrs. Walker as I did, believe me, I never touched that table. If Mrs. Lucille Walker told you not to do anything, you didn't do it--plain and simple! So, for months and months I would clean. Everything else in the house would be shining and sparkling like new, and there that table would be, in the same state as I originally found it. I didn't care if the dust on it got as high as Mount Everest, I wasn't going to touch it--and I didn't!

Mrs. Walker and I had many conversations, and one day she told me something that to this very day I have never forgotten. We got to laughing and talking about school, and I asked her about all those whippings she used to give me (and to half of the total population of black kids ever to grace those hollowed halls of Attucks). What I wanted to know was why in the world was it that I got so many of them. It seems like everytime I turned around, she'd be on my behind with that strap. She said to me, "Hortense, you know why I got on to you so much and gave you all those whippings? I gave them to you because you needed them. I knew you had good potential; I knew you could do your work and could be anything you wanted to be, but you didn't want to. You were lazy, and I had to show you--and all of you chill'uns that you could do it. And that's what I did. I made sure you did what you were supposed to do."

It was not until my adult years that I fully understood what she meant. And now, looking back on it all, and now that Mrs. Walker is gone, I understand what she was doing. That's exactly why our black kids are like they are today. They (the parents and teachers) have gotten away from spanking their little hind-parts, and now they are out of control.

Whenever I hear some say the name Lucille Walker, I think about the time I worked for her and the things she taught us black kids. That is why I hear so many of the old Attucks bunch always talking about Mrs. Lucille Walker and that famous strap of hers. And they all talk about her with love and respect. We see now just how much of herself she gave to us. We realize how much love it must have taken for her to deal with so many of us for all those years. Many of the old teachers are seldom mention, but the name Lucille Walker is never forgotten--she was truly a mother to us all.

"Raised up" at Olivet
by
Melvin L. G. Macklin

At Olivet there were so many wonderful people who worshipped and fellowshipped each Sunday. And I remember a few out of the long succession of preachers that occupied the pulpit. There was Reverend Crim, Reverend Banks, Reverend Hall, and later Rev. Sumner. However, when I was a youngster, what impressed me most about Olivet was our Sunday School.

"Aunt Tank," as she was known, was our Sunday School superintendent for twenty-five years. It was she, along with the dozens of other men and women, who made sure everyone learned their

Sunday School lesson. In Sunday School class, everyone had to read and recite. Then, the bell rang for general assembly. "Aunt Tank" would always ring the bell that sat on the superintendent's table, and that was our signal for everyone to regather back in the congregation area.

Some of us boys would dare each other to go up and ring the bell. We would wait until nobody was around--no grown-ups anyway--and then dash up to the table, strike the bell, and make a quick get-a-way before being apprehended. The Norman boys were especially good at striking the bell without being caught. Timothy Norman was tall and had long arms. He could strike that bell so fast nobody could see him, even with the adults sitting all around. To a group of nine and ten year old boys, that was a lot of fun--eventhough it was quite dangerous if you got caught.

"Aunt Tanks", who was the mother of Etta White, would call on individual members from the different classes to answer questions about the lesson. After that, she always said how proud she was that everyone had done such a good job, especially the children. Sometimes, a lot of us children just mainly focused on the candy we had just purchased from Mrs. O'Neal or on what we were having for Sunday dinner when we got home, and we really didn't give much thought to the Sunday School lesson. But still, that was all right. We still got complimented on how well we did on the lesson that day.

Mrs. Norman was my Sunday School teacher. She reviewed the lesson with us and then gave us candy because we were the youngest children. Needless to say, hers was my favorite class. Learning about Jesus was just fine, but a little candy bar now and again, somehow made Jesus a little more popular. My "Mama Martha," who was Grandpa Taz's wife, told me once that it was a shame for little boys to eat in Sunday School, but I figured if it was all right with Jesus, then it was all right with me. After all, if Jesus had something against it, then he wouldn't have given it to Mrs. Norman. I was always figuring up stuff like that for one reason or another.

There were two ladies at our church who were something of a mystery to me; yet, they were remarkable women: Mrs. Ida and Mrs. Mary Lou Jacobs. They were the sisters of Peter Jacobs. Not too much is known about their background, but they were at Sunday School every Sunday unless they were sick. Both of the sisters were stricken with hearing and speech impediments, but that didn't stop them from attending church. Mrs. Ida could read, and she could also write. She didn't write that well, but I would "talk" to her sometimes during church through the little short notes she would write. Sometimes she would asked about the Sunday School lesson or what a particular word meant. Other times she would want to know who the visitor was that just stood up for the "welcome" given by Mrs. Lillian Woods or Mrs. Arnett, or another woman of the church.

While the Sunday School teacher read and explained the lesson, Mrs. Ida would read and follow along with the others in the Sunday School class. She was very outgoing and also very intelligent. Mrs. Mary Lou was quiet and, since she didn't understand as well as Mrs. Ida, she mostly followed the lead of her sister. I would ask "Momean" how they could understand what was going on in church, and my grandmother would tell me simply, "They know."

When I was older, Mrs. Ida wrote me a note one time asking me if I would cut her grass. About two weeks later, I went to mow her lawn. I was paid seventy-five cents, but she fed me greens and cornbread and made me the best cold roast beef sandwich of my life. Maybe it was because I was hungry, or maybe it was because it was the first time I remember ever having cold roast beef, but it was truly the most delicious sandwich I had ever eaten. And right today, whenever I see cold cut sandwiches on a restaurant menu, I think back to the time Mrs. Ida served me that wonderful, thick slab of roast. And whenever I visit or pass by Olivet, the memory of how much these two ladies meant to our church family comes flashing back in my mind.

Then there were the other women of the adult classes. My "Mama Martha," "Momean," Mrs. Tiny Cavitt, Mrs. Etta Jackson, Mrs. Walker, and Mrs. Della Sykes, just to name a few. Then there was Cozette, who played piano, and later Virginia Young who also played for the church choir. And there was "Aunt Marie,: "Aunt Louberta," and "Aunt Fern." Almost everyone was either "Aunt" or "Uncle." And my grandmother and a lot of the other grown-ups even referred to each other as "Aunt" or "Uncle."

Voices Past and Present

This form of address or the use of nicknames was just one of the traditions of our small, close-knit community. Everyone was familiar with everyone else, and hardly anyone was a stranger "Mr." and "Mrs." were mostly used with people we didn't know that well or as a sign of respect for the elderly. Today, however, this unique mark of distinction specific to our heritage seems to be all but forgotten.

Today, no one knows anyone--not even his next door neighbor. Hardly anyone says "Aunt" or "Uncle" anymore unless the person addressed is really an actual family member, and the elderly are treated with no dignity at all. The younger generations of youth no longer say "ma'am" or "sir," to adults, and children now call their parents by their first names. In the Black society, for a child to address a parent or a grandparent by his or her first name was, at that time, one of the worst signs of disrespect a child could make toward his parents or a grown-up. That was one practice which was not tolerated at all, and one which brought immediate repercussions for the demonic child committing the offense--a swift back-hand across the mouth, if he were lucky. If not, a full fledged, dog killing type whipping immediately expelled all demons, imps, and minions of Satan from the heathen youngster during those demonstrative and established rites of exorcism.

Children now talk without being told to, and even worse, they actually dare to interrupt adults having a conversation with each other--another sin which was simply not permitted by our parents and grandparents. A family was measured by how well its children behaved. The well behaved child was thoughtful and courteous, and he or she did not speak without first seeking permission.

Besides the treats the adults would give us, another of the joys of Sunday School at Olivet was watching all the women dressed up in their beautiful dresses and hats. The women wore hats of all styles and fashions and colors. Mrs. Lucille Walker wore some of the loveliest hats of all. They were wide brimmed and would fall down over her forehead. She was one of the most dignified women around. Mrs. Hall, the wife of Reverend Hall, had hats with nets that dropped down over the face, and many of the other women wore "pillbox" types of hats. Dressed in their regal hats with a mink stole or fur collar draped about the shoulder, our parents were some of the most stately people any one could wish to see.

One of the most elegant ladies to me was "Aunt Mabel." I remember the bright colorful handkerchiefs Mrs. Franklin would always have. They would flow back and forth in time to the tempo of the church songs as she rocked and swayed with the rhythm of the hymns she would sang. She and Mr. Franklin were very devoted to the church, and it somehow didn't seem like church or Sunday School if either one of them was missing. Once, her grandson, David Dean, and I were playing out in Mrs. Mabel's front yard on Barnes Street, and I followed him into his grandmother's house. And sure enough, neatly folded on her table, were all sorts of beautiful handkerchiefs, done up with lace trim, embroidery, and taffeta. I don't know of too many women who had such stylish linens as Mrs. Mabel.

Mrs. Franklin, like all the other women at Olivet and the other black churches in our community, was a strong believer in discipline and didn't stand for any monkey business. And also like all the other women, she would always take time to give the children a smile and a hug. This, too--this great show of affection for the children--was another distinguishing mark of the past which has almost vanished today. Parents just don't hug and talk to their children like our parents did with us.

When it came to disciplining us children, there were three women at Olivet I always watched out for: one was my grandmother, "Momean;" the second was "Aunt Priss," and the third was "Aunt Louberta." Typically, our parents just didn't believe in a lot of talking; they took action! Mrs. Bell and my grandmother didn't allow any talking, moving, fidgeting, or inattention of any kind. If you messed up in Sunday School and any one of them saw you, it was time to pray that your soul went to Jesus, because your behind went to them. They would very calmly stand up and excuse themselves from their group, just as quiet as could be. They didn't say a word; but then, they didn't need to because it was almost as though you could see a cloud of death and destruction floating before them as they advanced toward the guilty child. With a crook of the finger or a sharp jerk of the head, they would summon their children and escort them out to the back of the church. The next thing would be the sounds of "whacks" exploding all throughout the congregation area. My grandmother didn't even bother to take you outside which, of course, was truly an embarrassment in itself. Now, you were right there in front of all of your friends, and every eye in the church got to watch the "crowning moment of Glory." "Momean" had this saying--actually, my grandmother had many sayings. Her favorite was, "Wherever you do your dirt,

Traces In The Dust

that's where I'll clean it up." And she did! In church, up town, in Ben Franklin's store, or in the grave yard, it didn't matter. She would clean house right there on the spot. I always envied Rodney and the other Cavitt children because, at least, Aunt Louberta would usually take them out to a private, secluded area before administering the justifiable punishment. Not Momean. Momean considered that a wasted effort. "I'm beating yo' ass right heah," she would say. Actually, my grandmother had a multitude of sayings--each of which was accompanied by its own separate switch. And over the course of time, I, along with my brothers and my cousins got to hear every one of them.

Sometimes, after sitting in Sunday School for a long time, you had to go to the bathroom, especially if you drank a lot of water beforehand. Well, when you had to go, you had to go, and you couldn't help but get fidgety. At first, you'd just sort of start to squirm around a little bit, and then you'd start sitting on your hands and twist your feet around. Then the next thing you knew, you'd be squeezing your legs together real tight. Well, when it got so bad that you could hardly stand it, you just had to start swinging your legs, and bouncing up and down.

Now, pretty soon all that internal buildup just became too much and you'd be there on the bench just like a wild ape, making all kinds of odd movements trying to do everything possible to ease your suffering. Well, after all that commotion, you were bound to be noticed, and right as rain, here came our parents again--the doom and gloom preceding before them as usual.

But mostly, when they found out this time you truly had a good reason for you barbaric behavior, and that you were just about to keel over from kidney failure, they let you go quickly downstairs to the toilet. This was one of the few times a body could move about without getting his limbs jerked into a bow knot or a fresh lump added to the ones he already had on his head.

When we did get a whipping, a curious thing always happened that I absolutely hated! It was the same routine practiced at school: the hug! It was the one unavoidable moment which followed every switching of legs and backs. At the end of such dispensations of justice, one always heard the inevitable, "Now, come and give me a hug." And like the promise made by the "Godfather," it was, indeed, an offer you couldn't refuse--not if you knew what was good for you. Sadly enough, this too, is one of the features uniquely characteristic of our Black history that has fallen by the wayside.

What we learned in Sunday School has carried us a long way today. We are who we are because of what our parents did. They cared for us: they made us mind, and they made us respectful. "Momean" always told me that because she had raised so many boys, she knew them like a book. She would tell me how she raised Floyd and Walter, and then me, her first born grandchild, and later, all the other grandsons.

My grandmother would explain how much she needed to stay on us. She said that she had raised boys all her life, and that girls were no trouble. But boys, she said, just had "tendencies" (for trouble), and it just couldn't be helped. She went on to explain that boys--and that included all boys everywhere--were just naturally "devilish" and "hard-headed" and "low-down" and "no account," and it took a good switch, laid across their "nappy headed asses" every now and then, just to keep them in line. That was the only way boys would ever be of some "account." And all this had to be done while they were little. "Train the tree while it was yet a sapling," my grandmother would say. She said things like that from the Bible a lot, and she used her switches to back them up even more.

She said a lot of other things about boys--and about men, too, most of which were anything but flattering. Most of the times I would be laughing so hard, I was almost crying. Other times I would be in a dead shock. Especially, when she talked about her own kin folks. Sometimes Momean would get mad at my Daddy James, and then she'd put together a string of adjectives that would make the Holy Roman Pope kneel down and say a couple of "Hail Mary's."

For a woman who never had any more than an elementary education, my grandmother was incredibly accurate and astute. Everything she said worked. When it came to raising off spring, she and most of the other women of our time could have written books. To me, women like my mother, my grandmother, "Aunt Louberta," and "Aunt Bertha" knew more about "young'uns" and had more common sense than half the psychologists around today--especially when you listen to some of the "nonsense" such scientists espouse. And "Aunt Bertha" had raised a whole bunch of boys, pretty close to a dozen of them. People would always tease her because they said she and Blue Mitchell always had enough boys to form just about any ball team they wanted.

To sum it all up, the Black women of our town knew their stuff when it came to discipline. You didn't see Black children cutting up and throwing fits all over the place. You didn't see them having temper tantrums and yelling and screaming in Sunday School or in all the stores like you see little white kids doing today. It may have happened one time, and it didn't happen any more--not after the mother or grandmother got a hold of the youngster.

And it was that way with all the women in our church. My mother, "Mama Ernell," and the other women all had straps or switches. Sometimes the switches looked like branches. Mrs. Bette Lou always walked down Allman Street with her children in front of her. And she always had two or three excellent switches swaying back and forth in her hand. (The good switches were freshly green and sturdy; they didn't break in half like the dry, rotten ones.) My mother and Mrs. Bette Lou didn't talk a lot either. They would be on you in a New York minute, tear your legs up with a few sharp stings of the switches, and then go on about their business, just as cool as a cucumber.

But it puzzled me about what my grandmother always said about us boys, and I couldn't get it out of my mind. What I just couldn't understand was, that with all the trouble boys caused, why "Momean" just didn't just raise girls? So, finally one day I asked her about it.

"Well," she said to me, "I would take your sisters, Debbie Kay and Sherlene, for a while when school was out. And, I would take them for good if something ever happened. But, girls just need to be with their mothers. God didn't place me here for them. No, sir. He put me here for you boys--for you, and Wendell James, and Larone, and all you knotty headed boys. That's the reason. I know God kept me here just for you boys, and I just always pray He let me live long enough see all my boys raised up and grown." Well, my grandmother got her wish. All of us--from me, Wendell James and Darnell, right on down to Little Jimmie Junior and Taz--had grown up when she died. Almost all of us even had kids ourselves by then. So her many hours and days spent in prayer worked. And all the things she and the other women in Sunday School said and did worked, too. We kids got the switches on our backsides, a few thumps up side the head, and we got a good scolding every so often; and in the end, we didn't turn out half bad. In fact, we turned out pretty good. It's just like "Aunt Louberta" said to me recently, "Just think where you kids would be--and what you would be like now--if we older folks hadn't done what we did back then."

Earning A Living
by
Annie Mae Dunlap Wakefield

I was born here in Carbondale in 1917. A lot of things were different back then as for as the colored people had to live. Most of the colored women worked across town in the white homes. But many blacks in the early 1900s began local neighborhood businesses of their own with what ever they could manage to scrape up and save. I remember when Douglas Garrett sold Barbecue sandwiches for fifteen cents, and you could purchase twenty-five cents worth of gas and go to work all week on it. Twenty-five cents ain't nothing now, but back then, you could do quite a bit with a quarter. My house payment was six dollars and ninety-five cents a month; you could buy a lot for twenty dollars.

As for jobs, well most blacks worked for the white people, but some began to have their own stores and shops. When a black person graduated from the eight grade, a lot of the smart ones started teaching. You didn't have to go to college or get certificates. Some of the blacks coming out of the eight grade were very intelligent, and if any of the persons with the schools thought you could do the job, well, you started teaching. Later on, blacks began to go to college out at SIU and started earning degrees and teaching certification.

When I was in the second grade, some of my classmates were Floyd Waters, Annedale Sumner, Harrison Gibbs, Pierce Sumner, Maggie Kenner, Ivy Mae Perkins and Clara Anders, and Elnore Reliford and Lola Autry. Harrison Gibbs and I are just about the only ones left out of that class, as far as I recall. Lola Autry was one of those that grew up and started teaching.

The black people used to have dances and parties at the Armory Hall. That was located where the Bank of Carbondale is now. Well known blacks and movie stars would give performances there. People like Duke Ellington, Cab Calloway, Louis "Satchmo" Armstrong, and Lionel Hampton used to come and play all the time. Every time you looked up, someone was coming in and out.

Between Chestnut and Birch Streets, there used to be what we called Twin Pond. The black churches used to baptize there. They didn't have water in the pulpits like they do now. If anybody got baptized they got baptized in the creek, or they didn't get baptized at all. In the winter time, the water would freeze over in the pond, and all the colored folks would get out on the ice and skate. It's all dried up and long gone now down there now.

Taz Green wired houses for the black folks; he went all over town. His wife, Martha did hair. Ora Holder and Mrs. King did hair also, and there were all other kinds of businesses. Mr. John Brown hauled water for twenty-five cents a barrell all the way from the tie plant to people all over the area. That's how the black folks got water. There wasn't any such thing as running water and toilets inside of the house. You didn't have pipes or plumbing. You had to "tote" water, as the old people used to say. Wherever it was closest to your house, that's where you had to tote it from. Mr. John had those kroger sacks that he covered the top of the barrel with to keep the water from sloshing out. In the winter time, you would just about freeze to death trying to get water to your house. The winters weren't like they are now. Back then ice and snow was so deep and so cold, everything would freeze and stay frozen for weeks. We had deep freezes! When winter came, it was winter--and it stayed winter! Nowadays, it's cold one day and hot the next. It's got so now you don't know if its spring or fall. When I was growing up, you knew it was winter! It would freeze solid, and it stayed cold for months--all winter long!

Another thing is that there were a lot more churches and preachers! Rev. Reid used to be at New Zion and Rev. Thomas had a church over on Green Street. And Rev. Gillespie was at Gillespie Temple on Wall Street down in Puppy Tail. That was just a few. Only about five or so of the big black churches remain now. But in the twenties and thirties, there was a lot of smaller black churches that popped up everywhere. There was a CME church on Jackson in addition to the ones there now and there were smaller Baptist Churches started by people who left the larger churches. If somebody got mad or if somebody didn't want to go along with the preacher, well they'd just break off and start another church. The preachers made a good living, and the church folks took care of them and their families. Dr. Westmoreland pulled teeth. Then there was doctor Bass and a lot of other professional colored folks. When I was married, I worked some doing housework off and on to help my husband out. But mostly, I stayed home and raised my children.

I used to have a picture of Boston Williams; he was the first black born here. He lived on Main Street. By the time I got to be a teenager, he was in his sixties, and he used to tell us stories about when he was a boy back in the 1800s. Making a living was hard for colored folks every since the railroad. Things are a lot easier now, and I thank God I lived long enough to see it.

Photography Notes

P. xvii. *Children on the Merry-Go-Round at the Attucks playground.* Included in the group are Vance and Alloysius Jackson; Stephanie Love (little girl); Mark Newbern; Phillip Mason, and Angela Sykes. Photo taken by the author; early 1960s.

P. 54. *Boston Williams.* Courtesy of Mrs. Stella Ivy.

P. 149. *The Bats Little League Baseball Team.* Courtesy of Calvin Scott.

P. 150. *The "Big House."* Home of Cecil and John Brown. Courtesy of Marilyn Brown-Tipton.

P. 157. *"Good Times."* Courtesy of Hortense "Tootsie" Edward.

P. 158. *Early Homestead of Robert and Della Matthews.* Courtesy of the late Mrs. Della Matthews.

P. 159. *Janet Johnson.* Courtesy of Mrs. Grace Scott.

P. 160. *The Cobras Little League Baseball Team.* Courtesy of James "Jasper" Boykins.

P. 161. *Jones Cafe.* Courtesy of Hortense "Tootsie" Edward.

P. 165. Versa Lou White at the Attucks Picnic at the City Park. Photo taken by the author during the Attucks High School Senior Class Picnic, 1963.

P. 168. *Earl Alexander and Alfred Hall at Attucks.* Courtesy of Earl Mitchell.

P. 329. *Robert A. Stalls.* Courtesy of Gwendolyn Cavit Gails.

P. 350. *Ida and Mary Lou Jacobs.*

Bibliography

Allen, John W. Jackson County Notes. Carbondale, Illinois: Southern Illinois Normal University, 1945.

Bethel A.M.E. Church. "The Chosen Soldier: Soldiers of Christ--Making a Difference in the 21st Century." In the Bethel A.M.E. Church 130th Church Anniversary. Carbondale, Illinois: Bethel A.M.E. Church, August 21, 1998.

Davis, Hardin Allen. A Capsulized History of Attucks High Under the Leadership of John Q. Clark (1943-1964). Research Project. History Department. Southern Illinois University. Carbondale, Illinois: 1973.

Development Services Department. The Historic Town Square: Carbondale, Illinois. Nashville: Thomason and Associates, 1997.

Donlin, A. Lyman. Carbondale City Directory, 1905. Donlin Publishers; November, 1905.

Executive Committee on Southern Illinois. Southern Illinois: Resources and Potentials of the Sixteen Southernmost Counties. Urbana, Illinois: University of Illinois Press, 1949.

Gildehaus, Valeire Phillips. Index to Death Records, 1844-1906. Murphysboro, Ill.: Jackson County Historical Society, 1996.

Griffith, W. " A Capsule History of Carbondale." In Century of Progress:The First 100 Years. Carbondale, Illinois: 1952.

Hodges, Carl G. and Levene, Helene H. "Growth of Anti Slavery Sentiment." In Illinois Negro History Makers. Chicago: Illinois Emancipation Centennial Commission, 1964.

--------------------------"The Best Known Underground Lines." In Illinois Negro History Makers. Chicago: Illinois Emancipation Centennial Commission, 1964.

Hoffman, C. R. Hoffman's City Directory. Quincy, Illinois: The Hoffman City Directories, 1957.

Jackson, Ronald Vern. Illinois State Census Index, 1830.

-------------------------- Illinois State Census Index, 1840.

Jackson County Historical Society. History of Jackson County, Illinois. Philadelphia: McDonough and Company, 1878. Reproduced by J.C.H. S., 1973.

Jones, Johnetta L. Jones. Negroes In Jackson County, 1850-1910. Master's Thesis. History Department. Southern Illinois University. Carbondale, Illinois: August, 1971.

Jones, P. M. Forgotten Soldiers: Murphysboro's African-American Civil War Veterans. Murphysboro, Illinois: P. M. Jones and the 1993/94 Murphysboro Middle School 6th Grade Class, 1994.

Jones, William Archie. "Facts, Facets and Consideration of Life." In <u>Success and Successful Living.</u> Carbondale, Illinois.

Morehouse, Louise. <u>Death Records for Carbondale, Illinois, 1877-1952.</u> Owensboro, Kentucky: McDowell Publications.

Musgrave, John. "Underground Railroad Ran Both Ways in Southern Illinois." In <u>The Daily Register.</u> Harrisburg, Illinois: Liberty Group Publishing, 1997.

New Zion Baptist Church. <u>A History of African American Churches in Carbondale and Surrounding Southern Illinois Communities.</u> Carbondale, Illinois: 1996.

Norton, Margaret Cross. <u>Illinois Census Returns, 1818.</u> Springfield, Illinois. State Historical Library, 1935.

----------------------------. <u>Illinois Census Returns, 1820.</u> Baltimore: Genealogical Publishing Company, 1969.

Rock Hill Baptist Church. <u>1871-1971 Centennial Bulletin.</u> Carbondale, Illinois: 1971.

Shelton, Herbert. <u>The First 50 Years: A History of the Carbondale Church of God. 1919-1969.</u> Benton, Illinois: Thomas Printing, c. 1986.

Smith, Thomas. <u>The Revised Ordinances of the City of Carbondale, 1905.</u> Carbondale, Illinois: Herald Printing, 1905.

Southern Illinois Achievers. <u>Southern Illinois Achievers Pamphlet.</u> Carbondale, Illinois.

Stalls, Madlyn. <u>A History of African Americans at Southern Illinois University at Carbondale, 1915-1987.</u> Doctoral Dissertation. Department of Education Administration and Higher Education, Southern Illinois University. Carbondale, Illinois: November, 1990.

Thompson, L. S. <u>The Story of Mattie J. Jackson; Her Parentage--Experience of Eighteen Years in Slavery.</u> (1866). Chapel Hill, North Carolina: University of North Carolina. 1st ed., 1999.

United States Census Bureau. <u>Ninth Census of the United States: 1870.</u> Washington, D.C.: Government Printing Office, 1883.

United States Census Bureau. <u>Twelfth Census of the United States: 1900.</u> Washington, D.C.: Government Printing Office, 1901.

United States Census Bureau. <u>Thirteenth Census of the United States: 1910.</u> Washington, D.C.: Government Printing Office, 1913.

Wright, John W. D. <u>A History of Early Carbondale, Illinois, 1852-1905.</u> Carbondale, Illinois: Southern Illinois University Press, 1977.

Wright, Henry T. <u>Laws and Ordinances Governing The City of Carbondale.</u> Carbondale, Illinois: Observer Book Printing Office, 1874.

Index

Author's note: Many names appearing in this index are copied as they appear in the original document(s) from whi taken. The only corrections made have been in cases where the name or spelling of the name was known be to incorrect. of the older documents of the 1800s and the early 1900s were hand written and often unclear--and because differences in caused differences in spellings--certain names have been found with multiple spellings, and in a few instances, the sam been found under two or three different names. For anyone doing research, names in this index should be compared to references whenever the need for clarification arises. The symbol (?) after a name indicates questionable spelling or identi

Aiken, H. Gloria Dean *See also* Brown, 178
   family of, 172, 179
Albritton, Delores and Chester, 180
Alexander, Alfred, 56
Alexander, Earl, Jr., 104, 168
Alexander, George, 51, 55
Alexander, Lester, 93
Algee, Delmar M., Sr., 73
Anders, Evelina, 91
Anders, Lillie Mae, 87
Anders, Quinella, 95
Anderson, Charles V., 80
Anderson, George, 56
Anderson, Gladys Malone, 144
Anderson, James E., 82-83
Anderson, Willie Dee, 83-84
Anthony, James "Swig," 163
Armour, Alfreda Mae, 96
Armour, Frances, 181, 345
   family of, 146, 162, 169
Armstead, Sam, 51
Armstead, Shelton, 51
Armstrong, Jackie, 166
Armstrong, Wardell L., 117
Arnette, Charles "Bear," 98
Arnette, Ella, 117
Ashberry, Louise, 61

B

Band, Edda, 51, 54
Bell, Flossie and Clifford, 182
   family of, 130
Bell, Cozette *See also* Spinner 164
Bell, Gregory Clint, 116
Bell, Henry and Mary ("Priss"), 135, 183
   family of, 161, 175, 184
Bird, Dolla, 56
Bird, Sora, 56
Blythe, Edward, 172

Blythe, Florence Hall, 107
Blythe, William LaVoyd, 93-94
Bostic, Leonard, 153
Bowden, Lovenger Hamilton, 332
Bowen, Elcosie, 87
Bowers, Frances Sadberry, 185
   family of, 170
Bowers, Wendell, 151
Bowers, Wilbert, Sr., 324
Boyd, Grace, 117, 315
Boykin, Evelyn and Everett, 128, 186
   family of, 161
Branch, Billy Gene, 89
Branch, Russell Lowell, 93
Brinson, Aaron Henry, Jr., 96
Brinson, Aaron Sr., 85, 88
Broadnax, Alvest, 113
Brooks, Aaron, Sr., 100
Brooks, Minnie M., 187
Brooks, Moses, Jr., 105
Brown, Arthur, 134
Brown, Bessie, 133
Brown, Betty L., 95
Brown, Beulah Mae, 188
Brown, Billy L, 87
Brown, Cecil Branch Woods, 51, 60
Brown, Charles 134
Brown, H. Gloria Dean *See* Aiken
Brown, Jeraldine, 311
Brown, John and Cecil
   family of, 148, 160, 161, 189, 332
Brown, Julian Ann Thomas, 170
Brown, Leota C. Nichols, 117, 318-319

Brown, Lillie and Cornelius, 190
Brown, Patricia Ann, 111
Brown, Ronald, 117
Brown Jr. Ronald
Brown, Willard E., 77, 313, 321, 332
Brown, William, 54
Buggs, Carl and Eva C. Ross, 134, 191
Burch, Freda O. Mosley, 81
Butler, Linda, 169

C

Campbell, Cora, 51, 56
Campbell, Osa Mae, 86
Carbondale
   African Americans in, (1880) 57-58
   African American Settlers in, (1865), 52
   African American Households in, (1905), 64-71.
   Early Downtown, 109-110
   First Negro Births in, 51
   Oldest Negro Families in, 51
   Populations, 48-52
   Real Estate, 53
   Unknown Deaths in, 61
Carson, Anna Bell, 90
Carter, Henry Lee, 108, 145
Carter, Percell, 59
Cavit, A. D. and Louberta, 192, 317
   family of, 193, 331
Cavitt, Edna L., 89
Cavitt, Louie and Celestine, 155, 194
   family of, 99, 138, 143
Cavitt, Robert L., Jr., 108, 143
Cawthon *See also* Couthon

Cawthon, James "Bud," 59
Chambers, Cora, 90
Chambers, David E., 112
Chambers, John and Everlene, 195
family of,
Chambers, William Lee, 95
Chappell, Edward E., 91
Chapell, Estelle Doretha France, 102, 155, 317
family of, 196
Chappell, Ida A., 77, 156, 246
Chappell, James Edward and Gloriastene, 173
Chappell, Jeff
Chappell, Jesse Albert, 114, 131
Chappell, Joe, 89
Chappell, Ruth Evelyn, 86
Chappell, Shelly M., 77, 79, 171, 313
Chappell, William, 196
Cherry, Cornelia, 55
Cherry, Henry, 56
Childress, Charles R., 94, 97
Clark, James W., 93
Clark, Josie B and James H., 78, 197
Clark, Virginia, 137
Clark, Walter H. Rev., 90
Clay, Aubra, 82
Clayton, Caurdie, 61
Clemmer, Annie Ruth, 156, 198, 321
Clemmer, Erma C., 115
Colbert, Curtisteen, 168
Cole, Robert Jr., 107, 147
Cole, William, 162
Cooper, Lucius, 105
Cooper, Lula Alexander, 86
Cousin Jenny, The Healer (Irene Haydene), 336
Couthon *See also* Cawthon
Couthon, Maude, 60
Crim, George Wesley, 63
Crim, Versa Lou, 95
Cunningham, Cora, 156
Cuningham, Dorcas *See also* Davis, 176

D

Daniels, Claudia, 139
Daniels, George, 99
Daniels, Jordan, 98
Daniels, Mary Francis, 199
Daniels, Olly, 59

Davidson, Alice Scott, 117
Davis, Dorcas *See also* Cunningham, 200
family of, 173
Davis, Ella Mandy Lula, 72
Davis, Ezekiel, 74
Davis, Hardin Allen and Ida, 104
family of, 201, 318
Davis, Luella McCall, 75, 321, 323
Davis, Unis Pearl, 80, 151, 311
Dedicated Teachers (Cleveland Matthews), 337
Deidley, Martha, 55
Denton, James "Doc," 139
De Soto Township
African Americans in, (1900), 22
Devers, Bobby G., 98, 101
Devers, Brenda, 166
Devers, Foice L., 97
Devers, Fred and Viola, 89
Devers, Wendell, 93
Dillard, Neil, Hon. 171
Dodd, John H., 117
Douglas, Vivian A., 117

E

Early Black Families (Albert"Flat Top Mason), 335
Eanes, Lovie Geneva Massie, 116, 142
Eanes, Willie Elmo, 116
Earning A Living (Annie Mae Dunlap Wakefield), 351
Edgar, Charlie"Po Charlie," 128
Edgar, Ida Marie Harris, 51, 63, 327
Edward, William "Popeye" and Hortense "Tootsie," 157, 202
Ellis, Lillian E., 63
Ellis, Mary, 91

F

Family Life in Carbondale (Louvenia McKinley), 339
Farmer, Earl, 116, 142
Farr, Alma Jean, 95

Favors, Mable Evelyn Meredith, 166, 203
Fisher, Annie Mae, 151
Fisher, Charley, 56
Fletcher, Edward, Jr., 106
Fletcher, Emma Ford,
Fletcher, Lane, Jr., 87
Fletcher, Louvenia, 136
Fletcher, Robert W., 91
Fletcher, William D., Jr., 99, 147
Ford, Araminta McCracken, 51, 60
Ford, Eule Lee, 92, 130
Ford, Emma May, 89, 137
Foster, Charles E. "Pancake," 118
Foster, Pearl Hudson, 118, 123
Foster, Robert Lee McCall, 239
Fowler, Chester Arthur, 118
Fowler, Samuel, 125
France, Ernell Marie
See also Green; Glasby, 140
France, George and Ann, 204
family of, 205
France, James Abe and Madelene, 102, 142,
family of, 104, 146-147, 163
Franklin, Abbott, Jr.
Franklin, Albert, Jr., 95
Franklin, Auralia, 86
Franklin, Clarence, 85
Franklin, Mabel, 248
family of, 247

G

Gails, Gendolyn, 175
Gains, William, 55
Gardner, Alice M. 111
Garrison, Isola, 140
Gibbs, Cora Lee Fletcher, 206
family of, 107, 207
Gibbs, Harrison and Jean Helen, 206
Gibbs, Jewel Eugene, 80
Gingery, Virginia Young, 89
Glass, Delona J., 90
Glen, Artie V., 76
Glispie, Naomi, 161
Glispie, Reginal, 118, 145.
Good Times! (Della Matthews), 344

Goodlaw, Adalade, 59
Gordon, Allean Davis Brown, 208
Gray, Ferne and Jeffrey, 209
Green, Daniel, 59
Green, Ernell Marie France
   See also Glasby
Green, James W., Sr., ("Pinto"), 84, 157
Green, James W., Jr., 115
Green, Jenola, 86
Green, Melvin *See also* Macklin, 162
Green, Sherlene, 172
Green, Taz E., 81, 313
Green-Jennings, Mary Helen, 210
Greer, Clayton, 153
Greer, Norma Jean, 95
Greer, Truley, 136
Grigsby, Warren and Gladys, 232
Growing Up in Carbondale (Barbara Greer Lemons), 337
Growing Up in the Hoodlums (Frances Armour and Mildred Harrington Jordan), 345

H

Hall, Alfred, 168
Hall, Charles E., 106
Hall, Minnie B. Brooks, 101, 106
Hamilton, Mary Edna, 56
Harkins, Milton, G., Sr., 118, 123
   family of, 118, 145
Haron, Mattie Green, 51
Harper, Abram Matthew, 169
Harris, Ben, 55
Harris, Charles E., 78
Harris, Johnny, 89
Harrison, George, 55
Harrison, Martha, 54
Hawkins, Margaret, 54
Hawkins, Virginia Mae *See also* Young, 156
Hayden, Irene Rice, 211, 336
Hayes, Eurma, 326
Hayes, Gerlean M., 111
Hayes, Jesse D., Jr. 95
Hayes, Lillie, 126
Hayes, Martha Lee, 93

Hayes, William Henry, 65
Hayes, William Richard, Sr., 73, 79, 153, 328
   family of, 145, 146, 212
Haynes, Dewitt, 119, 123
Haynes, Gloria, 156
Haynes, Josephine Mosley, 81
Haynes, Norvell ("C Junior"), 91, 314, 324
Haynes, Wanda Perkins, 213, 311, 333
   family of, 155
Hays, David, 61
Hays, Mary, 55
Hays, William Henry, 55
Henderson, James, 139
Hester, Thomas, 59
Higgins, Queen Esther, 114, 131
Hill, Delores Lilly, 175
Hillsman, Allen, 72
Hillsman, Genoa A. R., 72
Hillsman, LaVidas, 163
Hillsman, Mattie Lee, 72
Hinton, Minnie E., 103, 141
Hogan, Hattie A., 312
Hogan, Julia, 95, 101
Holder, James E., 96, 130
Holder, Ora, 136, 171
Holmes, Connie Elaine Cole, 111
Homes and Homesteads
   Cecil and John Brown, 150
   Charles Lilly, 162
   Robert and Della Matthews, 158
   Rev. Will Reed, 164
Howard, Doris *See* Mitchell
Hoyt, Delmar G. A., 108
Hudson, Archibald P., 84
Hudson, Beatrice and U.L., Jr., 155 214
   family of, 215
Hudson, Doris N., 75
Hudson, Ellis L. 119
Hudson, Hewitt C., 74
Hudson, Willie, 60
Hughlett, Corrine, 127
Hughlett, Willie C., 125, 127
Hunter, George, 59

I

Irvin, Sadie P., 85
Isbell, Alice, 56, 216

Ivy, Stella and Joseph, 133, 171, 217
   family of, 218

J

Jackson, Anabelle, 134
Jackson, Charles E., 78
Jackson, Etta Waddell, 72
Jackson, John Wesley, Jr., 113
Jackson, Lee Roy, 76
Jackson, Wilbert, 89
Jackson, Winona, 96, 314, 318
   family of, xvii
Jackson County
   African Americans in, (1870), 11-19
   African Americans in, (1900), 20-24
   African American Deaths in, 25-37
   African American Marriages in, 38-46
Jacobs, Ida and Mary Lou, 348, 350
Jacobs, Ora Lee, 103
Jamison, James A. and Willie Mae, 219
   family of, 146, 220
Jenkins, Julias B., 56
Johnson, Darnell, 172
Johnson, Janet, 159
Johnson, Marie, 144
Johnson, Vyonne Lynette, 170
Jones, Arthur and Annie, 56, 333
Jones, Beulah May, 51, 63
Jones Cafe, 161
Jones, Frances Bell (Fannie), 59
Jones, Franklin, 56
Jones, Helen Waters, 137
Jones, James, 85
Jones, William Archie, 119, 153, 321-322
Jordan, Mildred Harrington, 221, 311, 345
   family of, 175

K

Kelley, Grace L., 89
Kelley, John Eddie, 105, 129
Kelly, Thomas Ceaser, 119
Kenner, George, 157
Kenner, Maggie, 222

family of, 223
Kenner, Pauline Wills, 299
   family of, 300
King, Charles, 162
King, David L., 93-94
King, Dorothy Hamilton, 73
Kinner, James, 51, 54

L

Lane, Virginia Mae France, 346
Laster, Atlas and Rose, 224
   family of, 148, 225
Lee, Ernest, 86
Lee, Frances Rechel Meredith, 226
Lemons, Barbara Greer, 337
Lewin, Elizabeth Mosley, Dr., 331
Life in the Church (Cozette Bell Spinner), 340
Lilly, Charles Sr. "Papa Lilly,"
   family of, 160, 227
Lilly, Delores *See also* Hill
Lilly, Geraldine, 228
Lilly, Leatreasa M., 148
Lilly, Ora P., 115, 123
   family of, 229
Lilly, Willie Dee, 87, 157, 230
Lilly, Willie Mae *See* Thomas
London, Mittie Virginia, 60
Lucille Walker, Mother of Us All (Hortense Edward), 347

M

Macklin, Melvin L. G., 347
Makanda Township
   African Americans in, (1900), 23
Marshall, John, 56
Martin, Ellen, 128
Martin, Elna Mae, 76, 79
Martin, Joseph, 60
Martin, Magnolia Maggie, 311
Mason, Albert, 335
Mason, Edward, 76
Mason, Elizabeth "Liz," 138
Mason, Geneva, 114
   family of, 233
Mason, Kent, 175
Mason, Nathaniel, 59
Mason, Thomas and Edna, 231
   family of, 164, 174, 301
Mason, Tom, 120
Mason, Vance and Marie, 138
family of, 162, 175, 233, 234
Matthews, Cleveland, 312, 331
Matthews, Robert and Della, 235
   family of, 86, 92, 236, 237
Mattingly, William Rudolph, 111
Mayfield, Earnest and Beaudenual, 238
Mayfield, Lonnie, 60
Mayfield, March, 60
McBride, Dorothy Mae, 95
McCroy, Hal, Jr. and Jessie, 240
McCroy, Hal, Sr., 120
McCroy, Lillie Forest
   family of, 242
McCutchen, Mack, 125
McCutchen, Savannah, 314
McDaniel, Larry and Wilma, Sr., 106
McDonald, Anna V. P., 87
McDonnell, William, 59
McKinley, Enos and Louvenia, 243, 317
McKinley, Judy Ann, 108
McKinley, Ronald M., 97
McQueen, Shedret, Rev., 120
Meeks, Odessa McCroy, 241, 331
Memories (Marilyn Brown-Tipton), 338
Miles, Catharine, 55
Miller, Lee Anna, 244
   family of, 245
Miller, Louise, 144
Miller, Milton, 169
Mitchell, Bertha, 155, 249
   family of, 99, 142
Mitchell, Charles "Blue," 120
Mitchell, Doris Howard, 144
Mitchell, Harry, 176
Mitchell, Sola B. and Bernice, 247
   family of, 162, 248
Moore, James and Charlesetta
Mooreland, Amos, 112
Mooreland, Emma M., 112, 143
Mooreland, Floyd, 86
Mooreland, Minnie Helen, 77
Morgan, Arthur Louis, Sr. 125
Morgan, Evelyn, 120, 129
Morgan, Henry and Isalee
   family of,
Morris, Thomas Vesto, 120, 130
Morris, Wiley, 120
Morrow, Mary Elizabeth, 63
Mosley, Archibald, Rev. Dr., 325
Mosley, Statsie C. and Bertha I., 250
   family of, 166, 251
Moultrie, Darnecea, 160
Mousehart, Rena, 59
Murphysboro Township
   African Americans in, (1900), 20
Murray, Homer, 91
My Years At Attucks (Virginia Mae France Lane), 346

N

Negro, Usage of, 5
Nesbitt, Ruben A., 95
Nesbitt, Thomas and Margaret, 252, 314, 319-320
   family of,
Newbern, Arthur, 332
Newbern, Etta White, 297
Nicholas, Joseph H., 93
Nichols, Nina Mae, 74
Nigger, Usage of, 6
Nigger Pews, 6
Norman, Walter S., 92, 94
   family of, 255
Norwood, Anna Beatrice, 85

O

Ollie, Lucinda, 151
O'Neal, Booker, Jr., and Erie, 254
   family of, 89, 174
O'Neal, John Milton and Rosetta, 253, 313

P

Palmer, Thelma, 256
Parker, Estella Kelley, 103, 125
Parran, Betty Sue, 164
Parran, Lullu Bertha, 51, 55
Penn, Joseph C. and Lovia, 163
Penn, U. P., Rev., 100, 324
Penny, Monyette Rolene Mosley, 81
Perkins, Clyde and Geraldine,

121, 258
   family of, 259
Perkins, Francis E., 56
Perkins, Galveston and Leah, 257
Perkins, Lucy and Aaron, 163
Perkins, Mariam
   family of, 167
Perkins, Wanda *See* Haynes
Perkins, Woodrow W., 121
Perkins, Rayford, 171
Perry, Edna, 90
Phelps, Willie, 108
Pitts, James C., 51
Pollod, Andrew, 55
Porter, Ulis, 87
Powell, Felica, 115
Price, Dora Lee Armour, 85, 88
Price, Irma L. Gibbs, 121
Pulling Together (Everlene Chambers), 340

Q
Quigley, Franklin, 59

R
"Raised Up" at Olivet (Melvin L. Green Macklin), 347
Realty, 53
Reid, Albert S., 77
Reid, George Henderson., 121, 141
Reid, Will A., Rev., 121
Reid, Willie H., 122
Reliford, Charles, 90
Reliford, Charlie, 89
Reliford, Ruth H. 85
Ringo, Sarah, 55
Roach, Oscar Thomas, 59
Roberts, Milton and Grace, 261
   family of, 262
Robertson, Frances Marie, 87, 161, 263
Robertson, Levora D. L., 126, 319
Robertson, Vernell "Tater Bug," 91, 94
   family of, 155
Robinson, Russell and Veachie, 259-260, 312
Robison, Odell Barnett, 264
   family of, 154
Roseman, Verna Spriggs, 265

family of, 137, 266-267, 281
Ross, Arnold L., Sr., 85
Ross, Robert Lee, 122
Rowe, Julia and James, 268
Rowe, Lula Mae Roseman, 140

S
Sample, Irene, 108
Sanders, Frances Hall. 107
Sandford, Joseph, 56
Sanford, Donnell, 95
Schauf, Carla Denise, 114
Scott, Cardella, 269, 314
   family of, 174
Scott, Charlie and Lonnie C., 112
   family of, 270
Scott, Hazel, 313
Scott, Lucy, 80, 129
Scott, Ora and Grace, 271
Scott, Pervie and Lillie, 272
   family of, 273
Scott, Robert, 81, 135
Scott, Sarah, 61
Shird, Frank and Mary Liza, 107
Shoffner, Vantrece Russell, 319
Shoffner, Robert, 141
Silas, Mary, 274
Simon, Lit and Jeanether, 136, 275
Simpson, Kate, 55
Slaughter, Henry and Jean, 276
Slaughter, Henry and Vastulia, 119
Slavery in Jackson County, 2-7, 9-10
Smith, Addie B., 78
Smith, Andrew, Sr., 94, 126
Smith, Daisy L., 126
Smith, Dara, 176
Smith, Darnecea *See* Moultrie
Smith, Doris H., 84, 94
Smith, Irvin and Helen, 277
Smith, James Allen, Sr., 82, 94
Smith, John, 72
Smith, Nathaniel, 100
Smith, Ozell and Carrie, 278
   family of, 279
Smith, Rosetta, 280
Smith, Virginia, 164
Spinner, Cozette, *See also* Bell

340
Sports, Recreation, Activities
   Attucks Playground, 164
   Baseball, 149, 160
   Boy Scouts, 310
   History of Woods Park, 152
   Hunting, 153
Spriggs, Mary, 281
Spriggs, Shedrick, 122
St. James, Virginia Rose H., 83-84
Stalls, Robert Alvin, 312, 329-330
The Stand, 176
Stayton, Alice Woods, 129
Steele, Elsie, 122
Steele, Maggie, 94
Steele, Sylvester S. R., 91
Steele, Walter and Doris, 282
Stricklin, Carl Lee, 81
Sumner, Loyd, Rev.
Sutton, Bernice, 99, 101
Sutton, Wayne, 103, 141
Swafford, Elizabeth, 54
The Way It's Spozed To Be ("Grandtee") Dorothy Sykes, 132
Sykes, James Arthur, 126

T
Taylor, Marshall, 82
Tender, Barbara, 174
Terry, Bernard, 89
Terry, Wiliam, Jr., 87
Thomas, Guieula, 84, 138
Thomas, Hattie B., 114, 130
Thomas, Henry C. 124
Thomas, John and Juanita, 155, 315-316
   family of, 283-284
Thomas, John Wesley, 92, 131
Thomas, John Wesley, Jr., 92
Thomas, Robert and Rose, 285
   family of, 286
Thomas, Rosella Pearl, 287
Thomas, Willie Mae Day Lilly, 104
Thompson, Archie and Jewel, 288
Thompson, Julia Mae, 289
Thornton, George H., 96
Thornton, Kathleen, 317
Thornton, Lavern C., 80

Thornton, Mamie, 82, 128
  family of,
Thornton, Robert "Bob," 82, 140, 153
Those Were The Days (Hal McCroy), 343
Tipton, Marilyn Brown, 338
Tisdale, Iray Franklin Woods, 290
  family of, 173, 291
Traylor, Henry, 153
Turley, Lenus, Rev., 311
Turley, Roosevelt "Rose," 113, 313, 321

U

V

Valentine, Ima Mae Sparks, 97, 324
Valetine, James Arthur, Sr., 90, 131
Valentine, Janet, 163
Valliant, Ruben, Jr. "Jack," 133
Van Hook, Frances, 115
Van Hook, Louis Jr., 127, 143

W

Wakefield, Annie Mae Dunlap, 292
  family of, 148
Walker, Sylvester Miles, 112
Walker, Thelma and James, 293
Walker, Vivian Lucille, 72
Walker, William Harold, 76, 79
Walls, James E. and Wilma, 98
Walters, William F., 76
Ward, Clarence, 76, 151
Warren, Bessie N. S., 75, 88
Washington, Imogene Harris, 294
Watkins, Leora Hamilton, 125
Watson, Ella J., 63
Watson, Patsy Dean Kenner, 295
Waufford, Daughn, 55
Way It's Spozed To Be (Sykes, Dorothy), 132
Webb, Ida M. Armour, 86, 141
Westley, George and Mary, 296
Westley, Wilie Carl ("Fat Daddy"), 175
White, Charles O., 75
White, Etta Garrett, 172
White, Frances E., 72, 332
  family of, 173
White, Lorene Haynes, 87-88
White, Versa P. Hayes, 72
  family of, 165
White, William H., 76
Williams, Boston, 51, 54
Williams, Carolina, 46
Williams, Cleo Belle, 51, 72
Williams, Ernest, 124
Williams, Lola Bell, 139
Williams, Nat (Ga)
Williams, Sallie, 86, 298
Williams, Spencer, 61
Williams, Thomas (Tenn)
Wills, Edward "Ed," 83, 98
Wills, Fred, 333
Wills, James Edward, 127
Wilson, Andrew, 60
Wilson, Anna, 60
Wilson, Gary L. J., 78
Wilson, Willie Joe, 124, 135
Wimberly, Bobby J., 124
Wimberly, Curtis W., 124
Wimberly, Joe L., 126
Wimberly, Luther LeRoy, 124
Wimes, Zanie, 74
Wingo, Harry, 75
Wise, Beverly Gween, 104-105
Woods, Agnus F., 72
Woods, Delmar W.
Woods, Dorothy Lee, 93
Woods, George and Lillian, 302, 318-319
  family of, 135, 303
Woods, Hattie, 51, 59
Woods, James C., 91, 94
Woods, Josephine L., 75
Woods, Leonard, 51
Woods, Linda Marie Moore, 105
Woods Park See Sports, Recreation, and Activities
Woods, Paul Clayton, 73
Wooley, Francis and Marlee, 100, 141, 304
  family of, 305

X

Y

Yarbro, Arthur, 127
Yearkins, Alice, 51, 54
Young, Charles, 157

Young, Imogene, 85
Young, Tyler Sr., and Virginia M., 306,
  family of, 307

Z

Melvin LeRoy Green Macklin

After returning to his home in the spring of 1996 and seeing the multitude of changes taking place (particularly, the stark decline of the town's original African American families as well as the rapid loss of the city's Black history), the author decided to put down in writing much of what he remembered as a "young'un" growing up in the northeast section of town in an area known as "The Hoodlums." Recalling what had been taught to him and other wonderful childhood memories of his past, *Traces In The Dust* was thus conceived. Five and one-half years later--with the help of friends, neighbors, and family historians throughout the city--*Traces* became a reality.

Born in Carbondale in 1945, Melvin LeRoy Green Macklin, the son of James and Ernell Green, is a career educator. He has spent twenty-seven years in research, writing, and academic study. For the last fifteen years, he has taught literature and writing in the public schools of Texas. Currently, he is a doctoral student in the Department of Humanities at the University of Texas at Dallas. His areas of concentration are American Literature and Cultural History.

www.ingramcontent.com/pod-product-compliance
Lightning Source LLC
Chambersburg PA
CBHW081024240426
43671CB00029B/2894